FROM THE Library of

Marc S. Hochman

SCORPIONS

Also by Noah Feldman

After Jihad: America and the Sturggle for Islamic Democracy
What We Owe Iraq: War and the Ethics of Nation Building
Divided by God: America's Church-State Problem—And What We Should
Do About It
The Fall and Rise of the Islamic State

SCORPIONS

The Battles and Triumphs of FDR's
Great Supreme Court Justices

NOAH FELDMAN

TWELVE

NEW YORK   BOSTON

Twelve
Hachette Book Group
237 Park Avenue
New York, NY 10017
www.HachetteBookGroup.com

Twelve is an imprint of Grand Central Publishing.
The Twelve name and logo are trademarks of Hachette Book
Group, Inc.

Printed in the United States of America

First Edition: October 2010

10   9   8   7   6   5   4   3   2   1

Library of Congress Cataloging-in-Publication Data

Feldman, Noah
  Scorpions : the battles and triumphs of FDR's great Supreme Court
justices / Noah Feldman. – 1st ed.
      p. cm.
  Includes index.
  ISBN 978-0-446-58057-1
  1. Judges—United States—Biography.   2. Frankfurter, Felix, 1882–1965.
3. Black, Hugo LaFayette, 1886–1971.   4. Jackson, Robert, 1911–1977.
5. Douglas, William O. (William Orville), 1898–1980.   6. Roosevelt,
Franklin D. (Franklin Delano), 1882–1945   I. Title.
  KF8744.F45 2010
  347.73'2634—dc22
  [B]

                                                                    2010007788

To Daniel Aaron

CONTENTS

Book Nine   BETRAYAL AND FULFILLMENT

Epilogue   AFTER THE ROOSEVELT COURT

INTRODUCTION

A tiny, ebullient Jew who started as America's leading liberal and ended as its most famous judicial conservative. A Ku Klux Klansman who became an absolutist advocate of free speech and civil rights. A backcountry lawyer who started off trying cases about cows and went on to conduct the most important international trial ever. A self-invented, tall-tale Westerner who narrowly missed the presidency but expanded individual freedom beyond what anyone before had dreamed.

Four more different men could hardly be imagined. Yet they had certain things in common. Each was a self-made man who came from humble beginnings on the edge of poverty. Each had driving ambition and a will to succeed. Each was, in his own way, a genius.

They began as close allies and friends of Franklin Delano Roosevelt, who appointed them to the Supreme Court in order to shape a new, liberal view of the Constitution that could live up to the challenges of economic depression and war. Within months, their alliance had fragmented. Friends became enemies. In competition and sometimes outright warfare, the men struggled with one another to define the Constitution and, through it, the idea of America.

This book tells the story of these four great justices through their relationships with Roosevelt, with each other, and with the turbulent world of the Great Depression, World War II, and the Cold War. At the same time, another story emerges from the vicissitudes of their battles, victories, and defeats: a history of the modern Constitution itself. These four men reinvented the Constitution; and they did so along four divergent paths. The triumph of our Constitution is a story of controversy and competition—and of the greatness that can emerge from them in the realm of ideas.

The Supreme Court is nine scorpions in a bottle.
—ALEXANDER BICKEL, LAW CLERK TO
JUSTICE FELIX FRANKFURTER,
1952–53[1]

Book One

CONTACTS

CHAPTER I

In the Club

The mingled smells of oiled mahogany paneling, polished brass, and good tobacco were familiar ones to Franklin Delano Roosevelt. Folding his slim frame into a leather-upholstered chair in the new, three-story clubroom of the Harvard Club of New York, the recent graduate was exactly where he belonged. He had a job working in an elite Wall Street law firm, intended as a brief interlude before he sought political office. His starting position was enviable. The previous year he had married his cousin Eleanor, the favorite niece of the president of the United States.

Joining Roosevelt for lunch at the club on that spring day in 1906 was another twenty-four-year-old New Yorker, also a newly minted lawyer eager to become involved in politics. There the similarities came abruptly to an end. Rich and impeccably bred, Roosevelt was a favored child of the Hudson Valley aristocracy, educated at Groton, Harvard College, and Columbia Law School. His ancestors had come to what was then New Amsterdam before 1650. Felix Frankfurter had arrived in the United States from Austria at age twelve—in steerage, without a word of English. A dozen years later, after City College and Harvard Law School, he still spoke his acquired language with a noticeable Austrian accent.[1]

But speak he did—and with a passionate intensity that exempted no one. Frankfurter would grab his listener by the upper arm, squeezing hard on the bicep while pressing a point. Argument was his favored, almost constant mode of expression. He argued so well, in fact, that he had finished first in his law school class. That was his entrée into the corridors of power. It was the only way a recent immigrant could have been lunching on terms of equality with a Roosevelt.

The paths that Roosevelt and Frankfurter had followed to New York legal practice were as divergent as their backgrounds. Roosevelt had experienced a childhood of ease and privilege, spending time in Europe with his family before returning to the United States for his secondary schooling. His college peers liked him. If there was a hint of the spectacular class betrayal that Roosevelt's future held, it was only that he was perceived as trying a bit too hard. Socially prominent freshmen were publicly ranked by a series of elections to something called the Institute of 1770, which chose one hundred men in groups of ten, the most clubbable coming first. The lone setback Roosevelt suffered as an undergraduate was not being elected until the sixth group.[2] That signaled he would not be asked to join the Porcellian Club—the pinnacle of college social life, to which Theodore Roosevelt had belonged and which his sons Theodore Jr. and Kermit would join a few years later.[3]

Roosevelt, who acknowledged the slight as "the greatest disappointment in my life," looked for a different venue to distinguish himself. Unable to make the football team—at six feet one and 146 pounds he was far from solid—he made a run for the presidency of the *Harvard Crimson*. The membership of the student newspaper was more inclusive than that of the clubs, and it did not hurt that in the fall of his sophomore year, his cousin Theodore became president of the United States.[4] This time Roosevelt was successful. Choosing electoral politics over pure social status had paid off. He returned from summer vacation in 1903 not to go to class but to lead the *Crimson*.[5]

By coincidence, Frankfurter arrived at law school that same autumn, although the two never met in the year they overlapped in Cambridge. To Roosevelt's Anglo-Saxon contemporaries, prepared by their boarding schools to be leaders of an emerging great power, Harvard was simply the next training ground. Frankfurter, by contrast, found Harvard overwhelming—a land of giants: "The first day I went to my classrooms I had one of the most intense frights of my life. I looked about me. Everybody was taller."[6]

Frankfurter stood just five feet five inches tall, but his worry about stature was as much social as literal. He had been born in the Vienna of the late Austro-Hungarian Empire, the magical city that produced Freud, Wittgenstein, and Mahler. Yet Frankfurter's small-bourgeois family had little connection to the great world of Viennese arts and letters, which might be why Vienna almost never figured in Frankfurter's later reminiscences of his boyhood. Frankfurter's most accomplished relative was his uncle Solomon, a scholar who eventually became director of the State Library in Vienna. There were rabbis in the family's history, though nearly every European Jew could say as much.

On arrival, the Frankfurters had settled in the Lower East Side of New York, in a German and Yiddish-speaking part of the neighborhood that real estate agents would later rename the East Village. Frankfurter's pleasant and rather ineffectual father sold linens, silks, and furs, sometimes out of their apartment, sometimes door-to-door, and never to much profit.[7] Money was scarce. Frankfurter attended P.S. 25, and when he was offered only a half scholarship to the Horace Mann School—one hundred of the two-hundred-dollar tuition—he went instead to the College of the City of New York, which offered a combined high school and college degree.[8]

City College was already a hotbed of ambitious and brilliant young Jewish students. Frankfurter enjoyed his classes, and was an active and successful debater. The fervid atmosphere of intellectualism and leftism engaged him without overwhelming him. "I'd sit hours and hours in East Side tea shops," Frankfurter later recalled. Together he and his friends would "drink highball glasses of tea with some rum in it, or lemon, and a piece of cake, and jaw into the morning about everything under the sun."[9] Frankfurter read widely, browsing across a broad range of subjects and educating himself through the resources of the college and New York City's extraordinary public libraries.[10] While Roosevelt was averaging a gentleman's C at Harvard, Frankfurter finished third in his class at City College and left college (like Roosevelt) with the vague plan of becoming a lawyer.

An obsessive newspaper reader interested in politics and public affairs, Frankfurter did not yet aspire to an active role on the American stage. As a recent immigrant, it would have been odd if he had. Few Jews were then prominent in national affairs, and although Frankfurter had ceased to be religiously observant—he walked out of Yom Kippur services during his junior year and never looked back—his ethnic identity was obvious and permanently fixed. That he would soon become one of the country's best-known and most influential public figures was unimaginable.

Frankfurter spent the next year as a clerk in the Tenement House Department of the city government. While working, he sampled night classes at New York Law School and at New York University School of Law. If for Roosevelt Harvard was a birthright, Frankfurter ended up there by accident. He had been diagnosed with influenza, and the family doctor told him he should get out of New York City for his health. Frankfurter was considering applying to the University of Michigan, but a friend in the Tenement House Department had a brother who was studying at Harvard Law School. Assured by his soon-to-be roommate that the school was not only for the rich, Frankfurter, using the money he had saved while working for the city, decided to enroll. In a sign of his penury, he arrived in Cambridge a week after classes had already begun. He wanted to draw his final full month's salary from the Tenement House Department.[11]

Frankfurter flourished in the law school's exam-based meritocracy. At first he gloried in the intellectual riches of the campus, satisfying "a gluttonous appetite for lectures, exhibitions, concerts." Then came the first set of practice exams, on which Frankfurter performed badly. "That was the necessary jolt. I buckled down." Class standing was not revealed to the students, but Frankfurter knew that he had done well because he was made an editor of the law review, an indication of accomplishment that conferred status. Through his academic performance, Frankfurter overcame the insecurity that had struck him on arrival in Cambridge. The experience gave Frankfurter what he would call "a quasi-religious feeling about the Harvard Law School."[12]

The invocation of religion was more than an expression. His

law school success enabled Frankfurter to do things that other Jews of the time could not. Buoyed by enthusiastic letters of reference from faculty, Frankfurter managed to get a job at a prestigious Wall Street law firm previously closed to Jews. The hiring partner recommended that Frankfurter take the opportunity to change his name—"nothing the matter with it, but it's odd, fun-making." Frankfurter politely declined, remarking that he'd "better get along with what circumstances had given me."[13]

Proud as he was to have gotten the job, Frankfurter found private practice uninspiring. He soon received an offer to work for Henry Stimson, a Harvard Law School alumnus who had been appointed by President Theodore Roosevelt to be the United States attorney for the Southern District of New York. There was a pay cut involved, but Frankfurter was excited by the prospect of government work. Stimson, a distinguished lawyer, planned to reform the U.S. attorney's office. In the past, the U.S. attorney often kept his private clients and farmed out the work of the office to associates at private firms. Stimson proposed to make his own appointment full-time and to keep the work in-house. In Stimson, Frankfurter discovered a lifelong mentor, a member of the upper class who embraced the idea of merit.

Because the U.S. attorney's office did not yet have its own proper headquarters, Frankfurter would do his legal research in the library of the Association of the Bar of the City of New York on West Forty-fourth Street. Once there, he would cross the street to the Harvard Club for lunch. It was in that congenial environment that he was introduced to Roosevelt by a mutual friend, Grenville Clark, who had been a college classmate of Roosevelt's and a law school classmate of Frankfurter's. Clark, who would later become prominent for advocating international law and world peace, was part of the same circle of the wealthy and wellborn as Roosevelt. Effortlessly graceful, a member of the Porcellian, he once dove from a bridge to save a girl who was drowning in the Charles River.[14] In law school he had been an average student—Frankfurter described him as "one of those deep, but slow minds." Yet Clark had respect for the highfliers who sat in the front of the class and engaged the professors.[15] Now he was an associate at the same Wall Street law firm as Roosevelt, and it seemed natural for him to introduce his college friend to his law school colleague.

Roosevelt and Frankfurter did not become friends in New York. Though their circles now overlapped, they still occupied different spheres. They also belonged to different political parties. Roosevelt's political affiliation was the more surprising. It would have been natural for him to become a Republican like Theodore Roosevelt. Strengthening his connection to Theodore was one of the reasons he had chosen to marry Eleanor. She was ungainly and awkward where Franklin was handsome and highly eligible. Franklin's mother, the beautiful and imperious Sara Delano Roosevelt, tried hard to stop the match. Yet Franklin was insistent. He was in love, and the reflected glamour of the presidency must have been part of Eleanor's appeal.

Despite the ambition to bring himself closer to his cousin, Franklin did not want to become Theodore's direct political protégé. In 1910, he entered politics by running for the New York State Senate—not as a Republican but as a Democrat. The reasons for this fateful choice remain uncertain. Probably Franklin thought he would have more influence at the state capital in Albany if he belonged to the majority party there. In addition, Franklin Roosevelt's father had been a Democrat, and local Dutchess County Democrats were the ones who approached him directly and asked him to run.

Whatever the basis, Franklin's choice showed the political prescience that would become his hallmark. Once elected, Roosevelt's family name made him a natural leader for those reform Democrats who wanted to take on the corrupt Tammany Hall Democratic machine. By entering politics as a Democrat, Franklin managed to wear his relative's mantle of reform without tying himself too closely to Theodore's political fate.

Frankfurter, meanwhile, found himself powerfully attracted to the progressive politics of Theodore, the Republican Roosevelt. Frankfurter's mentor, Henry Stimson, was a close associate of Theodore's, and himself a lifelong Republican. When Stimson, with Theodore's encouragement and support, decided to run for the

New York governorship in 1910, he chose Frankfurter to manage his campaign. Thus, in the same election in which Franklin Roosevelt was elected to state office as a Democrat, Frankfurter made his first political foray as a Republican operative. He had the exciting experience of riding in a car with the former President Roosevelt, who had left office in 1908. Theodore asked if his speeches on Stimson's behalf were helping the cause; Frankfurter of course told the former president that the speeches were working. But in fact Theodore had overshadowed Stimson. Neither Stimson nor Theodore had read the prevailing political winds as well as Franklin had. It was a Democratic year in New York politics and nationwide, and Stimson lost.

Even in defeat, the Republican connection served Frankfurter well. With the New York governorship out of reach, Stimson agreed (with Theodore's blessing) to become President William Howard Taft's secretary of war. Stimson took Frankfurter with him to Washington as what today would be called his special assistant. The job did not exist then, so Frankfurter was officially made legal adviser in the Bureau of Insular Affairs.

This was a political appointment to the executive branch, one focused on America's recently acquired empire in the Philippines, Guam, and Puerto Rico. In his capacity as legal adviser, Frankfurter argued several cases in the Supreme Court, making a good impression there. For the first time in his life he also experienced notable social success. He roomed with a group of bright and energetic young men, most of whom worked in the administration. (One was a young lord who worked in the British embassy and provided extra tone.) The men dubbed their group apartment "the House of Truth," and invitations to their cocktail parties and dinners achieved a certain Washington cachet. Their regular guests included ambassadors, cabinet officials, and justices of the Supreme Court. Frankfurter got the thrill of his life when Justice Horace Lurton told him, "I hope you mix drinks as well as you argue cases." Then, sipping the cocktail Frankfurter had handed him, Lurton lowered the boom: "You mix drinks even better than you argue cases!"[16]

For a Jewish immigrant who was not yet thirty years old, Frankfurter's life in Washington was heady stuff—a sign of the opportunity that an increasingly egalitarian society could provide to a young man of promise. Not by coincidence, while in Washington Frankfurter first met and began to pursue the woman who would in 1919 become his wife. Marion Denman was a recent Smith College graduate. The daughter of a Congregational minister from an old New England family, she was high-strung and highly intelligent. She had studied social work and was interested in politics. Auburn-haired and hazel-eyed, Marion put admirers in mind of a Renaissance Madonna. Even in flats she was a head taller than Frankfurter.[17]

The relationship was rocky from the start. Denman was flattered by Frankfurter's attentions but worried that she might be overwhelmed by his dominating personality: "You threaten the securities of a person whose securities are only in the making, and will never be better than slow…and painful."[18] At first reassuring, Frankfurter then backed away, telling Marion he could not marry her because she was not Jewish: "I suppose it resolved itself into a choice between you and mother…To understand you will remember all that clusters around the traditions of thousands of years."[19] But Frankfurter then reversed himself again, and the two were eventually married. Frankfurter's mother did not attend the wedding.

In 1912, Taft ran for reelection, and Stimson supported the president who had appointed him. Frankfurter, still under Theodore Roosevelt's spell, supported the former president's third-party run quietly, without quitting the administration. When the split Republican vote helped elect Woodrow Wilson, a Democrat, Frankfurter's mentor Stimson was out of a job. Frankfurter stayed on in the War Department while he tried to figure out what to do next.

There Frankfurter reencountered Franklin Roosevelt, whose own rise to Washington prominence had been even more meteoric than his own. Despite his family ties to Theodore, Franklin had remained on the sidelines in the presidential election and was now a Democrat in good standing. Having spent all of two years in the New York State Senate, he went to Washington to seek a job in the new Democratic administration. He pulled it off, getting appointed assistant secretary of the navy—a plum position. At thirty, Roosevelt was a member of Woodrow Wilson's subcabinet.[20]

Frankfurter left Washington in 1914 to become the first Jewish professor at Harvard Law School.[21] In 1917, though, as the United States entered the war, Frankfurter was invited back to the War Department, where he had made Democratic friends. This time he served as chairman of the War Labor Policies Board, a body that had the task of handling labor relations for the production of munitions and other materiel during World War I. The job was especially delicate and important because many of the unions opposed the war. Roosevelt, still assistant secretary of the navy, served on the board with Frankfurter.

Now the acquaintances were colleagues. They saw each other professionally with some frequency, and their offices were near each other in the grand, high-ceilinged State, War, and Navy Building, which still stands next to the White House. Roosevelt even invited Frankfurter to lunch with his wife. Eleanor was still a long way from the broad-minded humanitarian she would later become. In a letter to her snobbish mother-in-law, she delivered a decidedly mixed verdict on Frankfurter: "an interesting little man but very jew."[22]

At war's end, the men's paths diverged again. Frankfurter went back to Cambridge. Over the next decade, he threw himself into a series of controversial and high-profile projects that would make him a national figure. The young professor was already identified with organized labor because of his role in the Wilson administration. At the president's direction, Frankfurter had participated in two high-profile investigations of wartime labor disputes. Each of his public reports reflected sympathy for workers. In one, Frankfurter detailed the way that copper-mine owners in Bisbee, Arizona, had deported a thousand striking workers to New Mexico and left them in the desert without water or supplies. In the other,

Frankfurter recommended a pardon for Tom Mooney, an important labor leader who had been convicted on questionable evidence of planning a 1916 bomb attack in San Francisco that killed ten people. Wilson ignored the report, and Mooney remained in prison until 1939, when he was absolved of guilt and pardoned after twenty-two years in San Quentin.[23]

Frankfurter's Mooney report had led to a split with Theodore Roosevelt. The former president wrote Frankfurter a furious letter, telling his one-time admirer that by encouraging a pardon, Frankfurter was "engaged in excusing men precisely like the Bolsheviki." In common with many pro-war Americans, Roosevelt was angry with the Bolsheviks who had pulled off the Russian Revolution because they had withdrawn Russia from the war effort, to the detriment of the United States and its allies. Frankfurter, Theodore charged, was "taking on behalf of the Administration an attitude which seems to me to be fundamentally that of Trotsky."[24]

Frankfurter did not back down. In his calm reply to Theodore, he wrote of his "great sadness" at finding "disagreement between us on an important issue."[25] Nor did Frankfurter shrink from causes associated with the left when he returned to Harvard. On Armistice Day, 1919, he chaired and spoke to a rally at Faneuil Hall in Boston in which he called on the Wilson administration to recognize the Soviet Union, a position that again left him open to the charge of Bolshevism.[26] It was an inconvenient moment to be identified as sympathetic to the left. The postwar Red Scare was brewing. It went into full gear after the events of June 2, 1919.

CHAPTER 2

Anarchy

That night, a few minutes after 11:00 p.m., a dapper Italian anarchist named Carlo Valdinoci, dressed in a suit and a polka-dot bow tie and carrying a leather briefcase, walked up to 2132 R Street, the Washington, D.C., home of Attorney General A. Mitchell Palmer. As Valdinoci mounted the front steps, the fuse attached to the explosives in his case went off prematurely, turning him into an unwitting suicide bomber. The explosion rocked the elegant residential neighborhood, blowing up the front of Palmer's house and breaking windows a hundred yards around. People were thrown from their beds in the mansions along Embassy Row, just a block away. [27]

Directly across from the Palmer town house, at 2131 R Street, lived the attorney general's neighbors, Franklin and Eleanor Roosevelt, in the house they had taken to accommodate their growing family during Roosevelt's tenure as assistant secretary of the navy. By chance, the couple was just returning home from a night out when they heard a blast so loud that their cook screamed that the world was coming to an end. Roosevelt ran upstairs to find his eleven-year-old son, James, out of bed, standing at the broken window in his pajamas. Relieved and unnerved in equal measure, Roosevelt wrapped his son in an embrace that, James remembered, "almost cracked my ribs."[28]

His family's safety assured, Roosevelt hurried across the street to the Palmers', where he was one of the first people on the scene. Roosevelt and Palmer, looking around, could pick out parts of the bomber's body. Valdinoci's torso ended up hanging from a cornice on S Street; one foot landed some fifty feet away. His scalp would be found on a nearby rooftop, with its long, curly black hair still attached. The next morning, James Roosevelt would find a piece of the bomber's collarbone on the Roosevelts' front steps. It seemed miraculous that no one else had been killed. Roosevelt drove Palmer's wife to safety. Then, with the police, Roosevelt helped gather the anarchist leaflets that the bomber had carried with him and that were now scattered along R Street.[29]

But the events of that night were not over. Within minutes after the stroke of midnight, bombs went off in cities across the country, including New York, Boston, Philadelphia, Cleveland, and Pittsburgh. Italian anarchists were behind these, too. All targeted government officials connected to the suppression of anarchism. "Midnight Bombs for Officials in Eight Cities," read the *New York Times* headline the next morning. It was easily the most serious coordinated terrorist attack in the history of the United States to that time.

In the six months following the bombing of his home, Palmer and his special assistant, J. Edgar Hoover, would order hundreds of raids arresting thousands of suspected radicals. A few of those detained could be connected to terrorist activities. Most, though, were socialists, communists, and other leftists of an idealist bent whose revolutionary impulses were more theoretical than actual. The overwhelming majority of those arrested and held without trial were immigrants, and many were deported or scheduled for deportation.

Frankfurter deplored the indiscriminate nature of the Palmer raids and arrests. With his law school colleague, the civil libertarian professor Zechariah Chafee, Frankfurter filed a brief in Boston's federal court on behalf of nineteen Communists who had been arrested and held for deportation. The friend-of-the-court brief was privately solicited by the judge in the case, who was himself outraged by the government's tactics. In it, Frankfurter condemned Palmer's Justice Department for denying the detainees access to lawyers and for obtaining evidence through illegal searches. The judge issued an order relying on Frankfurter's arguments. Then he freed all nineteen detainees, reasoning that the Communist Party did not, in fact, advocate overthrow of the U.S. government by force.[30]

In the political environment of the Red Scare, standing up for the civil liberties of Communists was unpopular, to say the least. Chafee was subjected to an investigation of his "fitness to teach" by the Harvard administration.[31] Frankfurter got off only a bit more lightly. Distinguished alumni warned him that any association with Reds could harm their fund-raising and the standing of the university. Frankfurter dismissed the criticism as absurd and misplaced. The purpose of the law school, he told his critics, was not to raise money, but to stand up for certain ethical principles.[32]

In the years that followed, Frankfurter also took a strong public stand on the most controversial radical cause of the time. The Sacco and Vanzetti case began on an ordinary Thursday afternoon, April 15, 1920. The paymaster of a shoe factory in South Braintree, Massachusetts, and his bodyguard were carrying two boxes containing $15,776.51 in cash from their office to the factory to make the weekly payroll. Suddenly, two men who had been lounging on the street sprung into action. One opened fire on the paymaster and the guard. The paymaster went down and stayed down; he died a few hours later. The bodyguard, wounded, struggled to pull himself up and reach for one of the cash boxes. The shooter grabbed hold of him and fired at least two shots into him at point-blank range, killing him instantly. At just that moment, a new Buick pulled up. The men grabbed the cash boxes, tossed them into the car, jumped in after them, and were driven away.

A few weeks later, two arrests were made in the South Braintree robbery. They came about after an immigration official in Boston asked the chief of police of Bridgewater, Massachusetts, to find an anarchist called Fioruccio Coacci. Coacci had been ordered to turn himself in for deportation on April 15 but had not appeared. The next day, the police chief sent an officer to Coacci's house. Coacci was home, and he agreed at once to be deported. Two days later, he was on a boat to Italy.

After the deportation, the chief began to wonder why Coacci

had failed to turn up for his deportation on April 15 but had been happy to go a day later. Suddenly it dawned on him: Perhaps Coacci had not been available to turn himself in on April 15 because he was robbing the paymaster in South Braintree. In a further twist, there had been an abortive robbery attempted in Bridgewater the previous Christmas Eve; rumor had it that the crime had been committed by Italians who hid their car nearby.

The police chief's hunch led him back to Coacci's house. It was now occupied by another Italian, Mario Buda, who was also an anarchist (although the police chief did not know it). The chief asked to see Buda's car. Buda answered that it was being repaired by a nearby mechanic. The police chief visited the mechanic and told him to call the police if anyone came to collect the car. One evening in early May, several men, including Buda, tried to pick up Buda's car. The mechanic told them that the car was not ready. Meanwhile, his wife went next door and called the police, who arrested two of the men on the streetcar from Bridgewater to nearby Brockton.

The men arrested were Nicola Sacco, a skilled worker in a shoe factory in Stoughton, Massachusetts; and Bartolomeo Vanzetti, a self-employed fish peddler in Plymouth. Both were members of the same anarchist group as Carlo Valdinoci, who had blown himself up outside the attorney general's house. They were Galleanisti, followers of the magnetic Italian anarchist Luigi Galleani, who advocated the overthrow of all organized government and had published a how-to manual for the manufacture of dynamite bombs.[33] The men later said they needed the car so they could move some radical literature they had been hiding. But it seems more than possible that they were planning to transport explosives. When they were arrested, both Sacco and Vanzetti were armed.

Eyewitnesses had reported that the South Braintree robbers looked Italian: That fact and the men's radical associations were all that linked them to the crime. After their arrest, various eyewitnesses came out of the woodwork to identify them as having been in South Braintree. Others, in contrast, offered alibi testimony that Sacco and Vanzetti had been with them at the time of the murders. The police were convinced they had found their men. Sacco was charged with shooting the paymaster and the guard, Vanzetti with sitting in the getaway car. Vanzetti was also accused and quickly convicted of the failed robbery in Bridgewater the previous Christmas Eve.

Meanwhile Buda, whose car the men had tried to pick up, disappeared. On September 16, a horse-drawn wagon carrying a hundred pounds of dynamite and five hundred pounds of cast-iron sash weights exploded in front of the subtreasury building on Wall Street. The blast killed thirty-eight people and injured four hundred. A note demanded freedom for anarchist political prisoners—presumably including Sacco and Vanzetti. It seemed that Buda had gotten his revenge.[34]

The stage was now set to try Sacco and Vanzetti for the South Braintree murders. The key factual question was whether the defendants could be connected to the crime at all. Beyond the eyewitness testimony, which was contradictory, the prosecution's key evidence came from the new science of ballistics. The state's main expert, a police captain named William H. Proctor, was called to testify on the all-important question of whether the bullet that caused the death of the bodyguard had been fired from the .32 Colt automatic found on Sacco when he was arrested. The prosecutor asked Proctor whether he had an opinion as to whether the bullet was fired from the Colt. Proctor answered, "My opinion is that it is consistent with being fired from that pistol."[35] The testimony sounded like a definitive yes, and the judge referred to it when he was summing up the case for the jury.

At least as important as the ballistics evidence was the effect on the jury of Sacco's and Vanzetti's radical political views. The prosecution made every effort to demonstrate what sort of people these immigrant anarchists were. The jury was told—accurately—that the men had dodged the draft during World War I, fleeing to Mexico and living there for half a year in a kind of anarchist training camp with a group of like-minded Galleanisti. (These, it later turned out, included the bomber Valdinoci, whom they knew.) Their belief in the overthrow of capitalism was also admitted into evidence.[36]

The trial was taking place in the aftermath of a national Red Scare and the Justice Department's Palmer raids. The jury could hardly have avoided being influenced by this background. The jury foreman, a former police chief, was discussing the case with a friend who said he was not sure that Sacco and Vanzetti were in fact the men who had done the robbery. "Damn them," answered the foreman, "they ought to hang them anyway!"[37]

The political nature of the trial was also underscored by the lawyer who represented Sacco and Vanzetti—Fred Moore, a well-known socialist lawyer for radical and left-wing causes. The judge at the trial strongly disliked Moore, whom he called a "long-haired anarchist from the West." Moore did not improve matters by insisting that his clients were being railroaded for political reasons—or by his habit of taking off his shoes in the courtroom. Given the ballistics evidence and the politics of his clients, Moore could not save Sacco and Vanzetti. It took the jury just five hours to convict them of murder and robbery. Sacco and Vanzetti were sentenced to die in the electric chair.

What Moore could do for his clients was to draw broader attention to the case, rallying national and eventually global support to the plight of men convicted on the basis of their ethnicity and political views. With Moore's encouragement, Sacco and Vanzetti continued to protest their innocence, and they began the arduous process of appeals through the Massachusetts courts. Over the next several years, claims of their innocence gradually attracted the attention of radicals and radical sympathizers who portrayed the men as unwitting victims of capitalist oppression. It would be 1927 before the cause of Sacco and Vanzetti became a preoccupation of American artists and intellectuals.[38] But already from 1920, the two attracted the serious attention of the remarkable woman who would eventually draw Frankfurter into the case. Her name was Elizabeth Glendower Evans.

Mrs. Glendower Evans, called Auntie Bee by her close friends, was a unique Boston figure—a Brahmin widow with deep sympathy for causes of labor and the left. After her father died, she and her siblings were raised in Boston as, in her words, "poor relations of a very aristocratic family."[39] At twenty-six she married Glendower Evans, an intelligent, wealthy Bostonian who was a former student and friend of the philosopher-psychologist William James.

After graduating from Harvard Law School, the newly married Glendower went to work in a prominent Boston firm. Four years later he died suddenly, leaving Elizabeth, who then added his full name to hers, in funds but without direction. Friends encouraged her to become a trustee of an industrial school. That reform effort launched her on a career as a social reformer. She studied philosophy; traveled to the Deep South to observe child labor conditions; went to England to learn about socialism; and became a regular participant in labor union strikes as an engaged supporter. For seventeen years she served on the national committee of the American Civil Liberties Union.[40]

With her prolabor, pro–civil liberties beliefs and connection to the Boston legal world, Auntie Bee gravitated easily to Sacco and Vanzetti. She not only attended their trial but befriended the two men, visiting them in prison and corresponding with them regularly in maternal tones. And Auntie Bee's efforts on behalf of the men went beyond treating them as substitute family. She put together petitions, set up committees, and raised money for their defense. From the start, her involvement with Sacco and Vanzetti was sincerely motivated, even if she remained in denial about the extent of the men's violent political commitments.[41]

Auntie Bee knew Frankfurter and his wife, Marion, from the worlds of the ACLU and progressive Boston. In the years after the men's convictions, Auntie Bee periodically asked Marion for Frankfurter's opinion about the Sacco and Vanzetti case—an implicit invitation for him to become involved. Several times, Frankfurter said no. He later claimed that he had simply not been following the case. This was almost certainly an exaggeration. Frankfurter would have been willing to help Auntie Bee, but despite the political circumstances of the trial, there seemed to be no new facts or arguments to undermine the conviction. That made the case legally hopeless—and therefore unattractive to a legal expert like Frankfurter.

In the fall of 1924, however, Frankfurter made a behind-the-scenes intervention—one that turned out to be decisive for him. With Auntie Bee's encouragement, Frankfurter guided the team representing Sacco and Vanzetti to hand over control of the appellate process to a new lawyer, William G. Thompson. Thompson was an "esteemed" Boston lawyer, Frankfurter thought, not "a blatherskite from the West" like Fred Moore. At least now the men would have the best defense available in the later stages of their appeals.[42] Deemphasizing the political angle that had preoccupied Sacco and Vanzetti's lawyers until then, Thompson took aim at the factual basis for the conviction, especially the ballistics report. What Thompson found astonished Frankfurter. It changed the case from a purely political issue into a miscarriage of justice, and gave him the opportunity to become deeply involved.

The new evidence that changed Frankfurter's view of the case was a sworn statement made by Captain Proctor, the ballistics expert. Now, several years after the trial, Proctor claimed that his ballistics tests on the bullet taken from the bodyguard did not prove it had come from Sacco's gun. And the prosecutors knew it. During pretrial preparations, Proctor said, the prosecutors had "repeatedly" asked him whether he could say that the bullet had come from the particular Colt automatic in Sacco's possession. Proctor told the prosecutors that he was not convinced by the ballistics test that the bullet had come from that particular weapon.

Instead of refusing to testify, though, Proctor had reached a compromise with the prosecution. To avoid having Proctor say on the stand that he was not convinced that the fatal bullet came from Sacco's Colt, the prosecutor had intentionally asked him only whether he had an opinion—not what the opinion was. For his part, Proctor had given the misleading answer that the bullet was "consistent with being fired from that pistol." Proctor now swore that he had meant only that the bullet was fired from *some* Colt automatic, not Sacco's gun in particular.[43]

When confronted with Proctor's allegation, the prosecutors did not specifically deny it was true. Instead they insisted that they had not "repeatedly" asked Proctor for his opinion during trial preparations. This answer hinted that they had in fact asked Proctor for his opinion and gotten his true answer—they just hadn't asked "repeatedly." The implication was that the prosecutors had known very well what Proctor's opinion was, and had crafted their questions as well as his answer to get around it.

As Frankfurter later told it, he was reading the newspaper one morning when he saw a scare headline: "Thompson Makes Motion, Charges Frame-Up." "When I read about that motion," he recalled, "something happened to my insides." Frankfurter had experience prosecuting criminals when working for Henry Stimson in the U.S. attorney's office in New York—and to him, this was an outrage. "I was propelled and compelled by the something in me that revolted against this conduct of a district attorney resulting in the potential death of two people accused of murder."

The "something" inside Frankfurter was revulsion at the smashing of his ideals about the rule of law. The prosecutors were not even claiming Proctor had lied; they were "practically in essence admitting" they had intentionally misled the jury. "If I didn't feel as strongly as I do about law, it wouldn't have had that effect on me," Frankfurter said later. "What moved me into action was not a nice, quiet determination, but the triggering of my convictions, my impulses to action, the triggering of my total being. . . . That outraged my sensibilities, outraged my whole conviction of what the administration of justice calls for."[44]

Frankfurter's passion had been unleashed. In a rush of near-manic energy, he plowed through "five or six thousand pages of the record" to produce a scathing article for the *Atlantic Monthly*. There quickly followed a book based on the article, which, Frankfurter said, "wrote itself."[45] Once he was on board, Frankfurter became an advocate. The deeper he delved into the case, the more he was repulsed by the biases of the trial judge, who had privately called the defendants "anarchistic bastards."[46] Frankfurter began to believe in the men's innocence, even crediting a confession to the crimes by another man on death row in Rhode Island.[47]

The timing of Frankfurter's engagement with the case was propitious. By 1927, Sacco and Vanzetti had become a sensation as far away as Europe. With professorial authority, Frankfurter took on the task of convincing the educated U.S. public that the Sacco and Vanzetti case was about more than leftist politics: It was about whether immigrants with unpopular views could get a fair trial in the American criminal justice system. Frankfurter's prominent involvement and compelling writing shifted the ground of public debate. As a result, Frankfurter also changed the incentives for those who wanted the anarchists executed. The initial conservative impulse had been for the punishment of dangerous radicals and the assertion of law and order. Now that the Red Scare had faded, the reason to show the convictions were warranted was to vindicate the legitimacy of the government.

Unlike the leftist movement to save Sacco and Vanzetti that had been in place before Frankfurter's article appeared, the pressure to reconsider their case now came from mainstream figures who could not be so easily dismissed by the establishment. Frankfurter became the key strategist for a committee made up of stockbrokers, clergymen, physicians, and other respectable Bostonians who believed that the Commonwealth of Massachusetts would be badly embarrassed if the executions went forward.[48] Matters came to a head when, on April 5, 1927, the Supreme Judicial Court of Massachusetts rejected Sacco and Vanzetti's final appeal. The men's only hope now lay with a last-minute commutation of their sentences by Governor Alvan T. Fuller.

The Republican Fuller was an utterly average politician. A successful car dealer who had held the Packard concession for Massachusetts and would take over the Cadillac-Oldsmobile dealership after leaving office, he had no particular interest in the high-profile Sacco and Vanzetti case—which would become his only historical legacy. Frankfurter and his well-connected committee knew that acting on his own, the mediocre Fuller would lack the confidence to commute the death sentences. They decided to pressure Fuller to convene a special commission of inquiry to help him decide whether to commute the men's death sentences. A commission would give Fuller the chance to pass responsibility for his decision to someone else. It would let him commute the sentences if he wanted to; and if it failed, they would be no worse off than they would be without the commission. A group of them went to see William Lawrence, the Episcopal bishop of Massachusetts, who was both the Commonwealth's leading Protestant clergyman and scion of one of its wealthiest and most socially prominent families. Bishop Lawrence agreed to propose a commission to Governor Fuller; and the committee coordinated other leading citizens to echo the suggestion. After some delay, Fuller acquiesced.

Now everything depended on the members of the commission. Fuller carefully chose men who were almost guaranteed to recommend leaving the sentence in place. The three members of the blue-ribbon panel came from the conservative Boston establishment. One, Judge Robert Grant, had been a probate judge, a writer of unimaginative fiction, and the first person to receive a Ph.D. from Harvard in English. As a retired judge, he had a keen interest in upholding the integrity of the judicial system. The second, Samuel W. Stratton, was the president of the Massachusetts Institute of Technology. He had previously served for twenty-one years as the founding director of the National Bureau of Standards in Washington, D.C., the body with the exceedingly important and equally dull job of making sure that scientific measurements of mass, length, and electrical charge were consistent across the country. Stratton was a scientist-administrator, not a politician. He had no real interest in the Sacco and Vanzetti case, and no important role in the committee's deliberations.

By far the most important and influential member of the commission was a cousin of Bishop Lawrence and a man whose name was extremely well-known in Boston and nationally. He was also, indirectly, Frankfurter's boss. This was Abbott Lawrence Lowell, the president of Harvard University.

Lowell belonged to the famous Boston family in the old rhyme:

> *And this is good old Boston*
> *The home of the bean and the cod*
> *Where the Lowells talk only to Cabots*
> *And the Cabots talk only to God.*[49]

He himself occupied a nearly divine position in the Harvard hierarchy. Trained as a mathematician and a lawyer, he practiced law,
then became an eminent professor of political science and finally
president. For twenty-four years, from 1909 to 1933, Lowell
immersed himself in the affairs of the university, transforming the
curriculum, the system of teaching, and the shape of student life
through the creation of residential houses. Almost single-handedly
he built the endowment to the unimaginable sum of $100 million,
the basis for the university's subsequent wealth. Just a year before
being appointed to the Sacco-Vanzetti commission, Lowell's picture, generously moustached, had appeared on the cover of *Time*
magazine for an article focused on developments in education.[50]

The selection of Lowell reflected the fact that Frankfurter had
been a central driving force in making the case into a mainstream
cause. Frankfurter and Lowell hated each other. Lowell considered Frankfurter an outrageous self-promoter who was hijacking
the name of the university Lowell loved in order to advance radical causes. Frankfurter thought Lowell was an imperious, narrow-
minded anti-Semite who could not overcome his prejudice against
immigrants. Neither was entirely wrong.

Lowell and Frankfurter had clashed before. When various
alumni of the university had told Frankfurter that he should back
away from leftist causes, Lowell had made it clear that he agreed
with them but had not tried to force Frankfurter to change his
positions or back down. When the law school deanship had come
open, Frankfurter had helped convince Lowell to appoint his preferred candidate, Roscoe Pound. Pound was an innovative legal
scholar (with a Ph.D. in botany!) who had come to Harvard from
a job teaching law in Nebraska. Lowell had preferred other, duller
candidates—mostly Wall Street lawyers. But he had accepted
Pound when he realized that the faculty broadly agreed with
Frankfurter.[51]

Lowell, for his part, had beaten Frankfurter on an issue that
mattered a great deal to both: the number of Jews admitted to Harvard College. When Lowell took office, admission was mostly by
open examination, and many Jews got in simply by scoring well.

Lowell believed the character of the college was being affected by the presence of the Jewish students, many of whom were the children of immigrants; and he sought to impose a quota. Because an explicit quota seemed too antimeritocratic, Lowell came up with the idea that the college should consider geographical diversity as a criterion of admission, rather than examination scores alone. The effect of admitting more students from outside urban areas would be to impose a de facto quota on the number of Jews.

As one of the few Jews on the faculty, Frankfurter opposed the new plan bitterly. But Lowell managed to keep him off the relevant committee. Frankfurter's influence in the broader faculty beyond the law school was not strong enough to beat the president on a matter of university-wide policy. Geographical diversity became a principle of Harvard admissions and remains so to this day.[52] For Frankfurter, this was proof positive of Lowell's anti-immigrant, anti-Semitic worldview.

As a result of their previous clashes in the realm of academic politics, both Frankfurter and Lowell saw the Sacco and Vanzetti case as a personal struggle between the two of them.[53] At one point in the controversy, John Wigmore, the dean of Northwestern Law School and the author of the leading treatise on the law of evidence, published an attack on Frankfurter in the Boston press. When Frankfurter demolished Wigmore's article, showing it to be full of errors and misstatements, Lowell erupted. "Wigmore is a fool! Wigmore is a fool!" he told the writer Norman Hapgood. "He should have known Frankfurter would be shrewd enough to be accurate."[54]

Frankfurter's published reply to Wigmore was just one of dozens of attempts that Frankfurter made to influence the commission and save Sacco and Vanzetti. As the planned execution date drew near, Frankfurter gave over his summer cottage in the seaside town of Duxbury, Massachusetts, south of Boston, to serve as a headquarters for efforts to stop the execution. The attorney general of Massachusetts was so worried about these efforts that he ordered a wiretap on Frankfurter's telephone.

The records reveal Frankfurter making nearly constant calls

to national journalists, sympathetic and otherwise, attempting to convince them to come out in support of commutation. He also directed petition drives, aiming to enlist prominent conservatives from around the country so as to show that the case was not a leftist cause. Meanwhile, at the same time, radical supporters of Sacco and Vanzetti conducted a parallel campaign from the North End of Boston. Their interests were not precisely the same as Frankfurter's; indeed, many radicals hoped Sacco and Vanzetti would be executed so that they could become martyrs for a global cause.

When it came to the ultimate outcome of the case, Lowell had the last word. Frankfurter had exerted enormous public pressure and made support of the defendants into a respectable position. His efforts had forced the governor to appoint the commission, but Lowell made sure that the commission's report reflected his views. The report to the governor essentially repeated that the trial had been fair.

Sacco and Vanzetti's lawyers made a final, last-ditch attempt to save them. After the commission report was published, William Thompson, the lead lawyer, drew attention to his clients' plight by publicly resigning from the case in "heart-broken" protest. With time running out, the defense was taken over by Arthur Hill, another elite Boston attorney who had assisted both Thompson and Moore before him.[55] Hill drove to the summer home of Justice Louis Brandeis in Chatham, Massachusetts, hoping he could convince Brandeis to issue a stay of execution.

Appointed to the Supreme Court by Woodrow Wilson in 1916, Brandeis had been the country's leading progressive lawyer before going on the Court. He was Sacco and Vanzetti's best hope. Hill knocked on Brandeis's door—but the justice would not even let him in. On the porch, Brandeis told Hill that his connections to the case were too close. Auntie Bee was a close friend of Brandeis and his wife. He could do nothing.[56]

Around midnight on the next day, August 23, 1927, Frankfurter, "unable to sit still," went wandering on Beacon Hill, beneath the golden dome of the State House. With him were a friend and his wife, Marion, who had thrown herself into the case with all her energy. A radio bulletin announced that the first of the executions had taken place: "Sacco gone, Vanzetti going!" Frankfurter "was very pale but said nothing." Marion Frankfurter "collapsed and would have fallen to the pavement if the two men had not caught her." Emotionally devastated, she plunged into a deep and painful depression.[57]

Frankfurter had lost, but not without a fight. Taking on the defense of Sacco and Vanzetti and forcing the establishment powers to confront his arguments further established him as a nationally known progressive activist. A civil libertarian, Frankfurter served as an adviser to the National Association for the Advancement of Colored People and as a member of the national committee for the American Civil Liberties Union.[58] Frankfurter was also close to Herbert Croly, the progressive who had founded the *New Republic* magazine. He largely shared the publication's reformist politics, frequently writing unsigned articles and editorials for it.

In short, during the 1920s, Frankfurter from his post at Harvard Law School established himself as one of the leading progressives in the United States. He wrote academic articles and taught immensely popular classes, but his horizon extended far beyond Cambridge. With no model and despite regular discouragement from the university administration, he invented the job of publicly engaged law professor.

A key element of Frankfurter's prominence—and the most important for his long-term legacy—was the constitutional philosophy that he developed and promoted. The starting point for his approach was the conviction that the conservative Supreme Court of the period had overstepped its authority when it reversed progressive state and federal laws that limited working hours, protected workplace health and safety, and established minimum wages. The Court's conservatives ruled that the Constitution protected individuals' right to make contracts and limited the federal government's role in regulating commerce between the states. Underlying the Court's approach was a deep commitment to the protection of private property, which it associated with the interests of employers and investors.

Two justices of the Supreme Court consistently dissented from these decisions, and Frankfurter made them his heroes. Not coincidentally, they were also the two people whom Frankfurter had cultivated most assiduously since he first went to Washington to work for Henry Stimson in the Taft administration. One was Brandeis, the first Jew to serve on the Supreme Court. The other was Theodore Roosevelt's appointee Oliver Wendell Holmes Jr., whom Frankfurter would help make the most famous Supreme Court justice of the twentieth century.

Brandeis was a natural model and mentor for Frankfurter. The child of German-speaking Jewish immigrants from Prague, in the Austro-Hungarian Empire, Brandeis had been born in Louisville, Kentucky, and begun his schooling there. When he was fifteen, his family went back to Europe for three years, during which time he studied with private tutors in Vienna and then enrolled at the Annen Realschule in Dresden—obtaining a broader higher education than was available in the United States at the time. After this stint abroad, Brandeis went to Harvard Law School, where he achieved the highest scores ever attained. His record would remain unmatched until the grading system was changed more than eighty years later.[59]

Brandeis entered private practice in Boston and quickly became a highly successful corporate attorney. At the same time, he took up popular, reformist causes, earning him the flattering nickname "the People's lawyer." On the side he coauthored a famous article calling for a right to privacy and wrote an influential, muckraking book on the depredations of the railroad-magnate robber barons of Wall Street, with the catchy title *Other People's Money and How the Bankers Use It*.[60]

By the time Woodrow Wilson named Brandeis to the Supreme Court in 1916, Frankfurter had established warm relations with the older man, who called him "half brother, half son."[61] Frankfurter had done all he could to support Brandeis in the confirmation battle before the Senate. (Lowell, among other Boston grandees, staunchly opposed the appointment.) Brandeis's ascent to the bench brought them closer still. As the most active, best-known progressive lawyer in the country, Brandeis had dozens of irons in the fire, causes he did not wish to abandon just because he had become a justice. His solution was to pass his active, public role on to Frankfurter—to anoint him as his successor, while maintaining a private advisory role through regular communication between the two of them.

Unlike Brandeis, Frankfurter had never made money as a lawyer and was chronically short of funds. So Brandeis regularly deposited money in an account for him to pay for his expenses and his time when he was pursuing Brandeis's projects. In contemporary terms, it would be highly irregular for a sitting Supreme Court justice to fund the political activities of a private citizen. And the arrangement remained secret during their lifetimes. But the ethical rules were not definitive at the time. Both men justified the arrangement on the grounds that Frankfurter would gladly have done what he did for free, that they were almost like family, and that Frankfurter needed the money. As he wrote to Brandeis in 1924, Frankfurter had to pay for the psychoanalysis of Marion, who had suffered her first nervous breakdown.[62]

Frankfurter vigorously pursued Brandeis's causes. Some, like labor reform, were already his own. Others, like Zionism, he took up mostly because of Brandeis, who played a leading part in the Zionist movement even after joining the Court. Brandeis's distinctive (and rather quirky) Zionism imagined the creation of an agrarian Jeffersonian republic in Palestine, one that reflected his own deep concerns about what was then called "the curse of bigness" in business and government alike. Brandeis split with the international Zionist movement only in 1921, a year after ceding leadership to Chaim Weizmann, who would later become the first president of Israel—and even then Brandeis continued to donate large sums.[63]

Frankfurter himself was never an ardent Zionist. He visited Palestine once, reluctantly, in 1934, when he was spending the year in England and so was already halfway there. But once he was acting on Brandeis's behalf in Zionist affairs, Frankfurter took full advantage of the opportunities that this connection offered.

Work for the Zionists brought Frankfurter to the Paris peace conference in 1919, at the close of World War I. He played a small
but meaningful role in this unique gathering of princes, presidents,
and kings-in-waiting, sitting down face-to-face with Emir Faisal
ibn Husayn, who would briefly be king of Syria and then of Iraq.
Faisal's translator and adviser was none other than T. E. Lawrence,
fresh from the exploits in insurgency that earned him the nickname Lawrence of Arabia. Working with Lawrence, Frankfurter
negotiated an exchange of letters expressing mutual support for the
national hopes of Jews and Arabs alike—a kind of hopeful entente
that prefigured later cooperation between the Zionists and the
Hashemite Kingdom of Jordan.[64]

Brandeis, then, had opened worlds for Frankfurter, and it made
sense that Frankfurter would be influenced by his judicial philosophy as well. Brandeis's reason for dissenting from the pronouncements of the property-protecting Supreme Court majority was
that it stood in the way of the popular cause of progressive reform.
Justice Oliver Wendell Holmes Jr., Frankfurter's other idol on the
Supreme Court, usually voted the same way Brandeis did—against
the conservative majority. But his reasons were altogether different, and his relationship with Frankfurter was correspondingly different as well.

Olympian, ironic, and disdainful of the notion of progress,
Holmes was an unlikely icon for the young Frankfurter. But his
brilliance, his roots in the American past (he was a decorated Civil
War veteran), and his contempt for the overreaching of the Court's
conservative majority made him the perfect public face of the progressive campaign against the Court.

As a young lawyer working in Washington, Frankfurter had
discovered in Holmes an aging figure without intellectual peers
who had concluded that he would die with his genius unacknowl-
edged. Frankfurter gave Holmes his adulation, sending him a steady
stream of lively, smart, and mostly Jewish admirers who told him
in perfect sincerity that he was the world's most important legal
thinker. In return, Holmes validated Frankfurter by offering him
his friendship. For Frankfurter, this meant a close association with

the person he considered the embodiment of the Anglo-American legal system.

As part of his effort to explain to the world why the Supreme Court was wrong to strike down progressive laws, Frankfurter turned Holmes into a saint of judicial restraint. A judge, according to this ideal, should not turn his favored political beliefs into legal doctrine, but stand aside and allow the people's representatives to pass the laws favored by the electorate. Holmes, a believer in minimal government who thought little of the progressive laws he voted unsuccessfully to uphold, did embody this ideal. But Holmes favored restraint less because he thought it was the judge's proper role than because he thought it was generally pointless to stand in the way of rising classes or social movements. Brandeis, by contrast, voted to uphold progressive laws because he believed in the improved working conditions and increased wages that the laws promised.

To mediate between these wholly opposite motivations, Frankfurter drew on the writing of James Bradley Thayer, a professor at Harvard Law School who had died shortly before Frankfurter arrived there as a student. Thayer had claimed that as a historical matter, judicial review of the constitutionality of state laws was unusual from the very outset of the Republic. Judges, he claimed, had traditionally overturned legislation only when it was clear beyond a reasonable doubt that a state constitution had been violated. Frankfurter would for the rest of his life insist that the essay in which Thayer laid out his view was the most important thing ever written about the Constitution.[65]

From Frankfurter's perspective, one of the greatest advantages of Thayer's essay was that almost no one else had ever read it. In his hands, Thayer's essentially historical analysis was transformed into the pointedly normative argument that courts should not intervene where the legislature had acted on behalf of the public. Historical precedent should be a guide to present practice: What had been done in the past was what now should be done.

Joining the diverse trinity of Brandeis, Holmes, and Thayer—progressivism, nihilism, and historicism—into a single godhead of judicial restraint was Frankfurter's most important intellectual accomplishment during his years as a professor. Indeed, it would be the single constitutional contribution that would shape Frankfurter's entire career. For nearly two decades, Frankfurter's theory of judicial restraint would become the unofficial constitutional philosophy of the movement that would itself become known as American liberalism.

CHAPTER 3

Disease and the Man

Those same years of Frankfurter's rise were extraordinarily difficult ones for Franklin Roosevelt. The period began with promise. After serving eight years in the same job in the Wilson administration, Roosevelt managed the amazing feat of becoming the Democratic candidate for vice president in 1920, when he was just thirty-eight years old.

Roosevelt did not expect the Democrats to win the election. Woodrow Wilson had ended his term in failure, and the Senate had rejected his plan to bring the United States into the League of Nations that had been his brainchild. Despite the appealing, progressive qualities of James M. Cox, the Democrats' candidate, the country was ready for a Republican, and Warren G. Harding won a landslide victory. But Roosevelt had made himself into a nationally known figure. He was now positioned to make a future presidential run of his own.

Then, less than a year after the defeat, Roosevelt was stricken with polio.[66] Both legs were paralyzed. The fact of the paralysis was kept from the public. Roosevelt's physician, the innovative clinician George Draper, affiliated with Presbyterian Hospital and Columbia University's College of Physicians and Surgeons, told the press, "You can say definitely he will not be crippled. No one need have any fear of that."[67] The cover-up was necessary in part because of the fear that the public would not embrace a crippled politician—but more important because Roosevelt had not yet accepted the fact of paralysis himself. It seemed that Roosevelt's promising political future might be over before it had properly begun.

Drawing on reserves of personal strength that even he did not know he had, the man to whom everything had come so easily rehabilitated himself until he was strong enough to run for governor of New York in 1928. It is a cliché of Roosevelt biography to say that his bout with polio transformed the arrogant, sheltered child of the elite into a sympathetic populist who would preside over the dismantling of the social class into which he was born. Like most clichés, this one contains a kernel of truth wrapped in a shell of oversimplification. Roosevelt's political instincts and desire to succeed ran deep, and they preceded his struggle with disability. And Roosevelt's response to the Great Depression that lay just ahead was designed as much to preserve the system of American capitalism as it was to transform it, no matter what his opponents believed.

Yet it is also true that Roosevelt's almost unbelievable accomplishment in returning himself to the political track at age forty-six, after eight midlife years in the wilderness, transformed the man within. Roosevelt's will was at the core of his rehabilitation. He never gave up the struggle to improve his physical capacities, and he never accepted that he would be limited in his political opportunities. Such resolve would be remarkable in anyone, and it reflects a kind of heroism that can only be admired. At the same time, though, Roosevelt did not make this journey alone. He had first-class professional help—and he got it through another of the lucky strokes that came from being a member of the highest stratum of the American elite.

The crucial medical figure in Roosevelt's early treatment was George Draper. A rising star, Draper had already published an important article on polio. But what proved more important to his role in Roosevelt's rehabilitation was that Draper already knew Roosevelt—and had known him since they were boys together at Groton and Harvard. Draper was, in fact, fully a member of Roosevelt's social circle. He had even been engaged to Eleanor's cousin, another niece of Theodore's, around the time Eleanor and Franklin had gotten married.[68] Given their social proximity, Draper's growing prominence, and the fact that Draper was based in

New York, it was natural for Draper to take the lead in Roosevelt's care.

As it turned out, the disease that crippled Roosevelt was, physiologically speaking, irreversible. What he needed, therefore, was not care oriented toward his physical recovery but psychological support in helping him recover from the shock of paralysis. Draper was just the man for this approach. In 1921, Draper was deeply enmeshed in the process of developing a medical philosophy he called "constitutional medicine." This approach insisted that treatment should engage the whole person—the whole human constitution—not only the disease.[69] Draper treated Roosevelt according to this view, paying close attention to Roosevelt's emotional state. Indeed, it is no exaggeration to say that Roosevelt received psychiatric care from Draper during those crucial years of his recovery. Without acknowledging it to himself, much less to others, Franklin Roosevelt was the first American president to have been treated extensively for his mental state.

Draper's combination of interest in human psychology and his personal knowledge of Roosevelt led him to realize almost from the outset that he needed to calibrate just the right approach to Roosevelt's care. "The psychological factor in his management is paramount," Draper wrote early in the treatment. "He has such courage, such ambition, and yet at the same time such an extraordinarily sensitive emotional mechanism, that it will also take all the skill which we can muster to lead him successfully to a recognition of what he really faces without utterly crushing him."[70]

Draper's solution to this quandary was not to force this recognition, but to hope Roosevelt would reach it on his own. During the years he treated Roosevelt, Draper never demanded that Roosevelt fully accept his paralysis as final. Remarkably enough—and in contradiction to Draper's expectation that recognition would eventually occur—Roosevelt seems never to have accepted the finality of his condition. To the contrary, he continually strove for improvement. He came to believe that swimming in the mineral waters of Warm Springs, Georgia, could actually improve his condition—and that the same treatment could work for others. Swimming,

of course, was excellent exercise, and by all accounts healthy both
for Roosevelt and those others who became devotees of the Warm
Springs treatment approach. From a physiological standpoint,
though, it is doubtful whether the swimming and exercises ever
increased Roosevelt's range of movement.[71]

What was significant about Roosevelt's commitment to treatment at Warm Springs, for himself and others, was that it represented his refusal to accept the impossibility of improvement. This
perspective can be usefully compared to Roosevelt's approach to
the problems of the Great Depression. Tinkering and adjusting as
he went, Roosevelt never lost the posture of optimism, even when
progress seemed to be slow, or things seemed to be getting worse.

From a broader psychological perspective, Roosevelt's obses-
sion with improvement could be interpreted as a species of denial.
If so, Draper made a clinical decision to facilitate that denial—and
it may well have been the decision that enabled Roosevelt to be
guided back to a full political recovery, and beyond. To be sure,
Eleanor and Roosevelt's political adviser, Louis Howe, also encouraged Roosevelt's efforts to recover. But Draper's was the expert
medical opinion; and Draper, despite his own medical judgment,
never gave in to the temptation to tell Roosevelt that his efforts at
recovering function in his legs were futile.[72]

Frankfurter and Roosevelt had not been close enough for
Frankfurter to have pursued the relationship while Roosevelt
was out of commission. But when Roosevelt got the Democratic
nomination for governor in 1928, he received a strange letter of
congratulations from his old acquaintance—the first written communication between them of which a record remains. The note
was addressed, with a combination of warmth and polite distance,
to "my dear Franklin Roosevelt." In it, Frankfurter first praised
Roosevelt's "pure-mindedness and real public zeal."[73] So far, the
letter was perfectly ordinary, if a little effusive coming from an
acquaintance who had been out of touch for almost a decade.

Then Frankfurter addressed a delicate matter. Roosevelt had
edged out Herbert Lehman for the Democratic nomination. Lehman was a Jew—and indeed would later become the first Jewish

governor of New York. Roosevelt's Republican opponent was
Albert Ottinger, who was also Jewish. Had Roosevelt not beaten
Lehman, therefore, the next governor would have been Jewish.
This was potentially awkward for Frankfurter, who as a Jewish
New Yorker might have been disappointed that Roosevelt's vic-
tory in the primary made this result unlikely.

Frankfurter decided to draw attention directly to the issue. "As
a Jew," he wrote to Roosevelt, "I am particularly happy that your
nomination prevented the New York contest from degenerating
into an unworthy competition for the Jewish vote. Now all good
and wise citizens ought to be drawn to your standard."[74] Frankfurter seemed to be expressing his relief that Jewishness would not
be the focal point in discussion of the campaign, the way it might
have been if two Jews had been running against one another. In
what would become his characteristic stance toward his religious
background, Frankfurter was acknowledging his Jewishness while
attempting to transcend it. He was asserting that as a Jew he was
pleased that a Jew had not been nominated.

There is no record of what Roosevelt thought of the note, and
Frankfurter did not again allude to his Jewish identity in his correspondence with Roosevelt. But when Roosevelt won, Frankfurter
sent another note—this time addressed to "Dear Franklin"—urging
Roosevelt to meet with Justice Brandeis to discuss unspecified
matters of importance to his forthcoming duties in Albany.[75] And
although Roosevelt declined to visit Brandeis in Washington, he
did write back to Frankfurter ("Dear Felix") inviting Brandeis to
see Roosevelt in New York. By the next summer, when Roosevelt
wrote to Frankfurter asking him to meet with a member of his
new Public Service Commission, it was "Dear Felix" and "Dear
Frank," as it remained in their private communications until
Roosevelt's death.

With Roosevelt once again in pursuit of the presidency, and
Frankfurter a leading liberal thinker, the two men needed each
other. Their earlier acquaintance paved the way for nearly immediate intimacy despite the stark difference in their backgrounds.
Their relationship would blossom naturally. Frankfurter would

take the role of an admiring yet independent academic, eager to give advice and to recommend policies and personnel, and always quick to offer a flattering comment on Roosevelt's latest speech or decision—no matter how small. "By holding out on your water power policy for New York, you have vindicated courage in government," he wrote on one occasion.[76] Roosevelt, who had never received much encouragement as a student, basked in the professor's praise. It did not seem fulsome to him, no matter what our current standards might lead us to think. Roosevelt also came to recognize the practical value of Frankfurter's advice, the quality of the people he recommended, and the value of Frankfurter as a conduit to the world of liberal ideas.

Four years later, Roosevelt was president. Calling Frankfurter to the White House, Roosevelt offered him the post of solicitor general, representing the executive branch before the Supreme Court. It was the most prestigious administration job possible for a law professor. But Frankfurter turned him down, arguing that he could do more good—and by implication, have more influence—as an informal adviser from Cambridge. Now it was Roosevelt's turn to raise the Jewish question. He wanted Frankfurter on the Supreme Court, he said, but it was impossible to nominate him directly from a professorship. He had never been a judge, had not actively practiced law in years, had defended Sacco and Vanzetti— and then there was, as Roosevelt put it, "your race."[77] By becoming solicitor general, Roosevelt was saying, Frankfurter would be seen as qualified to serve on the Supreme Court, overcoming skepticism about his Jewishness.

Even with this carrot held in front of him, Frankfurter said no. Frankfurter doubtless understood that Roosevelt's first solicitor general would inevitably lose some important cases as the conservative Supreme Court struck down new reforms. It is possible that he did not want a job that would make him into a public loser. Perhaps, too, he believed it would be difficult to influence broader policy questions from within the specialized office of the solicitor general. In any case—maybe because it showed Frankfurter could say no to the president—his refusal seemed to cement the relationship between the two men. "Felix is a stubborn pig!" Roosevelt commented, not without admiration. From Cambridge, Frankfurter's advice and protégés came fast and furious. Frankfurter drafted New Deal legislation and staffed the New Deal agencies. His closest associates enjoyed daily access to the president. Soon insiders would be describing him as "the most influential single individual in the United States."[78]

CHAPTER 4

Upstate

Robert Houghwout Jackson was a decade younger than Roosevelt and Frankfurter, and he too was a New Yorker—raised in the small town of Frewsburg, in the extreme western part of the state near the Pennsylvania border. Like Frankfurter, he met Roosevelt early, without forming a close attachment to him. The reason again was the stark difference in background. Ethnically, Jackson was not so distinct from Roosevelt. He even had some Dutch ancestors, as his middle name hinted. But if Roosevelt's family were rich people who moved in the highest echelons of American society, Jackson's were small-time farmers in a distant, poor corner of the Empire State.

The eighteen-year-old Jackson met the twenty-eight-year-old Roosevelt for the first time in Albany in 1911, as a result of the Jackson family's quixotic commitment to the Democratic Party, the perennial loser in upstate politics. They were introduced by a cousin of Jackson's mother, a lawyer called Frank Mott who was an active Democrat in the small city of Jamestown, which was just a trolley car ride from Frewsburg. Mott had taken on Jackson as his legal apprentice, and in this capacity Jackson had accompanied Mott to Albany on a political visit.

When Jackson first met him, Roosevelt had not yet served in Washington. He was a political neophyte, freshly elected as a Democratic state senator from Dutchess County, and he stood out among the rough, seasoned career politicians in Albany. With his light hair, blue eyes, patrician chin, and family name, the elegantly tailored Roosevelt was an instant celebrity. As Jackson remembered it, Roosevelt "looked and acted the aristocrat." He spoke differently than the other politicians—in a distinctive half-British, half-American drawl that was the mark of a self-confident, upper-class New Yorker who had spent time in Europe and didn't care who knew it. An "amateur" among the professional political class, Jackson later wrote, Roosevelt "was like a hothouse plant just set out among weathered and hearty rivals."[79]

Despite his matinée-idol appearance, though, he was making a mark in the state senate. Roosevelt had chosen as his signature issue an attack on the Tammany Hall Democratic machine, whose tentacles stretched deep into the state legislature. The field of battle was the selection of New York's U.S. senator—in those days still the job of the state legislature to elect, and effectively determined by the Democrats there. Roosevelt took his stand against Tammany's preferred candidate, a former state assembly speaker called William Sheehan. Other so-called independent Democrats, also unaffiliated with the machine, backed Roosevelt. After a brutal fight, Sheehan was replaced by a compromise candidate—an Irish-American with ties to Tammany, but at any rate not the man Roosevelt had initially opposed.

Upstate Democrats were almost by definition opponents of Tammany Hall, and so for Frank Mott, the fight for reform made Roosevelt an appealing figure, one worth meeting and introducing to his young cousin Jackson. It also definitively identified Roosevelt as a Democrat on the rise. The Sheehan battle quickly became national news. The most meaningful result of the fight was to draw attention to corruption in the selection of senators by the states, adding fuel to the progressive movement to elect senators directly. As for Roosevelt personally, the national reports showed him to be an independent-minded figure unafraid to challenge his own party. The comparison to Theodore, who had already begun his own insurgency against his onetime protégé, President William Howard Taft, was an obvious one.

The impression Jackson made on Roosevelt at this first meeting cannot have been much. Though pleasant-looking with even features, high cheekbones, and wavy dark hair, the youthful Jackson was by his own account a "countryman" compared to the polished Roosevelt.[80] To that point, the apprentice's education consisted of classes at Frewsburg High School, books he had managed to read while there, and a single postgraduate year at the larger high school in Jamestown.

Jackson must have read avidly, because decades later he could recall many of the books in the two-bookcase Frewsburg library collection. In particular, he remembered having read "a number of William James' works," and having done so "with great interest."[81] Apart from this tantalizing hint of Jackson's future pragmatism, however, the education he received was unsophisticated. He read Shakespeare with a beloved Jamestown teacher called Mary Willard; and while this literary encounter is often invoked talismanically to explain Jackson's wonderful prose style, the fact remains that at the time nearly every English-speaking high school student in the world read Shakespeare.[82]

Before beginning his year commuting to the high school in Jamestown, Jackson had come into contact with Mott and decided to become a lawyer. His father strongly objected and refused to provide money for law school. At the time, law school was not required for an applicant to take the examination and become a member of the New York bar. Three years of clerkship in a law office, or else some combination of law school and clerkship, qualified the applicant to practice. Roosevelt himself had taken advantage of this nearly obsolete rule, quitting Columbia Law School the moment he passed the bar examination and going straight into his law firm to complete the three-year requirement. The eighteen-year-old Jackson went into Mott's office with the plan of taking the apprenticeship route. It was during the first year of this rather arduous process that Mott gave him a break from sitting with the classic law books of the self-educated American lawyer of the previous century—Kent's *Commentaries* and "some Blackstone"—and brought him into Albany.

The young Jackson who met Roosevelt in Albany soon came to think that he needed at least a little bit more formal education before going into practice. After a year with Mott, he enrolled in the Albany Law School, where he spent a year enrolled in classes.[83] He took his certificate of graduation—not a degree, because he was not yet twenty-one—back to Jamestown to fulfill the required third year of clerkship in Mott's office. A year later, finally old enough to become a member of the bar and to vote, Jackson entered politics and was elected to represent his district on the Democratic State Committee. In that capacity he soon reencountered Roosevelt.

Jackson was never able to give any better explanation for his choice of the Democratic Party than heredity. His father, his grandfather, and even his great-grandfather had been Democrats, and that was that. But if upstate Democrats were distant in geography, ethnicity, and ideology from the great party machinery downstate, they still partook of the patronage that characterized the system of the U.S. government even after civil service reform began in 1880. Since the federal government still did not do much at the local level, the most important—often the only—federal patronage job available was that of postmaster. In 1889, for example, when Benjamin Harrison assumed the presidency, thirty-one thousand postmaster jobs turned over.[84] When Woodrow Wilson was elected in 1912, the local Jamestown Democrats wanted their piece of the pie, however small it might be.

To get it, the Jamestown contingent of the Democratic State Committee turned to Roosevelt. As assistant secretary of the navy, he had no authority to make postmaster appointments. But almost from the start, he was close to Wilson, and a participant in the "little cabinet." In Washington, access is the key surrogate for power. To be able to get into the room for the meeting is often 90 percent of the battle. With no small presumption, Jackson and Mott renewed their Albany acquaintanceship and approached Roosevelt for help. In 1913 and 1914, the two men made regular visits to the nation's capital, each time troubling Roosevelt with high questions of upstate postmaster appointments.

It worked. Jackson later wrote that "through Roosevelt we succeeded in getting our postmasters appointed in every place where there was a vacancy, including Jamestown, which is the largest and most important of the offices in my district."[85] To Jackson,

Roosevelt's help was further confirmation of his political independence, since the rest of the state party apparatus resented Roosevelt's meddling in patronage affairs that had nothing whatever to do with the Navy.

Visiting Washington, D.C., to meet with a major administration figure in an elegant Beaux Arts building next to the White House is hardly a typical experience for a twenty-one-year-old, regardless of education or provenance. Yet it is difficult to ascertain what effect, if any, these Washington forays had on Jackson. For Felix Frankfurter, the youthful years spent in Washington formed the paradigm for public engagement that he sought (and achieved) for the rest of his professional life. When Frankfurter went back to Cambridge, he stayed connected to the world of affairs he had sampled. Jackson, though, far from being entranced by politics, found that the visits distracted him from the legal practice he was trying to build. He was, he later recalled, "getting into fights over these little post office jobs that did not have any importance to anything that I was interested in, in a larger way."[86]

Jackson may conceivably have been spurred to future interest in high-level executive branch politics through his unusual exposure to Roosevelt. Certainly when he did enter the realm of the executive branch, he would have one of the fastest, most ambitious, and—up to a point—most successful runs in Washington history. But if he was bitten by the bug of power in those visits to Roosevelt's office, the incubation period was several decades long. When his term on the state committee was over, he decided he was finished with party politics and threw himself exclusively into the law.[87]

Back in Jamestown, Jackson married Irene Gerhardt, the daughter of a successful contractor, whom he had met ice-skating on Washington Park Lake during his year of law school in Albany. Irene had been working as a secretary in the state government. According to family lore, Irene's mother was skeptical: "He's too skinny, and he's never going to amount to anything."[88]

Indeed, Jackson's legal practice started small. "You tried lawsuits," he explained, "without too much regard for money."

Reputation was the coin of the realm. The client, who "usually was bitter at the adversary…expected a lawyer to protect his prestige as well as win the case."[89] With the financial stakes typically tiny, the cases Jackson took early in his career were as much theater as they were law. The local community treated a day's worth of trials as entertainment. Court was not held before a judge, but in front of a justice of the peace who was not a lawyer. Trials took place not in a regular courtroom, but wherever there was space to gather: in a school, a church, or the dance hall of a Masonic Temple. One time, Jackson recalled, when the justice of the peace did not have room in his house, "we put up some oil lanterns, put some boards across potato crates for people to sit on, and we tried the case in the barn."[90]

The barn was an appropriate venue, because livestock was frequently the subject of litigation. The humorous quality of these cases—throwbacks to a lost world of rural simplicity—was not lost on Jackson. Once, he represented a farmer who had bought a Holstein cow supposed to be with calf by a thoroughbred Holstein bull. When the calf was born, it was "obviously sired by a Jersey." Furious, Jackson's client filed a bovine paternity suit. For two days, as Jackson would later tell it, "we tried the love life of the bossie cow with the whole community attending." Jackson won his client fifteen dollars—and took home a fee of five dollars.[91]

Chicanery was also part of the game. In one of the many "horse lawsuits" that Jackson tried, he walked into a trap. His witness testified that the other side had doctored the horse in question before selling it. It was, Jackson recalled, a "perfect story," but "some way it didn't seem to be taking hold of anybody in the room." He soon found out why. Jackson had arrived in court late and missed jury selection. It turned out that his well-informed witness had claimed earlier that day that he had never heard of the case or the parties. He had been trying to sneak onto the jury to help his friend, Jackson's client. When the alert lawyer had kept him off, he had decided the next best thing was to testify as a witness.

Jackson assumed he would lose the case after this debacle, but there was a final twist. To his surprise, the jury stayed out for hours, and the lawyer for the other side agreed to a settlement of twenty dollars—which for the case was "pretty decent." When the settlement was a done deal, Jackson's client told him why: "I had a hired man on that jury." Jackson was surprised—hadn't the lawyer asked the jurors where they worked? "Oh yes," replied the client. "But he didn't catch him. You see he ain't going to work for me until next week."[92]

Notwithstanding their entertainment value, these small-time trials had a serious side, and Jackson never forgot it. "Lawsuits were conducted with great vigor and bitterness. Witnesses were impeached, litigants were abused roundly, factions were formed and the case tried over and over around the firesides of the neighborhood. Lawyers' sallies of wit were laughed over, their invective was repeated for days, and their oratory always brought out large attendance at court." In this world, "the trial was a battle of wits. A young lawyer that went out into that had to take care of himself and put on a good show."[93]

Jackson had what it took. He never wrote out his summations to the jury word for word, but instead favored a folksy, clear-speaking delivery that helped hone his distinctive literary style. To succeed in these justice courts was to be ready for a legal life full of improvisation and creativity. In later years, Jackson got good value from tales of his country lawyer's practice, as he did from the fact that he was the last Supreme Court justice never to have been graduated from law school. What he lightly called "Jamestown Justice" had something to do with the commonsense pragmatism that would become his constitutional philosophy.

As the Jamestown economy became more productive, Jackson's client base changed. His youthful experience of rural law gave way to the practice of a successful business lawyer in a small regional city. His legal career grew in tandem with the industrialization of upstate New York in that era. Representing local manufacturers and a local bank, he eventually built up an impressive personal fortune.

By the time he went to Washington, Jackson was earning $30,000 a year through his practice—something like $1 million in today's purchasing power.[94] Although this was substantially less

than the $100,000 a year commanded by the most senior Wall
Street lawyers at the time, Jackson kept a thirty-foot motor yacht
on Lake Chautauqua and took his family for vacations in Cuba,
Florida, Bermuda, California, and Arizona—in the midst of the
Depression. Jackson began his career in private practice as a country lawyer, but he ended it—without moving—as the most important and substantial lawyer in a small but growing city.[95]

That role was not without risks. The Depression almost reduced
Jackson to total ruin. As a prominent attorney, Jackson had joined
the board of directors of the Bank of Jamestown, one of seven
locally controlled banks. Jackson's bank had lent money conser-
vatively, and because it had large deposits it was able to overcome
the initial difficulties it faced when customers started to default
on loans. Once the other, more risk-taking banks began to get
in trouble, national banking authorities suggested that the Bank
of Jamestown take over two of the struggling banks in town, the
Farmers and Mechanics Bank and the Swedish-American Bank.
Jackson and his fellow board members agreed.[96]

Then in late February 1933, with Roosevelt about to take office
as president, there was a national bank panic, and depositors all
over the country lined up to demand their deposits, usually in gold.
The Bank of Jamestown, Jackson knew, was at grave risk. "Before I
went into my office in the morning," he recalled, "I went out more
than once to see if there was a line before the bank. I knew that if
there was a run on that bank we couldn't weather it."[97]

The danger of a run was not just that the bank would collapse
but that Jackson would collapse along with it. He had failed to
diversify his assets, and much of his wealth was tied up in the bank.
"My savings were largely in the bank either in deposits—we got
four percent interest—or in the form of stock, on which I would
have double liability," because he would be sued when the bank
failed. "I knew that if the bank went down, I would be ruined
financially," Jackson later explained. It would be the sort of failure
from which it would be difficult to bounce back. "To be a director
of a bank that fails in a small community is always to be marked as
a conspicuous failure who has caused other people great losses."[98]

Then, in a stroke of luck for Jackson and others in his position, Roosevelt, the day after his inauguration, declared a four-day banking holiday, starting March 6, 1933. Closing the banks temporarily had the effect of stopping the panic and the runs that were plaguing the country. On March 9, Congress passed the Emergency Banking Act, designed to close insolvent banks and save those strong enough to survive.

Again it was a close thing for Jackson and the Bank of Jamestown. "When the banking holiday came all of us concerned were badly alarmed and badly weakened. It was no comfortable position, I can tell you." The Federal Reserve wanted Jackson, along with two of his colleagues on the board, to undertake a personal guaranty of all the deposits in the bank before it would grant them a license to reopen. The men refused—one scare of that magnitude was enough—and the Fed backed down, allowing them to continue in business. The bank across the street, though, was not so lucky, Jackson recalled. The Federal Reserve forced it to close.[99]

This brush with the federal government aside, Jackson's political focus between 1914 and 1934 was local. As his legal practice prospered, he did little to involve himself in national affairs. He attended the 1924 Democratic National Convention, but not as a delegate. He did serve as a delegate to the state Democratic convention in 1928, where Roosevelt was nominated for governor. When his old mentor Frank Mott proposed Jackson as a nominee for attorney general, Roosevelt replied that it would be fine with him provided that "the balance of the ticket could be preserved."[100] *Balance* was code for candidates from both upstate and the city, and for a mix of Catholics and Protestants. Since Jackson was, like Roosevelt, a Protestant, and since neither was politically affiliated with New York City, this amounted to a polite way of saying no. Jackson made speeches upstate on Roosevelt's behalf anyway, and, after he won, Roosevelt offered Jackson a spot on his Public Service Commission. Now it was Jackson's turn to say no—apparently the commission spot was not sufficiently attractive to interest him.

During Roosevelt's second two-year term as governor, Jackson was proposed by the New York State Bar Association to serve on a

different state commission, this one aimed at improving the administration of justice in the state. Roosevelt wanted the commission
to be chaired by Professor Raymond Moley of Barnard College,
a political scientist whose expertise in criminal justice made him
a natural for the job. Moley, who was close to Roosevelt, would
soon become a key figure in Roosevelt's brain trust and an architect of the early New Deal.

Jackson and the state bar association opposed Moley. Lawyers
were and are deeply skeptical of legal reforms proposed by nonlawyers, and the struggle between lawyers and political scientists
would be repeated more than once in the years to come. Roosevelt
called Jackson to his office to ask him privately why he was opposing the governor's candidate. Jackson, who was doing the bidding
of the bar association, "could not give very substantial reasons."
Indeed, he later recalled, "Roosevelt laughed at the reasons I
advanced." But Jackson would not back down, and Roosevelt
became frustrated. He "left no doubt that he was much displeased
that I did not fall in line with his suggestions."[101]

The disagreement between the men explains why Jackson did
not go to the 1932 Democratic convention in Chicago to nominate
Roosevelt for president. He participated in Roosevelt's campaign
locally, and spent some time working at campaign headquarters in
New York. But this was not the service of a prominent Democrat
eager for a national position.

Yet somehow between the election of 1932 and 1934, Jackson
decided to make a run at Washington. Perhaps it had to do with
his increasingly prominent role in the American Bar Association,
which in 1933 led to his being elected to a national position in
the ABA. Perhaps, too, it had to do with the economic success he
had enjoyed in Jamestown. Whatever the cause, Jackson began to
believe that he was ready to enter the national stage.

The first inkling came in connection with his son, Bill, who
was set to enter Jamestown High School in 1933. Instead of sending him to the school he had himself attended, Jackson decided on
a private school. And he chose not just any private academy, but the
St. Albans School in Washington, D.C., the leading preparatory

school in the capital. Bill began to board there in 1933, half a year before Jackson took a job in Washington.

Although Jackson downplayed it in later years, the choice of St. Albans cannot have been accidental.[102] There were many excellent private schools closer than Washington. And the choice signaled more than geographical change. St. Albans was an elite school socially as well as academically, connected to those members of the political class who wanted to keep their sons near Washington. The Jacksons were moving out of Jamestown. Robert Jackson would arrive in Washington in 1934 as counsel to the Bureau of Internal Revenue. In the next six years he would become an intimate of Roosevelt's, solicitor general, attorney general, a potential candidate for vice president, and a justice of the Supreme Court of the United States.

CHAPTER 5

Southern Pride

Franklin Roosevelt had known both Frankfurter and Jackson when they were young men, relationships that laid the groundwork for their later intimacy. But the man who would become his first Supreme Court nominee, Senator Hugo LaFayette Black, was someone Roosevelt did not meet until assuming the presidency of the United States in March 1933. From the start, their relationship was competitive.

Roosevelt's first order of business was to stimulate the economy and put people back to work. But before he could propose legislation of his own, the president had to deal with a measure that had already been proposed in the Senate, and that was intended to achieve the same objective. In December 1932, a month after Roosevelt was elected but three months before he took office, Black had introduced an economic recovery bill of his own. The idea was simplicity itself: Limit the workweek to thirty hours in any business that shipped its products across state lines or out of the country. Existing jobs would be distributed more widely across the population, thereby "creating" millions of new positions. The labor unions eagerly supported Black's proposal, giving the bill a good chance of passing.

Black's December timing posed a serious problem for Roosevelt. He and his advisers had in mind a much more ambitious set of plans intended to control and restart the economy, not just spread existing jobs to more employees. But the specifics of the revolutionary program that would be adopted during Roosevelt's first hundred days in office had not yet been made public. Black's bill, introduced before the Senate went out of session, was setting the agenda. It sent a message to the newly elected president that Black was a man to be reckoned with, not a team player who would wait for an order before taking action.

Not wanting to reject Black's plan outright, Roosevelt waited until he was inaugurated, then invited Black to the White House and told him he supported "a measure of that kind."[103] It was the first time the two men had met. Beneath the surface pleasantries, these two skilled politicians were immediately playing hardball. In Black's presence, Roosevelt made a show of calling Joe Robinson, the new Senate majority leader, requesting that Black's bill be taken up right away. This guaranteed Black a public hearing with media coverage—which, Roosevelt knew, a junior senator early in his second term would appreciate.

Then Roosevelt sent his secretary of labor, Frances Perkins (the first woman in any cabinet post), to testify before the Labor Committee that was considering the bill. She made the very basic point that limiting the workweek might drive down pay unless a minimum-wage provision was added. She suggested that a one-size-fits-all hourly limit was inappropriate: Instead the government should be empowered to set hours more flexibly.

These politely formulated proposed changes amounted to the proposal of a wholly different kind of bill, one that instead of limiting hours to a single standard would set a baseline of pay and set hours industry by industry. Black's bill comfortably passed in the Senate. In the House of Representatives, however, various amendments were introduced that followed the administration's proposed changes and differed from Black's simple solution. In May, Black's bill died.

Black had been outmaneuvered by Roosevelt. Yet the operation had been carried out deftly, without discrediting Black or making him look bad. Black had gotten his ideas before the public. Roosevelt then offered Black a further carrot. When his advisers had finished drafting the National Industrial Recovery Act, the signature legislation of what would come to be called the first New Deal, Roosevelt offered Black the opportunity to introduce it before the Senate.[104] This would have made Black's bill look like the precursor to Roosevelt's, while marking Black as an administration loyalist and a full participant in the forthcoming reforms.

Black refused. The NIRA created industry-wide committees made up of representatives from management and labor. Entrusted with quasi-governmental power, the committees were authorized to enact regulations that set prices as well as wages and hours. Black believed that if the industries were given the power to set prices and wages, they would collude to raise prices at the expense of the consumer. He objected also on the constitutional ground that Congress was giving away its own lawmaking power to these newly created trade associations.

Black voted against Roosevelt's measure, which passed easily and was later struck down by the Supreme Court as an unconstitutional delegation of legislative authority. Black's vote sent a clear message to Roosevelt that Black was not prepared to fall into line. He was shaping for himself a reputation as a radical Democrat, but even this he intended to accomplish on his own terms.

Black's unwillingness to be co-opted by Roosevelt was an expression of the man's considerable pride—a jealous guarding of personal honor that would have been familiar to anyone who knew Black when he was growing up in the Deep South. Black was the eighth and youngest child of a storekeeper in Harlan, a hamlet in Clay County, Alabama, so small it does not appear on maps. When he was three, the family moved a few miles to the town of Ashland, where a cow, a horse, and some chickens lived just outside their five-room house.[105]

A photograph taken in front of the family home shows Black at six years old, standing between his parents with his hand resting on his father's knee. His mother is sitting in a cane-backed rocking chair with a plaid blanket over her lap, almost as though she were his grandmother. The house is clad in plain boards. The fence out front is constructed from irregular, hand-hewn pickets. Like the house, it is unpainted.[106]

Black left his high school, known as Ashland College, at fifteen. A teacher had punished his sister for whispering in class.

When Black intervened, two teachers tried to whip him. Black fought back, avoiding the whipping but precipitating a conflict that required him to withdraw from the school.[107]

This exercise in honor was not without consequences. Black's education was far from complete. He took and failed the state teachers' exam. When his family packed him off to Birmingham, some sixty miles away, to study medicine, he left after a year despite passing his exams. His parents agreed to send him to the University of Alabama the following year, but Black, who wanted credit for his Ashland high school courses, refused to start a college degree from scratch. That bit of self-assertion led him to the law school in Tuscaloosa, which did not require a college degree for entrance.

The two-year program at the University of Alabama School of Law that Black entered as an eighteen-year-old in the fall of 1904 was even more basic than the Albany Law School program that Jackson would attend a few years later. The forty-odd students in the school were taught by just two professors. The two faculty members would lecture and then send their students off to the library to study. Black was able to take courses elsewhere in the university, substituting somewhat for the later high school and college education he had not received. A professor of history and political economy exposed him to the works of Thomas Jefferson, and a professor of literature assigned him weekly essays to write. His grades were strong. He was one of seven students in his law school class to achieve highest honors.

But in truth Black's formal education was no better than Jackson's, which is to say, not very extensive at all—certainly not compared to Frankfurter's combination of City College and Harvard Law School. Black was acutely aware of this fact. When he was elected a U.S. senator at the age of forty, he set about remedying his deficiency with an extensive course of self-guided reading. Although he was not, strictly speaking, an autodidact in the sense of Abraham Lincoln, he believed his education was his own more than a product of the University of Alabama.

In the twenty years between the time Black entered the practice of law as a solo practitioner and when he went on the national stage as a senator, he gradually built a reputation as a successful general-practice trial attorney with strong populist sympathies. Fresh from law school, he set up his practice in Birmingham, then a booming steel town, and began with small cases, earning just a few dollars at a time. To drum up business, he joined civic organizations like the Masons, the Knights of Pythias, the Eagles, and the Shriners.[108] At the First Baptist Church in Birmingham, he became active in the Sunday school, lecturing weekly to enthusiastic men's classes.

Black spent a memorable year and a half in 1911–1912 as a police court judge adjudicating low-level misdemeanors like drinking, fighting, and petty theft. He was twenty-five years old, spare at not quite five feet ten and 125 pounds, and full of energy—and he enjoyed deciding as many as a hundred cases in a morning's work. A contemporaneous newspaper photograph shows an extremely young-looking man, with a high forehead, a prominent nose, a small mouth, and a smaller chin verging on weakness. The eyes alone (they were green-blue and sparkled throughout his life) reflect the intelligence, drive, and self-possession that Black already had begun to manifest.[109]

Black got a lucky break in the police court. A young reporter, Charles H. Mandy, made him the recurrent hero of a long series of humorous yet admiring stories in the *Birmingham Age-Herald*. Laced with African-American dialect and an exaggerated paternalism toward the defendants who appeared before the court, the articles were meant as lighthearted human-interest reporting.

In one, a drunk defendant stumbles onto the train tracks and is hit by a locomotive. When Black asks the man if there was any injury, he answers that "the cowcatcher was bent and a headlight had broke." Black explains that he meant to ask whether the man himself had been injured. The defendant answers that the only injury he received was when the white man arrested him and locked him up. The article then quotes Black's verdict: "I believe you guilty of trying to wreck the train by throwing it from the track...but the evidence is hardly sufficient, so I will impose a fine of $10, but take it from me, John, the next time you are brought to your senses by being struck by a locomotive with such dire results to the machinery, I will sentence you to life imprisonment, and if you outlive the sentence you will be hung. Next case!"[110]

The positive press coverage gave Black name recognition in a town to which he was a recent arrival. Two years after stepping down from the police court, he ran for the office of prosecuting attorney on a reform platform, and won. After two years prosecuting full-time, Black returned to private practice. He soon began to court Josephine Foster.

Charming and lovely, Josephine was the daughter of a genteel minister from a good family who owned nine or ten thousand acres of cotton fields. Through a combination of mismanagement and the boll weevil blight, her father gradually squandered a family fortune worth five hundred thousand dollars.[111] Josephine attended Sweet Briar College for a year, and her sister made it through several years of Wellesley College, but each had to drop out when their father could not afford the fees.

Penniless though she was, Josephine belonged to the highest social class that Birmingham had to offer. She and her sister attended debutante balls with the mercurial Montgomery belle Zelda Sayre, who married F. Scott Fitzgerald in 1920. Zelda "used to come up to the dances in Birmingham and she was just gorgeous. She had sort of a golden glow around her and when she would come into a ball room, all the other girls would want to go home because they knew that the boys were going to be concentrating on her."[112]

Josephine herself had remarkable appeal—as well as a dark side of her own. Josephine had been "an unusually sweet, beautiful child—everyone adored her." Her father worshiped her, treating her as "the love of his life." At the same time, she was recognized as "delicate," a euphemism that hinted at a future of serious, continuing depression.[113]

Black was (and remained) blissfully unaware of Josephine's disposition, and in 1921 the two married. He was deeply in love, and Josephine was a prize for a rising young man. The distance between the Clay County store where Black had started and Josephine's Jazz Age set was considerable. The Fosters spoke in the accent of the upper class of the suburb of Mountain Brook, while for the rest of his life Black spoke in the subtly different accent of the Lower South.[114] If Black was not quite as poor as Jay Gatsby and Josephine no longer as rich as Daisy Buchanan, it was certainly the case that Black, a man on the way up, was entering a social echelon higher than that from which he came.

Black's Birmingham legal practice prospered. He frequently represented victims of injuries against the railroads or other corporations that injured them. The juries liked Black's serious courtroom manner and related to his clients, who were ordinary people like themselves. Earning on a contingency basis, Black made a lot of money. In his best year, he earned the princely sum of sixty-five thousand dollars.[115]

Then, in 1923, nearing the height of his prosperity, Black joined the Ku Klux Klan. The decision was motivated primarily by Black's political ambition. Black had joined other civic organizations before leaving his native Ashland for Birmingham in 1907. None of these had taken much reflection: A young lawyer had to make connections and drum up business, and fraternal societies played an important role in economic and social mobility. Black was sociably inclined, and his participation in these various organizations had continued as he was becoming established.

By contrast, Black thought long and hard about joining the Klan. He became a member only after his legal practice was secure and apparently in anticipation of his run for statewide office. He was not greatly concerned about the Klan's views. But Black certainly understood, as did everyone in Alabama, that the Klan was not just another Rotary Club. After the original Klan, a Southern-focused terrorist movement, had been suppressed in 1874, the Klan had been refounded in 1915. In its second historical incarnation, it was now a national organization with some four million members. Secret, controversial, and immensely powerful in the mid-1920s, it exercised a major influence on Alabama politics.[116]

A couple of years earlier, Black had encountered the Klan while trying his most high-profile case as a defense attorney. A barber and sometime Methodist minister named Edwin Roscoe Stephenson had killed a Catholic priest who had married Stephenson's daughter Ruth to a Puerto Rican named Pedro Gussman.[117] Stephenson, a member of the Klan's Birmingham Klavern, was infuriated that the priest had accepted his daughter into the Church and had joined her to a man Stephenson considered racially black. Before shooting the priest, Stephenson told him, "You have acted like a low down, dirty dog....That man is a nigger."[118] The facts of the case presented the perfect opportunity for the defense to invoke two of the Klan's favorite themes, anti-Catholicism and racism.

Black obliged. He emphasized Gussman's race, parading him in front of the jury so they could see him, and asserting that Puerto Ricans were of mixed race and therefore black. He urged the jury to see that the minister's daughter had been "proselytized" into the Catholic Church and away from her parents' faith. Several of the jury members were Klansmen, as was the judge. Black left nothing to chance: In his closing argument, he even quoted from the Klan's official prayer. He then asked the jury to absolve the defendant and deliver a verdict of not guilty by reason of insanity. But the jury went further: In an act of irreversible nullification, it substituted its own verdict of not guilty by reason of self-defense. The lesson of the Klan's power was not lost on Black.[119]

Mere membership in the Klan, though, would not alone have satisfied Black's objective of political advancement across Alabama. For that he would have to take advantage of the fact that the Klan had local chapters all over the state. By speaking widely—generally on anti-Catholic themes[120]—he was able to raise his profile among a motivated subset of voters in places where his name had not been previously known. There were even parades and conferences ("Konklaves," in the Klan's nomenclature) to attend. In its shadowy mimicry of the forms of 1920s civic-political life, the Ku Klux Klan gave Black what he otherwise would have been unable to attain: a statewide network of audiences and contacts, free of charge and inclined to identify with him.

All that was left was to cash in the chips. Conveniently enough, Black was the only Klan member running for the newly open Senate seat in 1926. At the recommendation of the Grand Dragon, the senior Klan leader in the state, who functioned almost as a de facto campaign manager, Black submitted a secret letter of resignation designed to give him deniability at some future date. It was signed with a Klan formula, "I.T.S.U.B."—in the sacred, unfailing bond— "Hugo Black." Black's strategy of joining the Klan had worked. In the primary election, he won handily—by a large enough margin to avoid a runoff. Black's highest percentages were achieved where Klan membership was highest.[121]

Having risen to power on the strength of the Klan's support, Black proved unfaithful to those who elected him. The occasion arose in 1928, just two years after Black was first elected. After a rousing nominating speech by Franklin Roosevelt, the Democratic Party chose as its presidential candidate Al Smith of New York, the first Catholic ever on a national ticket. It would have been difficult for Black to support Smith, who was not only a Catholic but an opponent of Prohibition, which Black as a Baptist strongly favored. Yet Black, like many other Southern populists, shared Smith's other progressive values—a fact he was willing to admit to the Alabama press. Smith carried the state.

Smith's success in Alabama marked, among other things, the Klan's rapid decline there. A series of violent attacks by Klan members in 1927 had created backlash from the state's political elites, and its membership numbers collapsed. For Black, the timing was fortuitous. He opposed the Klan-backed Senator James Thomas Heflin in 1930; and by the time Black ran for reelection in 1932, the Klan actively opposed him.

Black was reelected by a comfortable margin. Having gotten what he wanted from the Klan without having had to give much in return, Black no doubt believed the relationship was now safely behind him. He might have been right. But as it turned out, the Klan, however reduced in influence, never forgot a member—and when Roosevelt decided to put Black on the Court in 1937, Black's membership in the most virulently racist organization in U.S. history would return to haunt him.

CHAPTER 6

Out of the West

When thirty-seven-year-old William Orville Douglas first came to the White House and met Franklin Roosevelt in 1935, he was brought by Joseph Kennedy Sr., one of the more colorful and controversial figures in twentieth-century American public life. Not yet famous as the patriarch of the Kennedy clan, Joe Kennedy was nevertheless nationally known for having made a fortune as a successful stock market operator and sometime Hollywood mogul. A Harvard graduate, Kennedy had known both Roosevelt and Frankfurter since their World War I days, when Kennedy had served as assistant general manager of the manufacturing giant Bethlehem Steel. In 1934, Congress had authorized the creation of the Securities and Exchange Commission to regulate the national financial markets. To chair the powerful new commission, Roosevelt picked Kennedy.

Kennedy brought Douglas to Roosevelt because he was eager to show off a remarkable new protégé. He could not have guessed that the unprepossessing Douglas—gangly, with light, sandy hair and a hick's "ungovernable" cowlick—would soon achieve the fastest career advancement in the whole of the fast-moving New Deal.[122] Douglas, a Yale Law School professor, was working for Kennedy in a minor position, directing a study of corporate bankruptcy and reorganization for the SEC. The way he got that post, and his leapfrogging rise to Joe Kennedy's job in the space of only two years, says a lot about the wide-open hiring practices of the New Deal—but even more about the extraordinary Douglas himself.

Douglas's path to a professorship at Yale was by no means obvious, direct, or easy. His father was an itinerant minister in Washington State who died when Douglas was five, leaving him to be raised by a mother who was by turns worshipful and demanding. Never prosperous, after the father's death the Douglas family struggled to make ends meet. Douglas was raised in the small town of Yakima, Washington, in an atmosphere characterized by the desperate, constant fear of bankruptcy and destitution.[123]

At Yakima High School Douglas was valedictorian and played center on the basketball team, but he was still socially awkward. He aspired to attend the University of Washington, but his mother could not afford to send him, and so he settled on tiny Whitman College in Walla Walla, Washington, which gave him a partial academic scholarship for his first year. To cover the rest of his tuition, room, and board, and send money back to his mother, Douglas took odd jobs at which he worked essentially full-time: as a clerk in a jewelry store, a janitor in an office building, and (for food) a waiter in a "hash house."[124] He debated skillfully and joined the Beta Theta Pi fraternity. In what would become a pattern for him, his grades started as above-average but not exceptional, and then he closed strongly, making Phi Beta Kappa in his senior year.

On graduation, Douglas had the ambition to do something great, but no particular plan for how or what. He had competed unsuccessfully for a Rhodes scholarship and believed, perhaps not without reason, that had he attended the University of Washington he would have been well placed to win.[125] Now he returned to Yakima, where he spent two years teaching English at his old high school. No clear direction had emerged until Douglas met Mildred Riddle. Blond and beautiful—a pattern that would recur in Douglas's attractions—Riddle was fresh from her degree at the University of Oregon, and had come to teach Latin at the school where Douglas taught and which he had attended.

Hoping to get out of Yakima with Mildred, Douglas applied to Harvard Law School and was accepted. Without money, though, he could not enroll. A local attorney advised him that he might be able to work his way through Columbia Law School, since there were more jobs in New York than Boston. As was the case for Felix Frankfurter, the happenstance of knowing someone who had attended a particular institution seems to have been the main reason for his choice.

Giving Mildred an engagement ring, Douglas got himself a job feeding sheep on a freight train traveling from Washington to the East and embarked. This was a means of transport well known to Washington State boys, and not perceived by them as especially onerous.[126] Nevertheless, it captures Douglas's background perfectly, and the story soon became a staple of his cultivated self-image as a humble Westerner. The train was stopped in Chicago by a rail strike, and after ten days Douglas had to wire his brother for fifteen dollars to get to New York. Arriving in the city disheveled, unwashed, and with six cents in his pocket, Douglas needed to convince the residents of the Beta Theta Pi fraternity at Columbia that he was actually a member of an affiliated chapter before they would let him sleep there as fraternity rules required.[127]

Douglas did not immediately distinguish himself academically at Columbia. As at Whitman, he had to work long hours just to pay tuition and fees. After a year he had not made the law review, which he understood to be essential to his future career success. In his second year, his grades were good enough to make the review. More important still, he was hired as a research assistant to a professor, Underhill Moore, who was a pioneer in the fields of commercial banking and business organizations. Moore's mentorship would exert a crucial influence on Douglas's career path and thinking. Although Douglas did not finish at the very top of his law school class, his relationship with Moore would turn out to be a substitute for the grade-based academic validation enjoyed by Frankfurter in his time as a law student.

Moore was a proponent of an influential and important school of legal thought known as legal realism, which was just hitting its stride at Columbia in the mid-1920s. The proponents of legal realism objected to the way law had generally been studied and taught until that time—as a body of rules and principles that could be found in legal treatises and used by judges to decide cases. To the realists, law was not what judges said in formal rulings. Rather, law consisted in what legal actors actually *did* in the real world. On the surface, the law might look like a body of rules. But social, psychological, and especially economic forces determined results. The notion that law was a neutral, scientific system, the realists believed, was an elaborate cover for enforcing the preferences of those in power.

Many legal realists took this descriptive view a step further, believing that law as a field should actively be remade to achieve desirable social consequences. This perspective infuriated conservatives. They feared that legal realism, taken to its logical conclusion, would mean the death of the rule of law and its replacement by governmental fiat.

Some progressive legal thinkers, like Felix Frankfurter, tried to carve out a middle ground. Frankfurter rejected the realists' extreme claim that the law placed no limit on judges—that the law was, as an influential realist glibly put it, whatever the judge ate for breakfast.[128] He believed that law was a social tool that should be used to achieve progressive change—but by legislatures, not judges. To the lions of legal realism, this middle ground was incoherent and even laughable.

It was the more radical position that influenced Douglas. Working for Moore, Douglas imbibed the application of legal realism to corporations, using the new method of studying businesses and the way they made decisions to understand the way the legal system was truly shaping the real world. On graduation in 1926, Douglas had impressed Moore sufficiently that the faculty appointed him as one of two lecturers in law for the following academic year.

The lectureship was not the greatest prize that the faculty could bestow—that went to the editor in chief of the law review, who was sent to clerk for Justice Harlan Fiske Stone, the former dean of Columbia Law School. Douglas was devastated to have missed the Supreme Court clerkship: "The world was black and I was unspeakably depressed that for all those years and all that work, I had so little to show."[129] Douglas took the part-time lectureship as a consolation prize, and decided to embark on a career in corporate law. He joined the Cravath firm in New York, then as now one of the leading law firms in the country.

He hated it. The hours were outrageous and the pay only adequate. The young associate was plagued by health problems, which included migraine headaches and debilitating stomach pains. After a few months, Douglas quit Cravath, relying on his Columbia salary to carry him. The following academic year, still teaching two courses as a lecturer at Columbia, Douglas tried Cravath again, this time putting in seven months before he left the firm for good. Columbia had offered him a tenure-track associate professorship for the fall of 1927, just two years following his graduation from law school. And though over the summer of 1927 he traveled to the Pacific Northwest to consider entering law practice back in Yakima or perhaps Seattle, in the end he took up the position at Columbia and threw himself into the world of scholarship.

In a sense, the psychological pressures of practicing corporate law drove Douglas into the academy. Struggling with his migraines and debilitating stomach difficulties, Douglas sought medical help. After unsuccessful visits to many doctors, he finally found it—in the person of Dr. George Draper, Roosevelt's physician, who believed in treating the whole man through a combination of physiological and psychological approaches.

Displaying diagnostic brio and psychological insight, Draper told Douglas his stomach pain was psychosomatic, triggered among other things by fear of peritonitis, from which Douglas had suffered as a child. Showing Douglas a fluoroscopic image of his stomach, Draper whispered the words "Rudolph Valentino died of peritonitis." Immediately Douglas's stomach began to ache terribly. On the scope, Douglas could actually see his stomach reacting to the words. There was no denying that the disorder was triggered in Douglas's mind. Acknowledging this reality helped Douglas get over the pains. Disguising Douglas's identity to maintain patient confidentiality, Draper later wrote up the case in a book called *Disease and the Man*.[130]

Douglas found the experience of confronting his fears under Draper's guidance to be utterly transformative. In a memoir published near the end of his life, he wrote that "Draper psychoanalyzed me and helped me discover and understand the stresses and strains that produced the headaches." As a result, Douglas believed, "the main seminal influence in my life was Dr. George Draper.... Having discovered that I had been launched in life as a package of fears, he tried to convince me that all fears were illusory."[131]

The word *tried* in Douglas's later account is telling. Douglas did not entirely overcome his fears, any more than Roosevelt "recognized" his paralysis. Douglas would never achieve the "complete integration" that Draper sought for him. In fact, despite remaining close with Draper, Douglas's life from his midforties onward would be characterized by a series of personal and relationship crises that would turn his personal life into a mess even as his career continued to grow and develop. But for the moment, Douglas did try to follow Draper's advice—including the advice that overwork was contributing to his difficulties, and that he should leave private practice for some position less taxing.

Having found direction under Draper's care, Douglas for the first time in his life now focused intensively on a single pursuit. The concentration of his ambition and intelligence paid off—and there followed a whirlwind rise up the academic ladder. At the end of his first year teaching at Columbia, Douglas met Robert Maynard Hutchins, an academic almost exactly his age, who had graduated from Yale Law School in 1925, immediately been named a professor, and then two years later become dean of the school at twenty-eight.

Hutchins was, very literally, a man in a hurry. He liked Douglas immediately and recognized in him a fellow legal realist. Without delay, Hutchins offered Douglas a job teaching at Yale, where legal realism was about to enter its heyday. The timing was perfect for Douglas, since the newly appointed dean at Columbia was not sympathetic to legal realism. He accepted the job, and in fact several of Columbia's legal realists left the school in the next few years, including Douglas's mentor, Moore, who moved to Yale as well.

From the fall of 1928, when Douglas joined the Yale faculty, until 1935, when he left academe, Douglas was extremely productive. He authored dozens of articles in the legal-realist mode. Perhaps most astonishingly, in 1931 and 1932 he published five casebooks. Not merely reworkings of earlier compilations, these were wholly new volumes designed to enable students to study the life cycle of a corporation, from formation and financing through management, profit and loss, and bankruptcy or reorganization. This categorical approach was quintessentially realist, organizing legal knowledge not through the abstract categories of traditional legal doctrine but rather through the way "business organizations" (known formerly to lawyers as partnerships and corporations) operated in the real world.[132] And Douglas's scholarly articles were heavily based in the analysis of actual business decisions. Only after the New Deal started generating new laws that had not yet been applied in practice did Douglas turn to formal legal analysis—and that was because the corporations needed guidance to help them apply the laws for the first time.

This scholarly productivity was quickly rewarded with tenure; but that was not all. After Douglas's first year at Yale, Hutchins, now thirty, was hired away from his deanship to become president of the University of Chicago. Hutchins tried to hire Douglas, who was reluctant to go but was tempted by the outsize salary that Hutchins offered him to join a law faculty that was desperately in need of new talent. Douglas went so far as to accept the offer while receiving extensions to remain in New Haven and finish ongoing research. To keep him, Yale raised his salary to its own maximum and made him Sterling Professor of Law, its highest academic ranking.

Having achieved this position when he was not yet thirty-four years old, after just five years as a full-time professor and two as a lecturer, it was not surprising that Douglas began to look to Washington. His motive was not any deep-seated horror when the Depression hit: "I remember walking the streets of New Haven with the great sum of ten dollars in my pocket," he later wrote. "I did not feel panicky; personally, it only appeared that the wheel had turned, taking everyone back to the conditions of poverty I had known in Yakima."[133] What drove Douglas was the urge to be in the center of things. With Roosevelt in office, the action had shifted from the academy to the real world. Now was the moment for innovative legal ideas to make their way into practice. Many of Douglas's realist colleagues were going to work for the administration, and Douglas, intensely ambitious and competitive, did not want to be left behind.

In 1934, when the SEC was being formed, Douglas lobbied for one of the five commissioner posts, but did not have the political connections to get it. Instead the academic who was appointed to the original commission was James Landis. Landis was a prodigy like Douglas. A student and mentee of Frankfurter's, Landis was a professor at Harvard Law School and an expert in the rapidly growing field of legislation. He was just thirty-five when appointed to the commission with Frankfurter's help. At the end of 1935, when Joseph Kennedy stepped down, Landis would become the commission's chairman. A year later, Landis would leave the SEC to become dean of Harvard Law School at thirty-seven.[134]

The child of missionary parents in Japan, Landis had traveled a relatively smooth path from Princeton to Harvard Law School to a clerkship with Justice Louis Brandeis and back to Harvard as a faculty member. But Douglas was something else again: an intensely driven, self-made scrapper who had overcome real poverty and profound insecurity to achieve professional success. Landis would burn out, become an alcoholic, and spend a month incarcerated for failure to pay federal taxes.[135] Douglas would parlay his own SEC chairmanship into a seat on the Supreme Court, where he would enter constitutional history as a leading participant.

As of 1934, Landis and Douglas were competitors—the only two young law professors in the country to have enjoyed comparable early success. Naturally they knew one another's work. To his credit, Landis recommended to Kennedy that he hire Douglas to run the bankruptcy study, which was directly relevant to his academic expertise. When Landis was promoted to chairman, he urged Roosevelt to give Douglas a seat on the commission.

The rest was up to Douglas, and he made the most of it. If his rise to academic stardom was generated by a combination of intense work and fortunate patronage, his rapidly achieved Washington success would result from high-stakes, real-world work that was no less intense—and from patronage more powerful still. The patron would be Roosevelt himself, who saw in Douglas limitless energy, personal charm, and a capacity for self-mythologizing that was essential in a politician. Of all Roosevelt's men, Douglas was the one he most believed had the talent to succeed him.

Book Two

POWER

CHAPTER 7

Collapse

In 1931, Hugo Black, still serving his first term as a senator, did something highly unusual: He took his wife, Josephine, and their three children and moved from Washington, D.C., back to his in-laws' house in Birmingham, Alabama. Publicly, he told people he was going back to his political base to begin the process of running for a second term.

The truth was otherwise. As a result of the Depression, Josephine's parents, whose finances were always precarious, were now "dead broke." It was just that the Fosters could not admit it. "Everything always had to be surrounded by all kinds of protection to save their pride," Josephine's sister, Virginia Foster Durr, later explained, "because they really both just had this terrible feeling of failure and shame at losing everything that they had."[1]

Although his presence in his in-laws' home was described as "sort of a favor," Black had in fact come back to Alabama in order to find a polite way to take care of his in-laws. Black's son, Hugo Jr., remembered his father asking him to mail a letter with a check in it to his grandfather. When Hugo Jr. offered to bring it to Mr. Foster—who was sitting downstairs at the time—Black told him, "No, son. He won't take it. Do as I say."[2] Black saved Josephine's childhood home, but he could not save the Fosters' land. Josephine's father sold his cotton fields at the meager price of eight dollars an acre, barely enough to cover back taxes.[3]

The Fosters were not alone in their extremity. Black had made his fortune in Birmingham. Now he found the city devastated. Four of every ten people were "on relief of some kind, some kind of

relief job, or support from the government." A quarter of the population was getting its food from charity. Before the Depression,
Birmingham boasted 100,000 manufacturing jobs. That number
had shrunk to 15,000, and it stayed there for most of the 1930s.[4]

As jobs disappeared, what had been a bustling, prosperous
city rapidly became a crime-plagued urban nightmare. Virginia,
Josephine's sister, lived in Birmingham during the terrible year of
1931, and remembered the city's descent vividly. "Around me," she
recalled, "was just ruin, ruin and more furnaces shutting up and
the town became poorer and poorer and more and more beggars
were coming to the door and then this whole fear of being mugged
in the night." Crime in turn bred terror. "You didn't want to go
from your door to the garage, because there were people lurking
in the alley. Just any number of muggings and robberies because
people were absolutely desperate. Well, things in the city were getting very bad indeed."[5]

The troubles extended into rural Alabama, where Black went
campaigning. "He was out all over the state," Virginia remembered, "finding things bad wherever he went. People were just
desperate." But Birmingham and its surrounding towns were especially hard-hit as the boom of industrialization contracted into bust.
Steelworkers who lived in nearby company towns found that when
the factories shut down, so did stores, running water, and electricity. One company, Republic Steel, evicted its workers by force.
"They drove them out and put in guards to shoot them if they
came back," Virginia recalled. The erstwhile residents took shelter
in abandoned brick ovens.[6] Roosevelt, running for president, said
Birmingham was "the worst hit town in the country."[7]

As the 1932 election approached, Black offered to hold one-on-
one meetings with any constituent who wanted to speak to him
directly. Choosing a morning in October 1932, he set up an office
in the Birmingham federal building and announced he would be
there. When Black arrived at 9:00 a.m., hundreds of unemployed
people had crowded the lobby of the federal building. Black's
nephew Hollis, who was helping him in the campaign, was worried they would riot if Black reneged on his promise to meet them

individually. Hollis hastily scribbled down numbers on scraps of paper to be handed out to the crowd. Taking them in numerical order, Black saw each in turn.

For four full days, Black listened to the men. Ranging from farmers to court clerks to businessmen, they were, Black said, "my oldest and best friends." And they were desperate. "Some...were threatening suicide if they didn't get a job."[8]

The talk of suicide was not just rhetoric. Black's close friend and co-investor, Albert Lee Smith, lost his father-in-law to suicide. The man, Charles W. Gold, had founded a major Southern insurance company, Jefferson Standard Insurance, with $300 million worth of insurance policies in force. The Depression "battered" the company as sales plummeted and its investments failed. On September 21, 1932, Gold died of a gunshot wound to the head. In keeping with the politesse of the age, the death certificate stated that Gold had been "In Country 'Squirrel Hunting,'" an explanation provided by the company and duly repeated by the *New York Times*. Black, though, knew otherwise, as he hinted to his friend Smith in a letter of condolence.[9]

To Black, witnessing at firsthand the human effects of the worst economic disaster in U.S. history, Roosevelt's candidacy seemed like the beginning of an answer. As 1932 progressed, he became a strong Roosevelt supporter. Meanwhile, the Depression deepened and broadened.

CHAPTER 8

Security and Securities

By the time Roosevelt took office in March 1933, the events Black had encountered firsthand in Alabama had become fully national. One in four Americans was unemployed. Some five thousand banks had failed. Across the country, people evicted from their homes had begun to live in shantytowns known as Hoovervilles, without running water, sewage, or electricity.

The Hoovervilles were not restricted to outlying areas. One sprung up in Central Park, in the expanse that would later be turned into the Great Lawn. The shantytown in Anacostia, across the river from Washington, D.C., had some fifteen thousand veterans living in it until President Herbert Hoover ordered General Douglas MacArthur to clear it out in a show of force.[10] The tremendous gains that the United States had made over the previous century seemed on the brink of being reversed. As if to underscore the sense of apocalyptic reckoning, a drought had hit the agricultural heart of the country and showed no signs of abating.

In his inaugural address, Roosevelt famously told the country it had "nothing to fear but fear itself." This opaque formulation, though, was not what grabbed the attention of the media. They were more impressed by Roosevelt's evangelical attack on Wall Street. "Plenty is at our doorstep," he said, but it was just out of reach. "Primarily this is because the rulers of the exchange of mankind's goods have failed... and abdicated. Practices of the unscrupulous money changers stand indicted in the Court of public opinion, rejected by the hearts and minds of men." The "money changers" were the titans of finance and the traders and speculators.

Restoring the nation to economic prosperity required reining them in.

Through the course of the New Deal, Roosevelt would ultimately make fundamental changes to the American system of government regulation. Alongside the successful conduct of World War II, these would become his lasting legacy. When he took office, however, he did not yet have a well-developed theory of how regulatory reform should work. He had been a governor for just four years, and although he was an intelligent man with preternatural political talents, "he had never," as Jackson would later put it, "devoted himself to much study of the economic processes of the country."[11] The chief advantages he brought to the problem were the conviction that something needed to be done and the willingness to go against the entrenched interests of the wealthy class into which he had been born.

To make matters more complicated, although Roosevelt instinctively felt that Wall Street was to blame for the world's financial woes (he even mentioned Brandeis's key phrase, "other people's money," in his speech), his closest advisers did not entirely agree. Three Columbia University professors formed Roosevelt's so-called brain trust in the early days of the New Deal. They were Raymond Moley, a political scientist; Adolph Berle, a law professor; and Rexford Tugwell, an economist. Frankfurter was not among them. Indeed, he tried unsuccessfully to send a surrogate, his former student Max Lowenthal, to participate in the brain trust meetings, and was rebuffed.[12]

The Columbia brain trusters believed that the Depression had been caused by overproduction. Manufacturers and farmers had expected economic growth to continue indefinitely. They had borrowed money to expand to meet the anticipated growing demand. When demand in fact slowed, the producers could not pay their debts. They laid off workers, which reduced demand again, since the workers were also consumers. The result was to put the entire economy into a downward spiral. Wall Street had lent the money for expansion, it was true. But to the brain trusters, the goal was to fix the problem of overproduction, not to control stock speculation.[13]

The solution that the brain trusters devised was truly radi-cal. Free market competition was at fault, Tugwell argued. So the government should step in to coordinate workers, producers, and the financiers who funded corporations. Together, under govern-ment supervision, these players would set hours, wages, prices, and quantities of production. The National Industrial Recovery Act embodied this philosophy. Its symbol was the Blue Eagle, depicted in 1930s modernist style, holding in its talons electric bolts and a gear in place of the familiar arrows and olive branch. Beneath was a motto: "We Do Our Part."

Devised to be displayed as a mark of pride by businesses who agreed to participate in the "voluntary" programs administered by the National Recovery Administration, the Blue Eagle also hinted at what some critics of the program considered its similarities to the corporatist economic programs advocated by Benito Musso-lini and Adolf Hitler.[14] The NIRA fundamentally changed the face of American business. Traditional adversaries—direct competitors and labor unions and employers—were supposed to sit together in one room and work out their differences, all in the pursuit of the common good. Government representatives hovered in the back-ground, but the decisions of these new trade associations had the force of law. To many, this represented the death of capitalism. It certainly meant the end of the independence and freedom long viewed by American business as crucial to its success.

Felix Frankfurter did not think much of the NIRA, or its sister legislation for controlling farming prices, the Agricultural Adjust-ment Act. But instead of criticizing them directly, as Hugo Black did from the Senate floor, Frankfurter held his peace. The brain trust was not focused on Wall Street—and there Frankfurter saw his chance.

As Roosevelt had intuited, the way Wall Street operated did have much to do with the dire situation of the Great Depression. In the heady years before the crash, stock ownership had become increasingly common. In 1929, 18 million Americans, out of a national population of some 122 million, owned securities. As the market declined until it had lost a full 89 percent of its value, nearly one in ten Americans found their investments nearly wiped out.

For most ordinary investors, buying stock was like playing the numbers—but with less assurance that the rules would be followed. "The chief business of many lawyers and bankers," Robert Jackson said in 1935, "was to put 2 and 2 together so as to make 10. The most profitable form of overproduction was the overproduction of stock certificates."[15] Financial insiders, organized into buying and selling syndicates, regularly drove prices up and down using rumor and hidden trading. Accounting was unreliable or altogether absent. There was almost no way an investor could know with confidence the underlying value of the company whose stock he was buying.[16] "We bought water and paid for it with wind," Jackson said in biblical tones.[17]

Frankfurter believed that Wall Street could be saved only by being reformed. "The real enemy of capitalism," he later wrote in a note he passed to Roosevelt, "is not Communism but capitalists and their retinue of scribes and lawyers."[18] Frankfurter's opening came in April 1933, a month into the new administration, when Raymond Moley asked him for help with a bill regulating the issuance and sale of securities, the single most basic transaction on which Wall Street was built.

As professors, Moley and Frankfurter had had their differences in the past. But reforming Wall Street required knowledge of regulatory law, Frankfurter's particular expertise. For this purpose, Moley was willing to bring Frankfurter on board. Moley apparently did not consider Frankfurter to be a threat to his own inner-circle position with Roosevelt.

A bill had already been drafted reflecting the brain trusters' views about centralized government control. In essence, it put an existing government agency, the Federal Trade Commission, in charge of deciding when companies could issue stocks and bonds and when they could not. Judgment about whether a given security should be for sale would rest with the FTC, not the company itself, which had to apply for permission to raise money in the market. Unsurprisingly, Wall Street rejected the whole idea as simply unworkable.

Accepting the task of amending this bill to make it acceptable to Congress—which also meant acceptable to Wall Street—Frankfurter headed for Washington. He brought with him two brilliant legislative draftsmen. One was Professor James Landis, who would soon become a member and then chairman of the Securities and Exchange Commission. The other was Benjamin Cohen, a New Yorker who would become the most respected technical lawyer in the entire New Deal cohort of great lawyers, as legendary inside the Roosevelt administration as he was unknown outside it. Cohen had studied at Chicago and Harvard, where he had met Frankfurter. He had also worked alongside Frankfurter at the Paris peace conference, where both men represented the Zionist movement.[19]

Frankfurter set up Landis and Cohen at the Carlton Hotel, just across Lafayette Park from the White House. To provide political insight, Frankfurter brought in another of his protégés: Thomas Corcoran, who would come to be known in D.C. circles by Roosevelt's nickname for him, Tommy the Cork. The three men worked well together; but the pairing of Corcoran and Ben Cohen turned out to be especially propitious.

Quiet to the point of diffidence—and a lifelong bachelor—Cohen needed an outgoing partner to put his outstanding legal work into the political mix. Talkative, smiling, with "Irish good looks" and skills as a social piano player, Corcoran was just the man to do it. Becoming friends and roommates, the two together would write dozens of statutes, solve legal problems throughout the New Deal, and be featured on the cover of *Time* magazine as "the gold-dust twins." One historian wrote half-jokingly that the pair "constituted a sort of semi-autonomous fourth level of government."[20]

Frankfurter had taught Corcoran at Harvard Law School and chosen him to clerk for Holmes, the greatest vote of confidence possible for a student. Corcoran had met Roosevelt for the first time the previous month, on Holmes's ninety-second birthday, March 8, 1933. Frankfurter had arranged a small lunch at the retired justice's house in Georgetown for Frankfurter, Corcoran, and Holmes's then clerk Donald Hiss, brother of the later infamous Alger Hiss, who had also clerked for Holmes. They drank a few glasses each of Prohibition-era champagne (Holmes called it "fizzle water"), and then Frankfurter sprung his surprise: The president of the United States, on his fourth day in office, had come to call on Holmes. The five men sat quietly chatting together as Holmes and Roosevelt savored their historic meeting. After Roosevelt left, Holmes delivered his assessment of the new president: "A second-class intellect. But a first-class temperament."[21]

Frankfurter gave Corcoran, Cohen, and Landis their marching orders, and told them they had the weekend of April 8 to draft a new bill from scratch. The structure that Frankfurter outlined, and that the three men shaped into the Securities Act of 1933, rejected the idea that the government should decide whether securities should be issued. That judgment, the men believed, belonged properly to the market itself, which would be much better at deciding whether to buy the securities than any government official would be at determining whether it was a good or a bad idea to let a corporation float them. The job of government was, instead, to ensure that the market would have clear and honest information in order to determine the value and marketability of the securities.

The men who drafted the Securities Act were deeply influenced by Brandeis's longtime belief that, as he put it, "sunlight is . . . the best of disinfectants." Disclosure, not direct government supervision, was the key to financial honesty. In practice, Frankfurter and his protégés recognized, the operation of the financial markets was deeply corrupted. But in principle, they believed, the structure of market capitalism was perfectly fine. The market, not government officials, should make decisions about the financial soundness of particular investments.[22]

In the 1930s, this goal of preserving market capitalism by regulating its potentially corrupt features acquired a name: liberalism. Socialism and communism called for transfer of the ownership of the means of production to the people, which meant, in effect, the state. The economic theory of fascism also depended upon the shifting of economic decision making to collective, quasi-governmental bodies.

Liberalism flatly rejected that proposition. Liberals wanted to save capitalism by fixing it. The solution they proposed was regulation that would allow free markets to operate the way they should, in the presence of accurate, complete information. In this way, liberalism represented a subtle development away from the progressivism to which it owed its roots. Progressives, too, had favored regulation; but they were less concerned with preserving free market capitalism and were often willing to see the government make decisions that liberals preferred to leave to the market.

The Securities Act of 1933 was the wedge that let the liberal Frankfurter and his "happy hot-dogs"—men like Cohen, Corcoran, Landis, and dozens of others—into the Roosevelt administration. Once there, they would eventually replace the brain trusters and their revolutionary aim of centralized government control.

Frankfurter was personally identified with the 1933 act, defending it at length before the House Commerce Committee, which was chaired by congressman Sam Rayburn, who would later become the longest-serving Speaker of the House. Cohen and Corcoran sat beside Rayburn when he presided over the House debates on the act, making changes as needed. "Taken together," Rayburn said, "those two fellows made the most brilliant man I ever saw."[23] Frankfurter's influence in the new Roosevelt administration was on the rise.

Over the spring and summer of 1933, the pace of letters from the professor to the president—and occasionally back—grew rapidly. Often Frankfurter would send Roosevelt passages or even whole letters from others with advice for Roosevelt or comments on the job he was doing. Sometimes Frankfurter's favored technique was the congratulatory telegram after a Roosevelt speech or proposal. On a couple of occasions, Frankfurter sent policy memoranda, especially regarding matters of tax reform legislation.[24]

Then, in September 1933, just when it might have been expected that Frankfurter would increase the frequency of his visits to Washington and draw more directly upon the many connections he had already built in the administration's first six months, Frankfurter did something rather surprising. After a visit to the White House, Frankfurter and his wife, Marion, boarded the M.V.

Britannic, a luxurious White Star Liner like the *Titanic*, and sailed for England. For the next academic year, Frankfurter would be three thousand miles from Washington, serving as Eastman Professor at the University of Oxford.

The decision to go to England reflected Frankfurter's powerful Anglophilia. His love of England was not based on snobbishness or any self-identification. It came, rather, from the conviction that the American legal system to which he had devoted his life was properly understood as a branch of a greater Anglo-American legal system that was the best the world had to offer. Holmes himself had held this view, considering not only the common law but even the American constitutional system to be born from British origins. Holmes also maintained throughout his life close personal and literary friendships with English men and women, no doubt a model for Frankfurter as well. From previous shorter trips abroad, Frankfurter already knew some of the leading lights of British public and intellectual life. The opportunity to develop those relationships and to spend a year in the heart of one of the great world universities was enormously appealing to him.

But there was another, more important aspect to the decision to sail. With the New Deal coming up to speed, American public attention was focused heavily on the domestic front. Not so Frankfurter's. He had a keen interest in foreign affairs, dating back to his earlier government service in the War Department. A year in England was an opportunity to see Europe up close, and to become a source for the president not only on economic recovery but on foreign policy as well. Before he left, Frankfurter sought and obtained from Roosevelt the privilege of sending him letters through the diplomatic pouch. This was a level of access not available to the ordinary visiting professor, and Frankfurter would use it regularly.

And just as he was planning his trip to England, the situation in Europe took a personal turn for Frankfurter. In March 1933, days after Roosevelt assumed the presidency, Adolf Hitler stage-managed his own takeover of absolute power in Germany. As a Jew who was among the closest advisers to the president of the United

States, Frankfurter felt a responsibility to confront the challenge of Nazism directly. From that moment onward, he would do what he could to ally the president and the country with Germany's adversaries, to help contain Hitler—or, failing that, to defeat him in war.

CHAPTER 9

The Subpoena

As Frankfurter sailed to Europe, he took the trouble and expense to send a telegram from on board the *Britannic* recommending James Landis for a seat on the new Securities and Exchange Commission that was even then being formed to administer the Securities Act.[25] As one of the three drafters of the 1933 act, Landis had a claim to the job. One of the other two, Benjamin Cohen, was Jewish, and Roosevelt was worried about an anti-Semitic response if he put a Jew on the commission.[26] As for Thomas Corcoran—who promoted Cohen for the job—he was on his way to an even more important role within the Roosevelt administration.

Corcoran and Cohen had reprised their drafting role in preparing the Securities Exchange Act of 1934, which gave the SEC the power to prosecute the people who bought and sold securities if they lied or cheated in the process of disclosure. With Frankfurter in England, Corcoran took his place as the leading public advocate for the new legislation. This time it was the thirty-four-year-old Corcoran, not Frankfurter, who sat at the oak table in Sam Rayburn's Commerce Committee room to answer the attacks of the congressmen who were influenced by Wall Street money.

Corcoran performed brilliantly. Technically his job with the obscure Reconstruction Finance Corporation had nothing to do with drafting securities laws. One congressman asked Corcoran if anyone had authorized him to write the bill before them. No, Corcoran answered with a light touch. His drafting activities were "something extracurricular."

In fact, in the waning days of the Hoover administration, after taking a Depression-sized pay cut, Corcoran had quit his New York law firm and gone to work in the RFC. He had left to serve as an assistant to Dean Acheson, another Frankfurter student and former Brandeis clerk, who briefly was Roosevelt's undersecretary of the treasury but resigned when Roosevelt ordered him to raise the price of gold by buying above the market price.[27] Corcoran did not mind. He barely worked for Acheson. Instead he was busy, as Acheson put it, "running the rest of the government" by finding jobs for Frankfurter's protégés and involving himself in important new legislation. When Acheson resigned, Corcoran had returned to the RFC: a "temporary strategic retreat," he told Frankfurter.[28]

Roosevelt had met Corcoran at Holmes's house and knew he was Frankfurter's protégé. The president had also heard Corcoran play piano at the White House as one night's after-dinner entertainment. That had come about through Frankfurter, too. Before leaving for England, Frankfurter had written a note commending Corcoran to the attention of the remarkable Marguerite LeHand.[29]

Miss LeHand, whom everyone called Missy, was nominally the president's personal secretary. But she was also much more. She had begun to work for Roosevelt in 1920, after he lost the vice presidency but before his polio. For twenty years she was a combination of gatekeeper and quasi-spouse to the incapacitated Roosevelt. Roosevelt's son Elliott would write that the two "shared a completely familial existence."[30] Whether they were lovers is unknown; but it is striking that unlike Lucy Mercer, the mistress whom Eleanor hated and forbade her husband from seeing, LeHand remained on good terms with Eleanor throughout her life.

LeHand had introduced Corcoran into the White House social world, where he had shone. She would remain fond of Corcoran for the rest of her life. But Corcoran's ability to convince congressmen was more than a sign of good fellowship. It was an invaluable skill to a president with the most ambitious legislative agenda in history. After Corcoran's success defending the 1934 Securities Exchange Act, Roosevelt called him on the phone: "By God, you're the first man I've had who could handle himself on the Hill."[31]

Corcoran's skill lay in his access to the president and his ability to deliver. Sam Rayburn, for example, asked Corcoran to see if he could arrange a regular weekly meeting between the president and the Democratic congressional leaders to coordinate legislative efforts. Rayburn, who was not yet Speaker, knew the proposal was a little presumptuous coming from him, so he told Corcoran, "Don't dare let him know I suggested it 'cause he thinks he 'borned' every idea that ever lived." The next time Rayburn was at the White House, Roosevelt said to him, "Sam, I've been thinking." He then proposed a weekly meeting with the vice president, the Speaker of the House, the Senate majority leader—and Rayburn. "Mr. President," Rayburn replied, "that's one of the smartest ideas I've ever heard."[32]

Corcoran had done his magic. "Little by little," he recalled, "I was the guy who handled the tough ones on the Hill." He was on his way to becoming the president's designated strategist, operative, and, in his sometime friend William O. Douglas's memorable description, "hatchet-man."[33] For nearly two terms of Roosevelt's presidency, Corcoran's fingerprints would appear on every major appointment—especially once Roosevelt got the chance to start naming Supreme Court justices. His influence within the New Deal was unparalleled. Eventually, it would make him both famous and notorious.

One of Corcoran's oddest jobs for Roosevelt was passing on a message to the unruly vice president, John Nance Garner, about a new piece of legislation that Corcoran was drafting in the spring of 1935. The legislation involved "public utility holding companies," private companies owned by rich and powerful financiers who used them to control power, water, and other crucial public services. The Roosevelt administration had introduced a bill requiring these companies to dissolve themselves by 1940 or face dissolution by the SEC.

Roosevelt needed Vice President Garner to keep his opposition quiet. Garner, a Texan who gloried in the nickname Cactus Jack, liked to play the role of hard-drinking good old boy. He installed a bar and urinal in the vice president's office; and it was he who famously said the job of vice president was "not worth a bucket of warm piss."[34] Garner had briefly been Speaker of the House of Representatives, and he epitomized business as usual on the Hill. He had no intention of supporting the administration's bill.

Garner demanded that the normally abstemious Corcoran have a whiskey with him. As Corcoran told it, "The message never got delivered, and I was stiff when I got back to the White House and reported to Frankie." So Roosevelt sent Frankfurter to see Garner. When he made it back to the White House, Frankfurter "wasn't just stiff, he couldn't stand up. He couldn't even remember what Garner said, or what he said."[35]

Garner had read the politics correctly. Lobbyists for the holding companies descended on Capitol Hill, fighting for their clients' lives against what they called the "death-sentence amendment." With pressure from the Roosevelt administration on one side and the lobbyists on the other, the fight on Capitol Hill was brutal—so brutal, in fact, that many observers thought it was the worst ever.

Corcoran was at the heart of the lobbying for the bill he had drafted. The night before the vote, in recognition of his involvement, Roosevelt invited him to dinner at Joe Kennedy's house— Marwood on the Potomac, a replica of the Château de Malmaison that Napoleon built for the Empress Josephine. The *New York Times* Washington bureau chief and columnist Arthur Krock was spending the weekend with Kennedy at Marwood. Roosevelt was angry with Krock for some columns critical of New Deal policies. Rather than making his houseguest leave or incurring the president's displeasure, Kennedy told Krock to stay upstairs—from which vantage point Krock eavesdropped on the entire evening's proceedings.[36]

The festivities included Corcoran, Roosevelt, Kennedy, Missy LeHand, her assistant Grace Tully, and John J. Burns, the general counsel of the SEC, who was a Bostonian Catholic with connections to Kennedy. Kennedy proposed that they drink mint juleps—which Roosevelt said would be "swell." After what Krock described as "a reasonable number" of the seasonally appropriate drinks, dinner was served. Then the guests watched a screening of *Ginger*, starring child actress Jane Withers. Roosevelt "said the movie was one of the best in years."[37]

After dinner, as Krock described it, Corcoran came into his own. He had brought his accordion with him, and in the absence of a piano began to play Irish songs, in which Roosevelt heartily joined "in a rather nice tenor-baritone." Roosevelt told the story of how after the 1932 Democratic convention, he went in search of campaign songs, and came up with "The old GOP, it ain't what it uster be." Corcoran then improvised a version of the tune, substituting the name of an Alabama Democrat who was opposing the public utilities bill for which they had been lobbying. "Old George Huddleston," he sang, "he ain't what he uster be." Roosevelt responded with a verse about another opponent of the bill.

When the music was over, Corcoran announced, "I've never been drunk in my life, but if this amendment goes through tomorrow, I'm going to get stinking." Roosevelt laughed and laughed. Krock drifted off to sleep well after midnight, "pondering the paradoxes of the men who occupy the highest office in the land." But the next day, in a rare outcome for Roosevelt and Corcoran alike, the bill was defeated.[38]

When the dust settled, Republicans called for an investigation into the lobbying techniques that the Roosevelt administration had used during the fight. Faced with criticism, Corcoran turned the tables. He convinced Senator Burton Wheeler, who had sponsored the bill in the first place, to seek a Senate resolution authorizing a special committee to investigate lobbying in connection with the holding companies legislation. When Wheeler declined to run the committee—a result Corcoran had anticipated—he turned to Hugo Black.

The senator from Alabama had already crossed swords with Roosevelt by rejecting the NIRA. From Corcoran's perspective, Black needed a project that would keep him busy while serving the administration's interests. Black smelled the chance to make headlines by investigating the public utility holding companies who had blocked the bill. He agreed to run the special subcommittee—and the hearings that followed would make Black nationally famous.

Black was assured of support from the administration, which believed that exposing the companies' lobbying practices would help Democrats reintroduce the original legislation. For the rest, he relied on a combination of his prosecutorial experience and his populist political instincts, and he turned a special Senate sub-committee into his personal forum for what his enemies called an "inquisition" into the shadowy practices for holding companies that controlled most public utilities in the United States.

Black knew that the public was not likely to care about any-thing so dull-sounding as "holding companies." He needed a face for his investigation—a bad actor who embodied the excesses and dishonesty of business, and had also been involved in lobbying to preserve his ill-gotten gains. After a few false starts, Black found his villain: "fat, flour-faced" Howard C. Hopson, the founder and president of a company called Associated Gas & Electric.[39]

Hopson had begun his career as a regulator of public utilities for the New York State Public Service Commission. After an inauspi-cious start—he was arrested and sentenced to thirty days in the work house for "accosting" a woman and her daughter outside a theater at the corner of Forty-seventh Street and Broadway—Hopson made good.[40] Taking advantage of his specialized knowledge of the utilities industry, he built AG&E into a regional conglomerate of electric and gas utilities spreading through New York, Pennsylvania, and Ohio.

But Hopson's financial success had a questionable smell, one Black could exploit. Between 1929 and 1933, the heart of the Depression, Hopson and his family had taken profits of some $3,187,064 from AG&E. During those same years, the company's shareholders had received not one penny in dividends. The money that Hopson had bonused to himself came from the monopoly profits that utilities automatically earned and that were supposed to make them safe, stable, and dividend-paying investments for ordi-nary stockholders.

Hopson had not wanted the bonanza of AG&E ownership to

come to an end as a result of Roosevelt's bill. He had deployed all the lobbying techniques he could. One of his lobbyists testified that he had spent the whole summer of 1935 working against the bill through "indirect salesmanship," which one senator called "contacts over the cocktail glass."[41] And Hopson, it transpired, had arranged for hundreds of telegrams under multiple names to be sent to various congressmen, all opposing the bill.

Using his powers as committee chairman, Black issued a subpoena ordering Hopson to appear before the Senate and to bring copies of the telegrams with him. Hopson naturally tried to avoid the subpoena. Black grabbed headlines by sending the sergeant at arms of the Senate to find Hopson and serve him personally. When Hopson still did not appear, Black called for his arrest on the charge of contempt of the Senate.

Hopson caved. But the telegrams, which became part of the record, were not what damaged Hopson most—or what made him so useful to Black. Using subpoenaed documents from AG&E's offices, Black examined Hopson himself under oath. He showed that Hopson had coordinated the lobbying campaign directly. Then Black went on to reveal, through Hopson's business records, how Hopson had enriched his family while defrauding his shareholders. The shenanigans of the rich businessman made national news. Black's successful efforts helped generate a compromise version of the bill. Hopson was eventually tried and convicted of fraud and tax evasion and sentenced to five years in prison. Ultimately, it turned out he had defrauded his investors of more than $20 million.[42]

Having tasted national prominence, Black had no interest in folding his special committee. Beginning in 1936, he undertook investigations against a series of anti–New Deal lobbying groups. Precursors of today's "astroturf" lobbying organizations, which are designed to appear to be springing from the grass roots, the groups were in fact funded by big corporations and rich families like the DuPonts, Mellons, Morgans, and Rockefellers.[43]

The technique of the subpoena was working for Black, and so he pushed it to its limits. His special trick was to subpoena

Western Union directly, demanding archived copies of telegrams to or from particular recipients. In one celebrated instance, Black ordered delivery of ten months' worth of telegrams to and from a prominent Chicago law firm. Black lost that fight when a federal court quashed the subpoena, convinced by the law firm's argument that Black's efforts were "inquisitional" and a "fishing expedition."[44]

But Black won another, more prominent fight with an even more powerful adversary in his expansive use of the subpoena power. One of Black's more astounding Western Union requests had been to subpoena copies of every telegram sent into Washington, D.C., during the period when the lobbying over the public utilities bill had taken place. Among the thousands of telegrams they reviewed, Black's staff found a particularly juicy cable from William Randolph Hearst, the nation's most powerful newspaper owner, to his staff in Washington.

Aging and erratic, the great Hearst would soon break with Roosevelt, whom he had supported for election in 1932. In April 1935, Hearst had become furious with Congressman John McSwain, a harmless South Carolina Democrat who chaired the House Armed Services Committee. McSwain had accidentally crossed Hearst while investigating the use of the Army Air Corps to carry airmail—a Roosevelt innovation that Hearst opposed so mightily that he deputed Roosevelt's son Elliott to lobby his father over it.[45]

In the telegram, the man who had once launched wars with his headlines addressed the editors with the directness of the yellow journalist: "Why not make several editorials calling for the impeachment of Mr. Swain [sic]. He is the enemy within the gates of Congress, the nation's citadel. He is a Communist in spirit and a traitor in fact. He would leave the United States naked to its foreign and domestic enemies." And there was a deadline: "Please make these editorials for the morning papers."[46]

Black passed the telegram on to McSwain, who read it on the House floor to gales of laughter and intermittent applause. Black had made himself a new enemy. "We are having some trouble with Mr. Hearst," he told a friend lightly.[47]

Hearst retaliated with a lawsuit, demanding that the courts declare Black's investigation unconstitutional and force Black to return the telegram to him. The case of *Hearst v. Black* was not a trivial one for the senator: His reputation was at stake. Black sent for his Birmingham law partner, Crampton Harris, to represent him.

The federal appeals court for the District of Columbia rendered a Solomonic decision. It held that the Federal Communications Commission, which had ordered the telegrams handed over, lacked the authority to pass them along to the Senate. But, the Court continued, once the telegrams were in Senator Black's hands, the Court lacked the power to make him give them back. Hearst had to settle for establishing the principle that telegrams were not open season for Congress to investigate, and Black got to keep the proceeds—in documents and in prominence.

The fame and power Black gained came, it must be said, in large part from his invasion of what the telegram writers believed were private communications. Unlike a criminal investigation, where probable cause of criminal activity would have to be shown before a subpoena could issue, the Senate's investigative powers were not in any obvious way subject to specific legal restraints. Black, in fact, argued at the time that the great advantage of such legislative investigation was that only it could reveal the kinds of lawful but shady lobbying techniques that distorted the lawmaking process.

Black was legitimately outraged by corporate wrongdoing—but he was also glorying in exploiting his power as a senator. That power could ruin reputations. Evidence unearthed could be used for criminal prosecution, as it was for Howard Hopson. As a result, Black's techniques ran into harsh criticism from advocates of civil liberties, who noted that unrestricted investigative powers into private communications posed dangers all their own. Even Walter Lippmann, the eminent newspaper columnist whose own fame had been established in no small part by his criticism of corporate power, wrote a piece warning that legislative inquiry was in danger of becoming "an engine of tyranny."[48]

Challenged in the name of the Constitution, Black responded

by appealing to the people. He was, he said, protecting their interests against the distorting effects of rich lobbyists. Here he was speaking a language increasingly familiar to the Roosevelt administration itself. Critics of the New Deal were claiming Roosevelt's programs exceeded constitutional norms. The Supreme Court was blocking the administration and Congress from implementing its most aggressive reforms, such as the NIRA.

The Roosevelt administration had an answer to the constitutional arguments against its reforms. The rights to free speech, privacy, and property were being invoked by the richest members of society in order to protect the system that they had created and from which they profited. The courts, purporting to enforce these rights, were really using them as an excuse to stand in the way of change. That made the courts into enemies of the people.

The stage was being set for a confrontation over the Constitution: a confrontation between the president of the United States and the courts that were standing in his way. The decisive battle between the executive and the judiciary would take place in Congress. And the fight would prove decisive for the future of constitutional law in the United States.

CHAPTER 10

Art and Taxes

As Hugo Black was being sued by William Randolph Hearst, Robert Jackson was taking on another of the most powerful Americans of the Roaring Twenties: Andrew Mellon, the third richest man in the United States. The investigation and trial of Mellon on charges of tax evasion marked one of the most misconceived political undertakings of the entire Roosevelt administration.

Mellon was no ordinary wealthy businessman. Beyond his extreme wealth, amassed in banking, oil, and steel, Mellon had a distinguished record of public service. Appointed secretary of the treasury by Warren G. Harding in 1921, he had served for nearly eleven years, through the presidencies of Calvin Coolidge and Herbert Hoover. The third-longest-serving treasury secretary ever, he had presided over the boom years of the twenties as well as the crash of 1929 and the failed recovery effects that followed. More than any other single person, Mellon embodied the financial system of the United States.[49]

As the most visible and durable symbol of the Republican establishment of the 1920s and early 1930s, Mellon had come in for intense criticism once the Depression began. The chief target of his critics was Mellon's policy in reaction to the crash: he refused to bail out failing banks, insisted on fiscal discipline, and resisted the impulse to financial stimulus spending. This course of treatment had not healed the market or put the economy on the rebound. But it was hardly criminal—just mistaken.

A Democratic effort to impeach Mellon in 1931 had led to his resignation. Far from being disgraced, however, Mellon had been named by Hoover as ambassador to the Court of St. James's, traditionally the most prestigious appointment in the diplomatic corps. With Roosevelt's election, however, the Democrats had another chance to pursue Mellon, who remained a potent reminder of the broken financial system and the rule of the robber barons.

With his luxuriant white moustache and hooded eyes, Mellon even looked the part of the shadowy plutocrat. The young men of the New Deal were bright-eyed and clean-shaven. Flush with the success of Roosevelt's election, the righteous glow of reform, and the political desire to show their predecessors not merely incompetent but corrupt, senior figures in the Roosevelt administration made the decision to investigate Mellon. Roosevelt, full of zeal, approved the decision personally.[50]

The prosecution of Mellon began badly. Attorney General Homer Cummings publicly announced he would seek a criminal indictment against Mellon before a Pittsburgh grand jury for tax fraud. This grandstanding was highly unusual—the attorney general of the new administration declaring war on the secretary of the treasury from the previous three. It was also foolish. The Department of Justice had not given Mellon or his attorneys the customary opportunity to show privately that no intentional fraud was involved.

As a result of their aggressiveness, the government attorneys did not realize that Mellon had done nothing without seeking the advice of his tax lawyers. The choice of Pittsburgh as the venue was ill-starred, too. Mellon not only owned several banks there; he had given many millions of dollars to a local university (now Carnegie-Mellon) and other civic organizations. After the evidence was presented, the grand jury turned the government down flat. The saying goes that a prosecutor can indict a ham sandwich. But in Pittsburgh or anywhere else, Andrew Mellon was no ham sandwich.

The administration was deeply embarrassed by what Walter Lippmann, who was usually sympathetic, called "a low and inept political maneuver."[51] Now, as a matter of political cover, it became more important than ever for some government body to find

Mellon responsible for some tax-related wrongdoing. The search for a champion led circuitously to the Treasury Department, the Bureau of Internal Revenue—and its new general counsel, Robert Jackson.

Although Jackson had known Roosevelt for twenty years, his position in the government was not a high-profile one. Jackson and Roosevelt had clashed when Roosevelt was still governor of New York, and as a result, Jackson had not followed Roosevelt to Washington immediately. Instead, he had been recruited by James Farley, a powerful New York politician who was both chairman of the Democratic National Committee and postmaster general of the United States. Farley had arranged a speaking tour of prominent upstate Democrats in advance of state assembly elections in the fall of 1933. Impressed with Jackson, Farley urged him to come to Washington.

Jackson was picky, turning down legal positions in the Works Progress Administration and the Department of Agriculture. The job in the Bureau of Internal Revenue had a better title and more responsibility than the others, with a staff of almost three hundred lawyers. But even after meeting Henry Morgenthau Jr., the secretary of the treasury, Jackson still hesitated. Ultimately he agreed to take the position only if he could return to Jamestown on Fridays and spend Saturday, Sunday, and Monday working at his law practice there. This unrealistic arrangement did not last. That Jackson attempted it at all showed how reluctant he was to give up his thriving practice—and how inexperienced he still was in the ways of the world beyond Jamestown.

Unbeknownst to Jackson, the Bureau of Internal Revenue was something of a minefield. The outgoing general counsel was E. Barrett Prettyman, a talented, experienced, and extremely plugged-in Washington lawyer. (Prettyman later served on the U.S. Court of Appeals for the D.C. Circuit with such distinction that the courthouse was named for him.) Prettyman had been fired by Morgenthau—but no one had told Prettyman, much less Jackson, who arrived in the office to find Prettyman still behind his desk. Then the unknown Jackson had to overcome Senate opposition to his confirmation. The basis for the opposition was not Jackson's total lack of experience in the complexities of tax law—although that might have been a good reason. It was that Prettyman's father had been chaplain of the Senate. As a result, the senators took a fatherly interest in Prettyman, and resented his firing and its manner.

The bigger problem with Jackson's new job was the Mellon case. Once the Department of Justice had publicly failed to bring a successful criminal charge, the only remaining venue to catch Mellon was a civil hearing before the Board of Tax Appeals. Needless to say, no one—certainly not the Department of Justice, which had already been humiliated—wanted to present the case. Jackson had played no role in initiating this debacle-in-the-making. It had begun even before he arrived in Washington. It landed on Jackson's desk because he lacked the clout to say no.

To make matters worse, Jackson did not get to choose his own theory of the case he was to present. After investigating, Jackson believed that it would be almost impossible to prove fraud even in a civil proceeding. The best that could be hoped for was a ruling that he must pay taxes he had previously avoided. But Cummings, the attorney general, outranked Jackson, and he insisted that the fraud charge be included in the hopes of vindicating his ill-fated attempt at a criminal indictment. Roosevelt, who was in on trial strategy—so significant was the case—went along with Cummings in a meeting that Jackson was considered too unimportant to attend.[52]

Yet Jackson waded gamely into the Mellon tax prosecution, and through it he gained his first taste of national recognition. The case was tried in Pittsburgh, where, as Jackson later put it, he was "in the enemy country." On the other side was the legendary criminal-defense attorney Frank J. Hogan, who had once famously said that his ideal client was "a rich man who is thoroughly scared." The spectacle of Roosevelt's Treasury Department going after the former secretary of the treasury—who was also spectacularly rich and famous—made the case front-page news nationwide. Hogan appeared on the cover of *Time* magazine.[53]

Jackson, who formed a personal affection for the theatrical Hogan, gladly played into the scenario. When Hogan remarked to the press that Jackson was "just a country lawyer," Jackson "immediately picked that up and said, 'Yes, that's what I am. That's just what I am.'"[54] The "country lawyer" sobriquet became a Jackson trademark. In Jackson's appropriation of the phrase *country* did not imply simplicity; after all, he got the name trying an enormously complex tax case. *Country* meant common sense. For Jackson, the term became part of a narrative that also included his lack of a law school degree and the trials he had conducted in the justice of the peace courts. Eventually, invoking country common sense would provide context and cover for Jackson's willingness to dismiss accumulated doctrinal precedent when he did not think it led to results that were pragmatically sound.

The most serious difficulty faced by the government in the Mellon trial was that it was trying to change the rules of tax law to make them more focused on the substantive realities of financial control and benefit, and less on empty formalities. Mellon, it turned out, had scrupulously followed what he had been advised was the letter of the law. For example, on becoming secretary of the treasury, when he had to divest himself of his enormous financial holdings, he simply lent money to his brother to "buy" him out, and then continued to direct his business holdings as he had always done. Similarly, when it came to paying taxes, he had followed the practice of "selling" his profit-making securities at a loss to a shell company on December 31, and buying them back the next day. With the possible exception of continuing to run his business while serving as treasury secretary, nothing that Mellon had done was definitively illegal when Mellon had done it.[55]

Roosevelt's men were trying to change the rules, and hold Mellon retroactively responsible. The trial was criticized, Jackson later recalled, as "an attempt to judge past transactions by new standards that were not enforced when the transactions took place."[56] To pull this off, Jackson needed a strategy—one that would resonate with a public that was angry with anyone so rich that he was still unimaginably wealthy after the crash and into the Depression.

Jackson's approach was to emphasize that Mellon's wealth did not put him above the law. "It is Mr. Mellon's credo," Jackson memorably said, "that $200,000,000 can do no wrong. Our offense consists in doubting it."[57] He also focused on one of Mellon's more spectacular tax dodges—one that involved his collection of paintings, at the time "the finest collection of old masters in the universe."[58]

Mellon's art collecting had begun as early as 1896, under the influence of his friend and business partner Henry Clay Frick, who would himself amass the collection that is now housed in his former home at Fifth Avenue and Seventieth Street in New York City.[59] But Mellon's buying had been slow and inconsistent—not to mention poorly chosen—until 1921, when he began to buy excellent paintings handpicked for him by a British-Jewish dealer, Sir Joseph Duveen. This dealer extraordinaire had stalked Mellon in the hopes of making him a client. According to the story Duveen told, during one of Mellon's visits to London, Duveen rented a suite at Claridge's Hotel directly beneath Mellon's. He bribed Mellon's personal valet to call him when Mellon left his suite. Then Duveen appeared in the elevator, declaring a remarkable coincidence.[60]

Once Duveen had begun to influence Mellon's taste, the magnate's purchases grew bolder. He had reached his height in 1930, when the Soviet Union, buffeted by the crash of 1929 and desperately in need of cash for its next Five Year Plan, had decided to sell off some of the treasures of the Hermitage Museum in St. Petersburg. Duveen himself was eager to buy any of the incomparable pieces the Soviets were prepared to sell. But Mellon went around the dealer and bargained with the Soviets directly. In this Mellon had a huge advantage: He was secretary of the treasury of the United States.[61]

The Soviets welcomed the opportunity to combine cash sales with political influence. In particular, they were facing a potential embargo on cheap Soviet lumber, which American protectionists claimed was being harvested with slave labor. Mellon, whose Treasury position gave him control over much of trade policy, cleverly announced an embargo on any lumber that could be shown to have been produced using slave labor. The result favored the Soviets, since proof was hard to establish in any particular case. He also decided against American manganese producers who protested that the Soviets were dumping the metal at below-market rates.[62] These decisions might have been the right ones; both reflected Mellon's generally free-trade perspective. At the same time they were made, however, Mellon was spending $8 million (some $250 million in today's dollars) on twenty-three masterpieces from the Hermitage. The purchases were kept secret from the public.[63]

Having bought all these paintings, Mellon figured out that they could be used to keep his taxes low. He formed a nonprofit foundation, the A. W. Mellon Educational and Charitable Trust. Then, as needed, he donated paintings to the foundation that he himself controlled. Each time a donation was made, Mellon deducted the value of the painting from his income. The paintings themselves never moved. They stayed in a vault at the Corcoran Gallery in Washington—Jackson made a field trip to see them—or else on the walls of Mellon's own houses in Pittsburgh, New York, and Washington.[64]

To Jackson, seeking to prove that Mellon had engaged in tax fraud, the paintings formed a perfect target. Mellon had "donated" some $40 million worth of art—yet he had done nothing to suggest that the paintings were going to be used for educational or charitable purposes. Jackson depicted Mellon as a greedy old man, exploiting a tax loophole while he privately gloated at his haul of great works.[65]

For Mellon, there was just one way out of Jackson's charge that he had donated paintings to himself. On the first day of the trial, Frank Hogan, Mellon's lawyer, announced with great fanfare that Mellon intended to give his collection of masterpiece paintings to the federal government for the purposes of creating a national art gallery in Washington. Indeed, Hogan insisted, this had been Mellon's plan all along. The trust had been created so that Mellon could give his art to the people. Such a charitable impulse, Hogan maintained, was inconsistent with Jackson's depiction of Mellon as a tax cheat.

The truth was a little hard to determine. Mellon had at least flirted with some version of the national gallery idea before. In the winter of 1927, the newspapers had reported the rumor that a national gallery would be built on the Mall, and hinted that Mellon had offered to spend $10 million of his own money to build the building.[66] But Mellon also seems to have considered keeping the art in his own home in Pittsburgh and turning it into a museum after his death, on the model of his friend Frick.[67]

To prove Mellon's intent, Hogan called the dealer Duveen to the stand. A greater conflict of interest could hardly be conceived. Duveen, who was by now Baron Duveen of Milbank, stood to gain tremendously if the plan for a national gallery came to pass, since he would be able to sell a grateful Mellon more art to put in it. While he was testifying about one tough negotiation between himself and Mellon, the usually somber defendant actually winked at him.[68]

Jackson did his best to shake Duveen, whom he described as "about the most fantastic witness I ever saw on the witness stand."[69] By *fantastic* Jackson did not mean "wonderful"—he meant "full of fantasy." Indeed, Duveen rather wonderfully claimed he could not quite remember where Mellon had told him the gallery would go: "He showed me a little sketch on the back of an envelope," Duveen said impatiently. "I think it was by the pond, by the little obelisk." Jackson was dismissive. "A pond with an obelisk? What do you mean?" he asked. Duveen was talking about the Washington Monument and the reflecting pool. The laughter in the room went on so long that a court employee had to pound for order.[70]

Jackson's crucial moment during the Mellon trial came in his direct examination of the protagonist. Mellon, it turned out, wanted to talk, and Jackson encouraged him to do so. From a defense attorney's perspective, nothing could be more horrifying than watching one's client consistently go beyond yes or no answers, since each extra fact potentially provides grist for the prosecution's mill. But politicians are not ordinary defendants, and in any event Mellon was not facing a criminal prosecution. Eighty years old, and frustrated at having his integrity impugned after years of public service, Mellon's goal was to rehabilitate his reputation. He spoke fluently and without rancor, offering what was essentially an account of his entire life. To some extent, Mellon did vindicate his personal cause with the testimony.[71]

For Jackson, though, Mellon's digressive and detailed answers were a godsend. They showed that Mellon was sincere by his own lights. But they also demonstrated the outrageous chicanery that the rich could employ while claiming to obey the law. This served the political purposes of the New Deal, just like Hugo Black's investigation of the utility holding companies and their rich owners. Both inquiries revealed the extent to which the American system of government allowed the wealthy to do more or less whatever they wanted.

The result was a standoff between Jackson and Mellon. In response, the Board of Tax Appeals split the difference. As Jackson had predicted, it cleared Mellon of the fraud charges. At the same time, the Board found Mellon deficient for some eight hundred thousand dollars in taxes, a paltry sum to Mellon but significant enough for the Roosevelt administration to save face.

It was a career-making performance for Jackson. His small-town trial experience had paid off at the national level. Roosevelt was thrilled with how Jackson had turned a disaster into a victory. For Roosevelt, the prospect of a world-class national gallery of art on the Mall was highly attractive. It was not that Roosevelt had any great appreciation of the works that Mellon had acquired. Rather, breaking ground on a museum of international importance would symbolize optimism about America's future at a time when the economic situation was still very bleak.

Jackson, caught up in the prosecutorial spirit, urged Roosevelt to turn down the gift from a tax cheat. From the presidential standpoint, this attitude was absurd. In his occasional conversations with Jackson about the case, Roosevelt ribbed him about "your" art collection. The gentle teasing showed that Roosevelt understood perfectly well that Jackson's successful management of the trial both saved the administration embarrassment and helped secure what would become the National Gallery of Art—funded by Mellon and begun with his incomparable collection.

Jackson's promotions now began in earnest. After a brief

sojourn advising the newly formed SEC, he was appointed assistant attorney general for taxation in the Department of Justice. This was the job he held when, on January 29, 1937, he went to give what should have been a routine speech to the New York State Bar Association.

Jackson had many friends in the state bar association, and its members probably expected war stories about the Mellon trial. Instead, Jackson subjected his audience to a diatribe. The Supreme Court and the president, he said, were entering a period of deep struggle. Lawyers should be on the side of the progressive president, he told his audience. Instead, the national bar had allied itself with the reactionary Supreme Court. The speech was ill-received by Jackson's erstwhile colleagues. It was not Jackson's business to tell them what they should or should not believe. But the speech sent a strong message in Washington, one that would prove decisive for Jackson's career: When it came to attacking the Supreme Court, Robert Jackson was ready for a fight.[72]

CHAPTER 11

Court Packing

The clash between the Supreme Court and Franklin Roosevelt could have been predicted even before the more aggressive programs of the New Deal were introduced in Roosevelt's first hundred days. For most of the 1920s, the Supreme Court had stood in the way of forward-looking legislation. When Congress passed progressive laws, like those attempting to regulate child labor, the Supreme Court struck them down as beyond the limited power of Congress to regulate "interstate commerce."[73] When laws regulating hours or wages came from the states, the Supreme Court struck those down, too.[74]

The most famous example of the Supreme Court's intransigence eventually lent its name to the whole constitutional era. The case, *Lochner v. New York*, dated back to 1905. New York State had passed a law that limited bakery workers to ten hours a day and sixty hours a week on the job. Joseph Lochner, the owner of Lochner's Home Bakery in Utica, New York—a strapping man with an enormous walrus moustache—had struggled with the bakers' union over his workers' hours. After the union applied pressure to state inspectors, he was arrested for employing a journeyman named Aman Schmitter for more than sixty hours one week. It was Lochner's second offense. He turned to his trade group, the New York Association of Master Bakers, which agreed to take his case on appeal.[75]

The Supreme Court decided in Lochner's favor. It struck down the sixty-hour law as unconstitutional. It reasoned that such laws violated the "liberty of contract," a right said by the Court to be included in the "liberty" of the individual protected by the Fourteenth Amendment.

Underlying the Court's declaration of the liberty of contract and also its cramped view of Congress's power to pass laws was a unifying philosophy: that the primary purpose of the Constitution was to protect private property from being taken and redistributed to society at large. Critics of this constitutional philosophy liked to say that the Supreme Court was interpreting the Constitution to require the economic views preferred by the majority of its members. In his dissent to the *Lochner* decision, Justice Holmes wrote that "a Constitution is not intended to embody a particular economic theory, whether of paternalism and the organic relation of the citizen to the state or of *laissez faire*." In a practical sense, Holmes was right. The court was imposing its own economic beliefs on the country.

But as an account of the Supreme Court's constitutional theory in the *Lochner* era, the *laissez-faire* label was inadequate. Protecting property was in fact central to U.S. constitutional history. The framers of the Constitution believed, following John Locke, that property was an inalienable right alongside life and liberty, and just as essential to human flourishing. The framers were concerned about various practices in the state legislatures before the Constitution was ratified that they saw as deeply dangerous to the right of private property—practices like the systematic devaluation of currency to benefit debtors at the expense of creditors. The Fifth Amendment to the Constitution guaranteed that there would be no deprivation of life, liberty, or property without due process of law. That provision, originally applicable only to the federal government, had been taken up and repeated in the Fourteenth Amendment, extending the limitation to the state governments.

Furthermore, the idea that the federal government was a government of limited powers was itself intended to protect not merely the liberty of the citizen but his property. The framers did not anticipate the degree of federal intervention in commercial affairs that was advocated by progressives in the first part of the twentieth

century, to say nothing of the far more drastic regulatory intervention inaugurated by the New Deal. It was therefore not absurd for
the Supreme Court to have concluded that the protection of property was the core constitutional value—especially when socialist and communist ideals came to challenge the American way of
market capitalism.

Progressives, of course, did not see it that way. Frankfurter had
written as early as 1916 that "if ever an opinion has been subjected
to the weightiest professional criticism it is the opinion in the *Lochner* case."[76] At the time, he hoped the *Lochner* doctrine would die
a natural death. In the 1910s, the Court had occasionally shown
willingness to allow progressive legislation to stand.[77] But that
willingness eroded by the 1920s.[78] In 1927, Frankfurter wrote with
frustration that "we are, then, where we were in 1905," when the
Lochner case was decided.[79] The court was imposing "its views or
assumptions on social policy," thwarting the popular will in defense
of settled property interests.[80]

A modern manufacturing economy was different from an eigh-
teenth-century republic based on agriculture and trade. Between
them lay "the history of the emergence of modern large-scale
industry [and] of the consequent public control of business."[81] New
laws were needed to make sure labor was treated fairly. The public
had elected representatives who, in both the states and in Congress,
had passed laws intended to do just that. To limit bakers to sixty
hours a week was not to constrain their freedom or that of their
employers, but to protect health, safety, and wages. The Court,
Frankfurter believed, was putting a thumb on the scale to help
employers and other business interests exploit workers who used
the tools of democracy to improve their lot.

Led by Frankfurter, who was himself building on Supreme
Court dissents by Holmes and Brandeis and the writings of James
Bradley Thayer, progressives began to develop an alternative constitutional philosophy, one based on the principle of judicial restraint
or deference to legislative judgment. According to this view, the
Constitution must not be understood to embody an inflexible protection of private property, since it was designed to accommodate

different economic systems at different periods. Furthermore, charged critics of the Court, the words "liberty of contract," so central to the *Lochner* jurisprudence, were nowhere to be found in the Constitution. The concept had been smuggled into constitutional thought by a reactionary judiciary that stood in the way of progress.

When Roosevelt took office, then, it was hardly a surprise that the Court frowned upon his policies, which struck at what were perceived as core property rights. Roosevelt's earliest efforts at regulation pushed the federal government's power far beyond its previous bounds—and concentrated much of that power in the president. In 1935, the Court struck down the NIRA as unconstitutional.[82] Not only did the Court say that the law exceeded Congress's power over interstate commerce, but it objected to the way that Congress had given its authority to the president. Even its more progressive members agreed. Justice Benjamin Cardozo said the law was "delegation running riot."[83] Then, in 1936, the Court struck down the Agricultural Adjustment Act, which attempted to do for agriculture what the NIRA did for industry.[84]

The Court had now blocked the two signature reforms of the early New Deal. In essence, it was telling the president of the United States that it did not matter that the legislature passed his reform bills, that he had signed them into law, and that they had been designed to save the country from economic disaster. The changes to the system were too fundamental, and the Court was going to prevent them from being enforced.

When Roosevelt in 1933 ordered all the nation's gold to be turned in to the federal government, the conservatives on the Supreme Court saw this as the very property theft against which the Constitution was intended to guard. When the Supreme Court upheld the president's action, Justice James McReynolds, a former attorney general in the Wilson administration, dissented from the bench. Departing from his prepared text, he declared that "the Constitution is dead" and compared Roosevelt to "Nero at his worst."[85] McReynolds was a crotchety, nasty old man, but his remark reflected philosophy as well as pique: Roosevelt was, like a corrupt Roman emperor, expropriating the rich in pursuit of a policy of bread and circuses.

By the middle of the 1930s, the wealthy social class from which Roosevelt himself came had turned viciously against him. In September 1936, Roosevelt was the featured speaker at Harvard's three hundredth anniversary. Alumni complained about the choice, pointing out that "there are a great many Harvard men who feel very bitterly towards Roosevelt." Former Harvard President Lowell, Frankfurter's old nemesis, issued the invitation over his own misgivings—and practically ordered the president of the United States to "divorce [him]self from the arduous demands of politics and political speechmaking," while keeping his remarks under ten minutes.[86] The *Crimson*, of which Roosevelt had been president, disclaimed him, writing that "if even the fundamental character of Harvard had left its impression on Mr. Roosevelt during his undergraduate days, he would now find it impossible to lead the New Deal."[87] When Roosevelt came back to Cambridge later that fall to campaign, he met with "a chorus of boos from students whose rich fathers hated Roosevelt as a traitor to their class."[88]

Roosevelt came to believe, as did many observers, that the Supreme Court was speaking and acting on behalf of that same wealthy class. Correctly or not, he decided that the Court was the primary obstacle standing in the way of real change—or at least, it was the one obstacle that Roosevelt had not been able to overcome. On February 5, 1937, after behind-the-scenes discussions with Attorney General Homer Cummings, Solicitor General Stanley Reed, and a tiny circle of other advisers, Roosevelt announced his solution.

Justices could not be fired, since the Constitution gave them life tenure. But nowhere did the Constitution specify the number of justices who would sit at any one time. Over the years, the number had ranged from as few as six to as many as ten.[89] The solution was to pack the Court, adding new justices whose views would be congenial to the New Deal.

In a special message submitted to Congress, Roosevelt called for legislation that would empower the president to nominate a new federal judge—including a Supreme Court justice—for every sitting judge beyond the age of seventy. Six justices were then over seventy. If passed, the law would therefore have enabled Roosevelt to gain the support of a majority on the Court.

The court-packing plan was no more transformative than the other reforms that Roosevelt had proposed or that Congress had enacted. Over the course of the New Deal, Roosevelt would ultimately create a panoply of regulatory agencies that have come to be considered a fourth branch of government. The establishment of these changed the structure of American governance more than the addition of more justices to the Court would have done.

Yet Roosevelt's court-packing plan encountered greater resistance than any other single program he ever introduced. The reason was that it seemed to be an explicit attempt to change the balance of powers among the three branches of government that existed when Roosevelt took office. It looked, in other words, like a grab for power on the part of a president who would not take no for an answer. The brazenness of telling the Supreme Court that if it would not accept his policies, he would change its composition, ranked as one of the most remarkable pieces of constitutional one-upsmanship ever tried.

At the same time, the attempt to force the judiciary into line confirmed the worst fears of those Americans who had come to see Roosevelt as the most dangerous man in America—not merely a traitor to his class, but a dictator in waiting. James A. Reed, a former three-term senator from Missouri and a Democrat, charged that Roosevelt's plan was "nothing more nor less than a step toward making himself dictator in fact."[90] He was not alone. A letter to the *New York Times* made an explicit comparison to the contemporaneous rise of fascism: "Congress is already a mere 'rubber stamp.' Make the Supreme Court one and a dictator will reign supreme. Many, unable to read the handwriting already on the wall of Europe...will of course shout 'Heil, heil.'"[91]

Almost from the start, then, the plan looked like a significant political blunder by a man who rarely made any. Roosevelt could insist that it was the Supreme Court that had upset the balance of power, by standing in the way of duly enacted legislation. But this was a tricky argument to make to the public, which considered the Court to be a basically legitimate institution, even if its recent decisions were unpopular.

All the justices considered the plan an outrage—including those who had often been in dissent from the Court's more conservative decisions. Although Roosevelt may mistakenly have imagined that the more liberal justices would welcome a provision that would put them in a majority, in so doing he badly mistook the judicial personality. When pressed, most judges will admit that many important constitutional decisions made by the Supreme Court have a political component. But that is an entirely different thing from welcoming a legislative measure that announces publicly that the business of the Supreme Court is inherently political, and that the only thing needed for victory is for the president to add a few votes. This posture, which might have made sense to a professional politician like Roosevelt, was anathema to even the more liberal judges on the Court, precisely because it transformed them from independent judges into rubber stamps. To them, Roosevelt's proposal smacked of presidential self-aggrandizement at the expense of the judiciary whom they represented and led.

Roosevelt gave the opponents of his plan an easy opening in the oblique way he proposed it. Initially concerned about the appearance of attacking the Court for foiling his favorite programs, Roosevelt officially justified the program on the ground that the Supreme Court was unable to keep up with its work because of the advanced age of several of the judges, colloquially known as the nine old men. The problem with this explanation was not that it was patently a cover story—such things are common in Washington politics, and deniability is rarely a bad thing. The difficulty was that the charge was simply untrue.

It was accurate to say, as Roosevelt did, that the Court did not choose to hear the overwhelming majority of the cases that were brought before it. But, then as now, this was because almost none of those cases actually deserved a further hearing after having been dealt with by the courts of appeals. The Supreme Court was, in fact, up to date in its work. The ages of the justices might in some cases account for their conservative temperament—though Brandeis, the oldest, was the most liberal of the bunch—but old age did not seem to be interfering with their workload.

The direct result of Roosevelt's mistake in going after the Court in this indirect way was that it invited a response from the Court itself. The logical man to do it was the chief justice, Charles Evans Hughes. Senator Burton Wheeler, who was leading the opposition to the plan, asked Hughes to testify before the Senate Judiciary Committee. Hughes declined. But Brandeis, working behind the scenes, had Wheeler call Hughes from Brandeis's home and request a letter that could be read out before the committee.[92]

Hughes agreed. His letter, which was also signed by Brandeis and the conservative Justice Willis Van Devanter, refuted Roosevelt's claim that the Court was behind on its work. It insisted that adding more justices would make the Court's work less efficient, not more. The letter did more than reveal that the justices opposed the plan. Through Brandeis's signature, it signaled to liberals that one could disagree with Roosevelt about the court-packing plan without sacrificing one's credentials as a liberal.[93]

Many liberals now found themselves caught between the political will of the president who was bringing them to the promised land and the prophetic voice of the justice who had inspired so many of them to try and get there in the first place. Frankfurter embodied this dilemma. On the one hand, Frankfurter himself had been the leading national critic of the Supreme Court's mistaken constitutional jurisprudence. And Frankfurter was thoroughly committed to Roosevelt. On the other hand, Frankfurter himself had always idolized the Court as an institution even as he criticized the jurisprudence of the era; and his mentor, Brandeis, was devoted to blocking the plan.

Roosevelt seems to have intuited that he would be unlikely to get Frankfurter's public support. In a letter to Frankfurter on January 15, 1937, he had floated a trial balloon: "Very confidentially, I may give you an awful shock in about two weeks. Even if you do not agree, suspend final judgment and I will tell you the story."[94] To

a man with Frankfurter's desire—and capacity—to know everything all the time, this was something like an invitation for him to
try to find out what was going on. Three days later, on January 18,
Frankfurter wrote back: "Are you trying to find out how well I can
sit on top of a Vesuvius by giving me notice that 'an awful shock'
is in store for me 'in about two weeks'?...You certainly tease my
curiosity when you threaten me with something with which I may
not agree. That, certainly, would be a great surprise."[95]

Frankfurter may indeed not have known what Roosevelt was
planning. On February 2, Tommy Corcoran was told of the plan,
and he gave the impression that he was hearing about it for the
first time.[96] Alternatively, Frankfurter may have had an inkling,
in which case his note to Roosevelt was to hint that he would not
oppose the plan. In any event, on February 7, two days after the
announcement, Frankfurter wrote to Roosevelt to say that he was
shocked only in the dramatic presentation, but not by the proposal. "Risks had to be taken—for you had to consider the costs
and limitations of possible choices of action, as well as the risks
of non-action. And so it was clear that some major operation was
necessary."[97]

This general note of support was not enough for Roosevelt.
According to Frankfurter's later account, Roosevelt called him in
Cambridge. The president told Frankfurter that he planned to put
him on the Supreme Court some day, and sought a pledge of public
silence—supposedly to preserve Frankfurter's chances of confirmation. Roosevelt, according to Frankfurter, acknowledged Frankfurter's "strenuous dislike" of certain aspects of the court-packing
plan but nevertheless also asked for private advice on how to conduct the public campaign.[98]

Frankfurter may have shaped the story to emphasize the degree
of his disagreement with the plan. What is certain is that Roosevelt
wanted the country's leading Supreme Court expert on board. In
a letter to Frankfurter marked "Privatissimo," Roosevelt explained
that he planned a fireside chat about the court-packing plan and
asked bluntly, "Do you want to help me?" Keeping his involvement
secret, in keeping with Roosevelt's superscript, Frankfurter sent

lengthy and detailed notes to the president. Subsequently, Frankfurter maintained public neutrality about the plan, while remaining involved in private until the plan ultimately died in August.[99]

The compromise position that Frankfurter adopted was awkward for him and costly to his relationship with Brandeis. But it
was probably the best that Frankfurter could do under the circumstances. He seems to have been genuinely conflicted. Given
his frustration with the Court's intransigence, and the tenor of
his criticism over the course of the 1920s and into the New Deal
era, Frankfurter clearly did believe that something had to be done
about the Court. But there were other options that the president
had failed to consider, ranging from a constitutional amendment to
stripping the Court of jurisdiction in some cases to adopting a more
careful approach in drafting new laws. The ham-handedness of
Roosevelt's approach, especially the unwillingness to consult him
and give him the opportunity to try to bring Brandeis on board in
advance, must have been a source of major reservation.

Deprived of the public support of the man who could have done
most to help him, Roosevelt looked elsewhere for help. He found
it in a most unlikely place: in the person of Robert Jackson, the
upstate Democratic lawyer whom he had known years ago, who
was now, after his success in the Mellon case, an assistant attorney
general at the Department of Justice. For Jackson, the court-packing
plan would be his route into Roosevelt's inner circle, propelling
him into a series of higher and higher profile positions, and ultimately to the Supreme Court.

By all accounts, Jackson was not one of the small number of
administration officials who knew about the plan that the president was concocting. Jackson was a relatively new addition to the
Department of Justice team. But he had given a speech critical of
the Court to the New York State Bar Association in January, a
speech that had been noticed in the White House.

On February 22, Jackson took the initiative. He sent a letter to
Roosevelt arguing that although he supported the plan, he believed
Roosevelt had the wrong strategy in trying to sell it to the pub-
lic. The White House was claiming the Court was too old and

therefore behind on its work; it maintained that the Court had refused to hear many of the cases brought to it—in lawyer's parlance, it had "denied certiorari."

Jackson had just been in Jamestown, he told Roosevelt, where he had spoken to ordinary people about the plan. The administration, Jackson explained, "couldn't expect the general public to understand the significance of certiorari denied because they didn't know what certiorari was." What was more, Jackson added, the public "thought that the courts have reviewed too many cases anyway." Roosevelt's criticism of the Court had not struck the right note for so monumental an undertaking: "Nobody ever yet went into a fight over a set of statistics." The right way to proceed, Jackson argued, was to take on the Court directly, telling the public that the Supreme Court had gone too far in prohibiting any sort of law, state or federal, establishing a minimum wage or limiting workers' hours.[100]

Instructing the president on how to explain his own plan might have seemed presumptuous for an official who was not an intimate of the president. But as a result of his activities before joining the administration, Jackson had real stature in the American Bar Association—greater than any other member of the administration. The state and national bar would undoubtedly play a role in a national fight about the judiciary. That gave Jackson an angle; and having recently tasted the fruits of national recognition through the Mellon prosecution, he was eager to become a player.

The White House must have taken notice, because Jackson was soon told by the Senate Judiciary Committee that he would be the second witness called to testify in favor of the plan, after the attorney general. Pretending not to know why he had been asked to testify, Jackson asked for the chance to clear the invitation with the president. The ploy got Jackson a meeting with Roosevelt. Face-to-face, Jackson made it clear that he disagreed with the statistical approach and preferred challenging the Court directly on the merits of its decisions. Since this distinctive point of view must have been precisely why the White House had proposed him as a witness, Roosevelt unsurprisingly urged him to speak his mind before the committee.

The hearings began on March 10, 1937, and Jackson testified the next day. His approach, as promised, was substantive: The Court was not too old nor was it lacking in integrity. It was just consistently wrong and intransigent. Jackson marched through the cases where New Deal programs had been struck down, pointing out that eight of them had been decided by a 5–4 margin.[101]

Well-reasoned, well-delivered, and to the point, the testimony made a good impression, further enhancing Jackson's emerging national image. Walter Lippmann wrote that Jackson was "one of the ablest and most engaging" young men in the New Deal. The administration sent Jackson to New York where, on March 24, he gave two speeches supporting the plan, one to a conservative group and the other to a large audience at Carnegie Hall.

The plan, however, was still in trouble. On March 22, Chief Justice Hughes's letter, dated the previous day, was read out by Senator Wheeler before the judiciary committee. Then, a week later, on Monday, March 29, something happened that no one had anticipated. It changed the stakes of the fight in a basic way; but that was not all. The decisions announced that day created a fundamental challenge for constitutional law in the modern era.

CHAPTER 12

Switch in Time

The overflow crowd of ordinary citizens and distinguished visitors who filled the gleaming marble Supreme Court building on the morning of March 29, 1937, was entering a brand-new building. A visitor to the Supreme Court today could be forgiven for thinking that this temple of justice, with its stately columns and Greek motifs, was as old as the Roman-inspired Capitol or the gracefully columned White House. In fact, though, for almost 150 years of its existence, the Supreme Court had no building of its own. The justices had no offices, and the Court convened to hear argument in the old Senate chamber in the Capitol.

It had been the dream of William Howard Taft—a man who greatly preferred his years as chief justice to his term as president of the United States—to remedy this defect and give the third branch of government a home of its own. Under Chief Justice Hughes, Taft's plan ultimately came to fruition. In October 1935, the justices set up shop in this opulent space with its miles of burnished brass and expanses of polished stone.[102] The marble of the building is so white that when the Washington sun hits it directly, it is literally impossible to look straight at the Supreme Court without averting one's eyes.

The centerpiece of the new structure was the courtroom itself. The ornate friezes, in what may generously be termed eclectic style, depict lawgivers and lawmakers throughout the centuries, from Hammurabi and Justinian to Moses, Muhammad, and Blackstone. But from the perspective of the visitor to the courtroom, what actually dominates the visual field behind the bench is an enormous red velvet curtain, from behind which the justices emerge like stage actors or high priests of some mystery religion. Seats in the courtroom are set aside for distinguished visitors, and on March 29 these were full of luminaries, probably because the court-packing plan had thrust the Court into the center of national attention. On the right side of the courtroom, when seen from the audience's perspective, is a special box formally given over to the justices' spouses. That morning, the ladies' box was full, always an independent indication that something important is going to happen.

The first case to be announced, the one with all the action, turned on the constitutionality of Washington State's minimum wage law. The previous June, in a 5–4 vote, the Court had struck down New York's minimum wage law as violating the liberty of contract. That case had been surprising to liberals, who had hoped the doctrine was finally dead.[103] Indeed, it had provided some of the impetus for the court-packing plan, since it seemed to signal that the Court was not in fact budging from its earlier intransigence.

Chief Justice Hughes had been in dissent in the New York case. When he began to read the opinion for the Court in this one, *West Coast Hotel Co. v. Parrish*, those in the know immediately stirred with excitement. Even before Hughes got to the powerful language that was to come, they understood history was being made.

The Supreme Court of the United States had reversed itself. Hughes's opinion repudiated the core *Lochner*-era doctrine of the liberty of contract: "The Constitution does not speak of freedom of contract. It speaks of liberty and prohibits the deprivation of liberty without due process of law."[104] The decision upheld the minimum wage law, and by implication opened the door to all regulation of wages and hours that had previously been held to violate workers' and employers' right to contract freely without government inter-ference. The vote, as it had been the previous June, was 5 to 4—but this time to uphold the law, rather than strike it down.

The personnel of the Court had not altered, and eight of the justices had not budged from their earlier positions. One man had crossed the aisle, thereby accomplishing the most famous change of mind in the history of the Supreme Court. This was Justice Owen Roberts.

Quiet and unassuming, Roberts was an almost accidental justice. An obscure Philadelphia prosecutor, he had gained recognition after being appointed to investigate the Teapot Dome scandal in the Coolidge administration. He had then been nominated to the Court by Herbert Hoover as a fall-back option after Hoover's favored nominee, the Southerner John J. Parker, was defeated by a single vote for what were said to be racist and anti-union views.

Roberts was known to be the most wavering member of the Court. In 1934, over the dissent of the four hard-core conservatives, he had written a majority opinion upholding a New York law that set the price of milk. That opinion had stated frankly that the states were "free to adopt whatever economic policy may reasonably be deemed to promote public welfare."[105] This seemed to repudiate the *Lochner*-era notion of the liberty of contract. But then, confusingly, in the 1936 case involving the New York minimum wage law, Roberts had cast the decisive vote to strike down, joining an opinion that invoked the liberty of contract as its basis.[106] Now, in 1937, he had flipped again.

Roberts's reasons for the change have been analyzed more than any other vote in Supreme Court history. Defenders of the purity of the judicial process—including some serious historians—have argued that Roberts was not being inconsistent.[107] They maintain that in 1936, for technical reasons, the Court was not formally asked to repudiate the liberty of contract. And they point out that Roberts had reached his decision and voted on it in private conference in December, before the court-packing plan was even introduced.[108]

In the moment, though, that was not the perception of almost any observer. It seemed, rather, that the changed vote was designed to do what it did in fact do, namely weaken the court-packing plan by giving in to the Roosevelt administration's pressure. Roberts's vote would become known, perhaps inevitably, as the switch in time that saved nine.

Felix Frankfurter, once he joined the Court as a justice, would become one of the leading defenders of Roberts against the charge that he had been weak and unprincipled in reversing his earlier vote. In later years, Frankfurter went so far as to convince Roberts to give him a secret memorandum, for release after Roberts's death, describing the course of events that led to his vote, and explaining that there had been neither external pressure nor inconsistency involved.[109] On March 30, 1937, however, the day after the switch, Frankfurter saw things the way everyone else did. He wrote to Roosevelt that "with the shift by Roberts, even a blind man ought to see that the Court is in politics, and understand how the Constitution is judicially construed. It is a deep object lesson—a lurid demonstration—of the relation of man to the 'meaning' of the Constitution."[110]

It is telling that Frankfurter did not react triumphantly to the change, but with ambivalence. He had long argued that as a matter of reality, the Supreme Court's decisions were political; and, as he wrote to Roosevelt, the switch seemed to confirm this theory. The "meaning" of the Constitution was, in fact, what men made of it.

At the same time, however, Frankfurter believed that the Court should not involve itself in political decision making but should stay out of the way, leaving politics to Congress and the state legislatures. Thus, even the decision that could be seen as fulfilling Frankfurter's desired goal for judges was tainted for him by the political context in which it was reached. What was "lurid" about the decision for Frankfurter was that it seemed not to be made on principle. The decision was "one of life's bitter-sweets," he wrote to Brandeis, "and the bitter far outweighs the sweet."[111]

This concern for the appearance of principle would become fundamental to Frankfurter's later jurisprudence of judicial restraint once he was on the Court. To preserve the Court's legitimacy, it was not enough for a decision to be apolitical; it must also appear so. To maintain the Court's stature and independence, the judges must convince the public that the Court was not "in politics." But this task would be infinitely complicated by the underlying reality that even if the Court did not intervene in legislative politics, it was nevertheless a political body, and the decision not to interfere was in a sense political in itself.

Now that the Court had opened the door to progressive state legislation, it went further. On April 12, it upheld the new labor relations law.[112] Known as the Wagner Act, this signature piece of New Deal legislation created the National Labor Relations Board and gave the government full regulatory authority over labor-management relations nationwide. The basis for the 5–4 decision was that the law was a permissible exercise of Congress's power to regulate interstate commerce. Since limitations on interstate commerce were the primary tool by which the Supreme Court had restricted federal authority, this decision did for Congress what the March 29 decision had done for state legislatures: It signaled that the Court would not block future regulation.

The old jurisprudence of the protection of private property had now been repudiated at both the state and federal levels. The progressives had won. Frankfurter's reaction to the triumph of the constitutional philosophy he had advocated for nearly three decades was to reproach the Court—which meant Roberts, again the swing vote—for its unprincipled reversal: "After today I feel like finding some honest profession to enter," he cabled Roosevelt. The result was the one Frankfurter wanted. But he could not help feeling troubled by how the victory was accomplished.

Roosevelt, for his part, was so deeply committed to the political fight to pack the Court that he could not acknowledge that the effort was now unnecessary. On April 5, he had written to Frankfurter, spinning the breadth of the opposition to his plan as a sign that he would succeed: "It is quite clear that the utter confusion of our opponents among themselves means success for us even though it may be deferred until June or July." Jackson later reasoned that "the reversal impressed the president rather unfortunately, more as weakness than as strength."[113] A strategic retreat could always be reversed, and this, according to Jackson, fueled Roosevelt's impulse to see the Court's concessions as a reason to press forward.

On May 18, Justice Willis Van Devanter, one of the hard-core conservatives known as the Four Horsemen, announced his retirement. Planned or otherwise, the retirement looked like an acknowledgment of defeat. At the Court, at least, Roosevelt's victory was now total. In Congress, the court-packing plan was still on the floor.

On the evening of May 24, Jackson had a long one-to-one conversation with Roosevelt in the president's study. Jackson was now a key presidential adviser on the matter, and once again he urged a different course than the president was pursuing. Having earlier pushed the president to make the court-packing plan a matter of substance, Jackson was in a position to argue that Roosevelt had won. Now, Jackson advised, the president should declare victory and depart the field, withdrawing the plan on the ground that it was no longer needed.

To Jackson's surprise, Roosevelt told him that while withdrawal might be the wisest course of action, he had already made a deal to put the plan through. Before the retirement of Justice Van Devanter a few days earlier, Roosevelt had promised the first available seat to Senator Joe Robinson, the Senate majority leader, in exchange for his continued support. That promise, Roosevelt intimated, could not be reversed. Although he had taken the deal, Robinson was a constitutional conservative who could not be expected to vote Roosevelt's way. That meant Roosevelt would need the extra court seats that would be afforded by the passage of the bill in order to appoint liberal justices to counterbalance Robinson.[114]

If he accepted Roosevelt's explanation, as he appears to have done, Jackson showed considerable naïveté for someone who was now operating in the highest echelons of power politics. That naïveté that would later haunt him when Roosevelt gave him to believe on his own appointment to the Court that he would some day be made chief justice. Political promises can be broken. If Roosevelt had been prepared to withdraw the court-packing plan, he could have cancelled his agreement with Robinson and paid the political price.[115] Whatever Jackson may have thought, Roosevelt's comments to Jackson are best understood as suggesting that as of May 24, Roosevelt still believed it possible that the court-packing plan would succeed with Robinson's help—and that this was the result Roosevelt wanted.

Success became much less likely on June 14, when the Senate Judiciary Committee voted 10 to 8 against the bill. In the end, though, it was serendipity that delivered the final blow to the court-packing plan. On the night of July 13, 1937, Senator Joe Robinson, to whom the next Supreme Court seat had been promised, died of a heart attack in his apartment. His maid found him the next morning, lying next to his bed in his pajamas.[116] With imaginative license, associates said it was a result of overexertion in the fight over court packing. On July 22, the bill was sent back to the committee with a commitment that it would not be reintroduced in that session; this time the Senate vote to send the bill to oblivion was 70 to 20.

Roosevelt's persistence in pressing the court-packing plan offers a window into his political personality. In 1936, he had been reelected by an enormous margin, and some observers believed that this success had gone to his head. But the truth was more complicated than that. Roosevelt had undertaken the court-packing plan in the first place precisely because the Supreme Court was the only institution that stood in his way. Not to finish the battle would be to suggest weakness. By contrast, to defeat the Court altogether, even after it had already retreated, would mean total victory. The will to prevail was, in fact, one of Roosevelt's greatest strengths, the thing that had enabled him to overcome personal disability, and ultimately what would make him the right president to lead the United States during World War II. It was also connected to Roosevelt's willingness to break constitutional tradition, as he would do when running for not only a third but a fourth presidential term.

CHAPTER 13

Ambition

The court-packing plan strengthened Jackson's ties to Roosevelt. During the fight, he had shown himself to be an effective advocate in the Senate, not to mention a deft expositor of legal arguments to the president. His advice had not exactly been taken, but neither had it been rejected. More important, since Jackson had from the start claimed that the purpose of the court-packing plan should be to get the Court to change its views, the fact that the Court had in fact switched provided a basis for claiming that the whole undertaking had been a success. And since the plan had failed to be adopted, it became especially important to Roosevelt—always focused on winning—to explain that it had in fact been a victory.

Jackson was the natural person to take up this task. Within a few months, he began work on what would become a four-hundred-page book offering a historical justification for the plan as well as a detailed accounting of why it had ultimately been a success. Titled *The Struggle for Judicial Supremacy*, it was written over the course of the next four years, during which time Jackson was promoted from one assistant attorney general position to another, and then, in March 1938, barely a year after the court-packing plan was first introduced, to solicitor general of the United States.[117]

That Jackson would undertake such a project while serving in high government office was a mark both of the importance of the court-packing plan to Roosevelt's perception of his own legacy, and also of the personal stake that Jackson took in the plan that had brought him into Roosevelt's inner circle. In fact, it is difficult to think of a comparably significant and sophisticated book ever written by a senior administration official while in office. Although it naturally reflects Jackson's distinctive, substance-oriented view of the court-packing plan, the book is no simple political manifesto. It offers nothing less than a practical-minded account of the proper role of the judiciary in relation to the "political power, which is the power of the voters"; the economic power of property, "which is the power of its owners"; and the other branches of government.

When Felix Frankfurter sat down to write his own books and articles on the Supreme Court, he was already an eminent professor sitting in the very law school that had educated him, given him entrée to Holmes and Brandeis, and promoted him to the front of the legal elite of the nation. Jackson held high office, to be sure. He had the benefit of extensive advice and drafting help from Paul Freund, who worked in the solicitor general's office and later became an important Harvard professor and eventually solicitor general himself; and from Professor Louis Jaffe, then teaching at the University of Buffalo Law School, later also a Harvard giant. But Jackson's preparation for writing this book was no greater than his twenty years of legal practice and his brief run in Washington, none of which involved constitutional law, much less the Supreme Court. An author of legal briefs and many speeches, Jackson had never before written a law review essay, much less a book-length treatment of an important legal topic.

The Struggle for Judicial Supremacy was not merely an attempt to make sense of the court-packing plan in a way that would appeal to Roosevelt and to history, but equally important, it was Jackson's own intellectual effort to teach himself about the Supreme Court and its role in American public life. Like the well-prepared lawyer that he always was, when embarking on a career as constitutional advocate before the Court, Jackson wanted to have a deeper understanding of just what he was doing, and why. Seen in this context, the focus on the court-packing plan makes a great deal of sense, because the Court before which Jackson regularly appeared was the product of that fight.

The book is also the first attempt made by Jackson to offer

a comprehensive theory of what the Constitution is and how it should be interpreted—a theory he would later develop in a remarkable set of judicial opinions. In language so clear it could serve as a model for writing about constitutional issues for a general audience, Jackson begins by explaining that the Constitution itself nowhere gives the Supreme Court the authority to decide on the constitutionality of federal legislation. This power was the result of historical development, not the Constitution's text or structure. Constitutional difficulties cannot be resolved simply by looking to the document or to the intentions of those who wrote it. The right way to proceed must lie elsewhere.

In Jackson's telling, the key to constitutional law is to identify the function that the Supreme Court has developed over the generations: resolving conflicts between different actors in government and society. The court, he said, has "the duty of being...the voice of the Constitution speaking the final word in composing conflicts within our complicated political system."[118] *Composing conflicts*, he explained, meant the balancing of competing interests: citizen against citizen, state against state, citizen against state, national against state authority, civil rights against sovereign power, and the Court against Congress. Although this list is notable in omitting the necessity of striking a balance between Congress and the president—a subject on which Jackson's views would ultimately exercise the greatest influence of any justice ever to have sat on the Court—this can perhaps be explained by the fact that it was written by a man who still worked for the president.

The view of the judicial function as one of balancing competing interests would become central to Jackson's pragmatic constitutional philosophy, and so it is noteworthy that it appears already in the first chapter of his first effort to think about the topic. The contrast with the other constitutional theories that would emerge in the following decades can already be sensed. For Frankfurter, the job of the Court was not to balance competing political or economic interests, but to stay its own hand and allow those interests to play themselves out in Congress or in the state legislatures. Black would disclaim even the first premise of Jackson's book: that the answers to constitutional questions may not be found in the text as understood by the framers. For him, the words, supplemented by their authors' intent, sufficed to do the job.

Probably the closest position to Jackson's was the constitutional view that Douglas would develop, in essence the application of legal realism to constitutional questions. But even there, the views diverged sharply. As a legal realist Douglas believed that since the Court would inevitably impose its own preferences in any given situation, it should have no qualms about explicitly doing so. By contrast, Jackson from the outset believed that the job of the Court was not to impose its own preferences, but to mediate practically among different interest groups in the hopes of preserving a balance. Douglas would have considered that perspective simple-minded, even self-deluding. To a realist, it would be impossible to imagine that judges would somehow be neutral arbiters among other actors. Douglas believed that as individuals and as members of courts, the judges would inevitably favor some perspectives and interests over others.

Just as Jackson was developing his views about the role of the judge as an impartial conflict resolver, he was undergoing a change in his own personal makeup. Jackson's experience advising Roosevelt on the court-packing plan was what propelled him rapidly into the solicitor generalship. After the fact, therefore, it may appear that his promotion to that important job was the inevitable progress of an upward career trajectory. In fact, though, in the brief period before his appointment as solicitor general, Jackson's personality developed in a way that would prove crucial to his life from then forward. In the wake of the close access to the president that he enjoyed during the court-packing plan, Robert Jackson discovered ambition.

Jackson had never particularly lacked in self-regard. He had worked hard to establish his lucrative practice in Jamestown and had accepted a national role in the American Bar Association. Before coming to Washington he carefully considered various options, waiting for and then taking the best job offered. But these were the actions of a prudent, successful lawyer with no interest in wasting his time—not those of a man eager to leave his impress on the history of the country or the world. As his initial flirtation with preserving his Jamestown law practice while in Washington suggested, Jackson still expected to return home in relatively short order.

The experience of seeking and getting one-to-one meetings with the president in the White House brought home to Jackson that sometimes achieving proximity to power was no more difficult than asking for it. Sitting in the president's office, Jackson had been able to give valuable advice. More important, he knew that he had been right—and in the rare case where the president's vaunted political instincts had been wrong. In the course of the court-packing plan, Jackson must have realized that he was as intelligent and effective as anyone else in the administration. Such thoughts can be a powerful spur to wanting advancement.

The distance had shrunk between Roosevelt, who had once seemed to the teenage Jackson the embodiment of aristocratic privilege, and the country-bred Jackson. Where once Jackson had noted Roosevelt's "immaculate" and "rather formal dress,"[119] Jackson himself had over the years come to be impeccably tailored—to the point where he was eventually named the best-dressed man in America by the Custom Tailors Guild. Jackson was not a dandy who sought attention with his clothes: He dressed in perfect, "ultra-meticulous" taste in order to emphasize just how rightfully he belonged to the elite milieu that he had now joined. His clothes reflected his sense of self-worth—and his desire for his quality to be recognized.[120]

A family photograph from 1938 shows Jackson sitting in his garden on a rattan chair. He is wearing a slim-tailored, three-piece white linen suit, with white socks and immaculate white bucks, all brought out by a dark tie and pocket square. His wife Irene sits perched on the arm of the chair, her white dress complemented by a floral scarf and matching belt. Jackson's teenage son and daughter sit on the grass on either side, she in elegant polka dots, he in a light suit and saddle shoes. The family collie lies in front, completing the picture of domestic perfection. This, the setting tells us, is a family on the rise.

In the weeks before the court-packing plan, Jackson had just switched assistant attorney general positions, from being in charge of the Tax Division to the Antitrust Division. As a matter of protocol this was a promotion, a fact Jackson carefully noted in a later oral history interview, but in terms of title it was a lateral move.[121] As early as March 11, 1937, the day he had testified before the Senate Judiciary Committee about the court-packing plan, the newspapers had reported a rumor that Jackson would succeed James Landis as chairman of the SEC. But Douglas, already a commissioner, made a lengthy and concerted play for the position, and after gaining Landis's support he was named chairman on September 26. Jackson's options for promotion were running out.

Patience was not one of the new Jackson's virtues. In November 1937, Jackson for the first time adopted what would become his characteristic strategy for promotion. He went to see Roosevelt and announced that he was prepared to resign from the government and return to private practice in Jamestown.[122]

Roosevelt was in the habit of receiving certain visitors in the morning while he was still in bed—not quite as revealing as Churchill's notorious bathing audiences, but still a mark of closeness to the person attending the meeting. The president's response to Jackson was as flattering as the venue was intimate. Not only did Roosevelt urge Jackson not to quit, he proposed that he consider running for governor of New York. Roosevelt suggested that Herbert Lehman, his successor in 1932, might not be planning to run again. Jackson was savvy enough to know that Lehman had opposed the court-packing plan and was therefore out of Roosevelt's good graces. The implication was that Roosevelt would help get Jackson the job without much of a fight.

If that tantalizing possibility were not enough, Roosevelt sweetened the pot. "If you can be elected governor in '38," he suggested, "you would be in an excellent position for the presidency in 1940. I don't intend to run. Every once in a while someone suggests that I'm going to run, but I want to get up to Hyde Park."[123]

The suggestion that Jackson might ride a two-year term as New York governor all the way to the White House was not absurd.

Roosevelt himself had served just four years as governor before becoming president. And 1940 would mark the end of Roosevelt's second term—the unofficial term limit established by George Washington and followed without exception ever since. It certainly signified that Roosevelt believed Jackson was in his office seeking some sort of promotion.

Roosevelt meant business. Such was the reach of his influence in New York politics that Jackson soon found himself invited to speak at a Democratic dinner in New York which all the potential gubernatorial candidates were expected to attend. Clearly intrigued, Jackson went and spoke. There followed an invitation to speak at a Young Democrats dinner. Things were now getting serious. Roosevelt sent Tommy Corcoran, along with several other political aides, to introduce Jackson to a well-known New York political handler, Edward Bernays, and begin to get a gubernatorial campaign into gear.

Despite the formidable war team Roosevelt had assembled for him, Jackson was not enthusiastic. Perhaps he feared he lacked the statewide recognition to win. Or he may simply have enjoyed Roosevelt's courtship and wanted the president to do still more to make him governor without doing much on his own. Regardless, Roosevelt persisted, and Jackson's access increased. The president invited Jackson to accompany him on a fishing trip with several senior presidential advisers. On the water, Roosevelt again pressed Jackson to run for governor.

It was not to be. In a clever tactical move, the New York attorney general, John J. Bennett, who also planned to run for Lehman's seat, scheduled a dinner directly conflicting with the Young Democrats' dinner in order to flush out Jackson's support. The result was that neither dinner was well attended—a net loss for Jackson, who lacked an in-state base. Then various political organizations around New York State began to come out against Jackson's candidacy, probably because Jackson was identified as Roosevelt's candidate and therefore owed his allegiance to none of them. There was also opposition from James Farley, who had brought Jackson to Washington but was himself interested in running for the presidency in 1940. Like Roosevelt, Farley must have thought that a Jackson governorship would put him in a leading position to succeed Roosevelt. Finally Lehman decided to run again, effectively closing the issue. A popular incumbent who had earlier received Roosevelt's blessing could not be challenged, even at the direction of a sitting president.[124]

Later, Jackson would say that he was glad he had not become governor, "because it would have been a dead-end street" when Roosevelt ran for president again in 1940 and 1944.[125] Whether he knew it or not, however, the episode cost Jackson dearly. Roosevelt formed the view that Jackson "does not have political 'it.'"[126] He would be mentioned as a vice presidential candidate in 1940 and again, less seriously, in 1944, but each time Roosevelt balked on the basis of his 1937 impression that Jackson did not have the stomach for risk-taking political engagement. "The trouble with Bob" as a political candidate, he would say, "is that he is too much of a gentleman...He seems to lack some fundamental fighting quality."[127] With his characteristic judgment, Roosevelt was almost certainly correct. Jackson was immensely talented, deeply intelligent, and he spoke well in public. But he lacked the inner equanimity in the face of conflict that would have enabled him to succeed as a politician. On some level, Jackson knew this, too. Appointed office was his natural métier.

Roosevelt nonetheless wanted to keep Jackson in government, and he needed a post to give him. One opened when, in February 1938, Roosevelt nominated Solicitor General Stanley Reed to the Supreme Court. Roosevelt replaced Reed with Jackson—and the job fit him perfectly.

Jackson was an amazingly successful solicitor general, by far the greatest on record. He won thirty-eight of his forty-four cases, a record unlikely ever to be surpassed.[128] Some of that was due to his skill in advocacy. When Jackson was promoted to attorney general—another job he wanted so much that he threatened to resign if it did not come his way—Justice Brandeis commented to a friend that "Jackson should be solicitor general for life."[129]

But a good deal of Jackson's unmatched success before the

Court must be attributed to the changed composition and state of mind of the body before which he was arguing. In the direct aftermath of court packing, Roosevelt began to pick his justices. Eventually, he would choose nine men for the Court, including a new chief justice.[130] Stanley Reed, whom Jackson replaced as solicitor general, was Roosevelt's second Supreme Court nominee. His service, like that of several of his fellow Roosevelt appointees, would be adequate but undistinguished. The same could not be said for Roosevelt's first Supreme Court pick: Senator Hugo Black of Alabama.

Book Three

JUDGES

CHAPTER 14

The Skeleton

To call Hugo Black's nomination to the Supreme Court unorthodox understates the case considerably. He was by wide repute the most radical member of the U.S. Senate. He had never served as a judge, unless one counts his year as a twenty-five-year-old magistrate handling misdemeanors in the Birmingham police court. And he was from the Deep South. Since Reconstruction, only five other true Southerners had sat on the Supreme Court, including the rebarbative anti-Semite James McReynolds, who was still serving.[1] Since Black, only four have served—Jimmy Byrnes of South Carolina, who lasted just a year; Abe Fortas of Tennessee; Lewis Powell of Virginia; and Clarence Thomas, born in Georgia.[2]

It was not that Roosevelt failed to consider more traditional candidates to fill Willis Van Devanter's seat when it came open in May 1937. Alongside Black, the other finalist was Stanley Reed, who was representing the government before the Supreme Court as solicitor general—the job Roosevelt had unsuccessfully urged Frankfurter to take so that he could later go on the Court himself. Reed, who would get the next appointment after Black, had learned the business of the Court while appearing before it, and was prepared to become a justice. When Tommy Corcoran asked Frankfurter to give his opinion on the relative merits of Black and Reed, Frankfurter sensibly replied that Reed would be "thoroughly at home in the procedural problems that come before the Court." Black, by contrast, was a politician. He would "have to muster an immense amount of rather technical jurisdictional learning" to do the job.[3]

The difficulty in appointing Reed was in the timing, not in the substance. He had taken a leading role alongside Attorney General Homer Cummings in formulating the court-packing plan. Now that the plan had failed, Roosevelt's power in the Senate was at a low point. If Reed were nominated, Roosevelt ran the risk that opponents of the court-packing plan would cast the nomination as a final attempt by the president to vindicate his efforts. That gave Roosevelt a reason to nominate someone whom the Senate would have no choice but to confirm, and confirm quickly.

There is no one more confirmable before the Senate of the United States than a sitting senator. In the gentlemen's club that the Senate then was—and to a surprising degree remains—elaborate courtesies are extended to fellow members and an arcane protocol of seniority obtains. The senators are of course profoundly ambitious, a fact accepted by all as a necessary feature of club membership. They disagree among themselves on the full range of policy questions of the day. But when a senator is nominated for any job that requires confirmation, he remains a senator for the period of confirmation, and the members, looking hopefully to the day of their own elevation, tend to treat the nominee as a favorite son made good.

The idea of naming a senator to the Court was already in Roosevelt's mind. He had promised the first available seat to the now-deceased majority leader, Joe Robinson, in exchange for his help in trying to pass the court-packing plan. The fact that both Roosevelt and Robinson expected that he would be confirmed by the Senate—despite the obviousness of the deal involved—offers some indication of just how pro forma confirmation of a senator was expected to be.

Now that Robinson was out of the picture, Roosevelt no longer owed the appointment to anybody. He did not want to refight the unsuccessful court-packing battle again; but neither did he want to admit that the plan had been a terrible idea. By sticking with his original idea of naming a senator, Roosevelt could assure easy confirmation without appearing to compromise on principle. He considered Sherman Minton, another powerful Senate Democrat who had supported the court-packing plan. But Minton, who would ultimately be put on the Supreme Court by Harry Truman in 1949, turned the job down. Having criticized the Court harshly from the Senate floor, Minton thought it would be awkward to serve beside the justices who had been subject to his attacks.

That led Roosevelt to Black, who had supported the court-packing plan but had not been a leader in the fight. Black was a wild card. When it came to reforming the capitalist system, he was perceived as an unrestrained populist. Best known for taking no prisoners in the pursuit of corporate wrongdoing, he had paid scant attention to civil liberties in the process. Yet Black was not a pure Roosevelt loyalist. He had not been elected in the class of 1932, alongside Roosevelt, but six years before; and he had voted against the NIRA—the signature legislation of the first New Deal. Above all, Black's political persona of aggressive attack and radical change made him seem like the antithesis of the conservative Supreme Court justices against whom Roosevelt had fought from the beginning of his first term in office. Nominating him would shake up the Court and surprise the Senate—while sailing through without costing Roosevelt very much politically.

Apart from the practical advantage of naming a sitting senator, nominating an active politician underscored Roosevelt's view that the Court was essentially a political body. In choosing Black, Roosevelt was moving a generally reliable vote in the Senate to an equally reliable spot on the Supreme Court. He was, in effect, telling the Court and the world that he had not abandoned the political conception of the Supreme Court that informed the court-packing plan. A Supreme Court justice, according to this view, did not need judicial experience, nor was it a problem if he had not practiced law in more than a decade. What mattered was his political philosophy, demonstrated in this case through aggressive Senate service.

The fact that Black was a Southerner also counted as an advantage to Roosevelt. Southern Democrats were a loyal constituency he wanted to reward, and since Reconstruction, the South had been underrepresented on the Court. The only disadvantage of Black's Southern origins was his long-rumored connection to the Ku Klux Klan. Roosevelt either did not know about the problem or, in the light of the racial norms of the time, did not expect it to matter much.

Roosevelt never ordered or conducted any investigation of Black's background. There had been plenty of speculation in Washington about Black's connection to the Klan at the time he was first elected. A visit to Alabama to speak with any of his old associates would quickly have revealed that Black's one-time membership was an open secret. But no such visit was forthcoming by any representative of the administration before the nomination was made. Roosevelt's senior confidants who knew of the appointment included no Southerner who might have had the understanding of Alabama politics to know what was coming. And the president was taken with his own cleverness in presenting the Senate with a candidate it would have to confirm despite conservative misgivings.

For his part, Black gave Roosevelt no reason to worry that there was a hooded skeleton in his closet. The idea that he might be nominated was floated to Black through Senator Sherman Minton, Roosevelt's first choice. Black responded favorably, with no mention that he might have something serious to disclose to Roosevelt before an official announcement was made. On August 11, 1937, Roosevelt called Black to the White House to offer him the job.

For Black, the decision to accept the nomination was not obvious. He had not aspired to a career on the bench. His immediate political ambition was to succeed the new Senate majority leader, Alben Barkley—and then perhaps to run for the presidency in 1940 or beyond. These goals were speculative, but not unreachable for a man of Black's talents—especially for someone who said that "you shouldn't be elected to the Senate unless you want to be President."[4] Slightly balding, with penetrating eyes, Black had established a reputation in the Senate as scholarly (for a senator) and persuasive. With a strong political base and a growing national reputation, he was marked for long-term political success.

At the same time, for someone of Black's humble antecedents, with his deep sense of pride, the nomination to the Supreme Court was unquestionably a major life accomplishment. Although the framers of the Constitution did not anticipate it, the title *Justice* is the closest thing the U.S. system has to nobility. Black cared about honor. To be a justice—and potentially a great one—was to become a figure honored in the fabric of American life.

Beyond personal satisfaction, Black's wife, Josephine, wanted badly for him to take the job on the Court. Josephine suffered from intermittent bouts of serious depression, a condition she inherited from her mother. For a deeply self-conscious woman who craved being alone, the social scene of the wives in the U.S. Senate was a form of torture.[5]

The Senate wives played a major role in the creation and cementing of the interpersonal bonds that underlay political relationships. There were weekly wives' luncheons and constant rounds of home visits. To be a Senate wife was a full-time job. It would have been socially unthinkable—as well as harmful to Black's career—for Josephine to have been less than fully involved.

Josephine found her duties ridiculous as well as unpleasant. She wrote a humorous, parodic short story about a politician's wife—and tellingly titled it "The Fifth Wheel." *Harper's Bazaar* had accepted the story for publication before Black prevailed on Josephine to withdraw it.[6]

The opportunity for Black to go on the Supreme Court seemed to offer Josephine an escape from the intensity of political life. Josephine would have had to increase her social efforts had Black pursued promotion within the Senate. If he were to run for national office, her commitment would have had to be greater still.

The honor of the post and Josephine's concerns together determined Black's course. When Roosevelt offered him the appointment, he accepted on the spot. Black never raised the possibility that the confirmation process had the potential to embarrass the administration.

Today it seems unimaginable that Black believed his Klan membership would not surface when he became Roosevelt's first Supreme Court nominee. But confirmation could happen then

with a dispatch that is now difficult to imagine. Just five days
elapsed from the time Black's nomination was announced in the
Senate chamber on Friday, August 12, until that body voted to
confirm him on Wednesday, August 17—and two of those days
were over the weekend. The specific question of Klan membership
was not raised publicly by any senator until the seventeenth, when
the vote was already scheduled to occur.

The speed with which Black was confirmed reflected his colleagues' solicitude. But the casual nature of the process also reflects
the spirit of an earlier age. Hearings were not required. The confirmation of a Supreme Court justice did not necessarily involve the
intense scrutiny and the lengthy, partisan public debates that we
now consider inevitable.

Black's own approach to dealing with rumors of his past had
been honed during his years in the Senate. When the question
of the Klan was raised, he never precisely lied. Instead, he stone-
walled. Because the Klan's support for him in 1926 was publicly
known, journalists asked Black immediately after his nomination
if he was a Klan member. To them, Black simply answered, "No
comment."

In dealing with his fellow senators, Black was also cagey—and
he relied on the clubby norms of the Senate to get him through.
After he was nominated, several senators who liked Black deputed
William Borah, an influential Idaho Republican who served on the
Judiciary Committee, to ask Black to make a statement addressing
the Klan rumors. Black told Borah he intended to remain publicly
silent on the question. He was not now a member of the Klan, he
said. Then, choosing his words precisely, Black added that he "had
had no affiliations of any kind with the Klan since I had come to
the Senate."[7] Finally, said Black, if any senator was concerned that
he might once have been a Klan member, then that senator should
vote against him.

From these answers, the fact that Black had been a member
of the Klan could have been easily intuited by his colleagues, as
it could have been inferred by journalists. Yet because the Klan
was a secret organization with no public membership list, no one

could offer definitive evidence of his membership in the five days it took for confirmation to come to the floor. The absence of the ocular proof gave Black and his Senate colleagues the small quantum of deniability that they needed. The vote to confirm was 63 to 16, with 17 abstaining. Many of those who refused to vote for Black were Catholics or Republicans who had opposed the court-packing plan.[8] The beauty of a Supreme Court appointment was that once it was confirmed, it was constitutionally irreversible. Short of impeachment, Black now had life tenure.

Black, it seemed, had pulled off an amazing feat: He had come to Washington on the strength of his Klan membership, abandoned the organization, and then transcended it through his elevation to the Supreme Court. On August 19, two days after his confirmation, he had lunch with Roosevelt at the White House. According to Black's later reminiscence, composed to "correct for posterity any idea of President Roosevelt's having been fooled about my membership in the Klan," at lunch Roosevelt told him that "some of the best friends and supporters he had in the state of Georgia were strong members of that organization."[9]

Roosevelt's comment may have been tongue-in-cheek—the "some of my best friends" formulation was usually used to speak of racial or religious minorities, not the Klan members who disliked them. Or perhaps Roosevelt was simply using the phrase to put Black at his ease. Either way, it suggested that once confirmation had been accomplished, Roosevelt shared Black's sense that the question could now be put in the past.

The investigative journalists of the 1930s moved more slowly than do their contemporary descendents, but they were hardly without resources. Various journalists tried to elicit the truth from former Alabama Grand Dragon James Esdale. The one who succeeded was Ray Sprigle of the *Pittsburgh Post-Gazette*. The *Post-Gazette*'s owner was a Jewish Republican New Yorker named Paul Block, whose opposition to Black could be taken for granted. The newspaper sent Sprigle to Alabama in August with instructions to get the story.

Grand Dragon or not, Esdale was willing to talk to the reporter

from up North. In exchange for friendly conversation and an undisclosed sum, Esdale opened his safe and handed over the documents
that proved Black's Klan membership. He had preserved the full
record of Black's service, including the resignation letter Black had
submitted in anticipation of precisely the situation where he would
have to deny membership.

Esdale needed money. But more than that, he was getting even.
Black had turned his back on the Klan once he arrived in Washington. Having helped elect Black, the Klan had gotten nothing
in return; they had been used. Then in April 1937, after the Klan's
power in Alabama had collapsed, Esdale himself was subjected to
disbarment proceedings.

Black could have helped. A few years earlier, the senator had
hurried back to Alabama in order to defend a friend who was
charged with the murder of an African-American—a crime he
almost certainly committed. Black's imprimatur and public reputation had gotten his friend acquitted. When the friend thanked
God, Black told him, "Don't thank Him. Thank me. *God* knows
you're guilty."[10] By contrast, when the request came from Esdale,
Black spurned his former ally. In April, when Esdale needed him,
Black could not have known that a few months later he would need
Esdale to keep his mouth shut.

On August 26, believing he had avoided exposure, Black
embarked on a trip to Europe with his wife. On September 13,
though, the *Post-Gazette* published the first of a series of stories
detailing Black's membership in the Klan. The articles even argued
that Black was still a member. This claim was not entirely baseless.
Black's resignation letter, designed to be disclosed only in case of
crisis, was signed with a Klan salutation that referred to the "sacred,
unfailing bond"—implying that the bond outlasted the purported
resignation.

The public outcry that followed shocked Black; but in retrospect
it was inevitable. For a Klan association to be rumored in a nominee was one thing. For a sitting Supreme Court justice to belong
to the most racist, anti-Catholic, and anti-Semitic organization in
U.S. history was quite another. The calls for Black's resignation,

and even for impeachment, began to multiply. Roosevelt had miscalculated both in failing to investigate and by laughing off the problem after Black was confirmed. Now, in face-saving mode, the president maintained total silence on the issue. When the outcry continued, Roosevelt went on vacation.[11]

Meanwhile, hounded by the American press in London, Black interrupted his own vacation to sail home. He had little choice but to make a public statement. He opted to use the radio to make a direct public address—a course of action never before followed in the history of the Supreme Court and unrepeated since. Closeted with two advisers—Josephine's sister's husband Clifford Durr, and his old Birmingham law partner Crampton Harris—Black turned to the task of drafting a speech.

Now Black's political experience became invaluable. He needed to satisfy Roosevelt, who wanted him to issue an apology and renounce the Klan. But Black was not a man inclined to grovel. And he did not want to offend white Southerners, his constituency until this point in his career. Like him, many Southerners had unpleasant past associations that they hoped to minimize but of which they were not truly ashamed. Black also had to consider his new colleagues on the Supreme Court, who would not want their institution tainted. Beyond these obligations, there was Black's intense sense of personal honor, probably the most demanding of all the constraints on him.

The radio speech was politically masterful, more for what it did not say than for what it did. Black asserted that his Senate record showed he was not a bigot. He stated simply that he had been a Klan member, had resigned, and had not rejoined. In parallel to Roosevelt's earlier comment to him, Black took refuge in the time-honored assertion that among his friends were "many members of the colored race" and that "some of my best and most intimate friends are Catholics and Jews." That was all. Black never criticized the Klan, nor did he express regret for having joined. He preserved his pride without exposing himself to further criticism.

A Gallup poll revealed that the speech in fact turned the political tide. Public opinion swung from 59 percent favoring Black's resignation if he was a Klan member to 56 percent supporting his remaining in office.[12] The key seems to have been that the speech made clear that Black no longer belonged to the Klan. In those days, a poll was not broken down with the demographic precision that it is today. But it is easy to speculate on whose opinions changed, and why. While newspapers were saying that Black was still a Klan member in good standing, not only Catholics and Jews and African-Americans (assuming, as is unlikely, they were adequately sampled) but also mainstream Protestants thought he should resign. Once the question of present membership was off the table, Jews, Catholics, and blacks probably still thought he should quit, but a good number of white Protestants apparently changed their minds.

Sure enough, over time, the pressure to resign subsided and the Klan issue became a joke. At the annual Washington correspondents' dinner that year, the humorous skits included some reporters dressing up in white bedsheets and singing a song about Black and the Klan. It was not, however, a joking matter for Black, either then or later. He got up and walked out of the correspondents' dinner—a striking breach of etiquette at an event where the currency of the realm is the ability to laugh at oneself.[13]

The Klan explosion haunted Black the rest of his life. Whenever the issue arose in the future, Black took pains to distance himself from the Klan. He would tell his law clerks that membership was little different from joining other civic associations—a claim falsified by the fact he himself did not join until he was ready to run for office, and resigned soon thereafter. What is certain is that he never found a satisfactory public explanation for his actions. Perhaps that was because the truth was too brutal to be stated publicly: Black joined the Klan because it would get him into the Senate, because his views at the time were close enough to those of the Klan's membership that he was not deeply troubled by joining, and because he thought he could get away with it.

Had Black continued his career as a politician, it would have been hard enough to figure out whether his continuing populism reflected Klan attitudes or a broader tradition of Southern

Democratic politics. But because Black became a justice of the Supreme Court, his body of opinions—and his brilliant, original constitutional jurisprudence—can be almost infinitely scrutinized to see how they relate to the ideology of the Ku Klux Klan.

In some cases, it seems certain that his views were influenced by the desire to cleanse himself of the Klan association. Black would eventually become an unbending advocate of judicially mandated racial equality, regardless of the Southern opposition that he knew would follow. This attitude surely reflected Black's desire not to be seen as a Klansman, and it is indeed the best reason to absolve him of guilt for his past actions.

On other questions of constitutional law, the relationship is more complicated. Black would develop an extremely strong view of religious liberty and the separation of church and state. His decisions would ban Bible reading in the public schools and prohibit school-sponsored prayer, results which alienated many evangelical Protestants and certainly would not have pleased the Christian-oriented Klan.[14] Yet Black also wrote decisions that blocked many forms of state aid to Catholic schools, which has led some prominent scholars to argue that the anti-Catholicism of his Klan years played a role in his thinking.[15]

Black would put free speech at the center of his constitutional vision, often rendering decisions that gave aid and comfort to the civil rights movement. His nearly absolutist conception of free speech might seem on the surface to be at odds with the Klan's reactionary worldview. But at the same time, the Klan can also be seen as the very model of a disfavored political organization that needs the protection of the First Amendment against government regulation. In a landmark case, Black would vote to maintain the First Amendment right of an organization to the secrecy of its membership list.[16] The organization in question was the NAACP. Yet it was precisely secret membership that Black had relied on to hide his association with the Ku Klux Klan.

CHAPTER 15

Original Intent

The Supreme Court term began in 1937, as it still does, on the first Monday in October, just a few days after Black's speech. The transition from the Senate to the Court would have been difficult for anyone ascending to the bench, even someone intellectually and legally prepared to dive into the specialized business of deciding Supreme Court cases. Black was not so prepared. There is little evidence that he was even in the habit of reading Supreme Court decisions regularly before joining the bench—why should he have been, as a senator without any particular judicial focus? To begin crafting such decisions when he had never written anything longer than a political speech posed a serious challenge.

To his credit, Black waded right in. He could have relied on his hastily hired law clerk—who was Jewish, part of Black's effort to show he was not biased. The clerk's experience was as limited as his own, but he had at least graduated from law school more recently. Instead, Black set out to write his opinions by himself. From the start, he wrote in the clear, direct, nonspecialist language that would become both his literary style and the touchstone of his constitutional philosophy. The early opinions were desperately lacking in legal sophistication. They read as though they were written by an intelligent person with no particular idea of the genre of the Supreme Court opinion—which, of course, they were.

Remarkably, though, Black's very first independently authored dissent, in an otherwise obscure tax case, already contained the seeds of what would become Black's immensely influential theory of constitutional law: that the text of the Constitution means what it was originally intended to mean. This is the philosophy known as originalism. Black's version of this philosophy was that the original meaning should be found by looking at the text of the Constitution as it would have been publicly understood when written. It guided his pen from the very first months he arrived on the Court and for the next thirty-four years. Although earlier justices had occasionally used historical materials to argue about the original meaning of this or that provision of the Constitution,[17] Hugo Black was the first justice to frame originalism as a definitive constitutional theory and to explain why and how he was using it. In this sense, Black was the inventor of originalism.

Before going on the Court, Black's main experience with interpreting texts was his weekly job of reading Bible passages and applying them to ordinary life for the benefit of a large audience of adult men. The deep wellspring of Black's originalism was the distinctively Protestant method of biblical interpretation that he had used for two decades as a Sunday school teacher in Birmingham. There is an overlap between the Protestant idea that the Bible may be interpreted by any individual without the mediating authority of the Church and the originalist idea that the meaning of the Constitution may be ascertained without reference to binding precedent.[18]

Protestant Reformers like Martin Luther and John Calvin set aside the precedents of the Church in favor of interpretations that they believed corresponded to the original meaning of the words of the Gospels. Black had been a great success in Sunday school without any specialized training in a religious seminary. Now he would set out to become a success in interpreting the Constitution without formal training in the history of constitutional interpretation.

The case in which Black rolled out his theory was brought by a Connecticut-based insurance company that had been taxed in California and wanted the Court to find the out-of-state tax unconstitutional. The other eight justices saw the case as routine, and they held in favor of the Connecticut company. Black, though, disagreed. The Constitution, he declared, did not protect corporations—only people.

His reason was simplicity itself: The due process clause of the Fourteenth Amendment gave rights only to persons. "I do not believe the word 'person' in the Fourteenth Amendment includes corporations," Black wrote.[19] To include corporations was to invent new rights, rights that had "a revolutionary effect on our form of government."[20] Black was alluding to the *Lochner* era, when the justices had invented the liberty of contract to protect corporations and their property. He was saying that all this could have been avoided if the justices had only followed the original intent of the Constitution.

Black's opinion flew in the face of precedent dating back to 1886; but Black did not care. "A constitutional interpretation that is wrong should not stand," he insisted. After all, the Court had reversed itself the previous spring with its switch in time. Black was tactlessly reminding his new colleagues that when the switch had happened, he had been in the Senate, supporting the court-packing plan and adding to the pressure. The first Roosevelt justice, Black was presenting himself as a harbinger of greater change to come.

As someone with no judicial experience, Black did not identify with the collective body of judicial wisdom developed over the years. As a populist, he was attracted to the idea that the Constitution meant what the people had thought it meant in the first place, not what elite judges construed it to mean. What was more, it seemed that anyone could do what Black was doing, namely read the text of the Constitution and decide for himself. Black had, after all, educated himself during his years in the Senate. In fact, he had first expressed his radical idea about corporations not being protected by the Constitution three years earlier, on the floor of the Senate, though no one had paid much attention.[21]

Black's originalism was liberal in its orientation, and radical in its implications. Conservatism had traditionally meant a cautious attitude toward rapid social change—a caution embodied in the practice of judicial precedent. Black's originalism was designed to be the opposite of conservative. It flatly rejected the idea that the Supreme Court should act slowly or cautiously in introducing changes into the fabric of constitutional law. Past practice had no value in itself. It should be weighed only against its correctness as a matter of original meaning. What was wrong should be jettisoned—no matter how jarring the social change that might follow.

Reading Black's maiden dissent, his new colleagues did not notice a distinctive constitutional philosophy in embryo. They saw an inexperienced politician issuing a solo dissent that challenged the foundations of constitutional law. Black's first sentence rather grandly stated, "I do not believe that this California corporate franchise tax has been proved beyond all reasonable doubt to be in violation of the Federal Constitution."[22] This opening might have sounded good to a former trial lawyer. But to an appellate lawyer it was embarrassing. With the exception of a few archaic nineteenth-century references, the "beyond a reasonable doubt" standard is never used in interpreting the meaning of the Constitution.[23]

Justice Harlan Fiske Stone felt the most alarm at Black's lack of craft and experience. Stone, a moderate Republican, was a former dean of Columbia Law School. He considered himself the natural leader of the wing of the Court that had rejected the conservative jurisprudence of the *Lochner* era. Indeed, until he became chief justice a few years later, Stone convened a weekly shadow conference of like-minded justices at his home. They would discuss in advance the cases that would be considered at the regular conference of the justices—and at much greater length than was encouraged by Chief Justice Hughes, who liked to keep the conferences short. Stone was not only worried about the amateur quality of Black's work. He was concerned that Black, as Roosevelt's first appointee, might give liberal Supreme Court justices a bad name.

Stone decided to write to Felix Frankfurter, whom he knew from the legal academy and through whom he had on occasion communicated with Roosevelt. Stone saw himself, Frankfurter, and Black as loosely aligned in judicial orientation; what he wanted was help in making Black a team player. Perhaps Frankfurter could give some guidance to his fellow New Deal sympathizer on how to write a judicial opinion, and when to dissent or remain silent? By the spring, Justice Brandeis, too, was beginning to worry about

Black. Brandeis had been a great dissenter in his day, but Black was dissenting alone, and doing it too frequently—a total of nine times in his first Court term. Brandeis, like Stone, mentioned his concerns to Frankfurter.[24]

The idea that the professor could tutor the recent appointee in how to act as a Supreme Court justice might seem like role reversal. It was plausible only because of Frankfurter's preeminence as a constitutional expert, the connection to Roosevelt that both men shared, and their identities as fellow liberals. Frankfurter had in fact been an important supporter of Black's during the confirmation process. No doubt Frankfurter's positive attitude was shaped in part by that of Brandeis, to whom Black had shown respect during his Senate years through annual visits. Frankfurter had relied on Senator Borah's public statement that Black was not a Klan member. Although a civil libertarian, Frankfurter had defended Black against the charge that his Senate investigative techniques had gone too far. He had insisted that Black's dearth of legal experience was no fundamental impediment to later judicial success.[25] Most important, when the Klan story broke, Frankfurter—one of the most prominent Jews in the United States—did not call for Black's resignation. Instead he tried to help Black's image, urging a Catholic Alabamian student of his who had just graduated from Harvard Law School to accept a job as Black's law clerk. (The student refused.)[26]

At the prompting of Stone and a hint from Brandeis, Frankfurter reached out to Black in May 1938. Tea was arranged with Frankfurter, Black, and their wives, Marion and Josephine, at the Blacks' residence in Alexandria. Then they met again for dinner at the home of Justice Stanley Reed.[27]

Frankfurter believed the meetings were useful in what he considered the gradual process of socializing Black into the norms of Court life. In a letter to Roosevelt, he described Black as quick to infer hostility, even where none existed: "Various experiences of his life have been calculated to make him a bit of an Ishmaelite—to expect every hand is to be raised against him, and therefore, at times to be unwarrantedly suspicious when nothing but friendliness is intended."[28] The biblical reference hinted that Black was a bit of a wild man, uncultivated—at least where the Supreme Court was concerned.

Frankfurter's observation reflected his own unconscious insecurities. Despite his insider status, he was no more a natural member of the elite than Black. The hint of projection is deepened by the way Frankfurter in the same letter to Roosevelt praised Black's wife, Josephine, as "an altogether grand person, with a keen realization of the psychological aspect of the situation, and with unusual talents for mitigating difficulties and softening hard feelings."[29] This could almost have been a description of Marion Frankfurter. Both she and Josephine Black were the daughters of ministers and came from class backgrounds substantially more elevated than their husbands. Both had corresponding social graces that their husbands lacked. Yet both women suffered serious depression and disliked socializing; and Marion Frankfurter often took it upon herself to placate those whose feathers Frankfurter had ruffled.

Notwithstanding Frankfurter's belief that the meetings had done some good, the get-togethers were not a success from Black's standpoint. Frankfurter spoke pointedly of the necessity of picking one's spots in filing dissenting opinions; Black remained impassive. The two personalities could not have been less well-suited. The professor saw himself as an expert on the Supreme Court with all the qualifications in the world for advising a junior justice—and hadn't he been asked to do so by a more senior justice on the same court? Black was a man of deep pride who was, in essence, being reprimanded for his inadequacies by a teacher—not a class of persons toward whom he ever felt much sympathy. Since Black was not a man who missed a slight—or forgot one—the conversations had the potential to do real harm.

Meanwhile Stone, fearing that Roosevelt would now fill the Court with unqualified, politically oriented appointees like Black, took matters in his own hands. In the fall of 1937, Stone had a series of conversations with the Washington reporter (and later syndicated columnist) Marquis Childs, in which he expressed his fears about the direction of the Court. He told Childs that Black was amateur in his approach and was not keeping up with the judicial workload. An enterprising reporter who was treating the Supreme Court like any other Washington agency, Childs wrote an article in the *St. Louis Post-Dispatch* in January that included the comment that "a new man on the bench who has had no judicial experience and only a comparatively limited legal experience is not a help to his colleagues in the first two or three years."[30] Although he was not quoted, Stone was Childs's source.

Stone liked the piece, but he wanted his message sent even more clearly, and he advised Childs to publish "something of the sort in a magazine having national circulation."[31] Childs obliged with a longer essay in the May 1938 issue of *Harper's*. The article depicted Black as a man in over his head, who had committed "blunders which have shocked his colleagues," and who was not carrying his share of the Court's business. Childs also gave voice to Stone's particular concern that Black was out to make a constitutional revolution without knowing how: "It is as though, a comparatively inexperienced player, he had stepped into a fast game, say tennis... and, ignoring the rules, made vigorous passes at every ball with a piece of board."[32]

The essay caused a stir. When it came out that Childs had been taking long walks with Stone, it became obvious that the source within the Court had been Stone himself. Now the *Harper's* story itself became a story, with newspapers widely reporting that Stone had attacked Black. Realizing he had gone too far, Stone issued a public denial that he was the source of the story.[33] Then he went to Black and explained that his private words had been taken out of context and distorted.

It would have been upsetting enough for Black to hear that a senior colleague was bad-mouthing him to a prominent journalist. But on top of that, Stone's explanation was not credible. Childs would not have used such extensive excerpts from conversations with Stone if he had believed that Stone would be upset about it later—Stone was too important a man and too valuable a source for such casual betrayal. Inexperienced with the use of the press and seeking to influence Roosevelt, Stone had simply overplayed his hand. In the process, he had insulted Black. Black made no response to Stone. He simply took note of the betrayal and filed it away—to reemerge at an appropriate time.

CHAPTER 16

Anschluss

The year 1938 was a particularly difficult one for Felix Frankfurter. The fear of Hitler's Germany that he had harbored for years was beginning to be proven horrifyingly real. Already in February, Hitler had promoted the expansionist, pro-war Joachim von Ribbentrop to be his foreign minister, and awarded the country's highest military post to Hermann Goering, who had built the Luftwaffe into the world's most advanced air force. On March 12–13 came the Anschluss, which brought Frankfurter's native Austria under Nazi rule.

Frankfurter was not one of those Viennese Jews who constantly waxed lyrical about his birthplace. His brilliance and his talent for meeting everybody might have meant that he would have fallen in with the city's intellectuals and artists had he remained, but Frankfurter was only twelve when he left. When he returned to Europe for a year in 1933–34, it was to England, which he had adopted not as his own country of origin but rather as the origin of the American legal tradition in which he found a spiritual home.

Yet at the same time, Frankfurter felt no bitterness toward Austria, and always paid special attention to its affairs. In February 1938 he wrote Roosevelt a rather formal letter urging the appointment of Hamilton Fish Armstrong, the editor of *Foreign Affairs* magazine, as ambassador to Austria. Roosevelt had not asked for his opinion, and Frankfurter claimed in the letter that this was the first time in the Roosevelt presidency that he had offered appointment-related advice unbidden. Whether this was true or not, what is noteworthy is his explanation that he was breaking his rule "because of my special interests in Austrian affairs."[34] Armstrong was a foreign-policy intellectual who had published an incisive book about Hitler as early as 1933. Even before the war broke out, Frankfurter wanted him on the spot to help sound the warning about the dangers of the Third Reich. The takeover of Austria made the appointment of an ambassador moot.

In letters with his sister Estelle, who was working in the middle levels of the New Deal, Frankfurter expressed horror at the news of the Anschluss. He and Estelle were close. Between 1933 and his death, Frankfurter wrote her some 750 letters. Addressed to "Telly" and signed "Filly," they often discussed matters of Jewish interest.[35] The concern about events in Austria was familial as well as collective. The Frankfurters' uncle Solomon, now eighty-two years old, still lived in Vienna, where he had retired as director of the State Library.

On the morning of March 12, the day the Germans entered Vienna, Austria's new masters began arresting persons they deemed a threat to the Nazi regime, including army officers, socialists—and thousands of Jews. One of those arrested that day was Solomon Frankfurter. He was marked for arrest because he was president of a group of Jewish fraternal organizations and had made "unguarded remarks" against the Nazis' destruction of free scholarship. Word reached Frankfurter more than a week later.[36]

Frankfurter could perhaps have called Roosevelt and asked for help with his uncle. One friend suggested to Frankfurter that he should go through the State Department in the hopes of securing his uncle's release.[37] But personalizing his concerns might have compromised Frankfurter's broader strategy of moving Roosevelt in the direction of helping European Jews. Nor was it clear what Roosevelt could do to affect events on the ground in Austria. It was not as if the United States had any influence in the new regime there.

Instead, Frankfurter called upon a connection he had made in England: Lady Nancy Astor, who had entertained Frankfurter at Cliveden House, her spectacular country estate, during his time in Oxford in 1933–34. American born, and a famous beauty and wit in her day, she had moved to England after divorcing her first husband, married into the recently minted aristocracy, and become a committed Christian Scientist. Her husband, Waldorf Astor, was elected a member of Parliament; but when he inherited the title of viscount, he automatically became a member of the House of Lords and so had to resign from the House of Commons. Nancy Astor ran for his seat—and won it, despite a total lack of political experience. She became only the second woman ever elected to Parliament and the first to serve her term. She remained a member of Parliament from 1919 until 1945.

In 1938, however, when Frankfurter appealed for her help, Astor was both more and less than a glamorous, well-connected Tory. She had become a leading advocate for accommodation with Germany and a conciliatory attitude toward Nazism. Indeed, Cliveden House had recently given its name to a pro-German political movement. The Cliveden Set, as it was derisively called, was a group of wellborn Englishmen, some with Nazi sympathies, who believed that Germany had been unfairly crushed with the burden of reparations after World War I. Convinced that the best chance for Britain's future lay in striking some sort of separate deal with Hitler, several of the group enjoyed informal contacts with the Reich.[38]

By 1938, the Jewish adviser to Roosevelt and the woman widely perceived as a Nazi fellow traveler did not agree on much in the realm of world affairs. But Frankfurter had agreed with Astor about the excesses of the Versailles treaty when they had met five years before. In principle, they were friends, or at least warm acquaintances. And Astor was probably the one person in England who would be guaranteed to have an effect when she asked the Germans for a small favor.

Astor had something else to gain by helping Frankfurter's uncle: It was a perfect opportunity for her to try and demonstrate that despite her pro-German sympathies she was not an anti-Semite. Once Frankfurter asked for help, Astor sprung into action. By her own account in a letter to Frankfurter, Astor twice called the German ambassador to England on Frankfurter's behalf, the second time announcing that "unless I received good news of Herr Frankfurter, I should myself go to Vienna!"[39] Her démarche worked. Solomon Frankfurter was released on March 26.[40]

If Frankfurter was grateful, his appreciation was tempered by the desire to continue his argument with Astor and to make clear his disapproval of her pro-appeasement position. In a letter now lost, which must have been a masterwork of chutzpah, he criticized the politics of the woman who had just saved his uncle's life. Astor replied defensively that the charges against the Cliveden Set being bruited in the newspapers were propaganda. She was not a fascist, she insisted, despite supporting closer relations among Britain, Germany, and Mussolini's Italy.

Frankfurter wrote back to her again, this time with no mention of her kindness toward his uncle. He reassured her that "there's nothing conspiratorial about you—you are one of the most forthright, above-board people I know." But he nevertheless chided her for a speech she had made earlier that year in which she explained American anti-Nazism as a result of American Jewish control of advertisements in the press. "Since we are talking with the candor of friendship let me suggest to you that you must not be too surprised if you are widely misunderstood regarding the anti-Semitic aspect—an essential aspect—of Nazism." Statements like Astor's "not unnaturally make people who do not know your warm human qualities infer a sympathy on your part with Hitler's anti-Semitism which people like me, of course, know to be untrue." Then Frankfurter passed on copies of the correspondence to Roosevelt—excluding, surely not by coincidence, his initial letter to Astor in which he thanked her for saving his uncle.[41]

The whole episode suggests the extreme difficulty of Frankfurter's position vis-à-vis his uncle's detention. It would have been monstrous had Frankfurter not done everything he could to save a close family member from certain death. It certainly justified asking a favor from an acquaintance, even if the basis for her ability to help was her closeness to the regime that was endangering Frankfurter's uncle in the first place. Once he had made the approach, though, Frankfurter's conscience clearly bothered him. He wanted it on the record—not only for himself and his posterity but for Roosevelt and probably the intelligence officials who would undoubtedly be monitoring Astor's communications—that he rejected Astor's views and had made no concession on that front to enlist her help.

At the level of U.S. foreign policy, Frankfurter faced a parallel challenge in the period before the United States entered the war against Germany. National sentiment strongly wanted to keep the United States out of the war, and many of the liberals around Roosevelt thought similarly. Frankfurter himself was pro-war.[42] He thought that American intervention was inevitable and desirable. But he was keenly aware that his own particular concern for European Jewry was not a product solely of his American identity, but as much or more of his European Jewish one. At a dinner Frankfurter held in honor of Lord Lothian, the British ambassador to the United States, after Britain was at war but before the United States was, Robert Jackson and some others present said that Hitler "was satisfying the aspirations of the youth of Germany." Frankfurter became "almost angry" and "declared that we might as well say that Capone had given leadership to the youth of Chicago."[43] That he tried to repress what must have been genuine fury suggests the delicacy of his position. Frankfurter could not advocate too strongly for the war without being seen to compromise his position of objectivity—thus weakening his cause.

Frankfurter began pushing Roosevelt in some particular cases to use the American diplomatic corps to try to save select distinguished Jewish scholars in Europe. In a few instances, individuals were helped as a result of these efforts.[44] Frankfurter next sent Roosevelt a comprehensive list of scientists who had been purged from European universities or sent to concentration camps. This elicited a noncommittal response: "That list of scientists is amazing and I fear the dismissals have not ended yet."[45] No specific further action followed.

Then there was the larger issue of Jewish refugees. In the days after the September 1938 Munich Agreement between England and Germany, Frankfurter, like others, became concerned that the British were planning to limit Jewish immigration to what was then

Palestine. Although no one yet could anticipate the horrors that were to come, it was nonetheless already clear that some significant number of Jews would seek to flee Europe, and that no country was likely to accept them. Frankfurter spoke to Roosevelt about this matter on the telephone. Through Ben Cohen, Frankfurter gave Roosevelt a draft letter for Prime Minister Neville Chamberlain. The letter urged that "no decision may be made which would close the gates of Palestine to the Jews. Shutting the gates of Palestine to Jews would greatly embarrass efforts towards genuine appeasement and it would be interpreted as a disturbing symbol of anti-Semitism."[46]

The letter seems not to have been passed on to Chamberlain; it would have had little effect even if it had been sent. The British interest in Palestine was to maintain calm between the Jewish and Palestinian-Arab populations, and limiting Jewish immigration was the best way to accomplish that goal. Even Churchill, who sympathized with Zionism, never allowed significant Jewish immigration to Palestine when it might have made a decisive difference in saving the lives of fleeing European Jews. There is no record that Roosevelt said anything to Chamberlain on the topic of the Jews or on Palestine. With Europe on the brink of war, these were simply not the central issues of the moment from the perspective of either man.

One irony of Frankfurter's cautious repeated efforts to draw Roosevelt's attention toward the Jewish question in the fall of 1938 was that at precisely the same time, other leaders of the American Jewish community were using their influence with Roosevelt to try and keep Frankfurter off the Supreme Court. The issue had arisen when Justice Benjamin Cardozo died that summer, opening another spot on the Court. Roosevelt in 1933 had suggested that he hoped to make Frankfurter a justice some day. Now that Roosevelt had made two Supreme Court appointments—Black and Stanley Reed—it was only natural to think that Frankfurter's turn had arrived.

In October, Frankfurter and his wife were lunching with Roosevelt at Hyde Park when Roosevelt, uncharacteristically "ill at ease," blurted out that he wanted to tell Frankfurter why he could not appoint him to succeed Cardozo. As Frankfurter later recounted it, Roosevelt explained that he had promised several senators and others in the party that the next appointment would go to a Westerner.[47] According to Roosevelt's version of the same conversation, the president added that he "could not appoint another Jew."[48]

Why Roosevelt could not appoint a Jew to replace the Jewish Cardozo was not obvious. Since Cardozo had joined Brandeis in 1932, there had been two Jews on the Court without that fact exciting any particular anti-Semitic response. What Roosevelt did not say was that it was Jews, rather than anti-Semites, that he was worried about angering with Frankfurter's appointment. Roosevelt had asked Henry Morgenthau Jr., the secretary of the treasury and the most important Jew in the administration, whether he ought to appoint Frankfurter or the non-Jewish James Landis, then newly installed as dean of the Harvard Law School. Morgenthau advised that Roosevelt should "by all means" choose Landis.[49]

Morgenthau and Frankfurter did not like one another. Indeed, the dislike went back a generation. Frankfurter had a low opinion of Henry Morgenthau Sr., the father of the secretary of the treasury, who had once been the U.S. ambassador to the Sublime Porte of the Ottoman Empire. Frankfurter, who had accompanied the elder Morgenthau on a fruitless 1917 mission to Europe to try and get Turkey out of World War I, had been exasperated by what he considered Morgenthau's incompetence. He once said of him that "the froth was the man."[50] The Morgenthau family knew how Frankfurter felt, and reciprocated his dislike.

But Morgenthau's opposition also reflected his concern that Roosevelt not foment anti-Semitism by seeming obviously pro-Jewish. This was the explicit argument of a group of American Jewish leaders, including Arthur Hays Sulzberger of the *New York Times*, who came to visit Roosevelt at the White House for the sole purpose of arguing against Frankfurter's appointment.[51]

A possible answer to this concern about appointing a second Jew to the Supreme Court was for Louis Brandeis to announce his retirement and open the door for his longtime protégé, the man whom he called "half brother, half son." Brandeis was not well, and he would in fact announce his retirement in early 1939. That he did not do so in the fall of 1938, when Frankfurter's appointment hung in the balance, indicated the rift that had opened between the two men over the court-packing plan the previous year.

Brandeis felt that Frankfurter's public silence about the court-packing plan had been wholly inadequate, a betrayal of both Brandeis and the Court. Faced with a conflict between Brandeis and Roosevelt, Frankfurter had chosen the latter. Meanwhile, to Frankfurter, Brandeis had unjustifiably harmed the president's plan by signing Chief Justice Hughes's public letter defending the Court. Relations between Brandeis and Roosevelt had broken down completely. When Brandeis heard the suggestion that he should retire to open the door for Frankfurter, he commented bitingly that "he was not sure that Frankfurter could not do more by teaching the younger generation"[52]—a devastating riposte given the past closeness between the two and Frankfurter's lifelong aspiration to emulate Brandeis.

But in the end, almost six months after the vacancy was created, Roosevelt did appoint Frankfurter to fill Cardozo's seat. Brandeis's illness was obvious enough that the Jewish question could be circumvented. More important, Tommy Corcoran had gone to great lengths to convince Roosevelt that Frankfurter could easily be confirmed. Working tirelessly, Corcoran had recruited active support from administration insiders including Robert Jackson.

Then solicitor general, Jackson aspired to the post of attorney general, which had just come open. At a meeting with Roosevelt, however, Jackson put Frankfurter first: "I regard the Court appointment as infinitely more important than the Attorney-Generalship," Jackson told the president. "All I would ask of you for me personally is to leave me as Solicitor General, but give me Felix on the bench."[53] Roosevelt was inclined to agree. "Your greatest contribution in the light of history," he said to Jackson, "will be the change of Supreme Court's interpretation of the Constitution"— the switch in time. "What is urgently needed . . . is someone who

can interpret it with scholarship and with sufficient assurance...
in conference and hold his own in the discussion." When Jackson suggested that the new appointee should be able "to help give
direction to the action of the Court," Roosevelt replied, "I think
Felix is the only man who could do that job, Bob."[54]

Corcoran, who had risen to power in Washington with Frankfurter's patronage and help, saw the appointment as a personal victory. On hearing the news of Roosevelt's decision, he and other
important young liberals gathered for a victory celebration over
champagne at the Department of the Interior. Among those present were Secretary of the Interior Harold Ickes, Ben Cohen, Missy
LeHand, and another leading liberal who was becoming increasingly close to Corcoran: William O. Douglas of the SEC.[55]

Like the liberals who were the allies of both men, Roosevelt
understood that Frankfurter was the single person in the United
States most qualified for the job of perpetuating the constitutional
ideal to which Roosevelt was committed. Frankfurter was the
nation's leading liberal public intellectual and activist; and he had
been around long enough that even the more conservative elements
of the national bar now accepted his preeminence. The American Bar Association endorsed his nomination warmly, leading the
more radical legal realists to argue that the endorsement proved
Frankfurter was actually a conservative.

In a sense, they were right: Frankfurter had never been a total
realist. His belief in judicial restraint was rooted in the belief that
judges should not effect social change, a belief that coexisted with
his political liberalism. To this point, the two impulses had never
been contradictory. Although he could not have known it, once
he went on the Court, Frankfurter would find that the tension
between achieving desirable liberal results and maintaining judicial
restraint would be a constant source of difficulty.

On January 4, 1939, all this was still to come. That day at around
7:00 p.m. Frankfurter was in his bedroom, dressing hurriedly for a
dinner. Guests were already arriving. Marion had gone downstairs
to answer the doorbell. The phone rang, and as Frankfurter told it,
he skipped across the hall to his study "in my B.V.D.'s" to answer

the phone. There it was, he remembered vividly, "the ebullient, the exuberant, resilient warmth-enveloping voice of the President of the United States."[56]

Roosevelt decided to have a little "sadistic" fun with Frankfurter. "I told you I can't appoint you to the Supreme Court," he intoned. "Yes, you told me this," Frankfurter replied. Roosevelt repeated himself several more times: "I mean it, I don't want to appoint you. I just don't want to appoint you." Frankfurter acknowledged that the point had been made when Roosevelt changed his tone, saying, "But wherever I turn, wherever I turn, and to whomever I talk that matters to me, I am made to realize that you're the only person fit to succeed Holmes and Cardozo. Unless you give me an unsurmountable objection I'm going to send your name in for the Court tomorrow at twelve o'clock."[57]

Standing there in his underwear, Frankfurter was momentarily stunned at the fulfillment of the ambition he had held his whole adult life. "All I can say is that I wish my mother were alive," he told Roosevelt. With restraint that almost killed him, he waited until his guests left at midnight to tell Marion the news. "We sat and looked at each other and faced this thing."[58] As Roosevelt had intimated, Frankfurter would fill what was sometimes called the scholar's seat on the Court, which before Cardozo had been held by his idol Holmes.

There remained the matter of confirmation. Like all the justices who came before him, Frankfurter did not expect to have to appear before the Senate. Indeed, for the Senate to hold confirmation hearings at all was a rare event, initiated in the case of Brandeis to accommodate conservative and anti-Semitic opponents who wanted a voice. When the Senate decided to hold hearings on Frankfurter, he sent his friend Dean Acheson, who was now out of government, to appear for him.

By the end of the second day, it had become clear that Frankfurter would have to break the mold and appear in person to defend his reputation. The Senate heard testimony, the *New Yorker* put it, from "a strange assortment of crackpot crusaders, Fascists, professional Jew-haters, and others." Elizabeth Dilling, "a good-looking witch-hunter" and author of books like *The Red Network* and *The Roosevelt Red Record and Its Background*, testified that the ACLU, on whose national committee Frankfurter had long served, was a front organization for Communists. Making his appearance, Frankfurter dealt with most of the challenges easily. The ACLU, he pointed out drolly, had recently issued a statement in support of Dilling's right to free speech when a broadcasting company denied her radio time to attack a Methodist bishop.[59]

The mood turned serious only when Frankfurter was examined by Senator Pat McCarran, a Nevada Democrat and a fervent anti-Communist. Behind the scenes, McCarran had suggested that Frankfurter's citizenship was not genuine because his father had taken the oath of naturalization before being eligible. Frankfurter had to scramble to find a copy of the original ship's manifest giving the date of his father's arrival, eventually swallowing his pride and asking Henry Morgenthau to have someone search the Treasury Department's records, where the document was found. Despite the document, McCarran nevertheless brought up the subject of the date of Frankfurter's father's citizenship.[60]

Then McCarran began to question Frankfurter about his views on Communism, using as a pretext a book called *Communism* by Frankfurter's friend, the Canadian-British academic Harold Laski. McCarran demanded that Frankfurter state whether he agreed with the "doctrine" of the book. Frankfurter explained patiently that the book did not have a unified "doctrine"; then he turned the tables and asked whether McCarran had read the book. No, McCarran admitted, he had not. But he still would not give up. "If it advocates the doctrine of Marxism," he asked Frankfurter, "would you agree with it?"

Frustrated by McCarran's combination of anti-immigrant bias and foolishness, Frankfurter "took charge."[61] "Senator," he said, "I do not believe you have ever taken an oath to support the Constitution of the United States with fewer reservations than I have or would now, nor do I believe you are more attached to the theories and practices of Americanism than I am. I rest my answer on that statement."[62] When Frankfurter was done, Acheson recalled, "A great roar came from the crowded room. People shouted, cheered, stood on chairs, and waved. . . . Every time the uproar would begin to quiet, someone would start it up again."[63]

Success achieved, Frankfurter and Acheson retired to the private office of the committee chairman, Henry Ashurst of Arizona. Ashurst produced a bottle of chilled brandy. Within a few minutes, Frankfurter was tipsy on *fine glacée*, which they drank "well into the afternoon," as Frankfurter and Ashurst bonded loudly over their mutual fascination with the love affair between nineteenth-century New York senator Roscoe Conkling and Catherine Chase, daughter of Lincoln's secretary of the treasury.

Still giddy, Frankfurter proposed to Acheson that they go to the White House uninvited and tell the tale to Roosevelt. Acheson was nervous, since he had last seen Roosevelt on resigning from his administration some six years before. But Frankfurter insisted. Although they did not have an appointment, their taxi was waved through at the north gate, "since FF was a frequent caller." After protesting that the president was too busy, Missy LeHand snuck them in for a fifteen-minute appointment that turned into forty minutes as Frankfurter excitedly told Roosevelt about McCarran's challenge, his answer, and of course Roscoe Conkling and the brandy.[64]

Frankfurter would be confirmed unanimously. On January 30, Roosevelt's birthday, he wrote to Roosevelt on Supreme Court stationery that "in the mysterious ways of Fate, the Dutchess County American and the Viennese American have for decades pursued the same directions of devotion to our beloved country." Now the immigrant's "opportunity for service to the Nation" had arrived, and, he added, there was no one save Lincoln at whose hands he would rather have been given the chance.

Comparing Roosevelt to Lincoln was not mere flattery. It had the broader purpose of emphasizing to Roosevelt that he would have to bear further crisis, and very probably war. After a year in which he had seen the world pulling closer to disaster, Felix Frankfurter had triumphed.

CHAPTER 17

The Sheriff

As Hugo Black was struggling with his Klan past, and as Felix Frankfurter was agonizing over the fate of Europe and his own judicial prospects, their future colleague William O. Douglas was having the time of his life. In 1937–38 he embarked on an intensely confrontational, headline-grabbing term as SEC chairman. In a few short months, the job would propel him from anonymity into the front ranks of American politics.

Douglas became chairman with a brio that the newspapers loved and the promise of taking the fight to Wall Street. He was photographed in his office wearing a ten-gallon hat. An unholstered six-shooter rested by his right hand, the better to present Douglas as the new sheriff in town.[65] His clothes were rumpled and bought by mail order—as they would be for the rest of his life—the better to show a Westerner's contempt for the buttoned-down niceties of the East Coast. Offering a note of greater worldliness in his office was a portrait of Brandeis, with whom Douglas now began to associate himself. The fit was good. Brandeis's book *Other People's Money* was the seminal work on financial fraud. Douglas quoted it frequently, reiterating Brandeis's goal of disinfecting Wall Street through the judicious use of sunshine.

The way he had gotten the chairman's job was as audacious as the image Douglas was now projecting. A year and a half earlier he had been a total anonymity in Washington—a law professor with a part-time job running one of the commission's several research committees. From the time he was hired as staff, he told friends he would be chairman. Joe Kennedy would not serve long, he knew.

His departure would create a vacancy on the commission, and if Douglas could get the post, he would be well-placed to become chairman when the next chairman stepped down. The first step went smoothly. Kennedy resigned, James Landis became chairman, and he in turn recommended Douglas to Roosevelt, who offered the job to Douglas just before Christmas of 1935.[66]

Douglas did not have to wait long to execute the next phase of his plan. Rumors that Landis would resign from the chairmanship began in the fall of 1936. By that time, Douglas already had some supporters who planted his name in articles speculating about the identity of the next chairman. The appointment of Douglas was by no means a sure thing. It was also rumored that Robert Jackson would get the job—a rumor that appeared in the press, not by coincidence, on the day that Jackson testified in favor of the court-packing plan in March of 1937.

So Douglas began campaigning for the chairmanship. His strategy was one of high risk and high return. Kennedy and Landis had both been conciliatory toward Wall Street, calculating that the SEC needed to co-opt those it was trying to regulate. Douglas took the opposite approach. He went in front of rich, conservative audiences, and denounced the predatory tactics and subversive influence of those who manipulated financial markets.

On one such occasion, Douglas's friend and longtime booster Robert Maynard Hutchins, president of the University of Chicago, invited him to address the trustees of the university. Douglas called his speech "Termites of Finance," a direct attack on financiers who lived off the profits of the productive members of society. In another speech, he told the Stock Exchange Institute that the financial community had tried and would try again to corrupt the government. The capstone was an address to the Bond Club of New York, with every important banker in attendance. Douglas told them they could not be trusted with the money that belonged to ordinary investors.[67] The audiences hated him. Douglas was announcing openly that he distrusted the financial community and favored aggressive regulation of their business. For the confrontational Douglas, who had never had much money, angering the wealthiest Americans was fun.

It was also clever. By striking fear in the hearts of those it would be his job to regulate, he created a constituency devoted to opposing him. At the same time, Douglas was gambling that from the perspective of the president, these were just the enemies to prove that Douglas was the right man for the job. The emergence of a campaign for "Anyone but Douglas" made it appear that there was no one better suited to establishing mastery over Wall Street. If Douglas inspired so much fear on the Street, he must surely pose a major threat to the old ways.

Douglas's gamble paid off, if just barely. Toward the end, in September 1937, when he had not yet gotten the job, Douglas used the same technique that Jackson would employ a couple of months later with Roosevelt: He threatened to resign. In Douglas's case, the threat could not be made directly to the president, because he was not yet close enough to Roosevelt to make it work. So Douglas explained himself to Joe Kennedy. To make his threat to leave credible, Douglas had to be creative. Landis was resigning from the SEC to become the dean of Harvard Law School. The competitive Douglas now claimed he had a parallel offer to become dean of Yale Law School.[68] Kennedy took the proposition to Tommy Corcoran. The two convinced the president to support the appointment of Douglas to replace Landis.

In Western films, at least, the way the sheriff establishes credibility is by taking on the worst offender in town and shooting him dead. In the role of the bad guy, Douglas cast the New York Stock Exchange. Long a symbol of the financial markets, the Exchange was particularly vulnerable after a substantial stock drop on October 19, 1937.

Douglas operated by confrontation, not mediation. He told the management of the Exchange that they had to reorganize themselves to his satisfaction. "If you'll produce a plan of reorganization," he told them, "I'll let you run the Exchange. But if you just go on horse-trading, I'll step in and run it myself."[69] The businessmen thought this was a negotiating position: But it was not. To the surprise of the Street, Douglas simply refused to budge. After all, Douglas in fact did have the authority for a takeover, and he must have known that his public image could only be helped by it.

Then Douglas had a piece of luck. It involved Richard Whitney, the former president of the Exchange. Whitney was a legendary financier who had attended Groton and Harvard a little after Roosevelt. Famously cool under pressure, he had tried to reverse the crash of 1929 single-handedly by buying stocks at above-market prices, a gesture that in the popular imagination was supposed to have stopped the sell-off on Black Thursday. As an opponent of reform, Whitney once told the Senate commission investigating Wall Street, "You gentlemen are making a huge mistake. The Exchange is a perfect institution."[70] In 1934 he had appeared on the cover of *Time* as the "White Knight of Wall Street."

Beneath the gentlemanly façade, however, Whitney had always been lurching from one financial crisis to another—even before the crash. In 1926 he had secretly taken money from his wife's trust fund, just managing to replace it before being discovered. In 1929 he had borrowed half a million dollars from his brother to cover losses. In 1930, when he became president of the Exchange, he began to sell securities belonging to the New York Yacht Club— without permission. His biggest mistake came in 1933, when he bought the Distilled Liquors Corporation, a firm that made an applejack no one especially wanted to drink. Whitney borrowed heavily against the shares, and when they plummeted, he was in debt too deep to recover. Borrowing desperately, he eventually owed some $8 million on his personal accounts. To cap it off, Whitney, out of options, embezzled from the Exchange's own pension fund in the attempt to cover his debts.[71]

Now, in 1937, Whitney faced a crisis of a different sort. For the first time, as a result of the pressure from Douglas's SEC, the Exchange demanded that all its member firms make public disclosures of their financial statements. Whitney hoped to fake his way through, but the Exchange sent its accountants to his offices. They were horrified by what they discovered. Whitney appealed to the ultimate authority: J. P. Morgan himself, the acknowledged king of Wall Street, with whose firm he had done business for decades.

Morgan was "shocked beyond measure." He concluded there was no choice but to let Whitney go spectacularly bankrupt.[72]

Although Douglas had done nothing personally to bring down Whitney, it was a disclosure adopted under SEC threat that had made his collapse happen when it did. Douglas's war on Wall Street had, in effect, caused the humiliation of this titan of finance. As Douglas put it, with Whitney's collapse, "the Stock Exchange was delivered into my hands."[73] It was Douglas who got to deliver the news of Whitney's meltdown to the president. As Douglas later told it, despite his willingness to criticize Wall Street, Roosevelt was stunned that a man who shared his background could have sunk so low. "Not Dick Whitney!" he exclaimed to Douglas.

> "Yes," I replied, "Dick Whitney."
> "Dick Whitney, Dick Whitney," he kept repeating. "I can't believe it."
> The Old Man, as we affectionately called FDR, came close to tears.[74]

Whitney was barred from the Exchange, subjected to a lengthy SEC investigation, indicted, and convicted of embezzlement. The man who presided over the New York Stock Exchange from 1930 to 1935 spent three years and four months in prison. Five thousand spectators looked on at Grand Central as he boarded the train to Sing Sing. He ended his days running a dairy farm in Barnstable, Massachusetts, and never traded securities again.[75]

In the wake of the Whitney affair, Douglas went for a last bit of brinksmanship. He announced that he planned to reorganize the Exchange himself and called a meeting with the Exchange's lawyers. At the meeting, a lawyer offered technical help in running the complex machinery of the Exchange. Douglas thought deeply, then delivered the blow: "There is one thing you can do for me. Tell me where you keep the paper and the pencils."[76] This last threat was all it took. The amazement within the financial community at Whitney's collapse gave other senior members of the Exchange the cover they needed to act publicly to clean their own house. The Exchange caved in to Douglas's pressure. Its members adopted the full panoply of self-regulating measures that Douglas and the SEC had demanded.

With this process under way, Douglas turned to implementing the Public Utility Holding Companies Act, the same legislation that had, through the fight over its enactment, created the special investigative committee that Hugo Black had ridden to national prominence. That law as finally enacted had given the holding companies a five-year grace period to reform their affairs on their own before the SEC would be empowered to break them up. The five years were coming to an end. Douglas announced that he intended to act just as the law empowered him to do. If the holding companies failed to reorganize themselves by simplifying their corporate structure, Douglas promised he would dissolve them completely. The doomsday threat was effective. It prompted a wave of reorganizations. That meant headlines—and an appropriate payoff to a half decade's crusade of reform.

By the end of 1938, Douglas, now all of forty years old, was one of the most prominent and successful New Deal players. Having risen to the top with astonishing speed, he now needed some position that would correspond to the ambition he had long held. The only question was what that office would be, and no Washington job was presenting itself. The most promising option within Douglas's reach was the Yale Law School deanship, which was open as of January, and which could plausibly become his on the model of Landis becoming dean of Harvard after his term as SEC chairman. Then, on February 13, 1939, Brandeis resigned from the Court for reasons of health.

Douglas was an extremely young man by Supreme Court standards, but he was a New Deal loyalist coming off of an impressive stint that had put him in the public eye. And he did have one significant advantage over other figures within the administration. He was, by upbringing and constructed self-image, a Westerner; and the president had, as he told Frankfurter the previous October, promised that a Westerner would get the next seat on the Court. The drawback was that Westerners in the Senate were urging the appointment of Senator Lewis Schwellenbach of Washington State.

Then Arthur Krock of the *New York Times*, a close friend of Joe Kennedy's, took up Douglas's cause. As Krock told it, the day Brandeis retired, he saw Douglas at a dinner and "bull session" at the home of SEC commissioner Edward Pavenstadt. Douglas said he was going back to Yale after his stint on the SEC, and Krock asked him why. "Security," Douglas answered. When Krock asked Douglas whether the job of professor was really so secure as all that, Douglas reassured him. "Yes," he said. "The only way you could lose your job would be to rape the wife of the president of Yale University. But even then it would have to be on the campus at high noon." Krock replied that Douglas was especially qualified for the Supreme Court vacancy that had just opened. Douglas professed not to have heard that Brandeis had retired, but said he would be interested.[77]

The next morning, Krock proposed Douglas's name to Attorney General Frank Murphy. At the same time, he wrote in that day's paper that Douglas was a front-runner for the job. In Washington, then as now, unconfirmed reports have a way of becoming fact. To be rumored for a job is to be a serious candidate for it. With this boost, Douglas could now turn to an insider team in search of support. The men he sought out were Harold Ickes and Tommy Corcoran, whom he had met during his rapid rise at the SEC, and who saw in him a promising, ambitious, and like-minded figure.

Roosevelt, it turned out, was on the edge of naming Schwellenbach. But Corcoran, who was in a hospital bed recovering from surgery, swung into action by telephone. He pointed out to Roosevelt that Schwellenbach had an enemy in Homer Bone, the other Washington senator; and he proposed that Roosevelt's backup nominee, Iowa Law School dean Wiley Rutledge, ought to be named to the court of appeals before being picked for the Supreme Court, as he eventually was. Then Douglas's legal-realist ally, the brilliant and mercurial Jerome Frank, whom Douglas had put on the SEC, lent a hand. Frank went to William Borah, the acknowledged Western senatorial leader, and told him that he should consider Douglas, who was a true Westerner.[78]

The goodhearted Borah had played an important role in Hugo Black's confirmation by carrying the message that Black was not a Klansman. Now he played the nearly parallel role of announcing to the press that he considered Douglas a native son of the West. Both statements were true in some technical sense, and both statements reflected the careful crafting of men who skillfully shaped their own images. But Black, of course, *had* been a Klansman. And Douglas had not been to the West except on vacation since he left Yakima for Columbia Law School sixteen years earlier. Borah's reputation for sincerity in leadership, however, made him an ideal figure to vouch for other men. Douglas was duly nominated, and confirmed easily in April.

The liberals who had celebrated Frankfurter's appointment just a few months before were equally excited by the Douglas appointment. He was, after all, one of them. Frankfurter was enthusiastic as well. His friend Harold Laski wrote to Roosevelt, "I threw up my hat with joy over Bill Douglas's nomination. He is second only to Felix in the list of those I want to see there."[79] Laski was not himself a Washington insider, so his comments reflected the impression of Douglas that he had gotten from Frankfurter. Douglas was a law professor, whose legal expertise therefore would not be questioned. He had made his reputation by going after Wall Street corruption. He professed a devotion to Brandeis. He was, in short, the very model of the sort of ally whom Frankfurter expected he would need on the Supreme Court.

Douglas's success at the SEC was the only thing he had ever accomplished practically. But that success built on his academic expertise in the subject matter of corporate behavior. He had developed that knowledge through the legal-realist approach he had learned as a student and applied as a professor, focusing on what actual corporations really did rather than on the law books. For Douglas, it turned out, legal realism had cash value. Its knowledge could be turned to practical uses.

Knowledge alone, though, would not have been enough to

explain Douglas's success. His rise to importance also depended on a truly astonishing ability to stake a position and then refuse to budge from it. This talent could be taken as commitment to principle, or as virtuosic skill in the art of bluffing.

Douglas's bluffing skill had been on display as he got to know Roosevelt through the president's regular poker games. The games were an opportunity for Roosevelt to relax with colleagues who were also friends, and attendance was a sure sign of entrance into Roosevelt's charmed inner circle. Douglas was first invited the day after he was nominated to the Supreme Court, and from the start he made an impression.[80]

Notice of a game would come through a telephone message: "There will be a command performance Saturday night." The small group would congregate at the home of Interior Secretary Harold Ickes or Treasury Secretary Henry Morgenthau. (Frankfurter, who did not play cards, rarely drank, and could not stand Morgenthau, was never invited.) As he did at his daily cocktail hour at the White House, Roosevelt liked to mix the drinks himself and "press a second, and at times a third cocktail upon any guest who was willing." Some people, remembered Roosevelt's aide Sam Rosenman, "were a little nonplused at the nonchalance with which the president, without bothering to measure, would add one ingredient after another to his cocktails. . . . He seemed to experiment on each occasion with a different percentage of vermouth, gin, and fruit juice. At times he varied it with rum—especially rum from the Virgin Islands."[81]

The men played seven card stud, and stakes were low—a few dollars a hand compared to the five-hundred-dollar buy-in that Harry Truman favored when he became president. John Nance Garner, Roosevelt's first vice president—who played in both games—described Roosevelt's games not as serious poker, but "just for conversation." Missy LeHand, always at Roosevelt's side on such informal occasions, served the drinks and sometimes played. Government business was never discussed directly, which did not mean it never got done.[82]

Douglas flourished in this environment of banter and bluff. To

Roosevelt's delight, he introduced a hand that allowed for as many as seven wild cards, which was promptly named "Justice McReynolds" after the Court's most virulently anti-Roosevelt member.[83] But Douglas could be deadly serious, and he also knew how to stand on principle. As a justice of the Supreme Court, he would come to be known as the least compromising figure on the bench, fully prepared to announce opinion after opinion without caring that he was alone in his judgment. Assessments of Douglas as a justice are deeply divided between those who consider him arbitrary and outrageous, and those who judge him the most advanced exponent of liberal principle ever to sit on the Court; again, there is truth in both propositions.

And finally there was Douglas's charm. Because the older Douglas became increasingly irascible and unpredictable, and because he developed a raft of dislikable qualities, it has become increasingly difficult from a distance to identify this feature. But the fact is that again and again in his early career, Douglas came to be admired, respected, liked, and promoted by powerful and important men. First there was his law professor Underhill Moore, who so appreciated Douglas's work and his mind that he got him appointed to the Columbia Law School faculty. Then there was Robert Maynard Hutchins, who recruited Douglas to Yale when Douglas had just one full year of teaching under his belt. The two remained friends even after Hutchins failed to lure Douglas to Chicago, and Douglas later urged the appointment of Hutchins as one of the external board of governors of the New York Stock Exchange.

After Hutchins there was Joe Kennedy, who did not know Douglas at all when the young professor first appeared in his office. Kennedy introduced him to Roosevelt and supported him for the SEC chairmanship even though Douglas's approach was, to the public eye, in sharp contrast with Kennedy's. Through Kennedy, Douglas met Corcoran and then by extension a small group of extraordinarily intelligent, ambitious, and powerful men who would remain his friends for some years. These included Harold Ickes, a crucial Roosevelt insider whose secret diaries, written for posterity, reveal much of what we know about relations among those closest to Roosevelt; Clark Clifford, later Truman's right hand; and even the young Lyndon Baines Johnson, who had impressed Roosevelt as a first-term congressman and been rewarded by Tommy Corcoran's friendship.

Nor was the young Douglas lacking in impressive protégés. Having been a law professor for only a short time, Douglas did not have Frankfurter's extensive network of student mentees. But Douglas had a small group of Yale Law School students with whom he formed long-term bonds. The most important was Abe Fortas, his first SEC staffer, who would become a successful Washington lawyer and would ultimately serve on the Supreme Court, only to resign in scandal after his nomination for chief justice faltered. Another was Fred Rodell, who became an iconoclastic Yale Law School professor himself and wrote extensively on the Supreme Court of the era.

Journalists, too, liked Douglas—and not only hard-driving, hard-drinking journalists, such as Eliot Janeway, a long-time supporter, but even the dour Arthur Krock. Douglas, it was true, provided good copy. But these were not men easily impressed by surface publicity. The journalists of the time knew everyone in Washington personally, and knew nearly everything there was to know about them. They were professional judges of character, and they saw in Douglas enormous promise and flair. His Western manner may have been self-created; but whose manner was not? And what could be more American than a genius for self-creation?

Most important, of course, was Roosevelt, no mean reader of men, who considered Douglas the most potentially promising member of the New Deal. Roosevelt put Douglas on the Court at a preposterously young age, but that was not all. Roosevelt expected Douglas would not long remain there. In 1940, Roosevelt briefly considered Douglas for the vice presidency. Then, in 1944, in ill health during wartime, and making what he well knew could be the most important vice presidential choice in U.S. history, Roosevelt wanted Douglas for the job. Had he pushed harder, or had the political machine supporting Harry Truman been a little weaker, Douglas would have been president of the United States.

Book Four

ALLIES

CHAPTER 18

The Pledge

In the brief period between the fall of 1937 and the spring of 1939, Roosevelt appointed Hugo Black, Felix Frankfurter, and William O. Douglas to the Supreme Court. Robert Jackson became solicitor general of the United States, charged with the responsibility of representing the Roosevelt administration before the Court. These men were allies, appointees and close associates of Roosevelt, and there was every reason to expect they would remain so. All had contributed in essential ways to the grand and increasingly successful project that the New Deal had become. All considered Brandeis an important influence. All had built or bolstered their reputations by taking on Wall Street.

Bound by a common commitment to Roosevelt's political values, the men thought of themselves as liberals. The economic dimension of the liberalism they shared was devoted to saving capitalism by regulating it. As Jackson put it in October 1938, "The liberal accepts the main outlines of our existing economic system as desirable and as destined to endure at least for some generations. He accepts and champions the right to use one's talents and efforts to produce, acquire, and to keep property. And the right of capital to a fair return for its work. This means a definite rejection of communism, socialism, and fascism."[1]

In the constitutional realm, too, the four men shared a common liberal vision. Their constitutional liberalism was defined in opposition to the property-protecting doctrines that had dominated the Court's jurisprudence for three decades and had collapsed only in 1937 during the court-packing episode. To a man, they rejected the doctrine of the liberty of contract that the earlier Court had derived from the due process clause of the Fourteenth Amendment. As liberals, they believed instead that state legislatures had the authority to reform the relationship between workers and employees. They agreed that Congress's power to regulate interstate commerce gave it substantial, indeed almost unlimited authority to regulate the economy. These were the most important constitutional questions in the pre–World War II period. Roosevelt appointed these men to the Supreme Court because they shared his beliefs about them.

The Supreme Court's October term, 1939, was the first one in which the core group of Roosevelt justices would serve together from the beginning. It was not an ordinary term. On September 1, 1939, Germany had invaded Poland, and World War II had begun. Although the United States would not enter the war for more than two years, no observer could reasonably have thought that the business of the Supreme Court was of central importance to the Republic compared with foreign affairs. In the peacetime between the world wars, the Supreme Court had become a focal point for national attention because of the ways its decisions affected the economy. For the next five years, the influence would run in the opposite direction. The overwhelming significance and consequence of war would influence the decisions of the Supreme Court.

In this environment, new questions would arise to which liberals did not have agreed-upon answers. These were, above all, questions of civil liberties: What rights should individuals have against the coercive power of the government?

On the one hand, liberals were heirs to a tradition that valued free expression and basic rights. During World War I, when the government had suppressed antiwar speech, and afterward, when the Red Scare was at its height, brave dissidents like Frankfurter had rejected repressive measures. The American Civil Liberties Union had been founded to stand against the state. Brandeis and Holmes had written great opinions trying to protect free speech, and Roosevelt's liberal justices considered these men heroes. Seen against the backdrop of this past, liberalism favored robust judicial protection of civil liberties.

On the other hand, the liberals distrusted courts' intervention into controversial legislative decisions. The conservative Supreme Court had framed its property-protecting measures in terms of individual rights. That had given judicial rights activism a bad name. According to the theory of judicial restraint, judges should not interfere with the orderly political process, reflecting as it did the will of the people. It therefore seemed possible that liberals could favor civil liberties without believing that the judges were the right people to guarantee them. The most important case decided in the 1939 term posed this problem starkly. Fraught with political symbolism, it made sense only in the circumstances of a war that the United States had not yet entered.

The case had begun four years earlier in a small, mostly Catholic town called Minersville, located in the heart of Pennsylvania's coal country. On one otherwise ordinary October morning in 1935, ten-year-old William Gobitis, a fifth grader who was the son of the local grocer, refused to salute the flag during the daily Pledge of Allegiance at his elementary school. The teacher tried to force his arm up, but William held on to his pocket and successfully resisted. The next day, his eleven-year-old sister, Lillian, a seventh grader, decided to do the same. Before class, her heart pounding, she went to explain her reasoning to her teacher. "Miss Shofstal," she said, "I can't salute the flag anymore. The Bible says at Exodus chapter 20 that we can't have any other gods before Jehovah God." The teacher hugged Lillian and said she was a "dear girl."[2]

The Gobitis children did not act completely on their own. They were Jehovah's Witnesses and had chosen as a family to take part in a grassroots movement of Witnesses protesting the customs associated with the Pledge and flag salute. The movement had emerged almost accidentally. Judge George Rutherford, one of the national leaders of the Witnesses, had given a speech earlier in 1935 denouncing the Nazi "Heil Hitler" salute: "All people who have faith in God," he said, should hail "Jehovah and Christ Jesus," not Hitler "or any other creature."[3] After the speech, several young Witnesses around the country applied its logic to the flag salute, which at the time closely resembled the straight-arm Nazi salute, except that the palm was to be turned upward, not down. Rutherford then gave a radio address praising the students who were standing up for their faith. Lillian and William had heard that speech and had decided as a matter of conscience that they would not salute.[4]

The reaction among the Gobitises' classmates to this presumedly unpatriotic act began as astonishment and quickly turned to disgust. Lillian was shunned and had to resign as class president. "When I got to school each morning," she later reported, "a few boys would shout 'Here comes Jehovah!' and shower me with pebbles."[5]

The adults in Minersville were no better. The Gobitis family grocery store was threatened with a mob attack, then subjected to a boycott organized by a local Catholic church.[6] The school district enacted a new regulation making the customary flag salute into a legal duty. Then it expelled the children from school. After a delay during which the children attended a Witnesses school some thirty miles distant, the Gobitis family, with the help of the national legal counsel of the Jehovah's Witnesses, turned to the courts.

The Witnesses' motivation was religious. When they described the flag salute as idolatry, the Witnesses were criticizing patriotic nationalism. For them, placing the state and its symbols on a par with God was an act of blasphemy. The lower courts that considered their cases believed religious liberty required deciding in their favor. But as the late 1930s ticked by and their case made its way to the Supreme Court, their religious belief gained a political context. The Witnesses were pacifists. Their leaders had opposed American entrance into World War I and now were opposing U.S. involvement in World War II as well.

To its proponents, the flag salute meant something different with a world war brewing and a draft in the offing than it might have done otherwise. A child's salute has special significance when there is the prospect that the nation may go to war behind the flag. By the time Judge Rutherford argued the children's case himself before the Supreme Court in late April 1940, comparing the children to Daniel in the lion's den, the case had turned into controversy about wartime loyalty. France was poised to fall to Nazi Germany—and would fall just days after the opinion was handed down in June.[7]

By a vote of 8 to 1, the Supreme Court decided in favor of the school district and against the Witnesses. Frankfurter lobbied Chief Justice Hughes for permission to write the decision on behalf of the Court. He had multiple reasons to be engaged with the undertaking. As Frankfurter framed the issues, the case was an opportunity to expound the constitutional theory he had developed. Just as important, Frankfurter was a careful student of international affairs and a Europe watcher who had identified Hitler's threat early, and so was staunchly pro-war. Harold Ickes wrote in his diary at the time that Frankfurter "is really not rational these days on the European situation"—an opinion that captured Frankfurter's preoccupied state of mind while reflecting a war skepticism that was not uncommon even in liberal circles.[8]

Frankfurter's opinion made it clear that he believed the flag salute was closely connected to a potential war effort. "We are dealing," he wrote, "with an interest inferior to none in the hierarchy of legal values. National unity is the basis of national security." Patriotism, in turn, was the glue that held the nation together: "The flag is a symbol of our national unity, transcending all internal differences, however large, within the framework of the Constitution." As a coda, Frankfurter quoted Holmes: "We live by symbols."[9]

To produce a canonical opinion, Frankfurter needed to explain why deciding against the Witnesses was not a blow to civil liberties. Frankfurter saw himself as a civil libertarian. Before joining the Court, he had been a member of the ACLU's national committee. And the ACLU had filed a brief in the case—on behalf of the Witnesses. He explained that in his own individual view, the school board should allow the Witnesses' children not to salute the flag. The best way to establish national unity, he said, was not by forcing everyone to conform, but rather by tolerating idiosyncratic beliefs, however "crotchety."

But, Frankfurter went on to explain, the job of the Court was not to decide whether the school board had followed the best course of action. It was, instead, to ascertain whether the school board had made a reasonable choice in requiring the children to salute. This formulation of the issue led Frankfurter to the idea of judicial restraint. Frankfurter argued that the Minersville school board had to be treated as though it were the state legislature itself, reflecting the democratic will of the people. According to the philosophy of judicial restraint, the judiciary was supposed to defer to reasonable judgments made by legislators, not overturn them because it disagreed with their substance.

According to Frankfurter, the question before the Court was whether the Witnesses were entitled to a religious exemption from a law that bound everybody. On this point Frankfurter could offer a clear answer, one with strong constitutional precedent behind it: The First Amendment guaranteed the free exercise of religion, but it did not provide for any automatic exemption. Among the cases Frankfurter cited in support of this proposition were decisions rejecting challenges to the draft during World War I.

Frankfurter concluded that the school board could choose to give the Witnesses an exemption from the flag-salute requirement—and maybe even should do so—but that the Constitution did not require such an exemption. Leaving the decision up to the legislative body was the hallmark of judicial restraint. Frankfurter was proud of his opinion. He believed he had shown how liberal constitutional theory worked in practice. It respected civil liberties without interfering in legislative judgments. And it was able to recognize important political values, like the need to promote national unity.

The other Roosevelt appointees to the Court agreed. As Roosevelt had expected, his appointees were functioning as a team. Black joined the opinion gladly. Douglas told Frankfurter the draft was "historic" and "truly statesmanlike."[10] Also joining Frankfurter was the amiable, dull Stanley Reed, the former solicitor general.

Considerably more interesting was the newest justice, Frank Murphy, who had come on in the spring of 1940, giving Roosevelt a total of five appointees. A committed Catholic who never married, Murphy lived for most of his life with the same man, Edward Kemp, who also worked alongside him in a variety of jobs.[11] Murphy got his political start as a pro-union, pro-African-American mayor of Detroit. Spurred at least in part by Murphy's Catholicism, Roosevelt appointed him governor-general of the Philippines. Murphy presided over the drafting of the constitution of the Philippines and the transformation of his own job into that of high commissioner. He then returned to Michigan and was elected to a two-year term as governor. When he was not reelected in 1938, Roosevelt appointed him as attorney general, in which position he pursued Communists and political bosses, and created a civil liberties unit within the criminal division of the Department of Justice, aimed at enforcing federal civil rights statutes around the country.[12]

This was the career of a distinguished public servant—yet Murphy's fellow liberals discounted him. Robert Jackson had hoped to become attorney general when the job went to Murphy, and remained as solicitor general on Roosevelt's promise that he would replace Murphy soon.[13] At Murphy's White House swearing-in ceremony, a friend of Jackson's observed, "Bob showed no sign of regret, but if I ever saw regret it was written on the face of Mrs. Jackson."[14] Working under Murphy in the Department of Justice, Jackson was horrified by what he saw. Murphy had "the least knowledge of federal procedure, or federal law, or the limitations on the federal government, of any man in such a responsible position that I ever knew."[15]

To Jackson, who did not shrink from using anti-Catholic imagery in discussing Murphy, the latter was an ideological crusader, driven by fanatical, priestly pretensions to his own holiness. Jackson practically begged Roosevelt to fire Murphy from the attorney general post, but as a politician with a substantial Catholic constituency, Murphy could not be touched. The most Roosevelt could do was keep Murphy from becoming secretary of war, a post he craved. When the only Catholic on the Supreme Court resigned, Roosevelt put Murphy in his place.

If as attorney general, Murphy sometimes seemed like an inquisitor, on the Supreme Court he emerged as a thoroughgoing liberal. Siding instinctively with the underdog, he would go on to write many dissents—one of them among the bravest in the history of the Supreme Court. The other justices found him a figure of fun—there he goes, they would say, "tempering justice with Murphy." Perhaps as a result of his colleagues' ribbing—and his own lack of interest in the technical side of the law—Murphy was deeply unhappy on the Supreme Court. During oral argument, he would write notes to Frankfurter, wishing Frankfurter would get him appointed ambassador to India, or (another of his fantasies) to enable him to return to the Philippines and lead a rebellion against the Japanese who occupied the island in 1942.[16]

As a newly appointed justice, Murphy had not yet found his voice. Like the other Roosevelt appointees, he accepted Frankfurter's formulation of the liberal result in the flag-salute case and voted to deny the Witnesses an exemption from the rules. The dissent in the case, therefore, had to come from a Republican. And it did: from the pen of Harlan Fiske Stone, a holdover from the pre-Roosevelt Court, who had not yet become chief justice.

Stone began by asserting that the flag-salute law was "unique in the history of Anglo-American legislation" in that it coerced the children "to express a sentiment which, as they interpret it, they do not entertain, and which violates their deepest religious convictions." Then he gave the real reason for his decision. To defer to the legislature's judgment, as Frankfurter was urging, "seems to me no more than the surrender of the constitutional protection of the liberty of small minorities to the popular will."

In 1940, the idea that the Court should protect minorities from the majority was not the commonplace it would later become. Stone had first introduced it in 1937, burying it in a footnote.[17] To Roosevelt's justices, this viewpoint raised the specter of the judicial activism practiced by the Court in the *Lochner* era. At the time Stone wrote his dissent in *Minersville School District v. Gobitis*, he had no allies among the Roosevelt appointees. All shared the liberal philosophy that Frankfurter had developed during his years as a professor. Judicial restraint meant that the courts should not interfere.

It seemed right that Frankfurter should assume intellectual leadership on the newly formed Roosevelt Court. Yet this would turn out to be the momentary high point of Frankfurter's judicial influence among the Roosevelt appointees. Frankfurter believed the *Gobitis* decision was constitutionally sound. But as he was about to discover, the decision was also a serious political mistake.

After the *Gobitis* decision, sentiment against Jehovah's Witnesses spread fast. Multiple cities and towns adopted school flag-salute ordinances similar to the one at issue in the case. When Witnesses refused to salute, children were expelled.

Alongside the new flag-salute laws came violence. Between June 12 and June 20, 1940, the FBI received reports of hundreds of cases of anti-Witness violence, including attacks on Bible meetings.[18] On June 9, a mob of 2,500 surrounded the Witnesses' Kingdom Hall in Kennebunk, Maine, and burned it to the ground.[19] To some horrified observers, it appeared that the Supreme Court, by denying the children the constitutional right to be exempt from saluting, had declared open season on the Witnesses.

Beyond the instinctive moral reaction of liberals against this terrible bigotry, there was the realization that for the first time since Roosevelt appointees had controlled a majority on the Court, they had been presented with an opportunity to enshrine the liberal value of tolerance into constitutional doctrine—and had passed it up. It was one thing to be frustrated with a Court controlled by conservative justices. It was quite another to feel that a liberal court did not produce the results that liberals wanted to see.

Among nonlawyers especially, Frankfurter's distinction between what the Constitution required and what he as a civil libertarian would prefer was difficult to grasp, and maybe even wrong. The vast majority of newspapers condemned the opinion. The *New Republic*, for which Frankfurter had written dozens of unsigned pieces over the years, condemned the decision as verging on hysteria. Even Frankfurter's friend Harold Laski wrote Stone praising his dissenting opinion and telling him "how wrong I think Felix is."[20]

A final element in the broad condemnation of the *Gobitis* decision was that pro-war sentiment was not yet strong enough for liberals to be swayed by Frankfurter's argument about the importance of symbols in generating national unity. Just a few years later, the Supreme Court's refusal to protect the rights of Japanese-Americans against forcible internment would encounter little public outcry. But that was wartime. In the summer of 1940, most Americans still hoped the country could stay out of the war. Most of the mainstream Protestant denominations were strongly for neutrality, which was the official posture of the United States as of the outbreak of the war in Europe. When it came to anticipating public reception of his appeal to the value of national security, Frankfurter was some eighteen months ahead of the times.

Douglas and Black were attuned to the disastrous reception that Frankfurter's flag-salute opinion received. For them, as well as for Frank Murphy, himself a lifelong politician, the liberal outcry over the case could have only one interpretation: The Court had gotten the *Gobitis* case wrong. Condemnation in the liberal media meant that they had misunderstood not only the will of the people but the true meaning of liberalism. Frankfurter had led them astray. Stone's dissent was right. The Coolidge appointee had out-liberaled them.

The answer, for these politically attuned justices, was for the Court to hear a new case that would give them the opportunity to reverse *Gobitis*. The process would take almost three years, and when it came, the repudiation would mark decisively Frankfurter's fall from grace as a liberal leader on the Court. In the meantime, Black and Douglas learned the lesson that following Frankfurter was no guarantee of liberal approbation. His constitutional subtlety had badly failed to anticipate actual reaction on the ground—and that did not make for a winning political strategy.

CHAPTER 19

Of Gurus and Vice Presidents

Today the Supreme Court is the ultimate destination job. From it, justices go nowhere but retirement, often at a very advanced age.[21] But this was not always so. In the early days of the republic, justices sometimes quit to enter law practice. Other high government office was not unknown. Charles Evans Hughes, the chief justice on the Court that was joined by Black, Douglas, and Frankfurter, offered a model of a different sort. A nationally known and respected politician, and the former governor of New York, Hughes had first joined the Supreme Court in 1910 after declining President Taft's invitation to join the presidential ticket in the second spot in 1908.

Then, in 1916, while a sitting justice, Hughes allowed himself to be nominated as the Republican candidate for president. He resigned from the Court in order to run, losing to Woodrow Wilson by a slim margin. After the defeat he returned to private practice. But his prominence was such that Warren Harding, the president after Wilson, made him secretary of state, a job he held until 1925. Then, after serving on the Permanent Court of International Justice in the Hague, Hughes was renamed to the Supreme Court. He assumed the chief justiceship in 1930, succeeding Taft, who had become chief justice after having earlier been president.

Hughes's career, with its two separate Supreme Court stints, a prominent cabinet position, and the tantalizing shot at the presidency, was never far from the minds of the men whom Roosevelt named to the Supreme Court. As confidants of the president, they saw the enormous power and prestige of the office firsthand.

Significant as a Supreme Court seat might be, in terms of ambition it could never measure up to the overarching importance of the presidency.

In Douglas's case, the lure of national office first surfaced shortly after his arrival on the Court—and it would remain with him for another decade at least. In June 1940, Roosevelt announced his decision to seek an unprecedented third term. When John Nance Garner, Roosevelt's vice president, decided to run against Roosevelt in the primaries, speculation about the vice presidency turned to Douglas. He was now publicly validated as a Westerner, which would potentially help the ticket. More to the point, the president thought highly of him. He was smart, energetic, and ambitious. Roosevelt could not be president forever; and unlike Garner, Douglas seemed to him a plausible successor.

Douglas's strongest supporter for the vice presidential slot was Tommy Corcoran. A year earlier, there could have been no better backer. But Corcoran's political fortunes had shifted since he engineered the appointments of Douglas and Frankfurter to the Court. During his time as Roosevelt's chief political operative, he had made enemies in Washington. "Not only did congressmen resent Tommy's dictatorial issuing of orders," wrote an administration insider, "but even more bitterly were they incensed when they found the jobs they regarded as Congressional perquisites being filled by Tommy's nominees."[22]

Corcoran had become the victim of his own success. His effectiveness had begun to fade. As a result, his position in Roosevelt's inner circle had become increasingly tenuous, and the president had put some distance between them. If Douglas, with whom Corcoran was close, could become vice president, then Corcoran might be able to ride the association back into power.

Douglas was thrilled by the prospect of the vice presidential nomination. Yet he was concerned that as a judge, he must not appear to be seeking it. This posture was on display in a note that he wrote to Frankfurter in early July 1940, which Frankfurter preserved and later donated to Harvard Law School along with much of the rest of his correspondence. The note is handwritten on the thick stationery of the Yale Club, situated then as now across the street from Grand Central Station in New York. Although Douglas had not attended Yale, he had been a faculty member there—which would have qualified him for membership, or at least for stopping by and helping himself to a handful of notepaper. As if to emphasize that he was embarking on a trip West to avoid being caught up in the Washington speculation, Douglas put a line through the Yale Club return address, replacing it with a notation that he was on the train, headed West.

In the note, Douglas tells Frankfurter that the talk of his being nominated for the vice presidency just will not let up. Of course he wants nothing more than to stay on the bench, where he is very happy. He is writing, he says, to ask Frankfurter to "scotch" these rumors whenever he hears them.

Frankfurter was notoriously gossipy. Asking him to scotch a rumor was the same thing as asking him to repeat it—and if Frankfurter had been in Washington, D.C., then that would obviously have been Douglas's goal. But Frankfurter was not in Washington. He was visiting Cambridge, Massachusetts. And, as Douglas knew, Frankfurter was not just anywhere in Cambridge. He was staying with Professor Thomas Reed Powell on Sparks Street, to whom Douglas hand-addressed the envelope.

Powell, acerbic, brilliant, alcoholic, and a snob, was known to Douglas.[23] He had taught him at Columbia before moving to Harvard. As Douglas had reason to recall, Powell had given him his lowest law school grade—a C in constitutional law that left Douglas "stunned and humiliated." Neither man forgot it. When Douglas was nominated to the Court, Powell sent him a note reminding him of the grade:

In days of yore
In old Kent Hall
He took some law from me.
And rumor has it
That his grade was just a
Modest C.

Douglas replied (also in bad verse), but he went further, tracking down other prominent men who had also gotten Cs from Powell and forming the "Powell C. Club," complete with officers, notepaper, and an annual dinner.[24]

Douglas, then, had more in mind than assuring that Frankfurter had not missed out on the rumors that Douglas might be nominated to the vice presidency. He wanted his Supreme Court spot and his potential elevation to be discussed in the home of the professor who had given him such a poor grade. It would be hard to think of a better means to suggest to Powell the error of his ways.

Insiders speculating on the vice presidential pick considered Douglas one of the leading candidates, alongside Secretary of State Cordell Hull and Secretary of Agriculture Henry Wallace.[25] Choosing the candidate with more political experience, Roosevelt went with Wallace. Douglas had gone West in the hopes of reminding Roosevelt of his regional appeal and demonstrating that he was not campaigning for the ticket. He could do little to change the result.

But when he returned to Washington, D.C., Douglas took a final shot at displacing Wallace from the ticket. All his life, Wallace had been a searcher after religious truth or what he called the "inner light to outward manifestation." Wallace had for some years enjoyed a close relationship with a Russian-born theosophist named Nicholas Roerich. Roerich, an observer reported, was "'bald as a billiard ball,' with a Manchu moustache that drooped to his chest."[26] Photos show him wearing a Rasputin-like beard. He had begun his career as a painter of spiritually symbolic images, collaborating with Sergey Diaghilev in the original production of the *Rite of Spring*. A museum dedicated exclusively to his oeuvre occupied an entire Art Deco skyscraper at 107th Street and Riverside Drive in New York, and held a thousand of his paintings.[27]

Wallace and Roerich had corresponded since 1929, when they first met. Addressing Roerich as "Dear Guru," Wallace employed a fantastical code: Cordell Hull was the "Sour One"; Roosevelt was the "Flaming One"; Wallace himself was "Galahad," the spiritual name assigned to him by Roerich. In the letters, Wallace mused lyrically about his hopes for the coming of the Northern Shambhala of the heavens, a Buddhist ideal about which Roerich had written a book.[28] "I have thought of the New Country going forth to meet the seven stars under the sign of the three stars," Wallace mused in a representative sample. "And I have thought of the admonition 'Await the Stone.'" The Stone, it seemed, was Roerich. "We again welcome you," Wallace wrote. "To drive out depression. To drive out fear."[29]

Wallace had promoted Roerich's grand plan to fly a "Banner of Peace" above cultural sites around the world so that they would not be damaged in wartime. This had eventually led to a treaty, signed by Wallace on behalf of the United States in the presence of Roosevelt himself. In 1934, while Secretary of Agriculture, Wallace had sent his guru on a department-funded mission to Mongolia and Manchuria in search of plants and grasses that would fight soil erosion in the American Dust Bowl. The expedition cost seventy-five thousand dollars; Roosevelt had been aware of it and approved the expenditure. While in Central Asia—a politically volatile region since Japan had occupied Manchuria—Roerich's behavior had been so bizarre that Wallace eventually had to break ties with him.[30]

Roerich, though, preserved Wallace's letters, which fell into the hands of one of his American followers. In 1940, after unknown vicissitudes, the letters were acquired by Republican newspaper owner Paul Block and his reporter Ray Sprigle—the same team that had acquired the evidence of Black's Klan membership.[31] Not all the letters were genuine, but enough were real to make it clear that the relationship had existed. The correspondence revealed no crimes, but it made Wallace look at best gullible and at worst rather crazy. Worse, the letters connected Roerich to Roosevelt. Publication of what were quickly called the Dear Guru letters would certainly have embarrassed the Roosevelt campaign in a substantial way.

To the Republicans' frustration, Roosevelt found a way to stop them from making the letters public. Their own nominee, Wendell Willkie, had had a long-term affair with Irita Bradford Van Doren, a divorcée previously married to the critic and biographer Carl Van Doren. At Roosevelt's direction, the Democrats made it clear that if the Dear Guru letters were published, they would spread the rumors of Willkie's affair. Captured on tape in his own office, Roosevelt was philosophical about it. "Awful nice gal," he said of Van Doren, "writes for the magazine and so forth and so on, a book reviewer. But nevertheless, there is the fact."[32] Mutually assured destruction achieved its desired result of nonaction. Because both sides had something to use against the other, neither Wallace's foolishness nor Willkie's love life was brought into the campaign.

Nonetheless the letters did potentially have some use to Douglas, who heard of them through his friend, the journalist Eliot Janeway. With Janeway, Douglas decided to stage a kind of intervention with Wallace in the office of Secretary of the Interior Harold Ickes. Not only was Ickes another friend of Douglas's, he also disliked Wallace, with whom he had long fought turf battles inside the cabinet.

The idea behind the meeting was to elicit some sort of admission from Wallace and so impress Ickes with the authenticity of the letters. Ickes, Douglas hoped, would then go to Roosevelt and tell him that Wallace was unsuitable and had to be dropped from the ticket. In addition to Douglas, Janeway, Ickes, and Wallace, the other people who attended the meeting were Tommy Corcoran, Ben Cohen, and Robert Jackson, who had by now become attorney general.[33]

These were men to be reckoned with; but Wallace defended himself adequately. Ickes did not bring the issue to Roosevelt. The premise of the meeting was in retrospect naïve. Douglas mistakenly believed that Roosevelt did not know about the letters. Roosevelt did know; but he had decided it would be less embarrassing to keep Wallace than to dump him. So Wallace became vice president for four years, after which Roosevelt replaced him.

The upshot of the episode for Douglas was that he got a taste of coming close to national office. He expected to have another chance in 1944, whether Roosevelt ran for reelection or not, and he was young enough to know that 1944 would not be his last chance, either. Most significant for relations within the Court in the next several years, Douglas's colleagues, including Frankfurter, knew that he knew it.

Nor was Douglas the only member of the Court with aspirations beyond it. According to Douglas, Black had advised Roosevelt of his willingness to resign and work on the campaign, by which he presumably meant he would leave if a suitable office—say, the vice presidency—were offered to him.[34] Although in light of the Klan revelations it is difficult to take Black's continued political dreams seriously, he had been, after all, an elected politician with a regional base. He had reason to believe that he had put the Klan question behind him and emerged stronger than before. Besides, for the inner dynamics of the Court, it mattered less whether Black's aspiration was realistic than that it existed.

CHAPTER 20

Destroyers and Bases

World War II began for Robert Jackson on the evening of September 2, 1939, at one of Roosevelt's poker games in the president's private study. It was a typically intimate gathering. With Jackson were Roosevelt's press secretary; his doctor; his aide, General Edwin "Pa" Watson; and Harold Ickes, the secretary of the interior and a regular fixture on poker nights. Bill Douglas, who like Jackson was now part of the inner circle, could not attend but sent a note of apology.[35]

As Jackson remembered it, the president used the game, as he typically did, to try and relax himself. He interrupted the proceedings only briefly around ten o'clock to say that he had gotten a note from Joseph Kennedy, then the ambassador to the Court of St. James's, to the effect that Britain would officially declare war the next morning. The game resumed, and the men played until a quarter to midnight. Ickes won heavily—enough, he joked, so that he could now afford the baby that his wife was expecting.

Jackson's role as Roosevelt's most important legal adviser on the war began the next day. Ordinarily, that job might have belonged to the attorney general, then still Frank Murphy. As solicitor general, Jackson's primary job was to argue cases in the Supreme Court.[36] Murphy, a politician, was not a practicing lawyer. Roosevelt could not rely on him for legal advice and would not have chosen to do so even if he could. He needed counsel about the legal consequences of the declaration of war in Europe; and he turned to Jackson for it.

During the two years between September 1939 and the Pearl

Harbor attacks of December 1941, the United States was legally neutral. Under the rules of international law, any military support for one of the belligerent parties would have meant that the U.S. was entering the war. Determined to stop Roosevelt from bringing the country into the war unilaterally, Congress enacted laws explicitly committing the United States to a neutral position. Roosevelt wanted to support Britain. The job of explaining how that could be done without violating neutrality fell to Jackson.

Under the terms of the Neutrality Act that Congress passed, the president was obligated to issue a formal statement proclaiming that the United States was neutral in the new war. The same statement was supposed to list the belligerent nations to whom the United States would now be unable to ship war commodities. Roosevelt had Jackson review the proclamation. But the president was not content to restrict himself to a statement of the country's limitations. Roosevelt also asked Jackson to draft a further proclamation. This one would declare an emergency and detail the special powers that the president could deploy under the emergency conditions that now obtained. The goal was typical of Roosevelt's whole presidency: to give him more extensive authority than other presidents had ever exercised in order to meet global challenges that were themselves greater than any encountered before.

Jackson's important duties brought home how frustrating it was to work under Murphy. Murphy himself had never even wanted the job of attorney general, and now Jackson was doing it for him—but without the public credit. Jackson was the obvious successor to Murphy. In May 1939, Jackson had threatened to resign unless he was made attorney general, and Roosevelt had promised him the job would soon be his.[37] Several months later, in October, Harold Ickes observed at one of Roosevelt's poker nights that Jackson seemed to be very unhappy, "disappointed...that the President has not made him Attorney General as he definitely promised to do not later than July 1."[38] Then fate intervened with the death of Justice Pierce Butler. In early 1940, Roosevelt named Murphy to the Court and promoted Jackson to attorney general.

Jackson was now in an even better position to advise Roosevelt on how to deal with the problem of neutrality. Matters came to a head in May 1940, just after Germany invaded France. First the French premier Paul Reynaud and then Winston Churchill, who had just become prime minister himself, cabled Roosevelt asking for urgent help. As a neutral nation, the United States was not sending any war materiel to Great Britain. Churchill proposed that the U.S. change its legal status from neutrality to "non-belligerency, which would mean that you would help us with everything short of actually engaging armed forces." Churchill asked for a very specific form of naval assistance: "the loan of 40 or 50 of your older destroyers to bridge the gap between what we have now and the large new construction we put in hand at the beginning of the war."[39]

Roosevelt answered Churchill and Reynaud that he lacked legal authority to change America's war status without permission from Congress—and that he was certain that Congress would not approve. In June, France collapsed; by the end of July, all of Western Europe had fallen under German domination. In August, the Soviet Union signed a nonaggression pact with Hitler: Britain now stood alone against Germany. This time, when Churchill renewed his request for the destroyers, Roosevelt recognized that circumstances had changed. Help could not be delayed any longer.

Even in Britain's hour of need, Roosevelt wanted something in return. At a cabinet meeting on August 2, 1940, Roosevelt broached the idea of asking the British to lease naval bases in the Atlantic and Caribbean to the United States in exchange for the destroyers that Churchill wanted. Over the next few days, transatlantic negotiations settled the deal of destroyers for bases.

Roosevelt initially planned to bring the pact to Congress for approval. In principle, authorization should have been easy. Trading old ships for access to strategic bases located near the East Coast was a terrific deal for the Americans. It could even be said that Roosevelt was taking advantage of Churchill's terribly weak bargaining position.

But as the summer progressed, it became clear that Congress, where pro-war sentiment was not strong, might impose substantial delays. On June 28, just a few months before, Roosevelt had signed legislation providing that no war materiel could be sold that was "essential to the defense of the United States." Warships like the destroyers possibly fit that description. Between the new law and congressional fears that the deal would lead the United States closer to war, going through Congress was not an option. The question then became a constitutional one: Could the president go around Congress without violating the law?

On the surface, the answer seemed to be no. The United States was now neutral, and an act of Congress required it to stay that way. As a matter of international law, it would be hard to maintain that the United States was remaining neutral if it was sending destroyers to one of the warring powers. To make matters more difficult still, a 1917 law prohibited building and arming ships in the United States for a belligerent nation, which Britain was. The law, which dated back to the period before the United States had entered World War I, seemed archaic. But as attorney general, Jackson believed it was still in force. In June he had caused no small difficulty for Roosevelt by invoking that same law to block a shipment of agile "mosquito" boats that had been ordered by the British government from private American manufacturers.

Given Jackson's opinion about the mosquito boats, Roosevelt hesitated to ask him directly about the legality of the destroyers deal that he wanted. Instead, in mid-July, Harold Ickes—whether acting on his own or under Roosevelt's instructions is unclear—asked Ben Cohen, the administration's most technically skilled lawyer, to draft a legal opinion that would somehow distinguish the destroyers from the mosquito boats. In a densely packed legal memorandum, Cohen offered the view that since the destroyers were old and outdated, they were not covered either by the old statute or the Neutrality Act. Skeptical, Roosevelt wrote to a member of his cabinet that given the June 28 law, "which is intended to be a complete prohibition of sale, I frankly doubt if Cohen's memorandum would stand up."[40]

Unlike Frankfurter or some of Roosevelt's other advisers, Jackson was not a particularly strong advocate of involvement in the

war. Adopting a posture of caution, Jackson took no action on
Cohen's memorandum except to read it and refer it to the solicitor general's office for review. But the supporters of aid to Britain
did not let up. On August 11, the *New York Times* published a long
letter to the editor offering more or less the same theory expressed
in Cohen's opinion—that the destroyers were too old to count as
war materiel. The letter, drafted by Cohen and Dean Acheson in
Cohen's New York apartment, was signed by four prominent attorneys in private practice: Acheson, Charles Burlingham, Thomas
Thacher, and George Rublee. Acheson had convinced them all to
sign the letter.[41]

The moment that the letter appeared in the *Times*, Acheson
began lobbying Jackson by phone. Jackson was out of the office,
camping in the Pennsylvania mountains with his daughter. A messenger was sent to find him, and he called Acheson back within
a few hours. "To say he was in a happy state of mind," Acheson
recalled, "would not be truthful." Over the phone, Jackson would
only promise to consider the matter; but he gave up on his vacation
and went back to Washington.[42]

On Jackson's return to the capital, Roosevelt asked him what
he thought of the letter. Jackson remained noncommittal, but by
now he saw the writing on the wall: Armed with such a prominent,
public expression of the deal's legality, the president had grounds
to go ahead even without Congress's permission. On August 14,
Jackson told Roosevelt that the Department of Justice's internal
investigation of the question suggested it was legally permissible for
the overage destroyers to be sent to Great Britain without specific
congressional authorization.

According to the Department of Justice, one further difficulty
remained. The chief of naval operations would have to stipulate
that the destroyers were not "essential to the defense of the nation"
under the terms of the June 28 statute. Cohen's opinion as well as
that of the solicitor general's office was that this claim could be
made because the destroyers were overage. The claim was tenuous.
The destroyers were indeed old. But they were functional enough
to make them important to the defense of Great Britain.

Jackson offered a solution of his own, one that would prove central to his ultimate approval of the deal. The destroyers were being exchanged for bases that would be extremely useful for the national defense. The fact that the destroyers would bring "far more than their equivalent in actual defense facilities," Jackson argued, meant that they were themselves not essential.[43] In essence, Jackson was arguing that the June 28 statute should only be understood as prohibiting transactions that weakened the national defense, not those that enhanced it. Based on Jackson's opinion, the chief of naval operations certified that the destroyers were not essential.

Despite recognizing where Roosevelt wanted him to go, Jackson did not simply acquiesce in his plans. Requiring that there be an overt exchange to the benefit of the United States limited the president's freedom of action. Characteristically, Roosevelt used the condition that was being placed upon him as a negotiating tool in his conversations with Churchill. When Churchill balked at the idea of a public bargain—which would look bad for Britain—Roosevelt insisted that "I have an attorney general—and he says I have got to make a bargain." To this Churchill replied, in Jackson's retelling, "Maybe you ought to trade these destroyers for a new Attorney General!"[44]

Roosevelt took a personal role in working on the final details of the official legal opinion, a highly unusual form of involvement that could be justified only by the importance of the issue. But it was crucial to Roosevelt that the opinion be identified as Jackson's, not his own. As Jackson recalled it, Roosevelt told him that "they will get into a terrific row over your opinion instead of over my deal, but after all, Bob, you are not running for office."[45] Roosevelt was right. "The opinion," wrote Jackson, "became the focus of much of the public controversy that ensued, and opposing quarters with equal extravagance threatened the Attorney General with everything from immortality to impeachment."[46]

Jackson's opinion authorizing the destroyers deal to go through was the most important thing he did as attorney general. Given the importance of the destroyers to Britain's war effort, it was quite possibly the most important legal opinion of the war. With it, the question of presidential power became Jackson's signature issue, and the pragmatic approach he adopted became his trademark.

The opinion did not deal directly with a key problem of international law created by the destroyers deal: By aiding one of the belligerents, the United States was violating the traditional definition of neutrality. But Jackson did have the beginnings of a theory. He gave voice to it the following spring, when Congress was in the process of approving the Lend-Lease Act, which was a more formal and extensive plan to provide military equipment to Great Britain.

Jackson's argument was deceptively simple and yet far-reaching. He had to explain why providing aid to Great Britain was not an act of war against Germany. His answer was that Germany had itself violated international law by perpetrating the crime of "aggressive war." Because such an aggressive war was an attack on the entire international community, Jackson argued, "as responsible members of that community, we can treat victims of aggression in the same way we treat legitimate governments when there is civil strife in the state of insurgency—that is to say, we are permitted to give to defending governments all the aid we choose."[47] This principle, Jackson acknowledged, was essentially invented on the spot. It was not to be found in international law treatises or in treaties. But "such an interpretation of international law is not only proper but necessary if it is not to be a boon to the lawless and the aggressive."[48]

Jackson's pragmatic picture of international law was informed by the sense that the ultimate purpose of the law was far more important than its form. He was also expressing for the first time the view that World War II was not like other wars. Hitler's Germany, Jackson was arguing, had engaged in a uniquely unlawful form of aggressive war. International law would have to evolve in response. Both of these aspects of Jackson's conception of international law would be on display four years later, when Jackson would take on the job of chief prosecutor at Nuremberg.

In the meantime, Jackson once again aspired to higher office. In June 1941, Chief Justice Hughes announced his retirement. The chief justiceship had now come open—and Jackson was the natural front-runner for it. Starting as an obscure upstate Democrat, Jackson had tried Mellon, supported the court-packing plan, and become an intimate of Roosevelt's. He had been a highly successful solicitor general, and now he was the most important lawyer involved in the war effort. It was natural to expect that Roosevelt would want to name a chief justice who shared his beliefs and views—and Jackson was the lawyer closest to Roosevelt. The newspapers expected Jackson to get the job.

So did Jackson. The position of chief justice seemed, both to Jackson and Roosevelt, a satisfactory use for Jackson's talent. Jackson was, after all, someone Roosevelt had considered potential presidential timber, even if he had concluded that Jackson lacked the drive for campaign politics. With this background, an ordinary Supreme Court seat seemed a little bit meager. Earlier in the year, when Justice McReynolds had retired, Jackson told Harold Ickes that "he would be willing to go on the bench to succeed McReynolds," but he "would like some indication that the President had an interest in appointing him Chief Justice." When Ickes passed the message to Roosevelt, the president assured him that "he had the Chief Justiceship in mind for Bob."[49] Roosevelt had appointed a Southerner, Senator Jimmy Byrnes of South Carolina.

Now, in June, after Hughes's retirement, Ickes went back to the president, urging him to appoint Jackson chief justice as he had suggested he would.[50] At the last moment, though, on the brink of making Jackson chief, Roosevelt hesitated. At the time, it was an accepted courtesy that an outgoing justice would be invited to the White House to discuss a successor. Roosevelt and Hughes had clashed over the court-packing plan. The fact that Hughes had won only enhanced Roosevelt's respect for the retiring chief justice, whom he sometimes called "the second-best politician in town."[51] Like Roosevelt, Hughes was a former governor of New York. Indeed, the president of the United States and the chief justice of the United States enjoyed addressing one another playfully as "Governor." When Hughes came in to speak with Roosevelt, he expressed admiration for Jackson. But for the post of chief justice, Hughes recommended that Roosevelt promote Harlan Fiske Stone, who was already sitting on the Court.

Stone had been dean of Columbia Law School, which both Hughes and Roosevelt had attended. But Hughes had quite a different reason for urging his nomination. According to a persistent rumor that he was never quite able to shake, Hughes's own stint as chief justice had come at Stone's expense.

The story went back to the Hoover administration. When Taft had retired as chief justice in 1930, Hoover had asked Hughes to come and see him. At the time, Hughes, sixty-eight, was off the Court, having quit to run for the presidency in 1916. His son was serving as solicitor general and would have had to resign if Hughes took the job. According to the story, Hoover planned to make Hughes a pro forma offer of the chief justiceship. Hughes was expected to refuse politely, leaving the post to Stone, Hoover's true choice. As the story had it, the expectation that he would say no never reached Hughes. When Hoover offered him the job, Hughes accepted. Now there was nothing for Hoover to do but nominate him as chief justice.[52]

Hughes was a dignified, image-conscious gentleman of the old school. He wore a sweeping, carefully groomed beard and a wing collar, decades after they had both gone out of fashion. Douglas said that Hughes with his beard "looked like Jehovah."[53] Jackson thought Hughes talked like God, too.[54] For Hughes, the story that he had stolen the chief justiceship by a convenient faux pas was in equal parts mortifying and frustrating. By getting Stone the chief justiceship, Hughes would once and for all establish himself as Stone's supporter rather than his usurper.

As a politician who had grappled with Roosevelt before, Hughes knew enough not to propose Stone's name to the president without offering some powerful support for his recommendation. He encouraged Roosevelt to call Frankfurter. Playing his role perfectly, Frankfurter also enthusiastically endorsed Stone. His logic was that under these near-war circumstances, it would be desirable for Roosevelt to demonstrate bipartisanship by picking a Republican.

Frankfurter had originally favored Jackson for the position.[55] Yet he deeply respected Hughes and must have relied on his judgment.

Frankfurter had long thought well of Stone, and he knew that Stone aspired to leadership. He must also have believed that their clash over the flag-salute case did not augur any deeper trouble—after all, the vote had been 8 to 1 in Frankfurter's favor, and Stone had written alone. Perhaps, too, Frankfurter thought that Stone as chief might be more malleable to Frankfurter's interests than Jackson. Relying on candor to avoid friction, Frankfurter immediately explained to Jackson what he had recommended to Roosevelt. He told Jackson that he had advised Roosevelt that since Stone was old, Jackson should become the chief justice after him.

Frankfurter's advice to Roosevelt was decisive.[56] Roosevelt decided to promote Stone to the position of chief justice while nominating Jackson to fill the seat that Stone would be vacating. In a meeting with Jackson, Roosevelt followed something like the same line that Frankfurter had proposed to him. Although we do not know exactly what Roosevelt said to Jackson when they met at the White House, it is clear that Jackson emerged believing that he would succeed Stone as chief justice. That expectation would stay with him for the next several years—to disastrous effect.

Roosevelt believed that with the appointment of Jackson, he had accomplished his goal of transforming the Court. He had appointed seven new justices: Black, Stanley Reed, Frankfurter, Douglas, Frank Murphy, Jimmy Byrnes, and now Jackson. He had taken Stone, the leading moderate Republican on the Court, and made him chief. The only sitting justice who had not been appointed to his job by Roosevelt was Owen Roberts—and as the protagonist of the famous switch in time, his career had been influenced by Roosevelt as much as any of the others. The day Jackson was sworn in, July 11, 1941, Roosevelt expressed his satisfaction to a private gathering: "It may not be proper to announce it, but today the Supreme Court is full."[57]

In truth Roosevelt had put his permanent impress on the Court, and through it on the Constitution under its keeping. Not since George Washington had a president appointed more justices. Roosevelt would get one more, for a total of nine appointments, when he borrowed Byrnes for the war effort and replaced him with

Wiley Rutledge. Since no president will ever serve as many terms as Roosevelt, this record will never be broken.

Roosevelt's effect on the Constitution would turn out to be very different from what he anticipated. Four of his appointees—Black, Frankfurter, Douglas, and Jackson—would become great justices, measured by the way their ideas and opinions reshaped the Constitution and the country. But their visions would diverge. Their personalities would clash. Beginning as allies, they would become enemies, each with his own theory of how to understand the Constitution.

It is impossible to know how Jackson would have conducted the affairs of the Court had he become chief justice. The chief justice of the United States has no extra votes. His responsibilities are to handle the administrative duties of the Court, to assign opinions when he is in the majority, and to run the conference of the justices. His influence on the other justices is not necessarily any greater than that of his peers.

But it is certain that by choosing Stone, Roosevelt helped set in motion the disagreements among his appointees that were to follow. As chief, Hughes had ended the justices' Saturday conference by 4:30 p.m., insufficient time for lengthy debate.[58] As Douglas later explained it, Stone's approach differed. He would "not only take up with the main point" of a case, "but he would take up the five or six or seven collateral points that Hughes would always say that we can leave that to the writer of the opinion. And he would discuss them with the thoroughness of which a professor in the law school of the first-year class might proceed. Then he would turn to the senior judge . . . and have it out for five minutes, twenty minutes, thirty minutes and then go on to the next Justice [and] . . . have it out with him. And so around the table with these endless discussions."[59] Conferences stretched to all day Saturday, then to an additional conference during the week, when the justices also heard cases. As a result, Douglas complained, "we were almost in continuous conference, spent battling every single point, big ones, little ones."[60]

Extended conversation among intelligent, forceful people encourages the participants to develop their own ideas. Repeated discussions pushed the justices toward having consistent responses to make week after week. The way Stone ran the conference was not conducive to efficiency or unanimity. It may even have encouraged the conflicts that emerged. But it also created the ideal set of conditions for the emergence of comprehensive theories of constitutional law.

The disagreements among Roosevelt's justices were not those of distant enemies peering at each other across the field of battle, but of fellows with a common cause, each confident their plan offered the surest route to success. When it came to the meaning of the Constitution, they could not compromise or hold back. For them the stakes were too high.

Book Five

LOYALTIES

CHAPTER 21

The Sword

O n Sunday, October 5, 1941, Louis Brandeis died at his home in Washington, just shy of his eighty-fifth birthday. The timing was symbolic. The next day was the first Monday in October, when the Supreme Court's term opens. For the first time, Black, Frankfurter, Douglas, and Jackson would all sit together on the bench. The four men, poised on the edge of reshaping modern constitutional law, each owed much to Brandeis's distinctive philosophy. Each revered Brandeis as the leading constitutional progressive of his era. Yet each man had already begun to find differences between his own views and those of Brandeis; and those differences about the meaning of a liberal constitution would eventually drive them into starkly contrasting viewpoints.

Frankfurter had been closer to Brandeis than were the others. Speaking at a private memorial service held in Brandeis's apartment, he quoted from *Pilgrim's Progress*: "My sword I give to him that shall succeed me in my pilgrimage." Those present understood that Frankfurter saw himself as that successor. Yet since 1937, Frankfurter's relationship with Brandeis had cooled. Frankfurter's implicit choice of Roosevelt over Brandeis during the court-packing plan had created the first meaningful rift between him and Brandeis in almost forty years, and Frankfurter's best efforts had not fully bridged the divide.

As if to help heal his own wound, Frankfurter now sought a reconciliation between Roosevelt and Brandeis, even though one of them was dead. After Brandeis's funeral, he wrote to Roosevelt "to tell you some of the things that Brandeis said about you the

last time I saw him—a day before the blow came."[1] According to
Frankfurter, Brandeis had called Roosevelt "greater than Jeffer-
son and almost as great as Lincoln."[2] These words sound more like
Frankfurter than like Brandeis—Frankfurter, after all, preferred
Lincoln, while Brandeis was the greatest American Jeffersonian
since Jefferson himself. Frankfurter was reprising for a last time
the role of go-between that he had played to connect Brandeis and
Roosevelt as early as 1928.

Brandeis's death left Frankfurter without a living model of the
Supreme Court justice he wanted to be.[3] Frankfurter had set out
to become what Brandeis and Holmes were, or rather what he had
helped make them: mythical embodiments of their constitutional
ideals. Now he would have to do it on his own.

The job was harder than it looked. Great justices live double
lives. They are human beings with emotions, motivations, and
beliefs. Simultaneously they also represent coherent constitutional
values. Coming to stand for such ideals takes more than the writing of great opinions. It requires, too, the skills of a mythmaker to
make the justice great, as Frankfurter did for Holmes and Brandeis.
Though he mentored scores of the most brilliant and accomplished
legal minds the country could offer, Frankfurter never found someone able to play Felix Frankfurter for himself.

Felix Frankfurter as a young professor at Harvard Law School, 1917. *Harvard Law School Library Historical and Special Collections*

Franklin and Eleanor Roosevelt with their children, Anna Eleanor and James, around 1908. *FDR Library*

Nicola Sacco (right) and Bartolomeo Vanzetti as their appeals neared an end, 1927. *Trustees of the Boston Public Library/ Rare Books Department*

The Black family home in Clay County, 1902; six-year-old Hugo stands between his seated parents at left. *AP Photos*

Hugo Black as a young lawyer in Birmingham, 1925. *Library of Congress*

Josephine Foster Black around the time of her marriage, 1921. *Birmingham Public Library Archives, Portrait Collection*

Robert Jackson on his graduation from Jamestown High School, 1910, as he would have looked when he first met Roosevelt. *The Robert H. Jackson Center*

William O. Douglas in 1937, as chairman of the Securities and Exchange Commission; note sheriff's hat and six-shooter. *Yakima Valley Museum*

Louis D. Brandeis around
1916. *Harris & Ewing Collection,*
Library of Congress

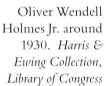

Oliver Wendell
Holmes Jr. around
1930. *Harris &*
Ewing Collection,
Library of Congress

Secretary of the Treasury Andrew Mellon between two presidents, Calvin
Coolidge (left) and Herbert Hoover. *Library of Congress*

A family on the rise: Robert and Irene Gerhardt Jackson, their children William and Mary Margaret, and their collie in front of the family home in Virginia in 1938. *Collection of the Fenton History Center, Jamestown, New York*

A public show of racial liberalism in the wake of a Klan scandal: Hugo and Josephine Foster Black speaking to then-Senator (later Justice) Sherman Minton at Marian Anderson's integrated Lincoln Memorial concert, April 9, 1939. *Harris & Ewing Collection, Library of Congress*

Felix and Marion Denman Frankfurter boarding the train from Boston to Washington, DC, on the occasion of Frankfurter's joining the Court, January 1939; note the difference in height. *Library of Congress*

Chief Justice Charles Evans Hughes, whose colleagues thought he looked like Jehovah. *Collection of the Supreme Court of the United States*

The Roosevelt Court in 1941 (seated, from left): Stanley Reed, Owen Roberts, Harlan Fiske Stone (Chief Justice), Hugo Black, Felix Frankfurter; (standing) Jimmy Byrnes, William O. Douglas, Frank Murphy, Robert Jackson. Including Stone, whom he made chief, Roosevelt had appointed all but Roberts; he would appoint one more justice, Wiley Rutledge, to replace Byrnes in 1943. *Harris & Ewing, Collection of the Supreme Court of the United States.*

Chief Justice Harlan Fiske Stone. *Harvard Law School Library Historical and Special Collections*

Mitsuye Endo at her typewriter in the Department of Motor Vehicles, Sacramento, California. *California State University Sacramento*

Robert Jackson and Mrs. Elsie Douglas at the prosecution table, Nuremberg, 1945–46. *Office of the U.S. Chief of Counsel, Courtesy of Harry S. Truman
Library*

Hermann Goering on trial at Nuremberg, 1946. *Harvard Law School Library Historical and Special Collections*

Benjamin Davis (right center) and his fellow CPUSA national committee colleague Robert Thompson, at a rally during their trial, 1949. *Library of Congress/New York World-Telegram and the Sun staff photographer C. M. Stieglitz*

Hugo Black, Robert Jackson, and Felix Frankfurter (left to right) at Chief Justice Fred Vinson's funeral, September 1953. *Getty Images*

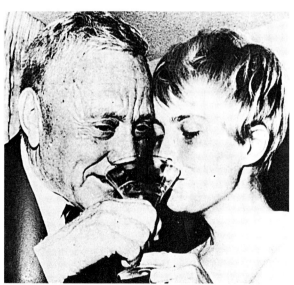

William O. Douglas and his fourth wife, Cathy Heffernan, at their wedding, July 15, 1966; the groom was forty years older than the bride. *Yakima Valley Museum*

CHAPTER 22

And the War Came

O n December 7, 1941, two months after Brandeis's death, Japan attacked the United States at Pearl Harbor, destroying much of its Pacific fleet. The possibility of war with Japan had certainly been in the air. In mid-November, Frankfurter, a minor master in the art of capturing Washington gossip, had written Roosevelt with the rumor that the true purpose of special envoy Saboru Kurusu's diplomatic visit from Japan was not to smooth the waters between the two countries, but to ascertain whether "we mean business in case Japan moves." Frankfurter, in other words, was reporting the theory that Japan wanted to know whether the United States was prepared to enter the war in case of aggressive action by Japan.[4]

But despite such rumors, and the strategic probability that Japan would seek an early advantage if it deemed a war with the United States inevitable, Roosevelt was genuinely surprised by Pearl Harbor. Jackson had attended cabinet meetings in which he had heard "repeatedly" that Pacific war "would not amount to much, that our Navy would 'knock Japan out of the water' in no time." He wrote later that Pearl Harbor "was a great shock to the president— that with all the war talk there had been, he did not believe Japan would make a surprise attack."[5]

Other astute observers were equally surprised. General Douglas MacArthur's aircraft were destroyed on the ground in the Philippines, fully nine hours after he had been informed of the Pearl Harbor attacks.[6] As the consequences of the attack became clear, the American entrance into the war increasingly forced the solemn realization that the U.S. role would not be what it had been in World War I. The United States was not sufficiently prepared for war, had suffered devastating naval losses at Pearl Harbor, and was going to have to fight hard and long to win.

Roosevelt had appointed nearly all of his justices from the heart of the government. With the exception of Frankfurter, the professor, and Wiley Rutledge, who would be appointed after serving as a law school dean and then briefly as a judge on the court of appeals, the appointees came either from high executive office or else from the Senate. For men like these, the war made the Supreme Court feel peripheral. The real action was elsewhere, and they felt it.

Ordinarily, the Supreme Court is its own little world. Problems of great import present themselves in the form of cases that, on paper, look exactly like the cases that matter to only a handful of people. The important consequences of a decision are often only dimly felt, based on the justices' predictions about how their precedents will apply to other cases in the future. As a result, it is easy for the justices to see themselves as equally powerful in the disposition of national affairs as they are in the decision of quotidian lawsuits. The Court spins its constitutional web. Different creatures, great and small, find themselves caught in it; and one by one, the Court deals with them.

Wartime is the great exception to this spider sense. When compared to guns, bombs, and bullets, the frailty of the Court's power is always and immediately obvious. In war, initiative is everything; and the Supreme Court, limited to the cases that come before it, lacks the power to take the initiative. The Court in wartime becomes a protector of the values that war necessarily threatens. It is the body that decides, often after the fact, whether the president and Congress have gone too far in doing what they have considered necessary to achieve victory. During and just after hostilities, this job can feel minor compared to planning, making, and supervising the war. Inevitably, though, when the judgments of history are made, the Supreme Court's actions turn out to be crucial to how the country comes to think of its own collective wartime actions.

Of Roosevelt's justices, only Frankfurter seems to have been fully satisfied with where he was sitting, and for good reason. His role in executive matters had always been advisory. Now that he was a sitting justice, he showed no inclination whatever to withdraw from this accustomed position. Indeed, his seat on the Supreme Court gave him even broader reach within Washington than he previously had.

Ten days after Pearl Harbor, Frankfurter sent Roosevelt a lengthy and detailed memorandum arguing for the creation of a war mobilization board in order to coordinate disparate defense efforts within the executive branch.[7] Drawing on his experiences in the War Department during and before World War I, Frankfurter reasoned that to overcome bureaucratic divisions of labor designed for peacetime, there must be a single coordinator of war mobilization, responsible to no one but the president.

Roosevelt listened. The War Mobilization Board was brought into being, and with it the single most important wartime civilian job. Frankfurter still was not finished. He recommended a specific candidate: Justice Jimmy Byrnes, appointed by Roosevelt from the Senate in 1941. Again, Roosevelt agreed, and Byrnes was plucked from the Court to run the Board. With its vast scope and direct responsibility to the president himself, the post gave Byrnes tremendous influence. Some people called him the assistant president. It was the proximity of the two men on the Court that had given Frankfurter his sense of Byrnes as the right man.

In another clever deployment of the Court's personnel, Roosevelt picked Justice Owen Roberts, the Republican appointee famous for the switch in time, to chair a commission of investigation into the causes and consequences of the Pearl Harbor attack. Roberts was a Republican appointee, so the selection looked bipartisan. As a justice, Roberts would have the aura of impartiality. Yet Roosevelt knew that Roberts was the sort of person who could be influenced by pressure. Though Roberts remained on the Court, he was in close contact with Roosevelt over the commission's report.

Again, Frankfurter's fingerprints could be discerned. In January 1942, Frankfurter wrote to Roosevelt urging him to meet privately with Roberts to discuss the Pearl Harbor commission. He told Roosevelt that Roberts was "forthright," "modest," and "truly shy." The purpose of a meeting, he suggested, was so Roberts could "tell [Roosevelt] of things that have no proper place in their report—particularly on matters of personnel pertaining not to the past but to what lies ahead."[8] In fact, Roberts did brief Roosevelt privately—and in essence gave him control over what information would be published or released to Congress.

The selection of Byrnes and the use of Roberts enhanced the other justices' feeling of irrelevance. In April 1942, Jackson told Roosevelt he would gladly resign from the Court to take on any useful function in the war effort. Roosevelt thought otherwise— and he had decided some time ago that Jackson was best in a legal role, not a more broadly political one. He fielded Jackson's suggestion by once again hinting that he would eventually make him chief justice.[9]

Roosevelt wanted Douglas in the administration. Since the summer of 1941, he had repeatedly offered Douglas a job coordinating defense efforts on his behalf. Douglas, meanwhile, wanted only a job that would propel him to the vice presidency or beyond. Before war was declared, the defense job did not seem sufficiently influential to Douglas, and he had declined. Once Pearl Harbor had happened and Byrnes had gotten the job of defense coordination, it was too late. (In fact, Frankfurter may have recommended Byrnes in part to make sure the post did not go to Douglas.) In the summer of 1942, Roosevelt asked Douglas to handle some unspecified projects for him—without resigning his seat. Douglas again declined. He did not want to accept responsibility with no clear route to promotion. Yet his reluctance did not alienate Roosevelt, who continued to think of Douglas as potential presidential timber—and would until his death three years later.[10]

CHAPTER 23

The Saboteurs

Meanwhile, in the summer of 1942, the Court for the first time became formally involved in the war. It started, improbably enough, in the Hamptons. On Saturday night, June 13, a German submarine slipped past American defenses and dropped four German soldiers onto the beach at Amagansett, a quiet Long Island town. This New York landing was followed a few days later by another drop of four more soldiers at Ponte Vedra Beach, Florida.

The eight Germans had all spent significant amounts of time in the United States before the war, and they spoke English—several with perfect American accents. Two of them, Herbie Haupt and Ernst Peter Burger, were naturalized U.S. citizens. All had chosen to return to Germany to become part of the war effort. Hand-picked by the Abwehr, German military intelligence, the men had been trained in explosives in a monthlong course at Quenzsee, a lake in Brandenburg, Prussia. Their instructions were to rendez-vous in Cincinnati on July 4 to await further instructions. Their superiors had chosen a series of bridges and manufacturing plants for them to destroy.[11]

The infiltrators were carrying fuses and TNT. They had been instructed to wear their uniforms upon landing so that they would not be considered spies if caught.[12] Fulfilling this directive, the men who landed in New York wore navy uniforms while clambering onto shore.[13] On the beach, under cover of darkness, they changed into civilian clothes, leaving the uniforms in a seabag that they halfheartedly tried to bury in the sand. The Florida party was less precise. They wore bathing suits but put on German marine uniform caps while landing. Within moments of making shore, they threw away their hats.[14]

The would-be saboteurs in Florida landed and got away undetected. The Amagansett landing ran into trouble. On the beach around midnight, the Germans' leader, George John Dasch, bumped into a lone Coast Guard foot patrol—twenty-one-year-old John Cullen, who until the year before had been a furniture deliveryman for Macy's. Dasch told Cullen that he and his friends had gone night fishing from East Hampton but that their boat had run aground. Another of the Germans approached, speaking a language Cullen did not understand but that he thought was German; Dasch told him in English to shut up and get back to the others. Then Dasch handed Cullen what he said was three hundred dollars and told him to forget what he had seen.[15]

Cullen ran through the night to the shingled Amagansett lifeboat station that functioned as the Coast Guard base. He woke the other coastguardsmen and told them there were Germans on the beach. His boss was incredulous until Cullen showed him the money. He broke out rifles, and the team of eight headed down to the beach. By the time the Coast Guard team got there, the saboteurs were gone. After walking for several hours, the Germans made their way to the Amagansett train station. At 6:59 a.m. they were on the Long Island Rail Road, headed for Queens.[16]

Having escaped detection, the saboteurs would have been in a position to do serious damage had they been so inclined. But Dasch, the leader of the New York group, had other plans. He told Burger that he had never planned to carry out his orders. Instead he would turn himself in to the FBI in the hopes of helping the U.S. war effort against Germany. Burger agreed to help.[17]

Dasch and Burger went to a phone booth in a hotel lobby on Madison Avenue, and Dasch called the New York branch office of the FBI. His call was routed to the "nutters' desk." Dasch told the field agent that he was a German who had arrived from Europe the previous day and that he had important news for J. Edgar Hoover. When the agent gave his note of the call to his supervisor, the supervisor commented, "Napoleon called yesterday." No further action was taken.[18]

Dasch decided he would take a train to Washington, D.C., to see Hoover in person. First he embarked on a marathon session of pinochle, his favorite card game, that lasted two days and left Dasch up by several hundred dollars.[19] Then he boarded the train. Once in D.C., Dasch checked into the expensive Mayflower Hotel, where, as he could not have known, J. Edgar Hoover lunched every day on fruit salad.[20] After a good night's sleep, he called FBI headquarters from the phone in his room and asked for J. Edgar Hoover's office. After he had stated his business, his call was directed to two more offices, each of which transferred the call to another department.[21]

Finally, as he was about to hang up, Dasch reached an agent who had heard a report of possible infiltration on Long Island. The agent asked Dasch to come in and meet him. When Dasch arrived at headquarters and began to tell his story, the FBI sent agents to his hotel room, where they found the $82,500 in cash that he had brought with him. That convinced them that he was a real saboteur and not a crank.[22] On June 27, the FBI announced it had arrested the eight men. For purposes of national security and self-aggrandizement, Hoover concealed the fact that Dasch had turned in himself and the others.

The problem, now, was what to do with the infiltrators. Roosevelt, who had not been told how the Germans were caught, had no doubts on that score. The two Americans, he said, were guilty of high treason—"just as guilty as it is possible to be." The other six, he noted, had landed in naval gear but had been arrested in civilian clothes. This, he said in a memo that he wrote himself, was parallel to the famous Revolutionary War cases of the British spy Major André and the American spy Nathan Hale. Both of them had been hanged. The infiltrators should be tried by court martial and executed immediately.[23] The only question, he said to an aide, was whether they should die on the gallows or by firing squad.[24]

Roosevelt's aim in demanding a fast execution was to send a signal both to Germany and the American public that the United States would not tolerate infiltration. The fact that it had been so

easy to introduce saboteurs into the United States revealed a huge
hole in American civil defense. A strong message was needed to
counteract this gap, or at least direct attention away from it.

Roosevelt had no intention of allowing the courts to stand in
the way. "I want one thing clearly understood, Francis," he told his
attorney general, Francis Biddle. "I won't give them up.... I won't
hand them over to any United States marshal armed with a writ of
habeas corpus. Understand?"[25] Biddle understood. As he himself
wrote, "it was obvious that the reliance of the public on their government would be immeasurably strengthened if these would-be
saboteurs were disposed of promptly."[26] The difficulty was that
despite Roosevelt's certainty, it remained unclear just what crime
deserving the death penalty the men had committed—or what sort
of court should put them on trial. The infiltrators had not blown
anything up nor taken any steps after landing that indicated they
might. Biddle put the problem succinctly: "If a man buys a pistol,
intending murder, that is not an attempt at murder."[27]

The scion of an old Philadelphia family and a graduate of Groton
and Harvard like Roosevelt, Biddle was a liberal and, by the standard of government service, a sensitive person.[28] Roosevelt enjoyed
teasing him. On one occasion, while the president was preparing
his State of the Union message, he sent for Biddle and told him in
the presence of his closest advisers that he was planning to suspend
freedom of speech for the duration of the war. The group watched
impassively as Biddle, who was completely taken in, "declaimed
and declaimed against the idea," offering a "vehement" defense of
civil liberties in wartime while "pacing up and down."[29] Biddle
now understood the likelihood that the saboteurs' case would come
before the Supreme Court—and he welcomed the chance to argue
it there. "We have to win in the Supreme Court, or there will be a
hell of a mess," he told Roosevelt. "You're damned right there will
be, Mr. Attorney General," Roosevelt replied with a grin.[30]

Biddle adopted an aggressive legal strategy that was aimed at
making the conviction fast and sure and keeping the courts out
of the case. In lieu of a court martial, which would have to follow
rules dating back to the eighteenth century, he proposed creating

a special military commission, which could set its own rules of procedure and impose the death penalty without requiring the unanimous agreement of its members. Roosevelt agreed. For good measure, Roosevelt's order declared that the saboteurs' case could not be reviewed by any court.

Over the protest of the War Department, Biddle chose to prosecute the case before the tribunal himself—so that he could appear before the Supreme Court if the defendants tried to reach that Court. Following Roosevelt's lead, Biddle charged the men with violating the international laws of war by entering the United States without their uniforms. Then he added several other charges, including conspiracy to commit violent acts, which of course the saboteurs had not yet performed when they were caught.

A special military commission needed special members. Biddle decided to ask Henry Stimson, the secretary of war, to sit on the commission as its chair.[31] On June 29, Stimson had dinner with Felix Frankfurter, and asked his opinion on how to proceed.[32] Stimson, easily the oldest person in the cabinet, owed his post to Frankfurter. Frankfurter had repaid the man who gave him his first government job by urging Roosevelt to bring Stimson into the cabinet for his second stint as secretary of war, more than twenty years after his service under Taft. The argument had been that Stimson had the most relevant experience of any living American—and that he was a Republican, assuring bipartisanship.

Even though he was now a justice of the Supreme Court, Frankfurter did not hold back from advising his old boss. He told Stimson that the secretary of war should refuse to serve on the commission, which should be made up exclusively of military officers. A civilian serving on the commission would complicate matters when the time came for the administration to argue that the trial was a purely military matter and therefore beyond the reach of the courts. Frankfurter was advising a member of Roosevelt's cabinet about how Roosevelt could avoid the jurisdiction of the Court on which Frankfurter sat.[33]

Judged by contemporary standards of noncommunication between judges and the executive branch, Frankfurter's advice to

Stimson was obviously improper. The saboteurs were almost sure to appeal to the Supreme Court, and Frankfurter had no plans to recuse himself if they did. It is anachronistic, however, to apply this standard to the Roosevelt Court. Roberts had been chosen to chair the sensitive Pearl Harbor commission. Douglas and Jackson were intimates of Roosevelt who attended regular poker evenings in the White House. Frankfurter himself was busily engaged in advising the president directly. There is little doubt that Frankfurter gave this advice simply because Stimson was asking for his opinion, and as a regular unofficial adviser to the president, Frankfurter was accustomed to giving it.

There was, after all, a war on. The United States had been attacked, and now it had been infiltrated by men intent on destruction. For Frankfurter, the overarching goal of winning the war clearly took precedence over any nicety of the separation of powers or judicial impropriety. That the question was coming from his last living mentor guaranteed that he would make a useful response.

Indeed, Frankfurter was not the only justice who became privately involved in the saboteurs' case. After making the decision to go forward with a trial by military commission—a commission to be made up exclusively of generals—Roosevelt also ordered the appointment of defense counsel for the saboteurs. Two colonels in the judge advocate general's service were chosen. As part of the defense team, they in turn selected Major Lauson Stone, a lawyer who was the son of Chief Justice Harlan Fiske Stone.

The defense team assigned Lauson Stone to research the question of whether a military tribunal was constitutionally permissible. He told them that it very possibly was not. The defense lawyers then concluded that their best bet was to go directly to the Supreme Court and seek an order declaring the entire idea of trial by military commission illegal. If they succeeded, the saboteurs would then have to be tried in an ordinary civilian court—which might help their case, and certainly could do it no harm.

Ordinarily, having settled on a legal strategy, the defense would have filed a motion stating its position. But this was no ordinary case. Instead of filing a motion, Kenneth Royall, one of the two colonels leading the defense—a North Carolinian, trained at Harvard Law School—first contacted Hugo Black. Black told him, "I don't want to have anything to do with that matter." Royall then went to Justice Owen Roberts. Off the record, Royall asked Roberts if it might be possible for the Supreme Court to convene over the summer and hear the case on an expedited basis.[34]

Far from rebuffing this irregular procedure, Roberts invited the colonels to talk it over with him at his Pennsylvania farm, where he was spending the summer. Black, with whom Roberts then enjoyed a close relationship, would be there, too. The men were to be joined by the judge advocate general, the undersecretary of war, and Biddle. At this private conference at Roberts's farm, the justice served crackers, cheese, and fresh milk. Roberts and Black agreed to ask the rest of the Court to convene a special session. With the agreement of Chief Justice Stone, the Court decided to meet on July 29.[35] By then, the saboteurs' trial had proceeded to closing arguments. Its outcome was not in doubt.

The intimacy between the judiciary and the executive branches, underscored by the cozy meeting at Roberts's farm, was further emphasized in the first moments of the hearing at the Court. Stone noted that his son had been assigned to work for the defense and ceremonially offered to recuse himself. Attorney General Biddle—representing the government, not the saboteurs—answered that Lauson Stone had only worked on the defense of the military commission, not on the constitutional issues that were before the Court, and that therefore the government did not seek Stone's recusal. This was partially true; Lauson had been removed from working on the constitutional issues as soon as it became clear there were any worth raising. But by contemporary standards, artificially dividing the defense's legal issues as in a student moot court would have absolutely no effect on the question of judicial recusal. This was, in fact, a kind of theater, in which roles were assigned and all had implicitly agreed to act them out.

There was at least one extremely important precedent on the saboteurs' side of the case, a decision known as *Ex Parte Milligan*,[36] decided just after the Civil War. In it, the Supreme Court had held that a defendant charged with aiding the enemy could not be tried by a military commission in the state of Indiana while the civilian courts were open. The courts of the United States were open, and the saboteurs were being tried by a military commission. If the precedent were applied, it seemed possible that the trial had been unconstitutional. Biddle himself, who had dreamt up the prosecution strategy, thought the *Milligan* case was "troublesome" and "seemed to stand in our way."[37]

But the Supreme Court of 1942 gave scant attention to the precedent. Worried that Roosevelt might order the execution of the saboteurs before it even issued a ruling, the Court reconvened on July 31, two days after hearing argument. It announced in a single unanimous order that the military commission had the authority to try the saboteurs. No opinion was issued to explain the order. Instead, the Court promised that it would issue an opinion explaining its decision some time in the future. Its immediate task accomplished, the Supreme Court resumed its vacation.

A few days later, the military commission found all eight infiltrators guilty, and sentenced all of them to death by electrocution. When it came to Dasch, who had turned in the others on the expectation that he would go free, the commission recommended commutation to a sentence of thirty years. His associate Burger, who had agreed to help him, was recommended for life in prison. Roosevelt took the recommendations, turning down the infiltrators' pleas for clemency. On August 8, less than two months after they had landed, six of the eight men were executed—including twenty-two-year-old Herbie Haupt, one of the two U.S. citizens. Dasch and Burger remained in prison only until 1948, when President Truman pardoned them and deported them to Germany.[38]

For the justices, writing the promised opinion justifying the military commission turned out to be more difficult than anticipated. Chief Justice Stone was able to convince himself and his colleagues that the saboteurs were unlike the defendant in *Ex Parte Milligan* because they were soldiers, while Milligan had been a civilian. According to this theory, the saboteurs' true crime was crossing enemy lines without a uniform—a violation of the laws of war.

But there were other legal difficulties that could not be circumvented so easily. The special military commission had not followed the rules laid out in the Articles of War passed by Congress. Roosevelt had ordered the verdict delivered to himself for review, not to the judge advocate general. And Roosevelt's initial order had also included the striking statement that no court would have the authority to review the commission's verdict.[39]

In principle, all the justices wanted to issue a unanimous opinion. After all, the entire goal of legitimizing Roosevelt's decision could be undercut if there were to be a dissent. What was more, the Court had acted in a highly unusual fashion by its summary approval of the commission, and the Court itself might be embarrassed if it turned out that there were good reasons to doubt the constitutionality of the trial now that the defendants had been executed. Behind the scenes, the justices began to squabble over Roosevelt's failure to follow the rules set out by Congress, as well as the question of whether he could tell the courts that they had no right at all to hear the saboteurs' case.

On one side, Hugo Black was inclined to think that Roosevelt had overstepped his bounds in ignoring the Articles of War laid down by Congress. Congress, not the president, had the constitutional power to declare war. For Black it followed that Congress could tell the president how to conduct that war, including how he might conduct military commissions within it. Black's preference for a close textual reading of the Constitution supported this perspective. Although Black did not then know it, further research would have revealed that at least some of the framers of the Constitution shared this rather formalistic view of the distribution of wartime powers.[40]

On the other side of the issue was Jackson, fresh from his job as attorney general. While serving Roosevelt, Jackson had made history by arguing for broad presidential power. Now, consistent with that perspective, Jackson circulated to his colleagues a proposed concurring opinion of his own. In it he maintained that the Supreme

Court had no business reviewing any aspect of Roosevelt's decision on what to do with the saboteurs. His basis was not so much constitutional doctrine as practical necessity: "Experience shows...the judicial system is ill-adapted to deal with matters in which we must present a united front to a foreign foe."[41] To Jackson, allowing the Supreme Court to sit in judgment of the president's actions during war was an unreasonable interference in operations crucial to the national defense. Far from seeing, as Black did, a president subordinated to the will of Congress, the pragmatic Jackson saw a president who sometimes had to act outside of ordinary legal bounds under wartime conditions.

For both Black and Jackson, the backroom wrangling over the opinion in the saboteurs' case offered a dry run for what would become their more fully developed views of presidential power— views that were in each case consistent with their broader beliefs about how to interpret the Constitution. As it turned out, neither published an opinion in the case. Along with the other members of the Court, both were convinced by Frankfurter. In this secret debate among the members of the Court, it was Frankfurter's own constitutional philosophy, the theory of judicial restraint, that would prevail.

Frankfurter's ability to convince the other justices was occasioned by their collective fear of losing unanimity. As it became increasingly clear that it would be difficult for the Court to issue a single opinion justifying its earlier order to let the executions go forward, Frankfurter produced a strange memorandum that he sent around to his colleagues. It took the form of an imaginary dialogue between Frankfurter and the saboteurs themselves. In it he excoriated the Germans in harsh terms, emphasizing that they deserved no rights and no consideration whatever from the Court or indeed the United States.

But the crucial passage, which Frankfurter's entire document was designed to emphasize, charged the saboteurs with the rather outré allegation that they were sowing dissension between the branches of government: "You've done enough mischief already, without leaving the seeds of a bitter conflict involving the President, the Courts and Congress."[42] Then Frankfurter delivered his judicial-restraint punch line: "It is a wise requirement of courts not to get into needless rows with the other branches of the government by talking about things that need not be talked about if a case can be disposed of with intellectual self-respect on grounds that do not raise such rows."[43]

Almost any case can be disposed of on nonconstitutional grounds. Whether this can be accomplished "with intellectual self-respect," however, is in the eye of the beholder. In any event, following Frankfurter's circulation, the justices agreed not to make their differences public. Stone's opinion for the Court simply ducked the issues of whether Roosevelt had to follow the Articles of War and whether he had the power to put a case like the saboteurs' beyond judicial review. When pressed, the Court had shown wartime loyalty to Roosevelt—loyalty that would again become crucial in 1943, when the first cases about Japanese-American internment came before the Court. Frankfurter could still function as a leader of the Roosevelt Court, swaying his colleagues to the national cause and the man who led it.

CHAPTER 24

Faith

In the spring of 1943, with the war raging in Europe and the Pacific, Felix Frankfurter found himself delivering an impassioned lecture to his colleagues in the privacy of the Supreme Court's conference room. The topic was one very close to Frankfurter's heart. He was explaining the difference between a true immigrant patriot—someone who had become a citizen and loved his country above all else; and a fundamentally disloyal immigrant—one who subscribed fully to the beliefs of the Communist Party, and took the oath of naturalization in bad faith, in the hopes of undermining the country that had welcomed him to its shores.

The villain of the piece was one William Schneiderman, whose case was being heard by the Court for a second time. Schneiderman, a Jew by birth, had come to the United States from Russia as a boy of two, and had been raised in Chicago and later Los Angeles in circumstances of dire poverty. He had joined the Young Workers League at sixteen and the Workers Party—predecessor to the Communist Party U.S.A.—at eighteen. At twenty-one he had been naturalized as a citizen. By that time he had become a committed Communist, rising to the rank of secretary of the Party in California. Schneiderman believed U.S. citizenship was perfectly consistent with Communist belief; but the government disagreed. After a disgruntled former Communist denounced him to the House Un-American Activities Committee, the federal government tried to strip Schneiderman of his citizenship. He had been a citizen for twelve years. But the government reasoned that, as a Communist, he could not have taken the oath of naturalization

without lying, since he must logically be a "disbeliever in organized government" who was devoted to the overthrow of the U.S.
government by force and violence.[44]

The foil to Schneiderman was Frankfurter himself. Frankfurter was the only justice who had immigrated. He was the only
one to have had his citizenship impugned at his confirmation hearings. And he was the only one to have been asked at those hearings
whether he was or ever had been a Communist. The superficial
similarities between his experiences and Schneiderman's impelled
him to differentiate the two of them. He had known innocent fellow travelers, Frankfurter told the other justices—and Schneiderman was no innocent. He was the real thing: a dangerous traitor,
whose citizenship should be revoked.[45]

Frankfurter had special competence on the subject, he maintained, not only because he had known many radicals in his lifetime, but because he, too, was an immigrant. He spoke of his own
naturalization as a conversion. Loyalty to the Constitution, he said,
was his religion—and "it is well known that a convert is more zeal-
ous than one born to the faith."[46]

Indeed, Frankfurter suggested, Americanism had replaced
Judaism in his spiritual life: "As one who has no ties with any formal religion, perhaps the feelings that underlie religious forms for
me run into intensification of my feelings about American citizenship." Such citizenship was, he said, a "fellowship which binds
people together by devotion to certain feelings and ideas and ideals." These could be "summarized as a requirement that they be
attached to the principles of the Constitution."[47] Schneiderman was
not attached to those principles. Therefore, he was no true citizen.
The conditions of loyalty had not been met.

Ultimately, Frankfurter's colleagues did not agree with his
assessment of Schneiderman. The Soviet Union was by then allied
with the United States against Hitler; and although the Court's
opinion protested that there was no connection, it was not an
opportune time for the country to be stripping Communists of
their citizenship. The Court held that because Schneiderman had
been a law-abiding citizen for five years after taking the oath, his

citizenship remained valid; and Frankfurter joined a dissenting opinion by Chief Justice Stone.[48]

But the significance of Frankfurter's protestations on the subject of loyalty were important for another reason: He was being subjected to almost unbearable pressure to admit that he had been wrong in the case of the Jehovah's Witnesses and their refusal to salute the flag. The claim was being based not simply on the principles of liberalism, but on his Jewish origin. When Frankfurter had written the opinion ruling that towns could require children to salute, it had seemed like a patriotic decision. As a Jew, he had been especially concerned that children not be treated differently in schools on the basis of religion.

Since then, the politics had shifted. The United States was now at war with Nazi Germany—a country whose policies were aimed precisely at suppressing a religious minority. To liberals, tolerance, not saluting, had become the American form of patriotism. Even the previously innocuous-seeming form of the salute, with the right arm extended straight ahead, palm up, was now perceived as too similar to the Nazis' straight armed, palm-down, "Heil Hitler."[49]

In the spring of 1942, in a case that involved the Jehovah's Witnesses' right to be exempt from a tax on the distribution of pamphlets, Black, Douglas, and Frank Murphy had filed a highly unusual dissent openly regretting their earlier votes in the flag-salute case.[50] Then, a year later, the Court overturned Frankfurter's earlier judgment—the first time the Roosevelt Court had reversed itself.

The opinion, elegantly written by Jackson, became an instant classic, famous as much for its aphorisms as its holding. Jackson had not been on the Court when the first flag-salute case was decided, but he had told Frankfurter that he strongly disagreed with his opinion.[51] Now he embraced Stone's argument in his original dissent that the goal of judicial review was to protect minorities. "The very purpose of the Bill of Rights," he wrote, "was to withdraw certain subjects from the vicissitudes of political controversy, to place them beyond the reach of majorities and officials and to establish them as legal principles to be applied by the courts. . . .

Fundamental rights may not be submitted to a vote; they depend on the outcome of no elections."[52]

Jackson's opinion also made it clear that he understood the political symbolism involved in protecting free speech for all—not just the religious liberty of the Witnesses. In particular, Jackson wrote, the children were being protected against having to declare a belief which they did not hold: "If there is any fixed star in our constitutional constellation, it is that no official, high or petty, can prescribe what shall be orthodox in politics, nationalism, religion, or other matters of opinion, or force citizens to confess by word or act their faith therein."[53]

Frankfurter took the reversal of his *Gobitis* opinion as a professional and personal calamity. It was bad enough that the Court had rejected the philosophy of judicial restraint on which he had built his reputation. But it was much worse that the Court was using the flag salute as a metaphor for the Nazis' oppression of Jews. Frankfurter's birthplace and childhood home were now under Nazi control. He believed that he had voted in favor of equal treatment for all, regardless of religion. Now he was being told that, as a Jew, he had made a mistake. Not only his jurisprudence but his selfhood was on the line.

Frankfurter responded with the most agonized and agonizing opinion recorded anywhere in the U.S. reports. Over weeks, Frankfurter compiled pages upon pages of disjointed arguments in his barely decipherable longhand. When circulating a draft could no longer be avoided, his law clerk, Philip Elman—who would later play a key role in the famous desegregation decision, *Brown v. Board of Education*—strung Frankfurter's notes together over a single long night at the typewriter. In the morning, Frankfurter circulated the unedited draft to the other justices.[54]

To his colleagues' horror, the opinion began with an excursus into Frankfurter's own identity as a Jew: "One who belongs to the most vilified and persecuted minority in history," he wrote, "is not likely to be insensible to the freedoms guaranteed by our Constitution." He went on to refer to his career as defender of civil liberties: "Were my purely personal attitude relevant I should wholeheartedly associate myself with the general libertarian views in the Court's opinion, representing as they do the thought and action of a lifetime."[55]

Several justices begged Frankfurter not to publish the opening lines of his opinion. Frank Murphy, closely identified with the Catholic Church—and the only other non-Protestant on the Court—told Frankfurter that his opinion was "too personal" and that his words "would be 'catapulting a personal issue into the arena.'"[56]

Frankfurter replied to Murphy that his self-reference would be personal if he were using his identity as a basis for his decision. But in fact, Frankfurter insisted, he was doing just the opposite by asserting that the Constitution required the judge to put aside his particularity. "As judges," he had written, "we are neither Jew nor Gentile, neither Catholic nor agnostic. We owe equal attachment to the Constitution and are equally bound by our judicial obligations whether we derive our citizenship from the earliest or the latest immigrants to these shores."[57]

Owen Roberts also came to Frankfurter, telling him that on reflection he considered the words "more and more a mistake." Frankfurter gave Roberts a lengthier explanation. He had, he said, been "flooded" with letters criticizing his original opinion in the flag-salute case on the ground that "I, as a Jew, ought particularly to protect minorities." Since the issue had come back to the Supreme Court, he had received "a new trickle of letters" telling him that as "a Jew and an immigrant" his duty was to reverse his vote. The letters, said Frankfurter, convinced him that he needed to tell the world that individual background was irrelevant to the business of the Supreme Court.[58] Frankfurter was trying to express his own tortuous identity: The more anyone told him that he had judicial obligations "as a Jew," the more crucial it became to insist that as a judge he was no more and no less than an American.

Roberts said that he accepted the answer—what else could he say? As he brooded about it, though, Frankfurter found that he was unsatisfied with the exchange. Murphy's concerns about Frankfurter's opening lines could be explained by his desire to deflect attention away from his own Catholic identity. But Roberts was an ordinary white, Republican Protestant who had no particular stake in such matters, and who was easily influenced by others. Why had he asked Frankfurter to change the text of his opinion? In his diary—written with future biographers in mind—Frankfurter surmised that Roberts had been put up to it by Black.[59] Although Roberts and Black would later split violently, they were, at the time, good friends; Black and his wife, Josephine, regularly visited Roberts at his Pennsylvania farm.

Black's motives for trying to stop Frankfurter from drawing attention to the personal domain would have been complex. As a former Klansman, he had a reason to want the justices' personal backgrounds to be kept out of Supreme Court opinions. Frankfurter made the point obliquely if ungenerously: "What moved Black I do not know except his general philosophy about not mentioning such things—he is a great fellow for keeping things under cover." This was a reference to Black's hiding his Klan membership from Roosevelt (and everyone else) before becoming a justice. Then Frankfurter pushed it still further: "To me, on the contrary, to keep all reference to anti-Semitism and anti-Catholicism hidden is the best kind of cover under which evil can operate."[60] Anti-Catholicism was, alongside racism and anti-Semitism, a mainstay of the Klan's worldview. In the interests of posterity, Frankfurter was justifying his very public reference to his own Jewishness as a blow against the secret bias he was ascribing to Black.

If Frankfurter's opening was driven by the challenges of his innermost identity, the rest of his opinion sought, fatefully, to defend the principle of judicial restraint. Although he sensed it only incompletely, Frankfurter was facing the most important crossroads of his judicial career. For more than a quarter of a century, while conservatives controlled the Supreme Court, Frankfurter had argued that judges must allow democratic majorities to act as they pleased, even when their decisions were fundamentally flawed. Now liberals had a majority on the Supreme Court—and they were arguing that the Court should intervene to protect the rights of minorities. Frankfurter realized that if he remained a stalwart of judicial restraint, he would be condemned by the liberals whom he had hoped to lead. But having made a career arguing against judicial interference in the majority's decisions, Frankfurter chose to stick to his guns.

The beauty and also the tragedy of Frankfurter's constitutional vision were captured in this stance. Consistency was, for him, the hallmark of good judging. The error of the Court in the *Lochner* era had been to overturn legislation when it served the interests of property owners and capitalists to do so; and Frankfurter had criticized the majority for following its economic and class interests. Now, he felt, he had to show commitment to a principle, regardless of whether he liked the consequences. If judicial restraint had been appropriate when conservatives controlled the Court, it must still be the right doctrine now that the liberals had the votes. Having articulated the theory of judicial restraint echoed by other liberals when they did not control the Supreme Court, Frankfurter found himself the sole liberal advocate of keeping to that theory when it was no longer politically expedient.[61]

For other liberals, judicial restraint had been simply the right idea for the right moment—a powerful way to criticize a conservative Court that stood in the way of progressive reforms. Now that the conservatives were out of power, the liberals saw good arguments for treating civil liberties as very different from property rights. They already believed the Court should not impose its economic values on the majority. But for the Court to protect religious or racial minorities was different from protecting the minority made up of property owners. These minorities, the liberals came to believe, needed the protection of the courts.

As the other liberals on the Court shifted ground, Frankfurter—to his astonishment—found himself transformed into a conservative. Frankfurter's critics, then and later, have tried to explain how it could be that the country's best-known liberal became its leading judicial conservative. But the source of the change was not Frankfurter, whose constitutional philosophy remained remarkably consistent throughout his career. It was the rest of liberalism that abandoned him and moved on once judicial restraint was no longer a useful tool to advance liberal objectives.[62]

The question remains, of course, why Frankfurter chose consistency once the writing was on the wall. He was not an ideologue in the years before he went on the Court. If Frankfurter's liberalism was open to revision, why did he not revise the ideal of judicial restraint?

The answer lay in what Frankfurter had told his colleagues during the *Schneiderman* case: that the Constitution had replaced Judaism as his religion. The obligation of the judge was to demonstrate loyalty not to any one particular identity, but to the Constitution itself. When Frankfurter said that "as judges we are neither Jew nor Gentile, neither Catholic nor agnostic," he was using the language of religion (and a reference to St. Paul) to say that "attachment to the Constitution" was his overarching religious commitment.[63]

All religions put their adherents to the test and require sacrifice. Frankfurter's constitutional religion demanded that a judge reach results that contradict his political preferences. Only then could he be certain that his allegiance was to the Constitution, not the false idols of partisanship. Disinterest could be proven only by way of sacrifice—the sacrifice of voting against one's political preferences.

To Frankfurter, Holmes personified judicial disinterest. But Holmes's disinterest derived from world-weary acceptance of the inevitable victory of whatever social forces were destined to prevail. "If in the long run," he once wrote, beliefs "in proletarian dictatorship are destined to be accepted by the dominant forces of the community, the only meaning of free speech is that they should be given their chance and have their way."[64] From this it followed that the judge's job was to stand by and allow social processes to run their course. "If the people want to go to Hell, I will help them," Holmes liked to say. "It's my job."[65]

By contrast, Frankfurter's judicial restraint was driven by a deeply romantic conception of the nature and tendencies of the American people living under conditions of democracy. For Frankfurter, the most astonishing fact about the United States was the liberalism of its people—a liberalism manifested not simply in the public's embrace of progressive ideals, but also in toleration and a commitment to basic rights. His deep loyalty to the country that had taken him as an immigrant led him to downplay the racism, prejudice, and other types of illiberalism that could be found in America.

Frankfurter worried that assigning to the Supreme Court the job of protecting liberal rights would relieve the public of the responsibility to protect basic rights on its own, through influencing the legislature. If the courts should become the institution charged with protecting rights, he feared, the public would cease to care about protecting rights itself. Legislators might enact laws that they knew to be unconstitutional, passing the buck to the courts in the expectation they would strike those laws down. What was more, the courts might eventually lose their legitimacy, since they would be seen as acting against the public, not in fulfillment of its most deeply held values. The right thing to do, therefore, under our basic constitutional structure, was to rely on the democratic polity to preserve rights, not for the courts to intervene. In his dissent in the second flag-salute case, Frankfurter laid out this argument for judicial restraint as explicitly as he ever would again in his career.[66]

Ultimately, Frankfurter's loyalty to the American people as he imagined them to be trumped the concern he had for the Jehovah's Witnesses whose loyalty was being impugned—just as it trumped any concern he might have had for Schneiderman. Frankfurter preferred to wait for the historical moment to pass and for the public to realize the error of its ways. To the extent he believed that loyalty to American values was itself a condition of liberalism, he may even have felt that the Witnesses' children would be better served by saluting the flag than by abstaining from that ritual. The alternative, he feared, was for the courts to assume a new role, one that he had rejected when his political views were not those of the majority of the Court. Loyalty to Frankfurter's distinctive vision of the Constitution was the transcendent principle for him here—and his sacrifice was proof of that loyalty above all else.

CHAPTER 25

Internment

Late on the evening of March 28, 1942, Minoru Yasui, a twenty-six-year-old lawyer from Portland, Oregon, went for a walk in the hopes of getting arrested. He passed a policeman—but instead of arresting him, the officer told him, "Run along home, sonny boy, or you'll get in trouble." So at 11:00 p.m., Yasui presented himself at his neighborhood police station and demanded to be booked. The desk sergeant obliged. The fact that he had walked in was proof enough of his crime.

Yasui had been born on an apple and asparagus farm in Hood River, Oregon, and lived in the state most of his life. He had earned his undergraduate and law degrees from the University of Oregon in Eugene, where he had also been enrolled as a candidate in the Reserve Officers' Training Corps. On graduation in 1937, he had been commissioned as a second lieutenant in the Army Reserve. But Yasui was a Japanese-American. Although he was a citizen of the United States and had been his whole life, it was illegal for him to be out of his house after dark, by order of Lt. Gen. John DeWitt, commander of Western defense. Violation of the order was a federal crime. Yasui was soon joined in his goal of testing the curfew law by another Japanese-American: Gordon Hirabayashi of Seattle, a Christian pacifist who voluntarily turned himself in to the FBI.[67]

The curfew, it turned out, was only the beginning. In the weeks that followed, the Army's West Coast curfew against people of Japanese origin was transformed into a full-on program of expulsion and detention. Some 120,000 ethnic Japanese—most of them U.S. citizens—were ordered to report at dawn to detention points with just a few of their possessions. Luggage was labeled and piled for shipping. Sometimes local churches or the Red Cross would provide coffee and doughnuts.

Then the Japanese-Americans were put onto trains or buses to "assembly centers." One recalled seeing a young man saying good-bye to his girlfriend who was being boarded onto a train. "An MP guard shoved him away from the train as the train tooted its whistle. . . . The man ran to the other side of the train to kiss her once more. The MP cocked his shotgun and ran after him. When the MP reached the young man, he clubbed him with his rifle butt. The young man was taken away with blood running down his face."[68]

From the assembly centers, the Japanese-Americans were sent to one of ten "relocation centers"—temporary, military-style camps located hundreds of miles inland, mostly in the Western desert. From 1942 until 1945, these Americans lived in tin shacks behind barbed wire. Conditions were terrible, with little running water, less privacy, and minimal food. Whole families crowded into tiny spaces. Sand from the frequent sandstorms poured through cracks in the walls, coating everything with fine dust. Temperatures went below zero in the winter evenings and over 100 degrees in the summer days. Meanwhile, the internees' businesses were shuttered and their farms lay fallow, unless purchased at deep discounts by white neighbors.

The overwhelming majority of Japanese-Americans peacefully obeyed the deportation orders. A few followed the example of Yasui and Hirabayashi and challenged the law. The only woman among them, Mitsuye Endo, was a stenographer working for the California Department of Motor Vehicles in Sacramento. Contemporary photographs show her in a shirtdress at her typewriter, her hair pin-curled and rolled back to her shoulders in the classic 1940s style. Her brother was serving in the U.S. Army.

After Pearl Harbor, Endo was dismissed from her job because of her Japanese ancestry. Then, when she was sent to the Tule Lake War Relocation Center, near the Oregon border, she brought a lawsuit demanding to be released. After a year at Tule Lake, Endo was transferred to the internment camp in Topaz, Utah, where a government official offered her a permit to leave the camp and relocate somewhere outside the West Coast. The government wanted Endo to drop her suit. Endo bravely refused—and remained in detention for a total of three years.[69]

The resister whose name would become most famous, Fred Korematsu, provided an unintentional test case. Korematsu, an Oakland native who had worked in his family's flower nursery, was deeply in love with his girlfriend, an Irish-American woman named Ida Boitano. When the order came to report for relocation, Korematsu hid. Then, in an act of real desperation, he subjected himself to plastic surgery to try and hide his Japanese origin. But he was nevertheless turned in after being recognized on the street near the family business, and charged with the crime of failing to report. He made bail—only to be rearrested and shipped to Topaz, where his room was a converted horse stall with a single bare bulb.[70]

The government of the United States could not have interned the Japanese-Americans were it not for the tradition of anti-Asian prejudice in the country in general and on the West Coast in particular. Although historically the bias was predominantly anti-Chinese, there was no hesitation in deploying stereotypes of the shifty, untrustworthy Oriental onto both first- and second-generation Americans of Japanese origin. Racialized bias was a familiar feature of wartime propaganda going back to World War I, when German-Americans were called "Huns" and subjected to systematic discrimination. The headlines of the period in mainstream newspapers like the *Los Angeles Times* refer constantly to "Japs" and "Nips"—the latter a derogatory contraction of the word *Nipponese*.[71]

The official report on Pearl Harbor, produced by the commission under the chairmanship of Justice Owen Roberts, also helped lay the groundwork for internment. The report asserted that in preparation for the attacks, Japanese spies in Hawaii had gathered information regarding Army and Navy bases there. The report never stated that any of the spies were Japanese-Americans. It said only that "some were Japanese consular agents and others were persons having no open relations with the Japanese foreign service."[72] The effect of this vague statement about private individuals was to legitimize fear of disloyal Japanese residents of the United States engaging in espionage on behalf of the Japanese government.

As the East Coast submarine landings suggest, foreign saboteurs could arrive on U.S. soil. On the West Coast, military concern focused primarily on the possibility that Japanese agents could make radio contact with Japanese naval forces, allowing Japanese submarines to attack ships departing from Pacific ports. Such submarine attacks did occur in the early days of the war with Japan. By February 1942, not quite two months after Pearl Harbor, General DeWitt was reporting to his superiors in Washington that he believed the attacks were facilitated by reports from Japanese spies.[73]

The FBI, then and later, would maintain that there was no real evidence to support this interpretation of events. Attorney General Francis Biddle opposed the evacuation of U.S. citizens of Japanese origin from the West Coast.[74] But the standards of evidence for wartime judgment are very different from those used in ordinary criminal investigations. Soon after Pearl Harbor, General DeWitt began to advocate a systematic evacuation from the West Coast of all people who were ethnically Japanese. Battlefield paranoia was not the only motive driving DeWitt. He came under intense pressure from leading politicians including the governor of California and the state's highest-ranking Republican, Attorney General Earl Warren.

Warren was the fastest-rising figure in California politics. He had been nominated attorney general with bipartisan support. Less than a year later, he would be elected governor of the state; he would eventually become chief justice of the United States. His influence was significant. After a conversation with Warren, Walter Lippmann wrote one of his nationally syndicated columns calling for the removal of Japanese-Americans from the West Coast. That there had as yet been no attacks, wrote Lippmann, was simply "a sign that the blow is well organized and held back until it can be struck with maximum effect." Even the *New York Times* called for serious action.[75]

The legal structure adopted to facilitate the internment was a masterpiece of political buck passing. It began with President Roosevelt, who issued an executive order proclaiming the need to prevent espionage and sabotage, and then authorizing his generals to issue orders of their own accordingly. The order was vague enough that subsequent decisions could not be attributed to the president personally.

The military, in turn, ordered the curfew, the exclusion, and the detention. Finally, Congress made it a crime to violate the military's order of evacuation. All this added up to exclusion and relocation to camps under the threat of prison. The whole scheme was designed so that no single legal pronouncement explicitly ordered relocation and internment on racial grounds. The Roosevelt administration and the Army expected legal challenges, and they wanted to win them.

For the internees, finding good legal representation turned out to be complicated. The Japanese American Citizens League, the leading national organization for Japanese-Americans, had adopted a policy of "full cooperation" with the government, the better to prove the loyalty of its members. The JACL decided that legal challenges to the internment would not comport with that policy, and so it did not represent the internees who wanted to challenge the law. The national ACLU had made a policy decision not to challenge the constitutionality of the executive order on which the detention rested—again, a manifestation of wartime loyalty. The Northern California local branch of the ACLU represented the pacifist Gordon Hirabayashi, focusing on the curfew order without attacking the detention. Individual lawyers with ACLU ties represented some others, like Mitsuye Endo.[76] Overall, however, the record of even civil libertarians in the history of Japanese-American internment is not gratifying.

The first cases to reach the Supreme Court were the challenges to the curfew brought by Minoru Yasui and Gordon Hirabayashi, which were argued in the spring of 1943, just as final opinions were being put in place in the landmark flag-salute reversal. In a unanimous decision, with three justices separately concurring, the Supreme Court upheld the curfew against the challenge that it violated the Constitution to impose restrictions on a single class of citizens based upon their racial origin alone.[77] The unanimity reflected both the justices' desire to maintain a united front on an important wartime measure and the powerful drive of loyalty to Roosevelt. Eight of the nine justices sitting on the case had been appointed by Roosevelt, including Harlan Fiske Stone, whom Roosevelt had made Chief Justice. Roberts, the lone Hoover appointee, had chaired the commission whose report had indirectly justified the internment project.

Stone took it upon himself to write the opinion. He rested the Court's legal position on the government's war power, which was, according to his predecessor, Charles Evans Hughes, "the power to wage war successfully."[78] Stone also felt the need to justify the curfew as a "reasonable" policy. To do so he cited Roberts's report, as well as the assertion that "social, economic and political conditions" had prevented the Japanese from assimilating "as an integral part of the white population."[79]

But for Stone, who had in 1939 proposed special scrutiny of laws targeting discrete and insular minorities, that was not the end of the matter. Upholding what was obviously a racially based measure, Stone insisted that "distinctions between citizens solely because of their ancestry are, by their very nature, odious to a free people whose institutions are founded upon the doctrine of equality."[80] This inspiring message demanded that Stone offer some explanation of why this particular discriminatory action was constitutional. His answer was that racial discrimination was ordinarily prohibited because race was "in most circumstances irrelevant." By contrast, in the case of Japanese-American loyalty, Japanese origin was relevant: "The danger of espionage and sabotage, in time of war and of threatened invasion, calls upon the military authorities to scrutinize every relevant fact bearing on the loyalty of populations in the danger areas."[81] This discrimination based on race was therefore permissible under the Constitution.

It is easy to condemn Stone for saying that racial discrimination was allowed under these circumstances. Justice Frank Murphy was sufficiently upset that he drafted a dissent—which he later changed into a concurrence—warning of the great danger of having "one law for the majority of our citizens and another for those of a particular racial heritage."[82] As the Court's only Catholic, Murphy was particularly troubled by Stone's suggestion that Japanese-Americans had not successfully assimilated—a recurrent Protestant accusation about Catholics in the nineteenth and even into the twentieth century. Murphy even went so far as to compare the curfew (and, by implication, the internment) "to the treatment accorded to members of the Jewish race in Germany and in other parts of Europe."[83] Yet Stone could have tried to avoid the question of racial discrimination altogether. His invocation of the principle of equality remained on the books alongside his situational justification of discriminatory treatment; eventually, it paved the way to judicial rejection of segregation.

The politics of the curfew were particularly important to Douglas, who like Murphy wrote a separate concurrence. As the Court's Westerner, and as a potential presidential or vice presidential candidate, Douglas was well aware of the strong West Coast political support for the internment program. In the first half of his concurrence, which Murphy considered to be "addressed to the mob,"[84] Douglas offered a justification for the Army's initial judgment. After Pearl Harbor, he wrote, "the threat of Japanese invasion of the west coast was not fanciful, but real.... If the military were right in their belief that, among citizens of Japanese ancestry, there was an actual or incipient fifth column, we were indeed faced with the imminent threat of a dire emergency."[85]

This sounded like a full-throated defense of universal internment; but it was not. At the same time as he showed sympathy for anti-Japanese sentiment, Douglas also expressed outrage that loyal Japanese-Americans were being interned. He wanted the military to institute a vetting process where loyal citizens would be released. "I think it important to emphasize," he wrote, "that we are dealing here with a problem of loyalty, not assimilation. Loyalty is a matter of mind and of heart, not of race. That indeed is the history of America."[86]

Under the cover of support for the military's decision, Douglas was looking for a real-world solution to put an end to the internment. In the first draft of his concurrence, he all but invited interned Japanese-Americans to file petitions for habeas corpus so that they could be freed individually upon acknowledgment of their loyalty.[87] Although Douglas drew back from holding out such an unfulfillable promise, the idea would remain with him. "Guilt," he wrote, "is personal under our constitutional system. Detention for reasonable cause is one thing. Detention on account of ancestry is another."[88]

CHAPTER 26

A Disaster

In the spring of 1943, when the justices approved the curfew, the war was going badly in Europe and the Pacific. By the fall of 1944, when they considered the constitutionality of the removal and detention in the infamous case of *Korematsu v. United States*, the D-Day invasion had already produced decisive momentum to win the war in Europe. The tide had turned as well in the war against Japan. Although people close to him knew his health was failing, Roosevelt was poised for reelection to a fourth term of office.

Under the circumstances, the pressures to maintain unity that had prevailed the previous year were now sharply reduced. The Court was still sufficiently loyal to Roosevelt that it did not want to issue an embarrassing judgment before the election. But beyond this concession, the impulse to maintain a common front in wartime was gone. This time, Justices Murphy and Roberts spoke out sharply in criticism of the internment policy, and Justices Jackson and Frankfurter gave the public a glimpse of a violent disagreement about whether the administration was adhering to the rule of law at all. In all, the decision generated five separate opinions from the nine justices.

Named for Fred Korematsu, the some-time flower grower who had tried to escape detention, the *Korematsu* decision is widely considered one of the two or three worst in American history. It was also one of the most important. The decision upheld the internment. Any law limiting the rights of a single racial group, wrote Hugo Black for the majority, is "immediately suspect," and must be subjected by the courts to "the most rigid scrutiny" to ascertain that it is not based on "racial antagonism."[89] But, Black insisted, the exclusion of Japanese-Americans from the West Coast was not based on racial prejudice. It occurred "because the properly constituted military authorities feared an invasion of our West Coast and felt constrained to take proper security measures.... There was evidence of disloyalty on the part of some, the military authorities considered that the need for action was great, and time was short."[90] As a result, Black concluded, the government's action was not unconstitutional: The real issue here was not race prejudice, but loyalty.

Understanding the opinion in terms of loyalty rather than prejudice explains how Black could have written it—and how Frankfurter, Douglas, Stone, Reed, and Rutledge could have joined it without sensing that it was fundamentally shameful. One key to the justices' mind-set was Black's demand that any law singling out members of one race demanded strict judicial scrutiny. This proposition later became one of the founding principles of the constitutional law of discrimination. The Court had never said it before, or indeed anything remotely like it.

In order to shift the issue from prejudice to loyalty, Black, the former Klansman, not only condemned racial prejudice, he also declared a judicial duty to ferret it out wherever it might be found. On some level, Black must have understood that the internment of Japanese-Americans was motivated by the very race prejudice he was condemning. Consider his own description of what he claimed the case was not about: "Our task would be simple, our duty clear, were this a case involving the imprisonment of a loyal citizen in a concentration camp because of racial prejudice."[91] That, of course, was exactly the situation before the Court: Loyal citizens were being imprisoned on the prejudicial assumption that their Japanese race made them security risks.

Black was trying to think away the truth. "We deem it unjustifiable to call them concentration camps with all the ugly connotations that term implies," he wrote.[92] Yet Black made no attempt whatever to explain why the camps were not places for the concentration of a disfavored racial minority behind barbed wire. Roosevelt had used the phrase on at least two occasions.[93]

In the very moment that Black was insisting that the judge's job was to scrutinize the law for evidence of racial discrimination, he was failing to do what he preached. This liberal, activist conception of the role of the judiciary was announced in the decision most frequently criticized for its abdication of the Court's duty to protect minorities. It was as if the justices had to form their sense of the obligation to ensure racial justice by engaging in a gross violation of it. Their impulse to deny that they were ratifying racial discrimination is precisely what would later, in *Brown v. Board of Education*, help them understand their job as blocking such discrimination when its reality could not be avoided.

If the overt denial of prejudice is the first clue to understanding the *Korematsu* decision, the second lies in the majority's embrace of the principle of loyalty. In the opinion, Justice Black took great pains to insist that the Court's holding did not authorize the government to detain loyal U.S. citizens once they had been removed from the West Coast. This was a legal fiction. The military order excluding persons of Japanese descent was paired with another order requiring them to turn themselves in for transfer to the internment camps. In practice, that meant that Japanese-Americans on the West Coast never had the chance to pack their belongings and move to another part of the country where they might live freely. The combination of the military orders was the reason the Japanese-Americans were forced into internment camps. What was before the Supreme Court, in other words, was precisely the question of detention.

Yet the same day the Court decided the *Korematsu* case, it also issued its decision in the case of Mitsuye Endo, the stenographer who had been detained at Tule Lake. Endo had gone through the bureaucratic process of applying to leave the relocation center. As part of the process, she had been vetted by the government, and found to be loyal.[94] Yet she had not been released—nor had many other detainees who had also been found loyal.

Endo's case is today much less famous than Korematsu's, but to the majority the two were meant to be read in tandem. In her case, the Supreme Court held that Japanese-American citizens who had been found loyal must be freed. In practical terms, this meant that the overwhelming majority of people in the internment camps would eventually have to be released.

When the Roosevelt administration got wind of the decision—possibly through Frankfurter, who had a former protégé working in the War Department under his old mentor, Henry Stimson—it announced its own plans to free those whose loyalty had been ascertained. The timing was no coincidence.[95] The *Endo* opinion was to be announced on a Monday. In violation of the business norms of the time, the War Department made its announcement the day before, on Sunday, December 17, 1944.[96]

Douglas wrote the *Endo* decision, which he intended as a continuation of his insistence in the curfew case that the government must not detain loyal citizens. His logic dovetailed neatly with Black's insistence in his *Korematsu* opinion that the exclusion was about loyalty, not race. The original evacuation of Japanese-Americans rested, Douglas said, on the fact that it was "an espionage and sabotage measure, not that there was community hostility to this group of American citizens."[97] Since loyalty was the basis for the whole program, the president could only have authorized the continued detention of persons still suspected of disloyalty, not loyal Americans. Correctly interpreted, the executive order, military orders, and the laws passed by Congress enforcing them did not allow loyal Americans to be detained.

As far as Douglas was concerned at the time, his opinion in Endo's case undid whatever wrong the *Korematsu* decision might have created. True, *Korematsu* upheld the original exclusion order and, by implication, legitimized detention of Japanese-Americans in internment centers. Yet Douglas expected the real-world effect of his *Endo* decision would be the release of nearly all Japanese-Americans detained. Justice would be done for the internees, and political cover would be provided for the Roosevelt administration's detention policy. As an added benefit, when Japanese-Americans returned to the West Coast, it would be because they had been declared loyal. This might conceivably reduce the anti-Japanese sentiment that the administration fully expected the internees would encounter on their return. Indeed, the expectation of such hostility—and its costs to the administration's popularity—was one of the main reasons that the administration had kept the Japanese-Americans interned for so long.[98]

But Douglas miscalculated in one fundamental and telling way. The principles of legal realism that Douglas had used as a law professor, and that he now sought to apply to his job on the Supreme Court, taught that what mattered was the effect the Court's decision had in the real world, not the legal logic used to obtain it. On this view, it did not matter that whereas Black's *Korematsu* decision had interpreted the Constitution to allow the exclusion, Douglas's *Endo* opinion relied on the president's order to demand the release of loyal Americans from internment. The difference was technical at best.[99] If this was right, then the detention approved in *Korematsu* was lawful only if limited to those found disloyal.

Ordinarily, legal realism has much to recommend it: Technicalities like the difference between a constitutional decision and one interpreting a presidential order are often less important than the real-world results of legal decisions. But landmark Supreme Court cases are different. Famous decisions take on a life of their own, both symbolically and legally through the precedents that they set. In these realms of symbol and precedent, Douglas's *Endo* opinion lacked the all-important heft of the constitutional decision in *Korematsu*. Interpreting a unique, time-limited presidential order is not the same as interpreting the Constitution.

Douglas, true to his realist impulses, did not bother to specify any broad principle that would emerge from his opinion. As a result, his *Endo* decision, with its emphasis on loyalty and its practical escape hatch for the internees, faded into obscurity. Meanwhile, the *Korematsu* decision has remained a stain on the reputation of the Court and those justices who joined Black's opinion.

Over time, Douglas came to see his decision to join Black's opinion in *Korematsu* as a major error.[100] Already during the war years, Douglas was eager to associate himself with Brandeis, the justice he had succeeded on the Court. He visited Brandeis's widow regularly, and it was "going round...that he is the great successor and follower of Brandeis."[101] For the rest of his life, Douglas would tell listeners that he had been "very, very close" to Brandeis and that Brandeis had urged Roosevelt to appoint him to the Court.[102] An association with the *Korematsu* decision was a blow to this liberal image—especially since other justices had dissented so vigorously while Douglas did not.

Years later, after he had learned the lesson of the huge symbolic importance of constitutional decisions, Douglas would say that he had hoped to gain support from the other justices to make *Endo* into a constitutional case.[103] Even according to this retelling, though, Douglas was willing to join Black's opinion in *Korematsu*. And there is little contemporaneous evidence to suggest that Douglas really tried to convince his colleagues to make *Endo* into a constitutional decision. The truth is that the young Douglas of 1944, though already interested in being seen as Brandeis's successor, was still driven by loyalty to Roosevelt, the Democratic Party—and his own political aspirations. He had not yet developed the commitment to individual liberty that would join with his legal realism to make him a great justice. Without a specific constitutional ideal to guide it, legal realism made a poor match with constitutional judging.

In contrast to Douglas, three justices were profoundly concerned about the effects of the *Korematsu* decision. Roberts, Murphy, and Jackson wrote dissenting opinions. Roberts was deeply troubled by the way a single sentence in his 1942 Pearl Harbor commission report had become the basis for systematic internment. His dissent eviscerated Black's formalistic and absurd insistence that the only issue before the Court was evacuation from the West Coast, not the internment itself. Roberts's opinion reflected the enormous frustration he felt at the way the Court was using legal technicalities—just as the president had—to legitimize the policy of detention.

Murphy's dissent focused still more bravely on the shameful character of the detentions. As a result of his experiences as mayor of racially polarized Detroit, governor of Michigan, and governor-general of the Philippines, Murphy had a powerful commitment to racial justice. At the time the curfew case was decided, Murphy had already been concerned about the racial motivation of the detention, but allowed his dissent to become a concurrence. Now he decided the time was right to make a stand. In impassioned terms, he argued that there was no real evidence of espionage, and that the detention was frankly racist.

The other justices were accustomed to writing off Murphy as a bleeding heart as well as a Catholic crusader who believed God was always on his side. Frankfurter went further. He addressed Murphy in a note as "Dear god." Another time, he wrote to him, "It is lucky, for God, that you are probably mortal, otherwise He'd be out of a job." After Murphy's death, Frankfurter said that Murphy was "a strange mixture of mystic aspirations and as extreme a case of self-love as I have experienced."[104]

Whatever its drawbacks, though, the self-righteous side of Murphy's personality served him in good stead when writing his *Korematsu* dissent. Moved by the plight of the detainees, he was unafraid to disagree with his colleagues, from whom he was already alienated. Standing against Roosevelt and his fellow Roosevelt appointees, Murphy spoke honestly and with considerable moral clarity about one of the worst episodes of racial discrimination in U.S. history. To the extent any justice preserved the dignity of the Court in one of its lowest moments, it was Murphy.

Jackson's dissent—one of his best-known, most powerful, and most enigmatic opinions—was different from the other two. While Roberts and Murphy focused on the treatment of the Japanese-Americans, Jackson was worried about the Constitution. The *Korematsu* decision, he believed, created a serious danger: The Court was sitting in judgment of a military order issued by a general in wartime. Military orders had to be made quickly and ruthlessly. Therefore, Jackson thought, they should not be subject to the ordinary standard of reasonableness that courts use to evaluate legality. Subjecting the military to judicial review would be bad for military decision making. The prospect of being reviewed by civilians who would be asking if their actions were "reasonable" might distort generals' judgment.

To make matters worse, once the courts approved the constitutionality of a military order, they would find themselves in the position of approving wartime deviations from constitutional norms that would have no place under conditions of peace. That would distort the fabric of the Constitution "for all time."[105] Jackson offered a memorable war-related metaphor: "The principle then lies about like a loaded weapon ready for the hand of any authority that can bring forward a plausible claim of an urgent need."[106]

Jackson's comparison of a bad constitutional precedent to a loaded weapon has become a classic of constitutional logic—and for good reason. According to Jackson's pragmatist view, constitutional law must be shaped to fit the particular needs of the case at hand. Above all, the Constitution must work. To work, it must be flexible, not dogmatic; driven by careful, balanced judgment, not by grand pronouncements or even by general rules.

Broad principles—like one approving detention—are by their nature difficult to limit to particular circumstances. They are, therefore, the enemies of constitutional pragmatism. And as enemies, such principles are not inert, but active. They influence justices in future cases. Through the work of precedent, said Jackson, the bad constitutional decision becomes an evil demiurge. It possesses "a generative power of its own, and all that it creates will be in its own image."[107] Jackson was recognizing that constitutional principles, though expressed by the judges who apply them, also have lives of their own.

Jackson, however, did not think that the right answer was for the Supreme Court to overturn the military orders. Looking back at the curfew decision, which he now regretted joining, Jackson predicted that most of the time courts would defer to military decision making, and so create bad constitutional doctrine. That led to a serious problem: How should the Court decide Korematsu's case? To uphold the military order would distort constitutional law; to strike it down would inappropriately second-guess military authority.

Jackson's answer to this legal puzzle was irregular, to say the least. Jackson proposed that the Court overturn Korematsu's criminal conviction. But at the same time, Jackson thought, the Court should not order the military to release the internees. Korematsu and the others would remain in military custody in their camps.[108] Jackson was saying that Congress lacked the constitutional authority to criminalize violation of the military order. But he was also saying that the Court lacked the authority to order the release of persons detained by the military pursuant to that order. When it came to war, the laws passed by Congress were to remain silent, without effect. Yet the Court was to remain silent about whatever measures the executive took in pursuance of that war. Outside the bounds of Jackson's pragmatic constitutional philosophy, his position would have been incoherent. But for him, the only relevant question was whether it would enable the effective functioning of the government.

Until he read a draft of Jackson's dissent, Frankfurter had intended to remain silent in the Japanese-American internment cases. No other justice combined, as he did, a general preference for judicial restraint with overwhelming support of the Roosevelt administration's wartime actions, not to mention ongoing contact with the War Department. His lengthy soliloquy to the other justices in the saboteurs' case, in which he was prepared to subordinate individual rights to the war effort, seems to have remained his position when it came to the Japanese-Americans. Given that his own aged uncle had been detained by the Nazis, Frankfurter's position with respect to the Japanese-American internees looks especially shameful.

What bothered Frankfurter about Jackson's dissent was that it condemned the internment as unconstitutional while nevertheless opining that the Court was powerless to block it. Frankfurter was not the kind of judge whose personality gave him room for a gnawing conscience. To the contrary, Frankfurter was both blessed and cursed with the absolute certainty that he was right on every occasion and that everybody else was missing the point. He decided to write a separate concurrence taking on Jackson's subtle dissent and demonstrating why it made no sense. His goal was to state clearly that the internment was constitutional, just like the curfew order had been the year before.

The core of Frankfurter's argument was that, unlike Jackson, he believed the Constitution did not break down in time of war. The Constitution applied. Through the vehicle of judicial restraint, it gave the military a scope of authority that it would never have in peacetime. The internment program, Frankfurter wrote, "is not to be stigmatized as lawless because like action in times of peace would be lawless."[109] To suggest otherwise would be to raise the dangerous prospect of treating the military as outside the reach of law: "Within their sphere, military authorities are no more outside the bounds of obedience to the Constitution than are judges within theirs."[110] It was therefore a mistake to call the internment orders "unconstitutional," as Jackson did. If the military had the power to issue them, then Congress had the power to make the violation of those orders into a crime. Any other interpretation "makes of the Constitution an instrument for dialectic subtleties."[111] To Frankfurter, the Constitution had to be an internally logical and consistent blueprint for government, or else it was not really law at all.

Whether one prefers Jackson's position here or Frankfurter's, the conflict is a useful litmus test for determining one's own constitutional philosophy. The great advantage of Jackson's pragmatism is its honesty about the overarching goal of judges who are interpreting the Constitution: to make the system work in a way that will have the best overall effects. The great appeal of Frankfurter's belief in judicial restraint and the rule of law is its commitment to principle and to ensuring the legitimacy of the courts. Both men would ultimately have allowed the internment, as of course did Black. Douglas believed, wrongly, that he had solved the problem using whatever judicial tools came to hand. For all four men, loyalty shaped their responses.

The scale of the Court's failure was noticed by some almost immediately. Barely six months after the Court issued its main decisions, Eugene Rostow, a law professor at Yale (later dean there and an important figure in the Johnson administration), published what is still the most important criticism of them. His essay was pointedly titled "The Japanese American Cases—A Disaster."[112]

In 1984, Fred Korematsu went back to federal court, seeking to have his conviction voided retroactively on the theory that the government had withheld crucial facts from the judiciary. The court agreed with him. The Department of Justice and the Army, it found, had distorted the record to make it appear that there was a legitimate security concern.[113] A few years later, Congress granted reparations of twenty thousand dollars to each Japanese-American who had been interned.

Neither of these efforts unsettled the Supreme Court's decision, which remains on the books to this day. If there was to be any redemption for the Court's mistaken judgment, it would have to come a decade later in *Brown v. Board of Education*, when the Supreme Court would consider the intentional racial discrimination of segregation—and repudiate it.

Book Six

BETRAYALS

CHAPTER 27

Succession

Franklin Delano Roosevelt towered over American political life as no president had before and no president ever will again. By 1944, however, he was failing, and those closest to him knew it. At one of Roosevelt's White House stag dinners that summer, Robert Jackson observed that the president seemed not to remember that he was no longer attorney general but had been put on the Supreme Court three years earlier.[1]

Nevertheless, Roosevelt's decision to run for a fourth term came even more easily than the one to run for a third. The traditional precedent of two terms had already been broken. This time the United States was actually at war. And there could be no doubt that this would be his last term.

The barely suppressed question of Roosevelt's health made the selection of the vice presidential candidate in 1944 into one of the most significant decisions of Roosevelt's presidency. As the choice of Henry Wallace in 1940 indicates, the degree of attention paid to such decisions, and the scrutiny attached to them both publicly and privately, does not come near the focus on the vice presidency that is common today. Vetting was minimal, or else a nearly open scandal like Wallace's letters to his guru could not have escaped notice. Roosevelt, who had dumped John Nance Garner in favor of Wallace, had no qualms about changing horses so long as it was not in the middle of a presidential race.

There was no question that Wallace would be replaced in 1944. Wallace, well to Roosevelt's left, had the support of labor. But he had clashed with other administration figures, and the president had relieved him of his war-related responsibilities. Roosevelt was sure Wallace would cost him votes among moderates. He considered Jimmy Byrnes, the Supreme Court justice who, with Frankfurter's support, had been made "assistant president" in charge of war mobilization. But Byrnes had converted from Catholicism to Protestantism and came from segregated South Carolina, both of which made him too risky as a national candidate.[2]

Whom Roosevelt should choose raised something of a quandary. He hoped for someone he knew well and who could be trusted to continue his work. But few prominent New Dealers who had been with Roosevelt from the beginning remained close enough to the president to make them viable. Roosevelt cycled through advisers (a trait not uncommon among presidents), and his administration had lasted so long that he had now run through everyone who was anyone in Washington. If the vice presidential candidate was not going to be a New Dealer, then more conservative political forces within the Democratic Party would unquestionably have a great influence over the selection.

Under these circumstances, two men emerged as leading internal candidates for the vice presidency in 1944. The candidate of the New Dealers—and the personal preference of Roosevelt himself—was Douglas, who had been a regular poker-playing companion of the president since joining the Supreme Court. Roosevelt "liked Bill's toughness"[3] and had considered him for various war posts. But he had not worked closely enough with him for their relationship to sour. Four years earlier, while already a justice, Douglas had been within striking distance for the vice presidency. Now forty-five, Douglas had added four years of Supreme Court service to his stint at the Securities and Exchange Commission.

If Douglas was not a household name, the other candidate was no more prominent. An unremarkable second-term Democratic senator from Missouri, he had begun to establish a national reputation for himself by chairing a committee to investigate war preparedness. Yet he was still identified with the Tom Pendergast political machine that had first put him in office. His name was Harry S. Truman.

Douglas's unofficial campaign manager was again Tommy

Corcoran. Corcoran was no longer Roosevelt's leading operative, as he had been during the New Deal years. Gone were the days when he would sneak into Missy LeHand's office by a secret White House staircase and give her daily political updates for the president.[4] He had not worked in the administration since 1941, when LeHand at the age of just forty-one had suffered a stroke that left her unable to work. Yet in the intervening three years, Corcoran had managed to create a powerful role for himself on the outside, functioning on behalf of private clients as one of the first modern lobbyists. Corcoran had played a central role in placing personnel all over the administration, and everybody owed him.

Notwithstanding his professional success lobbying the third Roosevelt administration, Corcoran wanted badly to be back in the executive branch. His reputation as an operator rather than a statesman had blocked him from a senior government position, and it rankled him to think that his political machinations had overshadowed his impressive intellectual abilities. Frustration that he could not apply his extraordinary placement skills to himself had led to a complete break with Frankfurter, his professor and mentor.

The fundamental cause of the quarrel had to do with Irish neutrality in World War II. Centuries of subjection to English rule had made Ireland anti-English, and there was little chance that Ireland would support the Allies. Corcoran acknowledged that he himself was "too Irish to trust the English."[5] Frankfurter, deeply committed to the war cause and an Anglophile to boot, asked Corcoran to encourage the leaders of the Irish-American community to pressure Ireland away from neutrality. Corcoran was understandably unsuccessful. When Corcoran came to Frankfurter's chambers to tell him, Frankfurter charged him with "half-heartedness." Then Frankfurter told his protégé that he was "behaving like Synge's *Playboy of the Western World* and murdering his father." The reference to the famous Irish play was factually inaccurate—the title character actually fails to kill his father, despite trying. Psychologically, though, it was precise. Frankfurter took Corcoran's war ambivalence as a personal repudiation.[6]

Corcoran considered Frankfurter's accusations absurd. But Marion Frankfurter, who had never much liked Corcoran, felt as her husband did. The childless Frankfurters had two English children living with them for the duration of the war. When Corcoran, in a conciliatory mood, came over to their house expecting to play the accordion and sing his usually popular Irish ballads, Marion became enraged—to her, even the songs had been tainted by Ireland's refusal to enter the war.[7]

The climax of the tension between Frankfurter and Corcoran had come when Corcoran was lobbying to become solicitor general, a job he badly wanted and that Frankfurter had once turned down. In an astonishing show of his ability to call in a favor, Corcoran cajoled four sitting justices—Black, Douglas, Stanley Reed, and Jimmy Byrnes—to write personal letters recommending him to Roosevelt for the job of arguing the president's cases before them. All these men owed Corcoran their appointments to the Court.

Corcoran had done much to help Frankfurter get there, too. But when Corcoran went to see Frankfurter for his help, Frankfurter rebuffed him—nor would he provide an explanation. Now it was Corcoran's turn to explode. He wagged his finger at Frankfurter and told him, "I put you here, now produce."[8]

Generally Frankfurter's mentorship lasted a lifetime. But in this case, after the confrontational meeting, Frankfurter actively went to work to block Corcoran. He told Roosevelt's assistant in charge of the appointment that Corcoran, though smart enough, was too politically minded and too controversial for the post. The message made it through to Roosevelt. Corcoran never got the job, or any other in the administration. Corcoran, naturally, knew what Frankfurter had done.[9]

As an erstwhile New Dealer who was now at war with Frankfurter, Corcoran had multiple reasons to back Douglas for the vice presidency. The tensions between Frankfurter and Douglas had been rising steadily for the previous four years. Frankfurter was outraged that Douglas was treating the Supreme Court as a jumping-off point for presidential politics rather than a forum of principle. In a letter to his friend Judge Learned Hand, he would later call Douglas "the most cynical, shamelessly amoral character I've ever known."[10]

Douglas, for his part, was convinced that Frankfurter was selling out liberalism and destroying the Bill of Rights by making its demands into "counsels of moderation," not binding laws. And Douglas's feelings extended beyond the professional to the personal. Despite, or perhaps because of his academic background, Douglas found Frankfurter's pedantic conversational style unbearable, and resented his condescension even more than did the other justices. Douglas quipped that Frankfurter's speeches to the conference were exactly fifty minutes long—the duration of a class at Harvard Law School. He thought that Frankfurter "was utterly dishonest intellectually, that he was very, very devious. . . . He spent his time going up and down the halls putting poison into everybody's spring, trying to set one Justice against another."[11]

Always attuned to the subtleties of interpersonal dynamics, Corcoran understood that supporting Douglas for the vice presidency was, among other things, a way to drive Frankfurter mad. More important, with his excellent political sense, Corcoran saw that if the aspirations of the New Deal were to be kept alive after Roosevelt was gone, Douglas had to become the liberal standard-bearer. Harold Ickes, also a New Dealer, nursed dreams of the vice presidency; he would eventually write Roosevelt a nearly delusional letter proposing himself for the job. But Ickes lacked the necessary charisma. Douglas was a Westerner, unquestionably brilliant, and devoted to achieving outcomes consistent with the New Deal philosophy he advocated at the SEC.

As it had so often in the past, Corcoran's way of thinking matched that of Roosevelt. In July 1944, Roosevelt sat down with the senior power brokers of the Democratic Party in what was then called the Oval Room of the White House to discuss vice presidential candidates. On his own Roosevelt brought up Douglas, who, he said, had the support "of the liberal left wing of the American people." Douglas, the president explained, was a Westerner who would have "appeal at the polls" and "played an interesting game of poker."[12]

The party bosses made it clear that they preferred Truman, who came from their world and whom they could expect to influence. Roosevelt seemed inclined to agree—one of his favorite operational gambits. "Douglas would have the greater public appeal," he said, but Truman "would make you boys happy, and you are the ones I am counting on to win this election."[13] As the men left, however, Roosevelt gave a handwritten note to Robert Hannegan, the Democratic National Committee chairman. In the note, Roosevelt wrote that he would be very glad to run with either Douglas or Truman.

No one in politics was closer to Truman than was Hannegan, the St. Louis, Missouri, machine politician who had helped Truman get reelected in 1940 after the tax fraud conviction of his first patron, Tom Pendergast. Hannegan had become party chairman earlier in 1944 when Truman told Roosevelt that he did not want the job and recommended his friend. By giving the note to Hannegan, Roosevelt was making sure to leave the issue formally unresolved.

Hannegan took Roosevelt's note with him to the convention, where he gave it to his wife, Irma, for safekeeping. She carried it around in her purse, and at night it went under the mattress where they slept.[14] When the moment was right, Hannegan leaked the fact that Roosevelt had written a letter endorsing Truman—without saying that the same letter also mentioned Douglas. The letter that was finally given to the press appeared not in the original handwritten version but in a typed version. Roosevelt's secretary later said that the original note listed Douglas before Truman, but that Hannegan told her to reverse the names in the typed version.[15] "I don't know why none of us asked to see the original note," Douglas supporter Eliot Janeway lamented. "We just didn't. You have to understand it wouldn't look good for us to be challenging the Democratic Party Chairman at the Convention on behalf of a Supreme Court Justice."[16]

In light of today's political norms, it may seem surprising that Roosevelt did not explicitly choose one of the two men. In the context of party politics as they were at the time, Roosevelt probably felt he could not force the urban political machines to accept his choice. The election could not be won without them, especially not by an infirm president who, citing wartime as his excuse, intended not to go on the campaign trail at all. By withholding an express endorsement of either man, Roosevelt was allowing the political process to run its course. Perhaps he believed that if the party bosses were powerful enough to get Truman nominated, that would be a sign that Douglas was not actually going to be an effective national candidate.

As it turned out, Corcoran's best efforts on Douglas's behalf were insufficient. The Democratic National Convention in 1944 took place in Chicago. Douglas, eager not to be seen as campaigning for a job he might not get, retreated to Washington State. Truman, by contrast, arrived in town six days early and went to work meeting left-leaning party figures whose support he would need, like Sidney Hillman, a founder of the powerful Congress of Industrial Organizations labor union, and Philip Murray, the CIO president. "I saw every political leader and labor leader," Truman later recalled.[17] The conceit of Truman's meetings was that he was supporting Jimmy Byrnes, the South Carolinian who had served as Roosevelt's "assistant president" in charge of war mobilization. The labor leaders told Truman that they had no use for Byrnes. They supported Henry Wallace, but if Wallace was not possible, they would support Truman. Since Roosevelt had already decided to dump Wallace, this was an endorsement of Truman.[18]

By the time Hannegan released his version of Roosevelt's letter, Truman had become the leading candidate. The tactics associated with the note were much less important than the underlying power dynamics between a Washington insider like Corcoran and the party bosses at the national level. Corcoran and his associates made last-ditch efforts to block Truman from being chosen too quickly, in the hopes that in a stalemate situation Douglas would have prevailed. "You were 20 minutes from being nominated," Eliot Janeway wrote to Douglas after it was all over.[19]

Yet when it came to a presidential election, Corcoran's specialized connections could not match up to the bosses' clout in delivering votes. In the absence of a direct demand from Roosevelt, the party leaders were free to choose Truman. Roosevelt "would have preferred Douglas," his confidant Harry Hopkins later wrote. "But nobody really influential was pushing for Douglas.... And Bob Hannegan was certainly pushing for Harry Truman."[20] Roosevelt had signaled the bosses that he was willing to live with their choice.

Truman maintained the fiction that he was not a candidate until the day Roosevelt was nominated. Hannegan, Truman's closest associate, then stage-managed a meeting in a large suite on the fifth floor of the luxurious Blackstone Hotel on Michigan Avenue. "The room was crowded," as Truman later told it. "Every damn political boss in the country was there, any of them you would want to name, and half a dozen governors." Hannegan put in a call to Roosevelt, who according to tradition was not at the convention when he was nominated. Over the phone, with his voice loud enough for those present to hear, Roosevelt told Hannegan that Truman had no choice but to take the job. "If he wants to break up the Democratic Party in the middle of the war and maybe lose that war it's up to him."[21] Hannegan had won, and Truman was the candidate for vice president.

To Douglas, coming so close to the vice presidency only to miss it again was deeply frustrating, but it was not a reason to give up on politics. To the contrary, it confirmed his belief that he was a national political figure, upholding the banner of the New Deal. It also gave him a permanently negative view of Truman, whom he thereafter saw as a rival.

Within the Court, Frankfurter and Jackson, who shared a dim view of Douglas, were relieved that their colleague had not attained high office. Jackson had nurtured presidential aspirations himself at one time and had his own independent reasons to be glad that Douglas had not outstripped him in the race for historical importance. But even for Douglas's enemies, there was a drawback to his defeat. The men would still have to serve together on the Court. For Jackson, the cost of that continued interaction would turn out to be almost unbearably high.

CHAPTER 28

The Death of Fathers

On April 12, 1945, less than three months into his fourth term, Roosevelt died in Warm Springs, Georgia. The business of the Court ground to a halt as the justices, like the rest of the nation, tried to absorb the shock. It had been understood that Roosevelt was not well. But no one, least of all the electorate, expected him to die quite so soon. Across the country, adults cried freely. It was difficult to imagine American public life without the man who had dominated it for twelve years.

All who knew Roosevelt found his death in the midst of the war overwhelming. Jackson was particularly affected. The next day, April 13, Jackson was asked to address the employees at the Department of Justice, where he still had many friends, and where Attorney General Francis Biddle recognized him as someone who had an especially close relationship to the president.

Jackson told the assembled employees, who packed the Great Hall, that Roosevelt had been "one of the most commanding figures of world history." But beyond the fact that he commanded a military force greater than any ever amassed before, "it was the moral forces and spiritual aspirations of mankind that he really typified, and they never were so passionately concentrated around a single person." Proceeding to the personal, Jackson spoke of the "innumerable little chits" that Roosevelt would write to all of those around him. "No father," said Jackson, "could be more solicitous of the personal and family welfare of those in his circle." By the time he got to the final paragraph of his speech, expressing gratitude that Roosevelt lived to see his country "on the threshold of victory," Jackson had broken down.[22]

When Roosevelt died, the tensions among his appointees to the Supreme Court were not yet a matter of public record. To be sure, careful Court watchers who read all the opinions knew that divisions were emerging. Merlo Pusey, the biographer of Charles Evans Hughes, could say in 1944 that the Court was engaged in "a sort of free-for-all battle of judicial intellects."[23] Yet the battle lines were far from clear. Frankfurter had been on the losing end of the flag-salute case, with Jackson writing the stirring opinion flatly rejecting the Court's earlier approach as expressed by Frankfurter. Meanwhile, Jackson had dissented in the Japanese-American internment case, while Frankfurter and Douglas had joined Black's opinion. The opinions of the Court had supported the Roosevelt administration when it came to the all-important questions of loyalty that lay at the center of wartime jurisprudence. The fact that Frankfurter and Jackson were forming a friendship based in no small part on their horror at the positions adopted by Black and Douglas was not visible to the general public.

All that was about to change. With the man who had chosen them gone, Roosevelt's justices were poised to splinter in full public view. The catalyst, though, was not an issue of great constitutional moment. It began with a dispute about wages. Should the men who mined bituminous coal be paid for the time it took them to travel up and down the thousands of feet to where the mining took place? The issue had become one of several in lengthy negotiations between the miners' union and the coal companies. When the federal government seized the mines as crucial to wartime production, the negotiations continued, now conducted between the union and the government.

The Supreme Court had taken up the problem on March 9, 1945, in the form of a lawsuit between the Jewell Ridge Coal Corporation and a local of the United Mine Workers of America. The next day in conference, the justices split 5 to 4. Black, Douglas, Murphy, and Rutledge sided with the miners. They reasoned that the travel time must be considered "work" under the Fair Labor

Standards Act, since travel down into the mine was tortuous and risky. If it counted as work, travel time should be paid.

The other five justices, including Jackson and Frankfurter, went with the coal companies. They pointed out that in years of negotiations between the coal mining industry and the miners, travel time had never been defined as work. They emphasized that the Fair Labor Standards Act was not, according to its drafters, intended to change any element of existing labor agreements. In support of that interpretation of the act, they could point to a 1937 debate on the floor of the Senate in which Hugo Black, a sponsor of the bill, several times stated explicitly that the law would not disturb agreements already reached between the unions and management. Chief Justice Stone decided that Jackson would write the opinion for the Court.

Two days later, though, on March 12, Stanley Reed, who was from Kentucky, a center of coal mining, changed his mind. The decision would still be 5 to 4, but now the Court would decide in favor of paying the miners for their travel time. Black was the most senior justice voting that way, which by tradition gave him the ability to assign the opinion. Black asked Frank Murphy to write it. Murphy was a natural choice. As a Michigan Democrat, he had always been reliably pro-union. The previous year, he had written the opinion for the Court in a similar case in the context of iron mining.[24] Now Jackson's draft opinion for the Court would become a dissent.

To this point, the case seemed to have nothing especially unusual about it, apart perhaps from the way that Black's vote as a justice seemed to be different from what he had promised as a senator. (Black, though, had also voted to treat travel time as work the previous year in the iron mines case.) The trouble started in behind-the-scenes squabbling about the timing of the opinion. Murphy came under pressure—from whom it is not clear—to write and release the opinion almost immediately, on the next day that the Court had scheduled to announce decisions. Murphy circulated a draft to the other justices on April 5. At the same time, he sent a note to Jackson saying that some justices had been talking about "forcing" him to get the opinion out the door. Nevertheless, Murphy said, Jackson should take his time with the dissent. Jackson replied equably enough that even if the opinion were released quickly, he could still file a dissent later. On April 11, before the opinion was handed down, the War Labor Policies Board approved a settlement between the government and the unions with regard to the bituminous coal industry.

In the distraction surrounding Roosevelt's death on April 12, the timing of the opinion in the Jewell Ridge coal mining case was momentarily forgotten. The opinion was announced, with Jackson's dissent attached, on May 7. Joined by Stone, Frankfurter, and Roberts, the dissent was pointed, but not out of the ordinary. Only the last two sentences reached for rhetorical force: "We doubt if one can find in the long line of criticized cases," Jackson wrote, "one in which the Court has made a more extreme exertion of power or one less supported or explained by either the statute or the record in the case. Power should answer to reason nonetheless because its fiat is beyond appeal."[25] Jackson was accusing the majority of acting without good legal reasons; and he was hinting, by his mention of fiat, that something else lay behind the decision in the case.

The game was not over. The mine owners who had lost the case decided to file a petition for rehearing. They had an unusual argument up their sleeves: They claimed that Justice Black should have recused himself from the case because it had been argued for the union by his former law partner, Crampton Harris.

The mine owners' lawyers were not expecting to win the case when they filed the petition. Such petitions are routinely denied.[26] What was more, even if Black had recused himself, the result would have been the same. The Court of Appeals had held in favor of the mine workers. Under the Supreme Court's rules, a divided Court cannot overturn a lower court decision. Without Black's vote, the split among the justices would have been 4 to 4, and so the appellate court's decision for the miners would still have been affirmed, albeit without creating a definitive precedent. It is conceivable that the mine owners filed the petition for the sole reason of embarrassing Justice Black. As it turned out, they succeeded, better than they could have anticipated.

According to Supreme Court rules, then as now, it is up to each individual justice to decide whether to recuse himself and whether to give any explanation for his decision. Ordinarily, the justices remain silent on such questions. Faced with the demand that he recuse himself because of the role of his former law partner, Black did what justices normally do. He simply voted to reject the petition for rehearing.[27]

Black's decision was, on the surface, straightforward. He and Harris had not been partners for twenty years. Their public legal affiliation since then was limited to one case. In 1936, Harris had represented Black when William Randolph Hearst had sued him regarding his ostensibly private telegrams to his newspaper employees. Yet the relationship between Harris and Black was also much closer than was publicly understood. Faced with the revelation of his Ku Klux Klan membership, Black had turned to Harris for advice and counsel, bringing him to Washington to weather the crisis. More than just former partners, Harris and Black were personal friends.[28]

It is not clear whether any of the other justices understood the depth of the relationship between Black and Harris. What is certain is that Jackson reacted badly to Black's decision not to recuse himself. The impetus seems to have been Murphy's note to Jackson indicating that he felt pressured to release the decision quickly. With the allegation of Black's closeness to Crampton Harris now before the Court, Jackson decided that it must have been Black who had earlier pressured Murphy. Black, Jackson now came to believe, had been trying to rush the decision in the case in order to help his friend and former partner who was representing the cause of labor.

Jackson's resentment of Black had been building for some time. The previous summer, Fred Rodell, a Yale law professor and Douglas's former student and friend, had published a laudatory magazine article about Black. Black, he argued, was "the ablest judge and the most brilliant legal mind among" the justices. Rodell was getting this from Douglas, who was happy to praise Black's legal acumen because he himself was focused on his political prospects, not his judicial legacy.

Still relying on his inside source, Rodell wrote that three of the sitting justices—Owen Roberts, Felix Frankfurter, and Robert Jackson—"fail to recognize" Black's preeminence. Jackson was singled out for his "dwindling hope of being named Chief Justice, an honor he once missed by a hair." According to Rodell, Jackson refused to acknowledge Black's leadership because "he is smart enough to see in Black the biggest threat to his ambition."[29] The implication was that Black's brilliance might some day make him chief, and that Jackson was jealous since he wanted the job.

Rodell's interpretation of Jackson's attitude toward Black was surely wrong. Jackson was sophisticated enough to understand that the scandal of Black's Klan membership precluded him from becoming chief justice. But Jackson's ego smarted at Rodell's elevation of Black to a position of preeminence on the Court. He considered it no coincidence that a close associate of Douglas was writing about him in this dismissive way.[30] Jackson's ambition to be chief justice was undimmed, and any negative press could only hurt his prospects.

The petition for rehearing in the coal mining case gave Jackson an opportunity to express his hostility toward Black. He could not comment directly on his suspicions about the pressure on Murphy, or even on the recusal decision itself. What he could do, however, with a lawyer's indirection, was to publish a separate statement on the general topic of recusal. The Court would issue a standard order denying the coal companies' request for rehearing. Alongside that order, Jackson would state that the decision whether to recuse was entirely up to the individual justice.

On its face, such a statement would be entirely banal—a description of a rule of Supreme Court procedure. But timing was everything. By saying that it was not up to the other justices to decide whether Black would recuse himself, Jackson would be implying that Black should have done so. To careful listeners, Jackson would be registering his implicit public disapproval of Black. And Jackson would not have to issue this unusual statement alone. After a discussion in conference, Frankfurter decided to join him.

Whether Jackson fully appreciated it or not, he was proposing to wound Black in the most sensitive spot possible: his honor. Black could take almost any sort of criticism. He had maintained his public equanimity even in the face of the press onslaught connected to the Klan revelations. But as a Southerner and a gentleman, his honor was another matter. Honor had made him leave his high school at sixteen, and would remain for him the dominating force in his inner life. Whatever disagreements with Jackson he might have had previously, Black now had a grievance that could not be passed over until revenged.

Frankfurter sensed the delicacy of Black's feelings, and in characteristic fashion decided to confront the issue directly. He was now firmly allied with Jackson and against Black and Douglas, and would not abandon Jackson. Yet he wanted to avoid being swept up in the battle that was now brewing between Black and Jackson.

On June 9, just a few hours before the justices were to meet in conference, Frankfurter sent Black a memorandum laying out in six numbered points why he was joining Jackson's statement about recusal. The thrust of his explanation was that it was objectively true that the decision to recuse belonged to individual justices, and that failure to join Jackson "would impliedly be denying the truth of what he stated." As an account of Frankfurter's actions, this was pretty weak stuff, and Frankfurter must have known it. But he added a further sentence that revealed the point of the whole exercise: "I had no share in creating the situation whereby Bob felt it should be his duty to make clear the issue of qualification," he wrote. Frankfurter was telling Black that he did not share Jackson's anger over the timing of the coal-mining opinion. Though joining Jackson's statement, Frankfurter was trying to distance himself from impugning Black's honor. To underscore the point, Frankfurter sent a copy of his note to all the members of the Court.

Frankfurter's ploy of circulating a last-minute memo allowed the justices to delay the issue for another week. But the conference on June 16 turned into an outright disaster. Chief Justice Stone had proposed a compromise in the form of a statement that could be issued by the full Court, without signatures, explaining that motions for disqualification were never considered by the full Court. But Black rejected the compromise. Any statement that even mentioned the subject of disqualification, he insisted, "would be a declaration of war."

Stone, taken aback by this extreme threat, withdrew his proposal. But Jackson insisted that he would not be intimidated. His statement would be published on Monday as planned. One writer later called this "the greatest fight in the nation's highest and most secret judicial conference room."[31] It was certainly an extreme case of private judicial confrontation. As far as Black was concerned, Jackson had been warned. Jackson, overcome with contempt for Black, decided to call his bluff. He seems not to have thought through what it would mean to have Black as an enemy and a declaration of war in force between them.

Jackson knew that Black was not a man who either forgot or forgave. In Black's first term on the Court, Harlan Fiske Stone had told the journalist Marquis Childs that Black was doing a bad job as justice. Black said nothing at the time. But when Chief Justice Hughes had died, Black had suspected (correctly) that with war in the offing, Roosevelt would want to appoint a Republican in a bipartisan gesture. That made Stone a serious candidate. Black and Douglas had gone to Owen Roberts and told him that they would support him for the position—even though their views were much closer to those of Stone. Jackson, who cared very much about who became chief justice, knew the story, and thought that Black had turned to Roberts in the hopes of blocking Stone's appointment.[32]

And even as the Supreme Court term was ending in June 1945, another example of Black's quiet vengeance was playing itself out. This time the target was Owen Roberts, once Black's closest friend on the Court. The year before, the two men had experienced a terrible falling out, in which Frankfurter had played a role.

The breakdown followed a broadcast by the Washington columnist and radio personality Drew Pearson on a Sunday in January 1944, in which Pearson purported to tell his listeners what the votes would be the next day in a particular decision.[33] The next morning Roberts arrived at the Court highly perturbed that someone seemed to be leaking case results to the press. Roberts demanded that Stone call an unusual Monday morning conference to discuss the matter.

Wisely or not, Stone agreed, assembling the justices for a hurried meeting before they had to ascend the bench at noon. Roberts told the conference he suspected Douglas or Murphy of speaking to the press. Frankfurter backed him up, implying that in fact the suspicions had been his in the first place. Douglas and Murphy flatly denied that they had leaked. Roberts, who was "very, very, very worked up" according to Douglas, insisted the case not be handed down that day at noon, and that the justices reconvene in the afternoon to continue the discussion. Douglas left court while the session was still going, "got home and went to bed," and did not return for the meeting. Frankfurter and Roberts took this abdication as evidence that Douglas was the source of the leak.[34] Douglas did have a history of psychosomatic illness—though perhaps accusation alone, without guilt, would have been enough to make him sick.

Now furious to the point of distraction, Roberts went to see Black. Roberts wanted Black to take a stand against either Murphy or Douglas, Black's regular voting allies. Black responded that he was "positive" neither had spoken to the press, and that he had "implicit confidence" in both men. Roberts refused to take his word; and as a result, Black's honor had been impugned. Black never visited Roberts's country house again, nor is there any evidence that Roberts ever asked him. Roberts became so embittered that he would not even come into the robing room before the justices went on the bench for the traditional exchange of handshakes.[35]

Roberts's decision to retire in June 1945 was the direct result of his alienation; and Black had not forgotten the incident, either. His revenge was deadly and difficult to trace. When Roberts announced his retirement, Chief Justice Stone circulated to the other justices the text of a formal letter of appreciation. Black refused to sign it. He had two objections. First, Black demanded that Stone take out a sentence regretting that Roberts would no longer be working with the other justices on a daily basis. Black said it would be hypocritical to express regret when he felt none.

More devastatingly, Black objected to a line in the letter to Roberts that said, "You have made fidelity to principle your guide to decision." Here Black was being particularly nasty: Roberts, the justices all knew, would be remembered forever for his famous switch in time—which some considered the least principled act in the Court's history. By telling the other justices that he would not say that Roberts was faithful to principle, Black was reminding everyone of the weakest point of a weak man. Ultimately, because of Black's intransigence, Stone sent no letter at all on behalf of the Court.

In the midst of the controversy over the letter to Roberts, Jackson should have weighed the risks of impugning Black's honor—but he did not. On June 18, 1945, the Supreme Court term ended. Roberts's resignation took effect, without any formal acknowledgment by the Court. That day, instead of going on to the bench at noon, as was customary, the justices convened at 10:30 so that they could then go across the street to attend a special joint session of Congress welcoming General Dwight D. Eisenhower back from Europe in triumph. Jackson's statement that recusal was up to the individual justice was issued alongside the Court's denial of rehearing in the coal-mining case.

It was to be Jackson's last official utterance on the Supreme Court for more than a year. That afternoon, Jackson got on a plane and flew to Europe. He had been appointed as chief prosecutor for the war crimes trials that were soon to commence at Nuremberg.

With Jackson went sixteen lawyers and secretaries. One was Jackson's son, William Jackson. A twenty-six-year-old ensign in the U.S. Naval Reserve, Bill had been graduated from Harvard Law School the previous year and appointed to his father's staff in May.[36] Another was Jackson's personal secretary at the Supreme Court, an attractive, forty-four-year-old divorcée named Mrs. Elsie L. Douglas. When Jackson was asked to travel to wartorn Europe to prosecute Nazis, she was the first person he asked to go with him. She agreed on the spot—without thinking about it or discussing it with her family. This was her first trip on an airplane.[37]

CHAPTER 29

Justice at Nuremberg

R obert Jackson's decision to take an unprecedented leave of absence from the Supreme Court in order to serve as the chief prosecutor of the Nuremberg Tribunal was the act of a man who did not want to lose the chance of a permanent place in history. The official request came from Truman in late April 1945, during the first few weeks of his presidency. Jackson accepted almost immediately. Taking the job, he later said, relieved "the sense of frustration at being in a back eddy with important things going on in the world."[38] Unhappy with his relations with the other justices, Jackson saw the appointment as a potential exit: "I wasn't at all sure that if I took it on I ever would return to the Court."[39]

Planning for some sort of war crimes trial had been going on in the War Department for months. Jackson had not been privy to the details, but he seems to have gotten wind of the idea. On April 13, the day after Roosevelt died, the same day as his tearful address at the Department of Justice, Jackson had given a lecture to the American Society of International Law. In it he had told the members of the leading organization of international lawyers that there were two options for the Nazi leaders: either summary execution under military and political authority, or else what he called a "good faith" judicial trial before "an independent body above obligation to any nation or interest."[40] The former option was not one his audience of lawyers would have found attractive; Jackson was floating an argument in favor of the latter.

Jackson's speech was too directly focused on the war crimes issue to be a coincidence, and it suggested he hoped to position himself to serve in some capacity on the new tribunal. As Jackson knew from his experience with the court-packing plan, giving a prominent speech on a topic of importance was a good way to get the president's attention. The approach to Jackson came through Sam Rosenman, one of Roosevelt's closest aides. Rosenman had been the White House point man on the war crimes issue and, just weeks after Roosevelt's death, remained as an aide to Truman.

Jackson agreed to take the job of chief prosecutor at Nuremberg, presenting the Allies' case to the world, recounting the Nazis' crimes, and in essence offering an after-the-fact justification for the war itself. Blocked in his own career, Jackson no doubt remembered that his first big break had come in a similar prosecutorial role, taking on Andrew Mellon in court and on the front page of the nation's newspapers. The Nuremberg prosecutor would have an even larger, global stage on which to act.

The propriety of assuming such an important position while sitting as a justice of the Supreme Court got short shrift from Jackson and Truman alike. Truman told Jackson that in his opinion, the justice would not have to resign his seat to take the job—and that if he felt he did need to step down, he should turn down the Nuremberg post, because it would not be worth it. For his own part, Jackson claimed to have believed that he could get the whole thing over with by October when the Supreme Court's term started again. Despite the potential consequences to the work of the Supreme Court if he were late, Jackson made his decision unilaterally. Exercising the prerogative of the life-tenured justice answerable to no one, Jackson did not raise the issue with his colleagues or Chief Justice Stone.

Jackson anticipated that Stone would disapprove—and he was right to think so. The Court might lose one-ninth of its workforce for an unknown duration. There was also the risk of future recusals from cases connected to the war. Jackson later admitted that "the difficulty with a judge of the Supreme Court getting into any of these things is that with the backwash of war there are pretty certain to be war problems that come before it. A judge's activities are apt to impair his reputation for impartiality, and perhaps his mental attitude of impartiality."[41] This proved to be an understatement.

When the time came, Jackson did not recuse himself from all of the important postwar cases that implicated his service at Nuremberg. The irony surely was not lost on Black, who had been chided by Jackson for his failure to recuse himself.

Stone's objections to Jackson's Nuremberg service went beyond his concerns about future conflicts of interest for Jackson or his annoyance at not being consulted. Stone thought the whole Nuremberg trial was itself a mistake—an operation unworthy of being called an exercise in law. "I dislike extremely to see it dressed up with a false façade of legality," he wrote to a friend. "The best that can be said for it is that it is a political act of the victorious states which may be morally right."[42] The basic problem, in Stone's view, came from the fact that there was no clear, preexisting legal rule that the Germans had violated. According to Stone, Jackson and the team of Americans, Russians, French, and British lawyers who designed the tribunal were making up rules of law and holding the Germans responsible for them after the fact.

The Soviets had no objection to making up new rules to try the Nazis. To them, a show trial was a show trial, and there was no reason to pretend otherwise. In a private dinner given by Jackson at the outset of the proceedings for a visiting Soviet dignitary— himself a veteran prosecutor in Stalin's trials—the Soviet jurist proposed a toast: "To the German prisoners, may they all be hanged!" The judges of the tribunal had already raised their glasses to their lips when they realized with horror what had just been said.[43]

To Jackson, though, dealing with this problem posed the main challenge in setting up the tribunal in the first place. The concern Stone voiced—and that others have echoed since—focused on the specific criminal charge leveled against the Nazi leaders. Today Nuremberg is remembered, somewhat inaccurately, as a trial of Nazi leaders for the crimes of the Holocaust. But in fact, the prosecution team was wary of focusing its legal strategy on crimes against Jews. The scope of the Holocaust was still not fully understood; the name had not even been applied to the killing of the Jews during World War II. The prosecutors wanted to convict the Germans of crimes that affected all humanity, not just one minority.

Moreover, traditional principles of international law considered a country's treatment of its own citizens or subjects off-limits. As Jackson put it to the planning conference for the trials, "It has been a general principle of foreign policy of our Government from time immemorial that the internal affairs of another government are not ordinarily our business; that is to say, the way Germany treats its inhabitants...is not our affair any more than it is the affair of some other government to interpose itself on our problems."[44]

American self-interest underlay the worry about charging the Nazis with crimes against their own minorities. Jackson admitted as much to his tribunal colleagues: "We have some regrettable circumstances at times in our own country in which minorities are unfairly treated."[45] The system of formal, legal discrimination against African-Americans in the Southern United States was the most obvious example of what Jackson was talking about; and the internment of Japanese-Americans provided another instance that could not be ignored.

Confronted with the difficulty of charging the Nazi leaders directly with the crimes of the Holocaust, Jackson and his colleagues took a different tack. The core criminal charge at Nuremberg was that the Third Reich had violated international law by waging "aggressive war." Aggressive war—a concept that Jackson had begun to develop as Roosevelt's attorney general—was, in essence, war without justification. The crimes of the Holocaust were included in the indictment only insofar as they were defined as part of the broader crime of aggressive war. According to Jackson's theory, "the reason that this program of extermination of Jews and destruction of the rights of minorities becomes an international concern is this: it was part of a plan for making an illegal war."[46]

The idea that war itself was against the law of nations marked a radical departure from the history of international law. As Jackson later remembered it, the British participants in Nuremberg initially objected "to taking such broad ground as to the criminality of a war of aggression."[47] The mere initiation of aggressive war had never been considered criminal before. The British were worried that by trying the Nazis for a crime that was only now being defined, they might no longer really be engaged in a legal trial.

Stone, too, considered the charge of "aggressive war" to be outrageous from a lawyer's standpoint. If the United States had lost the war, he wondered, could "the victors...plausibly assert that supplying Britain with 50 destroyers was an act of aggression"?[48] Jackson, of course, was the attorney general who had authorized the destroyers deal on the ground that it did not violate U.S. neutrality—a point clearly not lost on Stone.

As the year progressed, Stone became increasingly acerbic on the topic of Jackson and the trials. In December he wrote to a friend, "Jackson is away conducting his high-grade lynching party in Nuremberg." Stone's idea of a lynching was that the prosecution under Jackson was in an important sense lawless: "I don't mind what he does to the Nazis, but I hate to see the pretense that he is running a court and proceeding according to common law. This is a little too sanctimonious a fraud to meet my old-fashioned ideas."[49]

Stone's concerns reflected the most fundamental challenges that Jackson and the United States faced in Nuremberg. How was it possible to offer a fair trial when the outcome was all but a foregone conclusion? And how could the model of legality emerge from an undertaking that seemed to violate the basic condition of law, namely that the defendants knew in advance that their actions were illegal?

Jackson had one chance to offer an answer to these concerns. As an experienced trial lawyer, he knew that there are only a few moments in a trial that truly offer the opportunity to grab the attention of the public. One of these is the opening statement, when the prosecuting attorney frames the issues of the case for the court and the broader public audience. The opening statement would be particularly important in Nuremberg, because the commencement of the trial was the one event guaranteed to generate headlines all over the world. On November 21, 1945, Jackson gave a three-hour address, the substance of which was widely reported. It represented Jackson's best effort to justify the tribunal and to explain its purpose to the world.

The essence of Jackson's argument was that civilization itself had been wronged by the crimes of Nazi Germany, and that recourse to law was the way for civilization to be restored to its rightful place. He remained silent on the topic of justice, managing to avoid the word almost completely. Instead, Jackson offered a characteristically pragmatic account of the Nuremberg tribunal's nature. While "novel and experimental," the tribunal "is not the product of abstract speculations nor is it created to vindicate legalistic theories. This inquest represents the practical effort ... to utilize international law to meet the greatest menace of our times—aggressive war." Law, in this image, was a tool for accomplishing pressing real-world needs.[50]

Jackson refused to acknowledge that law might not be well suited to righting wrongs committed by national leaders: "The common sense of mankind demands that law shall not stop with the punishment of petty crimes by little people." According to Jackson, law itself was on trial in Nuremberg. If law could not accomplish the tasks that Jackson was setting for it, it would be incapable of sustaining civilization. In Jackson's telling, the rule of law would be tarnished to an even greater degree if the Nazis were punished *without* reference to law.

How, precisely, was law supposed to restore civilization? Here Jackson turned back to the theory of aggressive war. Such war, he argued, was itself a violation of the norms of civilization. To initiate war was to break the most fundamental law possible. What the Nazis had done was to wage "aggressive war, which the nations of the world had renounced. It was war in violation of treaties, by which the peace of the world was sought to be safe-guarded." Law would restore civilization by outlawing war itself.

Jackson needed to prove that the tribunal was not applying what he called "an *ad hoc* rule brought into being for that trial only."[51] He decided to claim that aggressive war had in fact been outlawed during the 1920s, even if it had not exactly been noticed by all the relevant parties. Jackson began by conceding that "there was a time, in fact, I think the time of the first World War, when it could not have been said that war-inciting or war-making was a crime in law, however reprehensible in morals."[52] But, Jackson continued, the idea that war-making could be lawful "was intolerable for an age that called itself civilized. Plain people with their earthy common sense...demanded checks on war immunities."[53] Jackson offered no evidence for the suggestion that the call to regulate warfare came from the bottom up, from the "plain people." His reference to "earthy common sense" was vintage Jackson, a combination of folksiness and the idea that abstract principles could give way to the demands of practical necessity.

Jackson reminded his audience that even before World War I, the Hague conventions had sought to regulate techniques of warfare. The aftermath of the world war, he maintained, had demanded limits on the decision to go to war in the first place: "The common sense of men after the first World War demanded...that the law condemn not merely uncivilized ways of waging war, but also the waging in any way of uncivilized wars—wars of aggression. The world's statesmen again went only as far as they were forced to go. Their efforts were timid and cautious and often less explicit than we might have hoped. But the 1920's did outlaw aggressive war."[54]

A period of time—the 1920s—is not a legal person with the capacity to outlaw anything. Jackson was using this strange and indirect formulation because it was so difficult to point to any one treaty or agreement specifically outlawing aggressive war. Several grand-sounding declarations to that effect had been made by international conferences and assemblies, and Jackson dutifully quoted them. But he and his audience knew that nonbinding resolutions were not the same thing as a law.[55] Jackson was arguing that during the 1920s, a new rule of international law had come into force that made the waging of aggressive war into a criminal act. The mechanism for the birth of this rule was custom.

Custom could only become law if it was recognized as the general practice of states. Germany, however, had obviously not recognized this new legal norm. Jackson offered a succinct rebuttal to this problem. If Hitler and his regime had not realized that war was now illegal, so much the worse for them: "A failure of these Nazis to heed, or to understand the force and meaning of this evolution in the legal thought of the world, is not a defense or a mitigation. If anything, it aggravates their offense and makes it the more mandatory that the law they have flouted be vindicated by juridical application to their lawless conduct."[56]

As a legal argument, this claim was exceedingly weak. If so important a nation as Germany had failed to realize that a new rule of customary law was coming into effect, this was evidence that the custom was not general, and therefore should not be treated as law. As a pragmatic argument to justify the tribunal's undertaking, however, Jackson's argument made perfect sense. By holding the Nazi leaders liable for a crime that may not have been fully recognized before the war, the tribunal would definitively establish aggressive war as a crime for the future.

Even if the Nazis were being tried under new law, Jackson insisted, "I still do not shrink from demanding its strict application by this Tribunal."[57] Since it had cost the United States a million casualties to win the war and restore the rule of law, Jackson reasoned, it was worth the lives of the Nazis on trial to make this new law stick: "I cannot subscribe to the perverted reasoning that society may advance and strengthen the rule of law by the expenditure of morally innocent lives but that progress in the law may never be made at the price of morally guilty lives."[58]

Here Jackson's ultimate justification for the tribunal was laid bare. He would make the best legal arguments that he could in support of the illegality of aggressive war. But the bottom line was that the ends justified the means. Law would restore civilization. The Nazis, with their obvious moral guilt, were perfect candidates to be punished in vindication of the law.

What one thinks of Jackson's argument reveals one's underlying philosophy of law. If the law is a tool designed to achieve good and moral ends, then it would be strange to think that Jackson and the tribunal overreached. The Nazi leaders had committed the worst wrongs imaginable. If law could not address such acts, it really would seem like a triviality, not a valuable mechanism for improving the state of the world.

If on the other hand law is conceived as not simply a tool, but the human method for applying justice, then Jackson's approach will seem sadly inadequate. According to this view, the formal structures of law, including the guarantee that no one will be punished for an act he could not have known was criminal, are precisely what makes law an exercise in justice, not an arbitrary exercise of power. Measured by the yardstick of traditional due process, the Nuremberg tribunal fell short.[59]

Jackson's own position could not have been more clear. His view of international law was precisely congruent with his understanding of constitutional law: Both were pragmatic tools for balancing competing forces and achieving the ends of civilization. With his basic theory in place, it remained for Jackson to make the tribunal into a criminal trial—and to convict the defendants in the name of civilization.

Having opened in late November, the tribunal was soon poised to take a two-week Christmas break. In a letter to his wife, Irene, Jackson explained he would have preferred to work every day except Christmas.[60] He would not be coming home himself—but neither would he be staying in Nuremberg. "The time is too long to remain here in waiting and not time enough to get home & back safely. I can't take a chance on the long delays now caused by weather over the Atlantic." Instead, Jackson requisitioned an Army plane and pilot. With Elsie Douglas, his son, Bill, and a handful of other staff, Jackson set off for Rome, Cairo, the French Riviera—and, on Christmas Eve, Bethlehem.[61]

Before they left, the group had an enjoyable dinner in the Nuremberg house that Jackson shared with Elsie, Bill, and Jackson's bodyguard, Moritz Fuchs.[62] Elsie, Jackson wrote to his wife, had decorated the tree with "nuts and cookies tied up in paper napkins, cut outs of horseshoes, the moon, stars etc etc." As Christmas gifts, Elsie gave Jackson and Bill each a pair of pajamas.[63]

From the Nuremberg trial until Jackson's death and beyond, many of those in the Supreme Court's small group of insiders believed that Jackson and Elsie Douglas were not only close friends and professional associates but also lovers. Several other Americans brought their wives with them to Nuremberg, while Jackson, enforcing Army policy for himself and his staff, did not.[64] If Irene Jackson was disturbed by her husband and only son celebrating

Christmas and travelling the Mediterranean with Elsie Douglas, we have no record of it.

J. Edgar Hoover, who specialized in discovering other people's secrets, told the *Chicago Tribune*'s Washington Bureau chief, a regular dining partner, that Jackson had a long-term affair with Elsie.[65] Fuchs, Jackson's bodyguard, would claim almost half a century later that any intimation of "a romantic link" between Jackson and Elsie was "totally without foundation."[66] By then Fuchs had become a Catholic priest, an indication no doubt of his honesty but perhaps equally of his innocence.

Elsie Douglas worked closely beside Jackson throughout the trials. In photographs of Jackson speaking from the podium, she can be seen sitting beside him at the counsel's table, in a tailored military uniform, a neatly knotted khaki tie around her neck. Gazing at Jackson, she looks happy.

CHAPTER 30

The Final Solution

If law was to succeed in Nuremberg—and be seen as a success—Jackson had to convince the world that the defendants were guilty of crimes, not merely of being on the losing side of history. His first attempt to address this challenge came just before the Christmas break, when he was eager to give the trial "a shot in the arm" and "to give the correspondents something to write about."

Although he had planned to save it for later in the trial, Jackson decided to screen film taken of the concentration camps by the American troops who had liberated them. "These pictures showed the heaps of the dead," he recalled. The footage "showed bulldozers pushing great heaps of naked bodies into trenches.... It showed the incinerators in which the bodies had been burned."[67]

The effect of the film was powerful. "The evidence was so dramatic and so gruesome, so sickening, that when the court adjourned there was just silence all over the courthouse.... It seemed as though the picture itself smelled of death and the signs and smells lingered with you."[68] The film helped remind those in the courtroom of the Nazis' abominable crimes. After the tribunal reconvened, Jackson had to connect those deeds to the defendants. For this task, there was no getting around Hermann Goering.

Goering was in practice the highest-ranking Nazi on trial, the most important Nazi still living, and the most important defendant at Nuremberg.[69] As Reich marshal he had been Germany's top military figure. He was also the man whom Hitler himself had designated as his successor for the entire period of the war, changing his mind only in the last days of his life. In manner, too, Goering was far more impressive than the other defendants. His father had been a German imperial governor in Africa. As a boy he had been close with his godfather, a minor aristocrat of Jewish descent—so close, in fact, that the godfather was rumored to be his biological father as well. To the polish of social class, Goering added a heroic World War I record as a fighter pilot who ended the war with twenty-two kills and the coveted Pour le Mérite, Prussia's highest military honor.[70]

A close companion of Hitler's from 1922 onward, Goering had held various senior political posts under Hitler's chancellorship, and then gained fame through his command of the German air force. Given to excess—he wore fur coats and togas, and was often accompanied by a standard-bearer carrying his self-designed flag—Goering was nevertheless, by debased Nazi standards, a man of relative education and culture. He was neither a crude propagandist like Julius Streicher nor a purely military figure like Admiral Doenitz. In Hitler's absence, Goering was the closest thing possible to an embodiment of Nazi Germany. Success at Nuremberg required not only convicting Goering but also demonstrating his centrality to the crimes of the Third Reich.

Here, once again, Jackson saw a rare chance to enter the annals of history by examining Goering on his own—a decision not without risk. The unrepentant Goering considered the trial an opportunity to justify himself and the Nazi leadership by denying their crimes and impugning the legitimacy of the tribunal. Even before the trial began, Jackson recalled, "it was apparent to those who were watching the defendants closely" that Goering would use the trial for propaganda purposes. "If Hermann Goering didn't choose to upset the trials, nobody would. He was the most reckless, arrogant, resourceful defendant in the dock. During interrogations Goering had indicated great skill in dodging and answering questions with long Nazi sermons. He was a difficult man to handle."[71] By creating a tableau in which the chief prosecutor and the chief defendant would interact face-to-face, Jackson opened himself to the danger that he might get the worst of the exchange.

Jackson's strategy was based on the dubious assumption that

Goering—"a reckless, boastful fellow, given to boasting of his exploits with women and men"[72]—would incriminate himself. The Mellon trial gave Jackson a precedent to this effect. Though the former secretary of the treasury and baron of finance was nothing like Goering, and had been accused of tax fraud, not crimes against humanity, there were certain superficial similarities between the two situations. Mellon's defense was that he was doing nothing out of the ordinary and following all the relevant legal rules, no matter how lax they may have been. Goering, for his part, maintained he had done nothing to violate the laws of Germany or of ordinary warfare. Mellon, too, had been enormously powerful, accustomed to de facto immunity from criticism. Letting him speak was the best way to draw him into damning admissions. He was not used to thinking defensively, and more important, his goal was to vindicate himself before the public, not to avoid the technical admission of a crime. Goering was a megalomaniac who had answered to no one but Hitler; and his objectives were political, not legal.

But as Jackson may not fully have realized, the goals of the prosecution were also quite different in the two cases. In the Mellon case, the only objective was to have enough material to obtain a favorable legal verdict. Any finding against Mellon would suffice to avoid the embarrassment to the Roosevelt administration that had arisen from the decision to bring the case in the first place. Jackson had not initiated the action against Mellon, and all he needed for his own success was to save face for Roosevelt.

With Goering, by contrast, a technically legitimate conviction was guaranteed based on the documentary evidence.[73] What Jackson needed from his exchange with Goering was a public relations coup, an opportunity to show the world that Goering was a monster and that the trial was justified. For these purposes, using the same tactic that he had used as a government trial attorney a decade before was a serious mistake. As one British judge noted to himself, "No one appears to have been quite prepared for [Goering's] immense ability and knowledge, and his thorough mastery and understanding of the captured documents" that Jackson sought to use against him.[74]

Jackson began his cross-examination by trying to draw Goering into general statements about his Nazi ideology; to "start by flattering him and induce him to display his Nazi attitudes as much as possible, instead of humiliating him."[75] Goering responded to Jackson's open-ended questions by starting to speechify. Jackson, in turn, directed Goering simply to answer his questions.

At this point, the cross-examination took a fateful turn. Francis Biddle, the American judge on the tribunal, whispered something to the British judge, Lord Justice Geoffrey Lawrence. From the bench, Lord Lawrence then instructed Jackson that Goering should be allowed to say whatever he wished in answering the question. Jackson was furious at Lawrence's intervention. He was more furious still that Biddle had apparently pressed for the ruling from the bench. "I thought he of all people," Jackson put it later, "ought to know the danger of the trial getting out of hand by permitting speechmaking from the stand by the defendant."[76]

Biddle and Jackson had a complex past. Biddle had been Jackson's successor as both solicitor general and attorney general, and the two had worked together at the Department of Justice. When Jackson went on to the Court, he recommended Biddle to succeed him, though Roosevelt took his time before making the appointment. Truman unceremoniously fired Biddle shortly after assuming office to make room for the Texan Tom Clark, who was close to Truman's backer Robert Hannegan, and whom Truman would later put on the Supreme Court. Biddle considered Clark totally unfit for the job.[77] This was not pure ego on his part. Eventually, Truman would come to see Clark's appointment to the Court as a terrible mistake. But Biddle felt he had been humiliated by the way he was fired. As attorney general, Biddle had helped plan the tribunal in its earliest stages, well before Jackson was involved. When Truman, hoping to make amends for what he realized was his shoddy treatment of Biddle, suggested putting Biddle on the Nuremberg tribunal as a judge, Biddle was eager for the job, as much for the public rehabilitation as for any other reason.

But unfortunately for Biddle's relations with Jackson, when Truman proposed Biddle's name for Nuremberg, Jackson had been disappointed. Indeed, Jackson told Biddle he would not have considered him for the job had it been his decision. Jackson's stated reason for concern was that Biddle might be subject to a conflict of interest because he had helped plan the tribunal in the first place. Truman initially offered the job to Jackson's preferred candidate, retired justice Owen Roberts, himself the victim of shabby treatment by his colleagues on the Court; Roberts turned it down. Biddle got the job by process of elimination and only after telling Jackson that he did not believe he was disqualified by reason of his role in planning for the trial. To make matters worse, Jackson had objected strongly to Biddle's request to bring his wife, Katherine, to Nuremberg—a request that Truman personally approved.[78]

It followed that Biddle had his own views about how the trial should be run. He also had good reason to feel at least mildly resentful of Jackson, to whom it seemed he was perennially playing second fiddle. Francis Biddle may have suspected that Jackson wanted him off the tribunal so that he would be the most distinguished American present. If so, giving Goering latitude to say what he wanted in response to questions put to him was not only a way to ensure that the trial would appear full and fair. It was also a subtle way to detract from Jackson's moment in the sun, turning his own trial tactics against him.

Jackson felt deeply aggrieved by the decision. Biddle, he thought, "might have endangered the trials very greatly."[79] The danger, though, was more to Jackson's reputation than to the trial itself. The outcome, after all, was predetermined. The charges against Goering related to the fact that the Nazis had pursued aggressive war, and nothing Goering could say would have made him less guilty of that. But Biddle's intervention did reduce Jackson's personal control over the cross-examination. Described as "political by-play" in the next day's *Chicago Daily News*,[80] the decision showed that in the courtroom the judges were in charge, and Jackson was not.

Goering made good use of the latitude he had been given. Those present in the courtroom thought that he had gotten the better of Jackson. "Suave, shrewd, adroit, capable, resourceful," one noted, Goering "quickly saw the elements of the situation, and as his confidence grew, his mastery became more apparent."[81] The day's newspapers reflected this perception. The *London Daily Express* reported that "for three hours this afternoon, Hermann Goering and Justice Robert H. Jackson, Chief U.S. prosecutor, fought a verbal duel across the flood-lit floor of the Nuremberg court—and Nazi No. 2 won."[82] The *Daily News* was much harsher: "At times it looked as though a competent district attorney was up against brains so superior to his that he could not cope with them." Some observers, according to the paper, said that "Goering had made a monkey out of Jackson."[83]

After this disastrous first day of cross-examination, Jackson was forced to abandon the tactic of asking general questions and turn instead to specific instances of wrongdoing by Goering. The next day, though, did not get much better. Jackson managed to elicit some more concise answers with more direct questions. But late in the afternoon, Jackson blundered badly. Trying to lay the foundation for the charge of aggressive war to expand territory, Jackson asked Goering about a German military planning document that, he said, spoke of "the liberation of the Rhine." Goering replied archly that Jackson had misunderstood. In fact, the document was not talking about the liberation of the Rhineland, but of the prosaic goal of clearing the Rhine River of extraneous boat traffic once military mobilization was under way.

Instead of backing down in the face of this mistranslation, Jackson bluffed. He challenged Goering to explain why, if this was so, the document was kept secret from foreign powers. Goering answered with cool irony: "I do not think I can recall reading beforehand the publication of the mobilization preparations of the United States."[84] Flustered, Jackson turned to the tribunal in protest: "This witness, it seems to me, is adopting, and has adopted, in the witness box and in the dock, an arrogant and contemptuous attitude toward the Tribunal which is giving him the trial which he never gave a living soul, nor dead ones either."[85] Then Jackson once again demanded that Goering be required to answer the questions put to him and not to make any explanation. Lord Lawrence refused: The tribunal had ruled on the same question the day before.

Jackson's growing frustration had led him into a series of errors. The mistranslation could have been excused—it was not, after all, Jackson who had done the translating. Jackson should simply have admitted error and moved on to a new topic. Goering's rejoinder about the secrecy of the document was clever but not particularly subversive or offensive to the tribunal. By attacking Goering, Jackson made it look as though Goering had won a victory, when in fact he had just scored a minor point. Then Jackson made the mistake of asking the tribunal to revisit its earlier ruling—which all but guaranteed that he would be rebuffed, making him look even worse. Recognizing Jackson's embarrassment and perturbation, Lord Lawrence decided to save him. He called a halt to the proceedings, and the tribunal recessed for the day. Jackson, Lawrence must have assumed, would cool off overnight.

But Jackson could not cool off. After the tribunal had left the bench, he went to see Biddle privately. He was, Biddle later recalled, "profoundly upset." Jackson said the tribunal was "always ruling against him, and intimated that I went out of my way to oppose him." Then Jackson declared that "he thought he had better resign from the trial and go home."[86] Biddle attempted to calm him; but the next morning, March 20, Jackson once more demanded that the tribunal instruct Goering to restrict his answers to yes or no. Lord Lawrence, speaking in a measured tone, explained that he had already laid down the general rule "that the witness must answer if possible 'yes' or 'no,' and that he may make such explanations as may be necessary after answering questions directly in that way, and that such explanations must be brief and not be speeches."[87] Jackson was unsatisfied. If Goering were permitted to make explanations that were irrelevant, he suggested, it would put "control of these proceedings in the hands of the defendant."

Now Lawrence started to get impatient. Was Jackson seriously proposing that Goering not be allowed to explain his answers? Yes, said Jackson. That was "the rule of cross-examination under ordinary circumstances." Lawrence, disbelieving, repeated the tribunal's judgment. Jackson, though, was a man on a mission. He now dropped the "ordinary circumstances" argument he had made a moment before, and insisted that the trial was in fact totally extraordinary. Goering, he asserted, intended to use his testimony for propaganda purposes. It was therefore necessary to keep him in line. Otherwise, Jackson insisted, "it does seem to me that this is the beginning of this Trial's getting out of hand, if I may say so, if we do not have control of this situation."[88]

If there was one thing that Jackson should not have done as a matter of tactics, it was to suggest in open court that the trial might be getting away from the tribunal. From a mistranslation, a failed bluff, and a single witty remark, Jackson now found himself in direct conflict with the judges. The trial was not getting away from the tribunal—it was getting away from Jackson. The fact that he could not let go compounded his earlier mistakes by revealing to all spectators just how badly Jackson thought things had been going. Jackson may have been out of practice, but these were not the mistakes one would expect of an attorney with thousands of trials under his belt, one who had argued and won dozens of cases before the Supreme Court of the United States. The pressures of Nuremberg were getting to him. Slowly but surely, Jackson was coming unglued.

Style, or rather a mismatch of style, had something to do with Jackson's uncharacteristic difficulty in mastering the situation. The country lawyer persona that Jackson had long adopted did not play well in the European context. Perhaps the ideal person to notice this was Janet Flanner, the daughter of an Indianapolis mortician who wrote the Letter from Paris for *The New Yorker* for fifty years. The one American abroad depicted the other as a kind of hick visiting Europe. "Even physically, Jackson cut a poor figure. He unbuttoned his coat, whisked it back over his hips, and, with his hands in his back pockets, spraddled and teetered like a country lawyer."[89] Flanner preferred the "physical dignity and sartorial elegance" of the British prosecutor Sir David Maxwell Fyfe, "impeccable in his foreign office attire." Lord Lawrence, too, Flanner praised for arriving at the tribunal daily "in a magnificent black limousine" wearing "a long, blue broadcloth coat and a bowler." These men, unlike Jackson, "unquestionably affected the Nazis, hypersensitive to formality and chic in the male."[90]

Costume and the manner of wearing it may not have affected the Nazis as much as it did Flanner, who wrote under the pen name Genêt.[91] In a dark, double-breasted suit with a conservative striped tie and a gleaming white handkerchief furled into a dramatic triangle, Jackson looked as well-dressed as ever by U.S standards. But personal manner provided an apt metaphor for Jackson's evident discomfort during the cross-examination phase of the trial. Gone was the image of the worldly jurist standing up for civilization that Jackson had projected so skillfully in his opening statement. A prepared speech was one thing; cross-examination in a political trial quite another. Jackson, ever attuned to his public standing, understood that damage to his reputation had been done.

As it turned out, Jackson's discomfiture could not have come at a worse time. On April 22, a month after the Goering cross-examination, Chief Justice Harlan Fiske Stone died. At the invitation of the Nuremberg tribunal, Jackson offered a few generous memorial words in memory of the man who had opposed his presence there and dismissed the tribunal as a lynching party.

Jackson's real and immediate concern, though, was the chief justiceship for which Stone had edged him out five years before. Logically speaking, Jackson was the front-runner for the job. It was an open secret that Roosevelt had all but promised Jackson that he would be chief after Stone. He was on good terms with Truman, who had chosen him for the Nuremberg post. Despite the difficulties of the Goering cross-examination, he had made world headlines with his opening statement.

And Jackson wanted the job—more than anything he had ever wanted before in his life. The validation of the chief justiceship meant, like success at Nuremberg, the validation of history. A hint at Jackson's desire had come as recently as September 1945, when the members of the Nuremberg Tribunal were choosing their own president, in effect their chief justice. According to Biddle, the members unanimously recommended him, the American judge, in recognition of the U.S. role in the war and in organizing the trials. Biddle demurred, insisting that the British judge preside— precisely so that the tribunal would not look like an American-run operation. Jackson, who believed Biddle was maneuvering to get the post, strongly wanted Biddle to turn it down and, according to Biddle, was "relieved" when he did so.[92]

Jackson, who was briefly back in Washington preparing for the publication of documents connected to the trial, seems to have been worried that Biddle would feel slighted. He cabled Biddle saying he wanted to publish alongside those documents a preface explaining that the tribunal members had chosen Biddle as their president and that Biddle had magnanimously declined. Biddle told Jackson pointedly not to publish this, since it would reflect badly on the British judge whom he had recommended—in effect undoing Biddle's gesture.[93] In Biddle's memoir, where the whole exchange is reported, there is a soupçon of disdain for Jackson's combination of eagerness to deny Biddle the post and his simultaneous solicitude about Biddle's feelings. None of it makes sense unless one realizes that for Jackson, the thought of becoming chief was never far from his mind, and he assumed others must feel the same.

Now that the chief justiceship was within reach, Jackson needed to be back on the scene in Washington to make sure he got the post. Friends sent telegrams advising Jackson to return to Washington immediately for Stone's funeral on April 25.[94] Now Jackson found himself in an impossible position. Having stayed away from Washington so long over the objections of the dead man, his chief, Jackson could not now fly home to advance his candidacy without looking like a vulture. There was no choice but to stay where he was and hope for the best.[95]

Jackson had a bigger problem than his whereabouts. He had enemies; and they were well-placed. First among these was Hugo Black, who had, ten months before, warned Jackson in the presence of the other justices that a statement about recusal in the coal-mining case would be a declaration of war. Black had tried and failed to prevent Stone from becoming chief in return for Stone telling a reporter about his limitations in his first year on the Court. This time around, Black was leaving nothing to chance.

On April 24, before Stone was even in the ground, the Washington columnist Drew Pearson mentioned in one of his radio broadcasts that if Truman nominated Jackson as chief justice, two other justices would resign from the Court in protest.[96] Through Tommy Corcoran, Pearson was connected to Douglas. And Douglas was in turn allied with Black. The message to Truman was clear: Black and Douglas would do whatever it took to torpedo Jackson's appointment.

Congressman Lister Hill of Alabama, then a good friend of Black's, went to visit Truman in the guise of supporting Black for the position. While with Truman, he referred to a report about possible resignations, thus confirming to Truman that the threat actually came from Black.[97] According to one source, Truman actually called Black directly to get his opinion on appointing Jackson, and Black said pointedly that he would prefer Douglas as chief justice.[98]

For the moment, Jackson remained the front-runner, as an article in the *Washington Post* indicated two days later.[99] In a classic piece of convoluted Washington intrigue, it was also rumored that Jackson could become secretary of state, replacing Jimmy Byrnes, who had quarreled with Truman. It was even reported that Jackson might have a shot at becoming Truman's vice presidential pick in 1948 if the spot were not offered to Douglas.

Then two things happened. First, Robert Hannegan, the influential Democratic National Committee chairman, began to tell people that Jackson would not be picked.[100] Hannegan had been the key figure in stage-managing Truman's selection over Douglas in 1944. His influence over Truman was strong, and when he said something was not going to happen, it probably wasn't. When he learned later of Hannegan's role, Jackson speculated that Hannegan's motivation was revenge for Jackson resisting a patronage appointee to the Nuremberg prosecution team—a St. Louis lawyer named Mark Eagleton, whom Jackson considered utterly unqualified.[101] Hannegan had cared enough to dispatch Byrnes— who became secretary of state in July 1945—to demand Jackson's acquiescence.

The power of men like Hannegan lay entirely in their ability to secure patronage jobs with a phone call. A secretary of state was no minor messenger boy. Honest, stubborn, politically flatfooted,

or all of the above, Jackson had turned Byrnes down flat. His interpretation of Hannegan's motivation was certainly plausible.

Trying to understand why Black and Douglas were so opposed
to Jackson, Truman asked Owen Roberts to the White House
to explain what was going on at the Court. Roberts had left the
Court the previous June a bitter man, having broken with Black
and having been denied even the courtesy of a letter of congratula-
tion on his retirement. He would not willingly have done Black's
bidding, but Roberts did not have a strategic cast of mind. He had
actually been in the room when Black and Jackson had clashed
over Black's nonrecusal in the coal-mining case. Perhaps believing
mistakenly that he was working against Black's interests, Roberts
was frank with Truman, laying out the difficulties between the
justices. Once Truman understood the acrimony between Black
and Jackson, he could not reasonably have made Jackson chief justice. Black's objective of blocking Jackson had been achieved.

At the Supreme Court, leaks were rare—so rare that an apparent leak had led to the breakdown of the friendship between Roberts and Black. At the White House, in contrast, leaks were normal.
Now that Roberts had spoken to Truman, someone gave the whole
sordid story to the journalist Doris Fleeson. In her May 16 column
in the Washington *Evening Star*, Fleeson reported that the "inside
story of the clash of strong wills has been laid before President
Truman." In Fleeson's essentially accurate telling, the precipitating event of the conflict was Jackson's unusual memorandum about
recusal in the coal-mining dispute, based on the fact that Black's
former partner, Crampton Harris, had represented the union in
the case. "Justice Black," Fleeson reported, "reacted with fiery
scorn to what he regarded as an open and gratuitous insult, a slur
upon his personal and judicial honor." According to her account,
Truman now knew what was going on: "the harassed president, a
southerner himself, was quick to perceive the affront which Mr.
Black feels he suffered. He has confided to a senator: 'Black says he
will resign if I make Jackson Chief Justice and tell the reasons why.
Jackson says the same about Black.' "[102]

This was a largely evenhanded account of the events leading

up to the conflict. Fleeson offered no comment on Black's decision not to recuse himself, but neither did she defend him against the fact that his former partner was representing one side in a case in which he was casting the deciding vote. Bending over backward to be fair, Fleeson quoted Jackson's statement about recusal in its entirety. Even in reporting Truman's reaction, she was careful to describe the insult that Black "feels he suffered," hinting that Black was an oversensitive Southerner.

The only notably doubtful point in the report was the statement that Jackson said he would resign if Black were appointed chief. But Truman could very well have said this to a senator, or a senator could have told it to Fleeson. There was indeed a kernel of truth to the possibility of Jackson resigning. Back in September 1945, when criticism of his decision to miss the Supreme Court term was brewing, Jackson had told Truman that he was prepared to resign if necessary. Of course Jackson knew perfectly well that Truman would tell him to stay on; this was just Jackson's usual strategy of offering his resignation to get reassurance. But the notion of resignation was nevertheless there for Truman or others to draw upon, however imprecisely.

Jackson, however, was in no state of mind to think of Fleeson's column as fair. Stuck in Nuremberg, far from the internal machinations of official Washington, Jackson could see the chief justiceship slipping away. A letter from one of his former Department of Justice employees underscored his suspicion: "I understand that for a few hours it seemed a sure thing for you. Then, Black got word to the president that there would be a row if you were appointed. At that he began to make wide inquiries and to appreciate, perhaps exaggerate, the rifts in the Court."[103]

Spurred by the column, Jackson put pen to paper and drafted a memorandum for Truman in which he tried to explain what he believed had really happened in the coal-mining case. Although Jackson went over the content of the decision and mentioned Harris's participation, his real focus was on what he considered Black's manipulative attempt to have the result in the case announced before the opinions were fully drafted. He added that in the Court's conference, Black had said it would be a declaration of war if Jackson were to write his memorandum about recusal.

These details, of course, had not appeared in Fleeson's column. They went beyond the backbiting and recrimination that had occasionally been leaked to the press by the justices in the previous few years. The facts about the proposed timing of the decision—if facts they were—and the details of what had been said in conference amounted to the inner workings of the Supreme Court. The confidentiality of such information had until now been sacrosanct.

For reasons that remain unclear, Jackson postponed sending the memo to Truman over the next two weeks. Perhaps he thought defending himself would only confirm Truman's perception that he was involved in a feud that would disqualify him from the chief justiceship. In all likelihood, it would not have mattered if he had. Black's threats, the Fleeson article, and Hannegan's backroom machinations had done their work. On June 6, Truman appointed his secretary of the treasury, Fred Vinson, as chief justice.

Jackson had been shaken by the difficulties of the Nuremberg prosecution. But now the news that the chief justiceship had eluded him pushed Jackson over the edge. Incorporating the memo he had been working on, he sent Truman an astonishing cable reflecting his agitated state of mind. It described Truman's choice of a different chief as either a naked concession to Black or a referendum on Jackson himself. Perhaps, Jackson wrote, "something sinister has been revealed to you which made me unfit for Chief Justice." Then came Jackson's trademark threat of resignation: "If that were true, I am also unfit for Associate Justice." Either way, Jackson insisted, he could not continue as a sitting justice unless something changed. He could not, he said, "allow the impression either that an associate 'has something on me' which is disqualifying in your eyes, or that my opinion in the Jewell Ridge case was a 'gratuitous insult' to an associate."[104] Finally, Jackson issued a truly outrageous demand: Unless Truman wanted him to reveal the contents of the cable, or "unless you can suggest some better method of making my position clear to the public and to the bar of the country," Truman must release the cable to the public.

The suggestion that the president of the United States make public a cable revealing the inner workings of the Supreme Court was nothing short of bizarre, and Truman reacted accordingly. He denied point-blank having spoken to any justice (including Black) about the appointment or having seen the Fleeson article. And he begged Jackson to keep his mouth shut: "The reputation and position of the Court are of paramount interest to me and no purpose can be served by making this controversy public."

But Jackson was by now too far off course to regain his bearings. He got Truman's response on June 9, and the next day, June 10, he cabled an edited version of his memorandum to the chairmen of the House and Senate Judiciary committees. On June 11, newspapers across the United States made the cable a front-page story. Many printed the text in its entirety.

The published document certainly counts as the most surprising public statement by any Supreme Court justice. Jackson's ostensible goal was to explain to the public that his feud with Black was no "mere personal vendetta" but directly relevant to "the reputation of the Court for nonpartisan and unbiased decision." Yet the central target of the document was Black himself, and the content and tone were unremittingly personal from beginning to end.

Jackson asserted that "in my absence, one of my colleagues made public threats to the president," which had been "exploited through certain inspired commentators and columnists to imply that offensive behavior on my part is responsible for the feud on the Court." In contrast to Black's "innuendos," Jackson wrote, he would reply "over my own signature." Jackson tried to refute Doris Fleeson's column of May 16, whose "omissions," Jackson claimed, "are more significant than its facts."

Then came the bombshell: "Since the confidence in which internal matters in the Court ought usually to be held has already been broken by partial disclosure, I shall reveal the undisclosed part of my story." There followed an insider's account of the *Jewell Ridge* case, complete with the allegation that there had been a proposal to announce the decision "in time to influence the contract negotiations." Jackson revealed that when he sought to issue his memorandum regarding recusal, Black announced in conference that "any opinion which discussed the subject at all would mean a declaration of war."

Jackson insisted that he had no intention of impugning Black's honor. "It is rather," he wrote, "a question of judgment as to sound judicial policy," namely the question of whether the justices' former partners could represent clients before the Court. "However innocent the coincidence of these two victories at successive terms by Justice Black's former law partner, I wanted that practice stopped." Jackson was building to a conclusion that was both rousing and a little unhinged: "If it is ever repeated while I am on the bench I will make my Jewell Ridge opinion look like a letter of recommendation by comparison."

The reaction to Jackson's disclosures and his tirade was shock. The *New York Times* reported that "the national capital was stunned to read of the bitter denunciation of Associate Justice Hugo L. Black delivered at Nuremberg by Associate Justice Robert H. Jackson, the chief American War Crimes prosecutor. Seldom in this city of recurring sensations has there been such surprise."[105] The strangeness of the cable was enhanced by its place of origin. Jackson was not merely another justice, but one who was representing the United States on the world stage. And the fact of the denunciation on such petty matters seemed particularly bizarre coming from someone whose job was to denounce Nazi war crimes.

Black, for his part, remained silent. Uniquely among the justices, Black had experience in being the subject of front-page attacks on his character. In the case of the Klan allegations, Black had little choice but to reply. This time silence afforded him an enormous advantage over his antagonist. Jackson had spectacularly breached judicial propriety. It was difficult for any observer not to think it resulted from his frustration at not becoming chief justice. Jackson was therefore publicly in the wrong.

Black's reputation was tarnished by Jackson's allegations. He did what he could to respond indirectly. The following April, the *Yale Law Journal* published an article by John Frank, Black's former law clerk, titled "Disqualification of Judges." Frank maintained that there was no reason for Black to disqualify himself when his ex-partner argued a case. "Justice Black heard an ex-partner twenty years after termination of the association," he wrote. "In so doing he seems to have done pretty much what all judges do.... Had Black disqualified [himself], he would have departed from the traditions of 150 years."[106] It was not quite accurate to say the association had ended twenty years before. Harris had represented Black in court in 1936, and he had secretly come to Washington to advise him during his Klan-related difficulties in 1937. It was true, however, that recusal practices were very loose at the time, and that many other justices sat on cases in which they had close ties to the lawyers.

Notwithstanding this only partial redemption of his reputation, the whole series of events could still be counted as a victory for Black. After all, in the final analysis, Jackson had offended Black's honor. A year later, in part through Black's agency, Jackson had failed to get the greatest honor he had sought in his life. What was more, Jackson knew it, could do nothing about it, and was so overcome by it that he was drawing enormous public attention to the whole affair. Betrayal had begotten betrayal, and measure had been given for measure. If ever anyone had a satisfying vengeance, it must have been Black.

The question remains, though: Why did Jackson walk right into it? How could so successful a man have inflicted such an injury upon himself and his carefully tended career? The answer inevitably comes back to his circumstances at Nuremberg in the late spring of 1946. Having taken his place in the crucible of world history, Jackson found that the pressures of his role were too much for him to bear. Far from home, far from reliable advisers, trapped in the paranoid mode of a man from upstate New York prosecuting the greatest criminal conspiracy in human history, Jackson's faculty of practical wisdom deserted him when it came to his own personal affairs. "Only someone who has lived the unreal life of an army of occupation," wrote Arthur Schlesinger Jr., who had, "can understand the violence of his response to the fragmentary reports of Washington intrigue."[107]

Biddle had a similar interpretation. "Nothing but a deep disappointment could have motivated his bitter outburst at Nürnberg," Biddle later wrote of Jackson. "He was strained and overworked in the trial of the German war criminals. . . . It was a foolish exhibition, and I felt sorry for him, stumbling like a child in pain. The British judges were profoundly shocked. They could not understand this washing of dirty linen in public, particularly by a judge."[108]

But that was not all. Biddle came to believe that Jackson's ambition came from a gap in his soul: "Later I became convinced that some more enduring sense of failure or a disappointment haunted him. It is not improbable that appointment as Chief Justice of the United States would have eased that brooding misery. But I do not think any achievement would have altogether banished it."[109]

This painful hint at Jackson's inner life provides another possible view of Jackson's strange decision in Nuremberg to bring his grievances to the press. To Biddle, Jackson's ambition, though kindled relatively late in life, had taken him over entirely, so that he could not conceive a purpose greater than grasping the next brass ring. "That wonderful year," Biddle wrote, "he had all the glittering acclamation than anyone could long for—degrees, decorations, the press almost universally won over to the adventurous value of his achievement. Why should he not have everything he wanted?"[110]

Perhaps it looked that way to Biddle, the aristocratic Philadelphian whose professional accomplishments came just short of Jackson's. But Frankfurter, a self-made man like Jackson, saw Jackson's character and legacy very differently. A decade after Jackson's death and only a few months before his own, he was still sending angry letters to Biddle defending not only Jackson's inner core, but even his tactics in the cross-examination of Goering. To Frankfurter, Jackson was a hero who acted out of principle, goaded on by Black's devious plot to deny him the office he most deserved—and that Frankfurter, his posthumously loyal friend, wanted him to have.

Book Seven

FRACTURE

CHAPTER 31

Things Fall Apart

Nineteen forty-six should have been a year of triumph for the followers of Franklin Roosevelt, whose liberalism had led them to victory over the Depression and the Nazis. With the war over and the economy rebounding, the time had come to fulfill the promises of peace. Instead they found themselves beleaguered. From the left, the labor unions, tired of compromise, were aggressively demanding a greater share of the postwar bounty. In the fall, John L. Lewis, president of the United Mine Workers of America, closed every coal mine in the nation for nearly three weeks. From the right, the Republicans were rising. In a sign of the times, Robert La Follette, a Roosevelt supporter who had served Wisconsin in the Senate for twenty years, was defeated by Joe McCarthy, an unknown, thirty-eight-year-old Republican. "This thing isn't running right," Tommy Corcoran observed as the election returns started to come in.[1] The Republicans took the House and the Senate back from the Democrats for the first time since 1930. A few years later, La Follette would kill himself in the shadow of one of his successor's investigations.

To the liberals who saw themselves as keepers of Roosevelt's flame, the source of the decline was Truman, a mediocrity surrounded by mediocrities. "We've got to have some brains in there," said Lyndon Baines Johnson, in the course of a thwarted effort to bring Douglas into the Truman administration as secretary of the interior. Corcoran, with the assassination of Caesar on his mind, remarked that Truman's motto seemed to be, "Let me have about me men who are not too smart."[2]

Meanwhile the Soviets' grip over much of Europe was growing stronger. Winston Churchill gave his "Iron Curtain" speech in
March 1946. Not until the next year would Truman settle on the
doctrine of containing the Soviet Union. Douglas, who considered
Truman a "pygmy" when it came to foreign policy, summed up
the contemporary view: "Truman was a very ignorant man about
world affairs. He was a precinct politician.... What he knew about
the world you could put into a peanut shell."[3]

The dispirited feeling extended to Roosevelt's justices. Frankfurter, who had no relationship with Truman, had lost the access
to the highest level of power that he had enjoyed uninterruptedly
since 1933. Jackson was trying to recover from his self-inflicted
humiliation over the chief justiceship. Douglas and Black, too, were
no longer in the loop. "I was out at Bill Douglas' with Hugo...and
some others," Corcoran told a friend, "and I couldn't help saying to
myself, 'Well, here's a bunch of guys...that had the world in their
hands last year, and now they're just a bunch of political refugees...
a helpless bunch of sheep.'"[4]

Frustration bred contempt. From allies sipping champagne
to celebrate one another's joining the Court, Black, Frankfurter,
Douglas, and Jackson had formed camps and become bitter enemies. Frankfurter despised Douglas, whom he called one of the
"two completely evil men I have ever met."[5] Reflecting the language of wartime, Frankfurter called Douglas, Black, and Murphy
"the Axis."[6] One-upping Frankfurter, Douglas called him "Der
Fuehrer."[7] The hatred between Black and Jackson ran so deep that
it threatened to ruin the reputations of both men. The friendship
between Frankfurter and Jackson seemed to depend more on disdain for Douglas and Black than any closer connection. Douglas
and Black voted together but were not intimate friends. For them,
common ground meant revulsion for Frankfurter and Jackson.

As their mutual distrust grew, differences of constitutional opinion began to emerge among the liberals.[8] In most of the important
wartime cases that came before the Court, these four had managed
to pull together. Now the bonds that connected them were broken.
The constitutional visions that each had begun to develop would

diverge into four distinct types, each claiming to be the true liberal position.

Alone among the justices, Black viewed the collapse of liberal consensus as an opportunity. Frankfurter's intransigence in the second flag-salute case meant that he had forfeited his natural position of leadership among the liberal justices. Jackson had been soundly defeated after his Nuremberg outburst. Douglas, his attention focused on politics, would provide a reliable vote for almost any position Black wanted to advance. So Black decided it was time to make his mark on the Constitution itself. He would set out to do what Frankfurter had done as a law professor and what Jackson and Douglas, each for different reasons, were predisposed not to do: Lay out a comprehensive theory of how the Constitution should be interpreted, and get it into the law books for the ages.

Black's early efforts at originalist constitutional interpretation were the work of an inspired amateur. After nearly a decade on the Court, he had developed the intellectual discipline and rigor to expound his theory. In 1947, he found an appropriate case in which to do so. On July 24, 1944, someone had broken into the apartment of Stella Blauvelt, a sixty-four-year-old widow in Los Angeles, California. Mrs. Blauvelt was at home when the break-in occurred. The intruder beat her badly, then strangled her with a lamp cord. Her purse was stolen, as were the diamond rings she wore on her left hand. Although she was not sexually assaulted, the top of one of her stockings had disappeared. The police concluded they were looking for a burglar with a stocking fetish.

A month later, the LAPD arrested Admiral Dewey Adamson, an African-American named for the hero of the 1898 Battle of Manila Bay. Adamson, forty-three, had been overheard in a bar offering to sell a diamond ring. In the dresser drawer of his apartment, the police found women's stocking tops—though none belonging to Mrs. Blauvelt. A police expert then matched Adamson's fingerprints with several latent prints found on the door to the apartment, which had been removed from its hinges so that the burglar could enter.

Adamson protested his innocence and insisted he had an alibi for the night of the murder. Yet at trial he chose not to take the stand. He had served time for two old convictions, one for burglary in 1920, and one for robbery in 1927. Adamson and his lawyer knew that if he testified, the jury of eleven women and one man would find out about his criminal record, which might well prejudice them against him. The stocking tops were admitted into evidence, over the objections of Adamson's lawyer.

In his summation to the jury, the prosecutor focused on the fact that Adamson had not testified on his own behalf. "He does not have to take the stand," the district attorney explained. "But it would take about twenty or fifty horses to keep someone off the stand if he was not afraid." The inference from Adamson's silence was clear. "If he wasn't there, where was he? Where was he?...He could explain how his prints got on there," the prosecutor went on. Adamson could have testified, "and he did not do it. You can consider that with all the testimony in this case, and I ask you to consider it." The jury wasted no time in convicting Adamson of murder and burglary. Adamson was sentenced to death. His attorney appealed.[9]

In most states, a prosecutor was not allowed to tell the jury that a defendant's refusal to testify should count as evidence of his guilt. In a federal court, the inference would almost certainly have violated the right against self-incrimination that was contained in the Fifth Amendment.[10] In California, however, the rules were different: The prosecutor was allowed to draw the inference. The important question raised by Adamson's case was whether the Fifth Amendment applied in state court. If it did, Adamson's conviction would be reversed. If not, he would be executed.

The Supreme Court decided against Adamson. The Bill of Rights had been added to the Constitution as a check on the federal government, not the states.[11] The only way one of those rights could be applied in state court would be if it were "fundamental to the concept of ordered liberty"—so basic that no system could be considered just if that right were not recognized. According to the opinion in Adamson's case, written by Justice Stanley Reed, there was nothing fundamental about the right not to have a prosecutor tell the jury it could infer guilt from the defendant's silence. Several years later, after exhausting every avenue of appeal, Adamson was executed in California's gas chamber.

Black filed a dissent in Adamson's favor. He maintained that the Fifth Amendment should be applied in state court as well. Adamson should get a new trial, one in which the prosecutor would not be allowed to tell the jury that the defendant's silence was proof of his guilt. It was not that Black thought the self-incrimination right was more fundamental than the majority did. The Constitution, Black argued, demanded that *all* the guarantees in the Bill of Rights be applied against the states. Black was doing much more than calling for a reversal of Adamson's conviction. He was proposing to transform the whole face of constitutional law. If the Bill of Rights applied to the states, then every action by a state government, including every conviction in a state court, would have to be reviewed to see if it complied with the Constitution.

Black's position flew in the face of precedent dating back to 1873. To back it up, he needed what every good constitutional theory demands if it is to gain followers: He needed a story. Drawing on months of historical research undertaken completely on his own, Black provided one.

CHAPTER 32

Originalism

Black's story began in a postwar era not so different from the one in which he was living. The war that had just ended was the Civil War. The defeated enemy was not the Axis powers, but the American South, Black's native soil. As the United States was doing in Germany and Japan, the victorious Union had imposed a military occupation on its defeated foes. As part of the occupation, it aimed to rid the occupied people of their practices of racial discrimination. And just as the United States in Black's own day would impose new constitutions on Japan and Germany, part of the project of Reconstruction was to create a new Constitution that would maintain racial equality in the Southern states—and give the federal government the authority to enforce it in perpetuity.

Black's story had a protagonist: Congressman John Bingham, who represented northern Ohio from 1865 until 1872. For a Southerner like Black, Bingham was an unlikely hero. He had made his reputation as a prosecutor in the military tribunal that convicted eight Confederate sympathizers for conspiracy in the assassination of Abraham Lincoln and hanged four of them, including a woman. Elected to Congress, Bingham became a member of the Republican majority. Although not a radical Republican who believed that the Union should reconstruct the South's entire political, economic, and social system from the ground up, Bingham supported Reconstruction in its essentials.[12] To most white Southerners, from the nineteenth century to the middle of the twentieth, Reconstruction was itself a conspiratorial plot, and the Republicans were the would-be dictators who had tried unsuccessfully to force it down their throats.

To Black, Bingham and his fellow Republicans were not villains. They were a second set of Founding Fathers. The amendments that they proposed in Congress—and that they insisted the Southern states ratify if they were to be readmitted to the Union—were, in effect, a new Constitution layered on top of the old one. The so-called Reconstruction amendments—numbers Thirteen, Fourteen, and Fifteen—had two purposes, according to Black. One was to "make colored people citizens entitled to full equal rights as citizens." The other was to turn the Constitution into a truly national document by making the Bill of Rights apply to the states.[13]

John Bingham had been the principal draftsman of the Fourteenth Amendment. As Black told the story, Bingham had introduced language into Congress that was very similar to the language finally adopted and ratified. It prohibited the states from depriving any person of life, liberty, or property without due process of law, or from abridging the privileges or immunities of citizens. Bingham had explained that his proposal was intended to extend the freedoms of the Bill of Rights so that they applied against state governments. When the amendments were ratified, Black insisted, contemporaries understood that this was the system they were putting into place.

Then Black's story took a dramatic turn. In 1868, the Fourteenth Amendment was ratified. But just four years later, the Supreme Court took up the first in a series of cases that would strip the amendment of its original meaning. Instead of acknowledging that the words "privileges or immunities" and the concept of "due process" were intended to incorporate the Bill of Rights by reference, the Court began to develop a new, deviant approach. It refused to apply the specific guarantees of the Bill of Rights to the state courts. Instead it began, slowly but surely, to invent different rights—rights protecting property—that appeared nowhere in the Bill of Rights but were attributed to the vague words "due process of law." This trend, Black hinted, led directly to *Lochner v. New York*, and the hated doctrine of the liberty of contract.

Black never said exactly why the Supreme Court had suppressed the original meaning of the Fourteenth Amendment. But his implication was clear enough. During the presidency of Andrew Johnson, the process of Reconstruction had been abandoned. Segregation had replaced integration. At the same time, in the industrialized Northern states, big business had started to dominate the institutions of government. The Supreme Court had gone along with Congress's abandonment of Southern blacks. And it had happily become an instrument of capitalism, using the Fourteenth Amendment to protect the property rights of corporations.

Black's story included one man who had seen it happening at the time—Justice Joseph Bradley, who in 1873 had written a dissent arguing that the "privileges or immunities" guaranteed in the Fourteenth Amendment must include those found in the Bill of Rights. For Black, Bradley was his frustrated forerunner. His 1873 opinion proved that Black was right about the outrage that had happened several generations before.

Having laid out his tale, Black had to explain why the Court had never told it before. The reason, he said, was ignorance. The Fourteenth Amendment's true "historical purpose," he said, "has never received full consideration or exposition in any opinion of this Court."[14] Before Black, no one had carefully studied the history of how the Fourteenth Amendment was drafted. "The Court had never had that kind of original research before," he proudly told his clerks later.[15]

In support of his claims, Black provided a thirty-page historical appendix. Prepared over the summer of 1946 in anticipation of a case like Adamson's, it cited numerous original sources, speeches taken from the Congressional Record and given context by Black's explanation.[16] For a self-taught justice whose first Supreme Court opinions had been subject to derision, the appendix was a powerful vindication. With it, Hugo Black established himself as both a justice in command of a major theory of constitutional interpretation and also as a constitutional historian of the first importance.

It was paradoxical that Black, who believed that any ordinary person should be able to understand the words of the Constitution, was now relying on unknown history to find out what the words originally meant. In Black's mind, however, his theory elevated the text of the Constitution over judicial speculation and invention. By showing that the Fourteenth Amendment's references to "due process" and "privileges or immunities" were really pointing to the words of the Bill of Rights, Black believed he could avoid *Lochner's* error of inventing new rights that were not actually contained in the Constitution. At the same time, Black's approach would expand constitutional rights for defendants like Adamson—a result that liberals badly wanted to reach. By discovering the original meaning of the Fourteenth Amendment, Black thought, he had solved the conundrum of liberal constitutional interpretation.

Frankfurter understood Black's historical foray in the *Adamson* case for what it was: a bid for intellectual leadership of the Court. Frankfurter would never stop thinking that Douglas was entirely unprincipled, pursuing his presidential ambitions from the bench and deciding cases solely on the basis of how they would play politically. He had once considered Black as little more than Douglas's henchman. Now Frankfurter saw that Black was actually a serious intellectual adversary—the only one he recognized on the Court.

Since the second flag-salute case, Frankfurter had understood that his leadership of the Court was in doubt. His diaries from 1946 to 1947 reflect the doldrums in which he found himself. He wrote regularly about long conversations with his old friend Dean Acheson, who was back in government as deputy secretary of state under Jimmy Byrnes. Looking for a judicial father figure, Frankfurter went regularly to visit the retired chief justice Charles Evans Hughes, with whom he discussed the rising threat from Russia as well as a mutual favorite topic: the great justices of the Supreme Court, their personalities, work, and reputations.

Frankfurter wrote an opinion of his own in the *Adamson* case, devoted specifically to refuting Black's claims. He pointed out that the Fourteenth Amendment never actually said it was incorporating the Bill of Rights by reference.[17] And he argued that the framers of the Fourteenth Amendment could not have meant to incorporate by reference the minor guarantees of the Bill of Rights, like the twelve-man jury, or the availability of a jury trial whenever the amount in controversy exceeded twenty dollars.[18]

But his separate, anti-Black concurrence, Frankfurter knew, was not enough of a counterpunch. According to Black's law clerk at the time, Yale Law School graduate and later judge Louis Oberdorfer, upon reading Black's *Adamson* opinion, "Frankfurter threw the dissent across the desk to Oberdorfer, scattering the pages on the floor and dismissing Oberdorfer with the words, 'At Yale they call this scholarship?' "[19]

The reference to Yale was no more an accident than Frankfurter's outburst itself. For Frankfurter, the former academic, the law schools were the real audience for Supreme Court opinions—and the primary venue for the making and breaking of judicial reputations. Black had neither attended a famous law school nor taught at one. But with Douglas as his conduit, Black was beginning to develop ties to Yale Law School that would eventually become his answer to Frankfurter's power base at Harvard.

Frankfurter's outburst at Black's historical work reflected the reality that Black had now done more important historical research on the Fourteenth Amendment than he had. Frankfurter liked to present himself as a great expert on the Fourteenth Amendment. In 1943, as Black was beginning to develop the theory of incorporation-by-reference that would emerge full-blown in *Adamson*, Frankfurter wrote to him a bit condescendingly:

> Dear Hugo:
>   For nearly twenty years I was at work on what was to be as comprehensive and as scholarly a book on the Fourteenth Amendment as I could make it. That book was aborted when I came down here, and now there is nothing to show for those twenty years except the poor things in my head and the mass of largely illegible notes.[20]

Whether Frankfurter's book in progress ever really existed outside his mind is doubtful. If it had, he would have been better acquainted with the historical materials connected to the drafting and ratification of the Fourteenth Amendment than he actually was. To his chagrin, despite his scholarly credentials, Frankfurter was not in a position to disprove Black's story on his own.

What Frankfurter needed was a surrogate who could provide a scholarly refutation of Black's historical claims. Frankfurter turned to Professor Charles Fairman, then of Stanford Law School and later of Harvard. Fairman had been Frankfurter's doctoral student at Harvard. He had written a book on Supreme Court justice Samuel Miller, author of the key 1873 decision rejecting the idea that the Fourteenth Amendment incorporated the Bill of Rights.[21] That expertise made Fairman the right man for the job.

Fairman understood that Frankfurter wanted him not only to refute Black's views, but also to deal a blow to an increasingly serious rival for intellectual dominance. He told Frankfurter a story about the nineteenth-century justice Miller, one that Frankfurter liked so much he repeated it to the retired chief justice Hughes. Miller had been complaining about one of his most distinguished colleagues—Justice Joseph Bradley, the man whom Black, in his story, had depicted as his own precursor. "The trouble with Bradley," Miller had said, "is that he does not recognize my intellectual preeminence."[22] The parallel to Frankfurter and Black was not lost on anyone.

Working for nearly two years, Fairman produced a lengthy article intended to show that Black's story was wrong.[23] He demonstrated that John Bingham, Black's hero, had wavered considerably over the precise effect he intended the Fourteenth Amendment to have. Then, collecting a much wider range of sources than Black had used, Fairman showed that supporters of the amendment said virtually nothing about incorporating the Bill of Rights by reference. In one particularly critical passage, Fairman maintained that Black had drawn unwarranted conclusions from an obscure 1908 book he had used as part his research.[24] Black's reliance on the book was perfectly natural, but the blow was effectively placed. To academic readers already inclined to doubt Black's unconventional conclusions, Fairman made Black seem once again like an amateur, corrected by a professional.

Black was frustrated and outflanked. Unlike Frankfurter, who had an army of professors he had been training for a quarter of a century, he did not yet have a large group of professional academics to defend him. He wrote to the one law professor with whom he was close, former clerk John Frank (then at Indiana Law School but soon to be at Yale): "I would thoroughly enjoy engaging in this debate with Mr. Fairman and his associates were I free to do so. I must say that Mr. Fairman's article reminds me of those advocates who come into court believing that strained inferences conclusively settle a matter. . . . By my agreeing with the conclusions of [Horace Edgar Flack, author of a 1908 text on the Fourteenth Amendment] in his nearly 300 page argument, it appears that I have committed an unpardonable sin."[25]

Frankfurter's recourse to a professional academic historian had worked—for the moment. He did not anticipate that just five years later, when the question of desegregation would come before the Court, that kind of history would become a much greater problem for him than it would ever be for Black.

CHAPTER 33

Crisis and Rebirth

Black had made great progress consolidating his position as an intellectual force on the Court. Yet he still harbored the fantasy of a return to political life. Truman was weak—extraordinarily so. By the end of 1947, talk of a rebellion from within the Democratic Party was rampant.

The source of the frustration was the liberals. New Dealers, Black among them, believed Truman had failed them. Roosevelt's legacy was on the line. Both Eleanor Roosevelt and Franklin Jr. were active in Americans for Democratic Action, a small but significant group aimed at rejuvenating the liberal cause within the Democratic Party. At their convention in February 1948, the ADA members made their insurgency public. They called for open primaries and a chance to unseat Truman.

In this environment, Black traveled back to Birmingham—where he had not lived full-time in fifteen years—to gauge whether he would have any sort of support were he to run for president. The reaction from his confidants was negative.[26] As Black should have realized, he no longer had a base in Alabama. Indeed, it is more a reflection on Black's ego than his political judgment that he even bothered to ask. The reason it was on Black's mind was that one of his colleagues had an altogether better chance at the job. As 1948 dawned, Douglas was gathering his forces for what would turn out to be his last chance to gain the one office he really wanted.

Douglas's political ambition had not dimmed since he fell just short of the vice presidency in 1944. Now the prospect of either the vice presidency or, if Truman continued to falter, perhaps

the presidency itself seemed entirely realistic. His friend Eliot
Janeway wrote to him that "an army of people...has welded
itself to you as a leader...The momentum of this army will accel-
erate at an increasing rate the next few years. Nothing you do can
stop it."[27]

The ADA's plan for a revolt against Truman was tailor-made for
Douglas. The liberals might have preferred Dwight D. Eisenhower,
a national hero of unparalleled stature whose political affiliations
were still unknown. But when Eisenhower officially dropped out,
Douglas appeared to be the liberals' natural choice. He had, after
all, been Roosevelt's own preference four years before; and since
then, no other liberal with comparable New Deal credentials had
emerged at the national level.

Frankfurter and Jackson had believed for years that every judicial decision that came from Douglas's pen was calculated solely to
advance his political career.[28] If this was so, Douglas's strategy had
apparently worked. When the ADA issued a pamphlet promoting
Douglas, it featured copious citations from his judicial opinions as
evidence of his liberalism.[29] From the Supreme Court, Douglas had
succeeded in keeping his political prospects alive.

But challenging Truman was exceedingly difficult. Whether a
failure or not, he was still president, with a strong influence over
his party. In the days before open primaries, the chances of displacing an incumbent as closely connected to the political machine as
Truman were slim. Either Truman would have to step aside, or a
miracle would have to happen at the convention. And as Douglas
should have known from his experience in 1944, the convention
was the worst possible place for a man with no substantial regional
constituency to mount a challenge.

To a rational observer—which Truman certainly was—it must
have seemed that in flirting with the ADA, Douglas was not running against him but was trying to become vice president, the spot
he had narrowly missed the last time. If this was his goal, it made
perfect sense for Douglas to welcome the sponsorship of the insur-
gent ADA. Truman badly needed support from the liberal wing of
his party, for which the ADA could plausibly claim to speak. If the

ADA wanted Douglas, then Truman could bring the liberals on board by offering Douglas the vice presidency.

That is precisely what Truman did. In July 1948, with the Democratic convention approaching, Truman sent a series of messengers to offer Douglas the number two spot on the ticket. Douglas rebuffed Robert Hannegan, Clark Clifford, and even Eleanor Roosevelt. Hat in hand, Truman called Douglas himself. Douglas equivocated, taking several days to make up his mind. But finally he declined. Truman settled on Senator Alben Barkley of Kentucky, a staunch supporter of Roosevelt as Senate majority leader and the closest thing Truman could find to a New Deal liberal.

It is puzzling that Douglas turned down the chance of becoming vice president of the United States when the overarching goal of his life had been the presidency. One possible reason is that he was relying too heavily on the advice of Tommy Corcoran, who was still trying to get back into power and still saw Douglas as the man who would bring him there. Corcoran wanted Douglas to defeat Truman, not join the Truman administration. Truman hated Corcoran. As a result, even if Douglas became vice president, Corcoran would not have real influence in the White House.

Corcoran therefore had reason to convince Douglas that it was worth taking a shot at the presidency, but not worth signing on with Truman. His method was to appeal to Douglas's ego. "Bill," he told Douglas in a phone conversation, "you don't want to play second fiddle to a second fiddle." Douglas, who had repeatedly resisted efforts to co-opt him into the Truman administration, could see Corcoran's point. Pretty soon Corcoran's line, often attributed to Douglas himself, was making its way around Washington.[30]

Truman knew all about it. Hating Corcoran even more intensely than Corcoran suspected, Truman had personally ordered a "national security" wiretap on Corcoran's phone. Three times a week, J. Edgar Hoover would send a special messenger to the White House with transcripts of Corcoran's phone calls.[31] The fact that Truman went on to offer Douglas the vice presidency despite knowing about the "second fiddle" crack was a mark of the president's humility—and his desperation.

Beyond Douglas's desire not to be subordinated to a man he considered inferior, there was also the question of whether Truman had a chance of winning. Some of Douglas's comments at the time suggest that he wanted Truman to lose so that he would be left as the party's standard-bearer in 1952. If so, the reason Douglas did not want to accept the nomination for vice president was that he feared Truman might win. Then he would be stuck with a close connection to Truman instead of being well-positioned to run the next time as his own man.[32]

At the same time, Douglas also seems to have feared that if he resigned from the bench to run and Truman then lost, he would find himself jobless. Joe Kennedy, his old mentor, reinforced this fear by asking him, "If you ran for vice president, and got licked, as you will, who will provide for your wife and children?"[33] Kennedy, of course, had the means at his disposal to promise Douglas the soft landing he needed. A lucrative corporate job would not have been hard to arrange. But by 1948, Joe Kennedy had other reasons for discouraging a vice presidential run by his former protégé. John F. Kennedy was serving in the House of Representatives and would try for a Senate seat in 1952. Counting ahead, Joe could see that putting the charismatic Douglas at the front of the Democratic Party might not serve his son's interests.

But for whatever reason—ego, fear, or the foolish expectation that the convention would dump Truman and draft him—Douglas turned down Truman's offer. After Truman's surprise victory, Douglas realized he had miscalculated. Although in theory he could have run again in 1952, Douglas probably sensed that having been so close to the vice presidency twice, he would not get another chance. Almost immediately, his life began to implode—and through actions of his own devising.

The first intimation of crisis had to do with romance, or what passed for it in Douglas's inner world. In common with Joe Kennedy and his sons, Douglas had for years been an inveterate womanizer. Now for the first time—though, as it would turn out, far from the last—he sought to turn one of his affairs into something more. In the summer of 1949, he proposed marriage to his mistress, promising to divorce his wife, Mildred.[34] Married herself, the mistress turned him down. But the mere fact that he had spoken seriously about getting a divorce signaled the beginnings of a personal transformation and the disintegration of his political ambitions. At midcentury the idea of a divorced president was still essentially unthinkable. No Supreme Court justice had ever been divorced. For a man who had for so long cherished hopes of the presidency, the willingness to accept a national scandal was remarkable, to say the least.

Spurned by his mistress and deeply unhappy in his marriage, Douglas traveled to rural Washington State. The trip itself was an opportunity for escape. Douglas often went to the Wallowa Mountains for personal retreat; he had been there the previous summer when he had rebuffed Truman's advances. In October 1949, just days before he was scheduled to return to the other Washington for the new Supreme Court term, Douglas went horseback riding alone on a dangerous mountain trail.

Douglas loved the solitude of the mountains and the challenges of nature. But he was not a skilled rider, and this time he overextended himself. While climbing uphill, the horse reared, and both beast and rider began to fall down the steep incline. The horse landed on its feet, but Douglas's injuries were severe. He broke twenty-three ribs and had to be carried off the mountain semiconscious and in shock.[35] At the Court, where Douglas was not much loved, the life-threatening accident was treated as the setup to a punch line. "Douglas fell off a cliff!" one law clerk told another. "Where was Frankfurter?" went the reply.[36]

Months passed before Douglas could return to work. When he did he was a changed man, at least with respect to his personal life. By 1954 he would leave his wife and file for divorce. He married his second wife in 1954, a blonde eighteen years his junior. In 1963, after divorcing her, he married his third wife, this one twenty-three years old to Douglas's sixty-five. The marriage—this time to a brunette—lasted only two years. In 1966, now nearly sixty-eight years of age, Douglas married a twenty-three-year-old college student who was, unsurprisingly, blond as well. He never divorced this fourth wife but he was consistently unfaithful to her. He spent most of his time with the one who got away, an artist and recent college graduate whom he met around the same time he married wife number four. With this last woman he maintained a long relationship despite (or maybe because of) her refusal to marry him.[37]

This pattern of behavior was erratic, to say the least. And Douglas's unusual personal decisions affected his professional activities. Burdened with multiple alimonies, he was chronically short of cash. His problems were made worse by an unusual clause in his divorce from Mildred, his first wife, according to which the more money Douglas made, the higher the percentage of his income he had to pay in support. The clause had been negotiated on Mildred's behalf by none other than Douglas's friend Tommy Corcoran, who called it "a hell of a deal."[38] At the time Corcoran had begged, cajoled, and finally ordered Douglas not to get a divorce that would end his political career. "You don't have to marry 'em, just sleep with 'em," he told Douglas.[39] When Douglas refused to listen, Corcoran decided to represent Mildred in the divorce, either out of legitimate concern for her plight, as Douglas's daughter believed, or sheer vindictiveness at Douglas for having wasted the political capital Corcoran had invested in him—the view of Eliot Janeway.[40]

As a fluid and fast writer with some political celebrity and increasing name recognition, Douglas found that the best way to make money was by writing books. Given his wide-ranging intellectual curiosity and impatience, Douglas would have written prolifically in any case. But financial pressure dictated the tempo. Working with astonishing speed, Douglas authored more than a dozen books on topics from the pursuit of liberty to exploring the Himalayas and the Soviet Union. Increasingly his favorite topics related to the protection of the environment—a cause for which he would later become a pioneer.

Yet even as his personal life spiraled increasingly out of control, Douglas's philosophy of the Constitution grew and developed. Realizing that he was going to spend his life on the Supreme Court concentrated his mind: And whatever else he may have been,

Douglas was brilliant. If fate had put him on the Court for the long haul, he would do what he could to make his mark on its work. Once a presidential future was no longer a realistic possibility, Douglas was freed to become a great justice.

According to the realist theory of the law in which Douglas had been trained and which he still espoused, judges inevitably make the law in their own image. Douglas needed a sense of who he was in order to know what the law should be. Until 1948, his self-image had been bound up in the aspiration to high office, and Douglas lacked a focused constitutional objective. If his opinions had a theme, it was trying to match popular opinion, as he had done in the Japanese-American internment cases. A constitutional realism based on the acknowledgment of judicial preference could get him nowhere so long as what he wanted as a judge was not to be a judge anymore.

Now, after 1948, Douglas's instinct to compromise principle for political gain began to fade. He was unmoored and adrift in his own life—and that freed him to make new constitutional law. Searching painfully for fulfillment and struggling with the norms of conventional society, Douglas settled on a picture of himself as a lone figure, riding toward the Western horizon, making his own fate without the interference of others. From childhood a loner, Douglas cast himself as independent.[41] Always struggling with authority, Douglas now self-defined as someone who made his own rules, governed by the Whitman-esque philosophy of "Darest Thou."[42]

This self-image gave Douglas a unifying constitutional goal: the pursuit of individual freedom. In his emerging vision, the Constitution should be interpreted to give each person the greatest room possible to shape his or her life autonomously, without the intervention of the government. The Constitution, properly understood, was a blueprint for personal liberty. In essentially every constitutional opinion he wrote from then on, Douglas sought to give individuals the maximum degree of personal freedom relative to the government. From 1948 until 1975, when he finally stepped down from the Court as the longest-serving justice ever, Douglas steadily expanded the boundaries of constitutional rights in the crucial areas of free speech, privacy, and reproductive and sexual freedom.

For Douglas, then, breaking the bonds of personal obligation provided the ideal of rights expansion that made him a great constitutional figure instead of an also-ran. Although he never found happiness in his own life, his personal chaos gave meaning and direction to his liberal constitutional values. Douglas eventually lost the credit for his revolutionary constitutional thought because of the unconventional character of his life. But it was his revolutionary, even unhinged life that allowed him to develop that thought in the first place.

Douglas's robust conception of civil liberties could be seen emerging in a decision he wrote shortly before his fateful ride into the mountains. The case had begun on a chilly evening in February 1946, in the tranquil neighborhood of Albany Park in northwest Chicago. The area was mostly Jewish (it now houses Chicago's Koreatown), but that night an event was planned in a local auditorium that would have few Jewish attendees. Members of an organization known as the Christian Veterans of America, affiliated with Gerald L. K. Smith, the founder and onetime presidential candidate of the racist, anti-Semitic America First Party, had received mailed invitations to a special rally. The featured speaker was to be Father Arthur Terminiello.

Terminiello was a Boston-born Catholic priest who had spent his pastoral career as a missionary to poor Alabama farmers. Terminiello blamed Southern poverty on a Communist-Jewish conspiracy. Like Father Charles Coughlin, the popular, anti-Semitic radio priest of the 1930s, Terminiello spoke and published widely on the subject of saving America from Reds and Jews. Like Coughlin and Smith, Terminiello sympathized with fascism and had opposed U.S. involvement in World War II. Spokesman for an organization that claimed to have forty thousand members, he was sometimes called the Father Coughlin of the South.

Father Terminiello's speech for the evening was titled "Christ or Chaos—Christian Nationalism or World Communism—Which?" When he arrived at the auditorium in Albany Park, a crowd of between two hundred and five hundred protesters—some reports said it was fifteen hundred—had gathered to express disapproval. Its composition would have confirmed Terminiello's worst suspicions: It was made up of labor union members, members of the Communist Party, and some of the membership of the usually staid American Jewish Congress. Armed with banners, the protesters tried to block access to the auditorium. Police had to escort attendees who were trying to enter, and some of them had their clothing torn on the way in.[43]

As Terminiello began to speak, the protest outside turned violent. The crowd threw rocks, bricks, and ice picks, breaking twenty-eight windows in the auditorium. A phalanx of forty boys rushed at the police, knocking some of them down. The door to the auditorium was forced open. Many people were injured in the mêlée, and nineteen protesters were arrested.[44]

Inside the auditorium, Terminiello soldiered on, connecting his remarks to the riot that was taking place outside. "I am going to whisper my greetings to you, Fellow Christians," he began. "I said, 'Fellow Christians,' and I suppose there are some of the scum got in by mistake...nothing I could say tonight could begin to express the contempt I have for the slimy scum that got in by mistake."[45] Terminiello then moved on to his subject: "the attempt that is going on right outside this hall tonight, the attempt that is going on to destroy America by revolution." That revolution, he said, was imminent. "My friends, it is no longer true that it can't happen here. It is happening here, and it only depends upon you, good people, who are here tonight.... The tide is changing, and if you and I turn and run from that tide, we will all be drowned in this tidal wave of Communism which is going over the world." The crowd inside the auditorium was cheering. According to some reports, shouts of "Kill the Jews" could be heard.[46]

After the speech was over and protest had wound down, Ira Latimer, the head of the Chicago Civil Liberties Committee, took the action that would lead to a Supreme Court case. Latimer walked to the nearest police station and, with the help of a judge whom he had met at the protest, rounded up a judge, a bailiff, and a court clerk. At 11:30 p.m., Latimer swore out warrants for the arrest of Terminiello and two of the meeting's organizers on the charge of breach of the peace. It was an unusual choice for a civil libertarian to seek the arrest of an unpopular speaker. The Chicago Civil Liberties Committee, however, was not a regular affiliate of the ACLU. The previous year it had withdrawn from the national organization after being threatened with expulsion for Communist tendencies.[47] Latimer wanted to deflect attention away from the violence of the protest and focus on Terminiello as the person who had provoked it.

The Chicago police arrested Terminiello. A local judge told the jury that a conviction for breach of the peace could occur when the accused "stirs the public to anger, invites dispute, brings about a condition of unrest, or creates a disturbance."[48] The priest was convicted and sentenced to pay a one-hundred-dollar civil fine. He appealed on the ground that his right to free speech had been abridged.

To Douglas, the case turned on the purpose of the First Amendment. The judge had told the jury that in Chicago, it was unlawful to invite dispute. It followed that the conviction should be overturned. After all, he wrote, "a function of free speech under our system of government is to invite dispute. It may indeed best serve its high purpose when it induces a condition of unrest, creates dissatisfaction with conditions as they are, or even stirs people to anger. Speech is often provocative and challenging."[49]

Douglas's analysis amounted to an aggressive expansion of the circumstances in which free speech could be used as a principle to limit government action. The Court had held several years before that a speaker's right to provoke his audience was not absolute. A speaker who used what the Court had called "fighting words" could be prosecuted for his speech.[50] All the lawyers in the *Terminiello* case had focused on whether or not the priest's speech should be counted as fighting words. All assumed that the Supreme Court's decision would depend on whether the Court thought that listeners would have been driven to use their fists when confronted by Terminiello's invective.

Douglas, however, sidestepped the issue completely. In his opinion, all that mattered was what the judge had said to the jury; that, he insisted, was where the constitutional analysis should be focused. The legal realists had long believed that court was where the law got done. The definition of law, according to Holmes, was "what the courts will do in fact." If a court could convict you for inviting dispute, then you lacked the right to invite dispute. Such a reality was not compatible with the Constitution, Douglas thought, and there was the end of it. It did not matter whether the lawyers had made this argument. What mattered was that the First Amendment should protect debate. Black joined Douglas's opinion, as did three other justices, giving Douglas a bare 5–4 majority.

Frankfurter saw the opinion as an abdication of judicial restraint. In his dissent, he criticized Douglas for ignoring what every lawyer and judge who had been involved in the case from the outset had thought the case was about. Ordinarily, appellate courts rule only on arguments that the parties make in court. Never before in the 150-year history of the Supreme Court, Frankfurter claimed, had the Court completely ignored the parties' arguments to overturn a state-court judgment on grounds it had invented out of whole cloth. Whether Douglas's decision was entirely unprecedented or not, Frankfurter was on to something. Douglas had a constitutional objective to promote. He could not care less what the rest of the world thought about it—and that certainly included the lawyers and the judges in the state courts who had dealt with Terminiello's conviction.

Meanwhile, from the pragmatic standpoint of enabling the police to control potential riots, the *Terminiello* decision seemed little short of crazy. Jackson fired off a frustrated dissent. To him, the events in Albany Park were the American version of the struggle between fascists (Terminiello) and Communists (the protesters). "This was not an isolated, spontaneous and unintended collision of political, racial or ideological adversaries. It was a local manifestation of a worldwide and standing conflict between two organized groups of revolutionary fanatics, each of which has imported to this country the strong-arm technique developed in the struggle by which their kind has devastated Europe."[51]

Jackson's railing about revolutionary fanatics may have sounded alarmist, but he had a reason for his concerns. At the Nuremberg trials, he had made a deep study of the rise of Nazism during the Weimar Republic. The Nazis had struggled with the Socialists and Communists for control of the streets. Jackson understood that whoever controlled the streets was halfway to controlling the state. Hitler had said as much in *Mein Kampf,* which Jackson quoted, the only time that work appears in the Supreme Court's reports. "It is not by dagger and poison or pistol that the road can be cleared for the movement," Hitler had advised, "but by the conquest of the streets. We must teach the Marxists that the future master of the streets is National Socialism, just as it will some day be the master of the state." They laughed at Hitler, Jackson noted, but "the battle for the streets became a tragic reality when an organized Sturmabteilung [i.e., Stormtroopers] began to give practical effect to its slogan that 'possession of the streets is the key to power in the state.' "[52] In Weimar Germany, Hitler's tactics had undeniably worked. The liberal state there had been, Jackson believed, too liberal for its own good, too fragile in the face of a fundamental challenge to its authority.

Of course postwar Chicago was not prewar Europe. Jackson was picturing an America threatened by forces whose consequences he had seen firsthand. Fascism was a spent force. As for Communism, the question of how serious the internal threat really was would preoccupy the justices in the years to come.

CHAPTER 34

The Constitution Abroad

Before the threat of Communism came to dominate the Court's worldview, the aftermath of World War II still had to be addressed—and here, too, Jackson's Nuremberg experiences would prove influential. The high-ranking Nazis who had been Jackson's targets were not the only enemies whom the United States decided to try for war crimes. Several Japanese generals were tried before military commissions; in each case, they appealed to the U.S. Supreme Court to review their convictions. Each time, the Court denied the petitions, citing different reasons to fit the particular circumstances.[53]

By 1950, just a single outstanding war-crimes case remained for the Supreme Court to resolve. At the time it did not make head-lines. But half a century later, in the wake of the terrorist attacks of September 11, 2001, it would turn out to have major historical sig-nificance, providing the blueprint for the creation of the American detention facility in Guantánamo Bay, Cuba.

The facts of the case were strange. A group of German radio operators, led by one Lothar Eisentrager, an espionage expert, had been lent by the German military to the Japanese government, which in turn deployed them in Japanese-occupied China to try and overhear U.S. military communications. They met with some success, feeding the Japanese intercepts of U.S. naval communica-tions during the battle of Okinawa. When Germany surrendered, the German radio men stayed on and continued their activities on behalf of the Japanese army.[54]

After Japan surrendered three months later, the radio operators were not sent back to Germany like ordinary soldiers. Instead they were arrested by the U.S. military and tried for violating the terms of the German surrender by continuing to fight after their army had raised the white flag. This, said the government of the United States, was a war crime, and the radio men would have to pay for it.

Their trial took place before a U.S. military tribunal in China. The men were convicted and sent to the Landsberg military prison in American-occupied Germany. While the radio operators were imprisoned in Germany, their lawyers filed a petition for a writ of habeas corpus, asking the U.S. district court in Washington, D.C., to reconsider what their lawyers called their illegal conviction.

The radio men's claims were serious. They had been operating under Japanese command, and Japan had still been in the war. It was far from clear that they had violated the terms of the German surrender. What was more, their situation arguably paralleled that of the free French, Dutch, and Norwegian soldiers who had fought alongside Britain throughout the war even after their governments had formally surrendered to Germany.[55]

What made the prisoners' request so unusual was that they were not in the United States and indeed had never set foot there— yet they were asking the U.S. courts to exercise supervisory power over their American jailers in Germany. The case therefore raised a novel question: Did the power of the U.S. courts extend overseas to protect people who were not American citizens yet had been tried under the auspices of the U.S. government? Did the Constitution follow the flag to occupied Germany?

It was not unrealistic to think that the German radio operators might possess the right to have a court hear their claims. The U.S. Court of Appeals for the D.C. Circuit, among the most prestigious courts in the country, held that they did have such a right. The Constitution, said the appellate court, guaranteed it. Anyone being detained by the U.S. government should have the right to challenge that detention in a U.S. court.[56]

Once the Supreme Court agreed to hear the case, one might have imagined that Jackson would have recused himself from sitting on it. After all, there was a certain similarity between the situation before the Court and Jackson's Nuremberg prosecution. Both involved the detention and trial of German nationals outside the U.S. by forces closely connected to the U.S. government. If the radio operators were entitled to a hearing in the U.S. courts, then the Nuremberg defendants might have deserved one, too. Jackson's role as prosecutor would certainly have been improper if the Court had the power to review the decisions of the tribunal. It would be as if a sitting Supreme Court justice had prosecuted a case in the state or lower federal courts. For Jackson to participate in judging a case that raised the possibility that his own conduct had been improper could have been understood as more improper still.

But as the whole world knew after the recusal controversy involving Black, it was up to individual justices to decide whether to recuse themselves—and Jackson not only chose to sit on the case but agreed to write the Court's opinion when it was assigned to him. There was a vaguely plausible basis to distinguish the two situations. Nuremberg had been an international tribunal, while the radio operators had been tried by a U.S. military commission. Several years before, in a case in which Jackson did not participate, the Supreme Court had held that international tribunals did not fall under its jurisdictional power. But in truth, this technical difference could potentially have been overcome in the case of the radio operators had the Court said, for example, that a substantial U.S. role in either detention or the trial gave a detainee constitutional rights.

Once Jackson was on the case, he left no doubt that he considered his expertise relevant. First he laid out the Court's holding: Noncitizens being held outside the United States had no right to a hearing before the U.S. courts. Then Jackson provided a series of practical reasons to back up his conclusion. The most powerful reason reflected his thoughts on the nature of occupation. Allowing access to the courts, he maintained, would make it extremely difficult to defeat and subjugate the enemy:

> Such trials would hamper the war effort and bring aid and comfort to the enemy. They would diminish the prestige

of our commanders. . . . It would be difficult to devise more effective fettering of a field commander than to allow the very enemies he is ordered to reduce to submission to call him to account in his own civil courts and divert his efforts and attention from the military offensive abroad to the legal defensive at home.[57]

As in the *Terminiello* case, Jackson was drawing on the lessons he had learned in Europe to shape American constitutional law. In effect, he was making constitutional law to fit the circumstances of his own participation at Nuremberg.

Justices Black and Douglas were having none of it. In a dissent that still resonates sixty years later, Black explained why noncitizens detained outside the United States possessed the constitutional right to have a U.S. court decide if they were being held lawfully. The answer lay in what Black called the principle of "equal justice under law." That principle, Black asserted, extended broadly. It meant "equal justice not for citizens alone, but for all persons coming within the ambit of our power."[58]

The source of this legal principle was less obvious than it might have seemed. The words *equal justice under law* appear nowhere in the Constitution, which avoids the word *justice* and instead specifies that no state shall "deny to any person within its jurisdiction the equal protection of the laws." In fact, the phrase *equal justice under law* appears inscribed on the lintel above the main entrance to the Supreme Court. According to the Court's own curator, the phrase was proposed by the building's architect.[59] Its origins lie, no doubt, in the language of the Fourteenth Amendment, and in an intellectual tradition reaching back to Athens. But the amendment is clearly limited to persons within the jurisdiction of the states, and the older tradition of equal treatment extended primarily to citizens. The captured radio operators were noncitizens held outside the United States.

The text that Black chose was thus a little bit misleading. But there was another constitutional provision on which he could and did rely: the guarantee of the writ of habeas corpus. The principle of habeas corpus, Black explained, subjects the government to legal standards no matter where it is acting and no matter whom it is acting upon. He dismissed Jackson's suggestion that such an expansive principle would make it difficult to fight wars and occupy foreign nations: "If our country decides to occupy conquered territory either temporarily or permanently, it assumes the problem of deciding how the subjugated people will be ruled, what laws will govern, who will promulgate them, and what governmental agency of ours will see that they are properly administered."[60] Germany, Black explained, was "a country we have occupied for years;"[61] and "we control that part of Germany we occupy." Under the circumstances, denying constitutional rights to noncitizens would make a mockery of the very idea of constitutional government.

Black insisted that it was not for the executive branch to decide "where its prisoners will be tried and imprisoned, to deprive all federal courts of their power to protect against a federal executive's illegal incarcerations." It followed that American constitutional values transcended American borders: "Our nation proclaims a belief in the dignity of human beings as such, no matter what their nationality or where they happen to live."[62] When the United States was exercising a governmental function under occupation conditions, the "mandate of equal justice under law should be applied as well when we occupy lands across the sea as when our flag flew only over thirteen colonies."[63] The radio operators deserved their day in court.

In contrast to Jackson's practical interpretation of the Constitution, under which U.S. commanders must be free to subjugate areas under their military control, Black's constitutional approach was expansive. At its core was the idea that the rule of law required judicial review of the government's actions. In extending this right to noncitizens who had never even set foot in the United States, the former Klansman was in effect repudiating the idea that the Constitution was designed primarily with the interests of American citizens in mind. Black's background had been parochial and local; but the idea of equality implicit in his opinion was cosmopolitan and universal.[64]

Perhaps most strikingly, by his dissent in the radio operators' case, Black was signaling that the ideal of equality to which he had paid lip service in the Japanese-American internment case was now poised to become a legal reality. In 1944, the attractive picture of equality had been trumped by wartime necessity. Now, in 1950, as Jackson was saying that similar pragmatic concerns should dictate the result in the case of foreign occupation, Black disagreed. Years had passed; the war was over; and now, Black was suggesting, the demands of equal justice deserved to make themselves heard. If noncitizens held abroad deserved equal justice, then African-American citizens at home deserved no less. Black had segregation in his sights. The decision in *Brown v. Board of Education* was just four years away.

Book Eight

COMMUNISM

CHAPTER 35

The Communist Councilman

Benjamin Jefferson Davis Jr. was not a typical member of the Harvard Law School class of 1930. For one thing, he was black, one of only nine African-Americans to attend the school during the 1920s.[1] For another, after graduation, instead of seeking a job on Wall Street or hanging out a shingle, he went into journalism, doing stints at the *Baltimore Afro-American* and in the offices of a Chicago advertising firm that specialized in the African-American market. Newspapers were a family legacy. Davis's father was the editor and publisher of the *Atlanta Independent*, a leading African-American-oriented paper with a circulation of 27,000.

On top of it all, Davis was privileged. His father drove a Packard, one of the first motorcars in Atlanta owned by anyone of any race. The family's brick home at 286 Martin Street was described in the family-owned newspaper as "palatial." He attended boarding school at Morehouse College, which then had a high school program, and got his B.A. at Amherst College before moving on to Harvard. He played classical violin as well as college football.[2]

For all his talent and relative wealth, Davis was still an African-American in the era of segregation. Once, on vacation from Amherst, he had sat down in the white section of an Atlanta bus wearing his varsity sweater—black with a purple A—and been arrested. At Harvard, students learned to argue cases in small law clubs that were known for mixing Jews, Catholics, and even Asians. Blacks were put in a club of their own. "The law school taught one thing and practiced another," Davis remembered.[3]

Davis's father was a Republican, like most African-Americans after Reconstruction and before Franklin Roosevelt. When Davis moved back to his native Atlanta in 1932 with plans to become a lawyer, the Republican Party offered to pay him to go on a campaign tour of the North making speeches for Hoover. But Davis's own politics were to the left. At Harvard, he recalled, he had heard lectures by William Thompson, whom Frankfurter had recruited to represent Sacco and Vanzetti. Since college he had been friendly with Paul Robeson, the famous bass-baritone singer and actor who was also by turns a member of Phi Beta Kappa, an All-American football player, a Columbia Law School graduate, and a committed leftist.

And Ben Davis's first major legal effort threw him directly into Communist politics.[4] The case that radicalized him was the trial of Angelo Herndon, an eighteen-year-old African-American member of the Young Communists League who was arrested while organizing a demonstration for poverty relief outside the Fulton County courthouse in June 1932, during the height of the Depression in the South. The Georgia authorities charged Herndon under an 1866 statute that made it a crime to incite insurrection. The maximum penalty was death.

Despite his lack of legal experience, Davis was recruited to take the case by the New York–based International Labor Defense, a Communist-linked organization that also arranged defense work for Sacco and Vanzetti. The ILD wanted an African-American to represent Herndon. It also wanted a lawyer who would help make the case into a cause by challenging the legitimacy of a segregated legal system that kept juries all-white. Davis agreed. "I was so outraged as a Negro, and partly by my Harvard idealism, that I volunteered my services in the case," he later wrote.[5]

Once Davis was on board, his recruitment to the Communist Party began in earnest. He began attending integrated weekly Communist meetings at an Atlanta foundry, led by an African-American worker.[6] He also began to read Communist literature, works Herndon was charged with teaching and believing. "In the course of defending Herndon," Davis explained, "I had to familiarize myself with these Marxist books. Their political philosophy in terms of my own status as a second-class citizen in my own country made more sense to me than anything I'd heard from the Republican and Democratic Parties."[7]

The racism on display in the trial did its part. The trial judge allowed the prosecutor to ask the jury, "Would you want a nigger to marry your daughter?"[8] Herndon escaped the death penalty, but was sentenced to twenty years on a chain gang. As Davis put it, "First credit for recruiting me goes not to the Communists but to the savage white supremacy assaults of the trial judge...against all Negroes."

At the same time, the Party's recruitment was systematic and logical, as Davis later acknowledged. It focused on the goal of transformational change in race relations: "The Communist Party...provided a rational, effective and principled path of activity and struggle through which the hideous Jim Crow system could be abolished forever in the U.S."[9] Indeed, it is no exaggeration to say that in the 1920s and 1930s, the Communist Party was the only organized political party in the United States that seriously addressed the problem of racism. The Supreme Court eventually freed Herndon, but Davis had already been radicalized. His client Herndon had become his Party mentor: "I entered the trial as his lawyer, but ended it as his Communist comrade."[10]

Once he had entered the Party, Davis left Atlanta, never to return. He moved to Harlem and returned to newspaper work, writing for the *Negro Liberator* and then the Communist *Daily Worker*. In 1943, he was elected to the New York City Council, filling the Harlem seat that had belonged to the legendary pastor-politician Adam Clayton Powell Jr. Davis ran openly as a Communist.[11] In the meantime he moved up the ranks of the Communist Party U.S.A. In 1945, while serving on the city council, he became a member of its twelve-person national board.[12] At the age of forty-one, the Harvard Law School graduate was one of the best-known Communists in the United States.

CHAPTER 36

The Battle of Foley Square

We tend to associate the virulent anti-Communism of the postwar era with Senator Joseph McCarthy, the House Un-American Activities Committee, and the Hollywood blacklist. But in fact formal efforts to combat Communism began earlier, in J. Edgar Hoover's FBI and the Department of Justice. In the summer of 1948, Attorney General Tom Clark ordered the arrest of a dozen senior figures in the newly reorganized Communist Party of the United States of America, or CPUSA. One of two African-Americans apprehended was Ben Davis.

The circumstances of the arrest were intensely political. The grand jury that indicted the Communists had been impaneled to investigate espionage. Running for reelection, Truman was caught between strident Republican anti-Communism and a third-party challenge from the left by Henry Wallace, who charged that Truman was overreacting to Communism. Neither Truman nor Clark wanted the grand jury to adjourn without taking some action. The indictment of the Communist leaders was the result.[13]

For nearly a year, eleven of these Communist leaders stood trial in the federal courthouse at Foley Square in downtown Manhattan. The proceeding was front-page news. Not since the 1918 trial of Eugene V. Debs, the Socialist candidate for president, had the leaders of an American political party been put on trial for the content of their beliefs.

The men on trial were, like American Communists generally, a mixed lot. The true believers among them were hard-core ideologues who accepted strict party discipline and the scientific certainty of Communist doctrine. They took orders directly from the

Comintern, and looked to the Soviet Union for "the answer" to workers' problems.[14]

Nor did they balk at working on behalf of Soviet interests. According to Soviet archives opened years later, one of the defendants, Eugene Dennis, the general secretary of the CPUSA, had met with agents of the Soviet secret police, then known as the NKVD.[15] Earl Browder, Dennis's predecessor as general secretary, had served for years as a talent spotter for Soviet intelligence.[16] (Browder had been purged from the CPUSA leadership under orders from Moscow and so escaped being charged alongside the other CPUSA leaders.) Historians who have studied the archives in Moscow have concluded that the CPUSA indeed "became an instrument of Soviet espionage" in this period.[17]

Other Communists, like Davis, had joined the party to find the solution to deep social grievances like racism and poverty. For these idealists, membership was often the result of a conversion experience. In Michael Gold's widely reprinted autobiographical novel, *Jews Without Money*, Communism appears as a salvation for the confused, miserable adolescent protagonist who has been suffering the brutal poverty of the Lower East Side: "O workers' Revolution, you brought hope to me, a lonely, suicidal boy. You are the true Messiah. You will destroy the East Side when you come, and build there a garden for the human spirit. O Revolution, that forced me to think, to struggle, and to live. O great Beginning!"[18]

The prosecutors, however, were not in a position to distinguish Communists who had participated in Soviet espionage from idealists who sought radical change in the American system. In the years before the trial, U.S. military intelligence had broken the Soviets' most secret codes for communicating to their operatives. Yet the prosecutors had no idea that another part of their own government had intercepted secret Soviet cables that might have implicated some CPUSA leaders and exonerated others. The military treated its codebreaking success as its most closely guarded secret. It did not even share the information with Truman himself.[19]

Because the prosecution had no direct evidence of collusion between the American Communists and the Soviet Union, it had to rely on a highly unusual and controversial law—one designed precisely to allow the pursuit of Communists within the United States. Known as the Smith Act, the 1940 law made it a crime to teach or advocate the violent overthrow of the U.S. government.

Even so, to prove the defendants' guilt was far from easy. The Communist leaders had never on their own made public statements advocating violence. That painful fact drove the prosecution to a three-step strategy. As evidence against the Communist leaders, the prosecution presented classics of Communist thought: Marx's *Communist Manifesto*, Lenin's *State and Revolution*, Stalin's *Foundations of Leninism*, and the *History of the Communist Party of the Soviet Union*. It then asserted that these works advocated violent overthrow of the government. Building on this "evidence," the prosecution asked the jury to conclude that by teaching these works, the Communist leaders had violated the Smith Act.[20]

That left the constitutional question: Did the First Amendment permit Congress to pass a law that in essence made it a crime to belong to the Communist Party? Here, too, the prosecution's case was on shaky ground. Pressed to say whether Congress possessed that power, the judge in the case, a Truman appointee named Harold Medina, ruled that it did. After Judge Medina's ruling, the outcome of the trial was never in doubt.

Medina, half Mexican and half Dutch, had attended New York public schools and put himself through Princeton and Columbia Law School. He had made his reputation in New York by teaching cram courses to law students preparing for the bar examination. If he had any sympathy for the left, it disappeared once the Communists' personal attacks on him began.

The Communists' lawyers attempted, with some success, to turn Medina's courtroom in the federal courthouse at Foley Square into a circus. They challenged Medina personally, calling him a racist; introduced hundreds of delaying motions; and offered thirty-five witnesses and 429 exhibits aimed at putting capitalism itself on trial.[21] Medina, thrust into the national spotlight, almost cracked under the pressure. In October 1949, *Time* put the worried-looking, bespectacled judge on its cover. The subheading, taken from his charge to the jury, read, "A certain calm and peace of mind"—but Medina's mental state was almost exactly the opposite

Like the trial lawyers who represented Sacco and Vanzetti, or Ben Davis representing Angelo Herndon in Atlanta, the lawyers for the Communists were not trying for an acquittal. Their tactics were aimed at swaying the public and the international community to see the prosecution as an outrage and the trial as a travesty. After the jury had convicted all the defendants on all counts, Medina sentenced the lawyers to jail terms for contempt of court. Then he sentenced the defendants to prison. Ben Davis got five years, of which he would serve three years and four months. As a convicted felon, he was automatically ejected from his seat on the New York City Council.

The leaders of the CPUSA appealed, challenging their convictions as a violation of the freedom of speech. The first stop of the appeal was the U.S. Court of Appeals for the Second Circuit. By chance, this court was the professional home of Judge Learned Hand, who would write the opinion in the case.

On the face of it, Learned Hand was the ideal judge for the defendants. As a young judge some thirty years earlier, during World War I, Hand had stood up to the government in a famous free-speech case involving a revolutionary Greenwich Village magazine called *The Masses*. The Hand of 1917 had gone out of his way to interpret the law so that the crime of incitement could only be committed by telling a listener that it was his duty or interest to break the law. Hand's opinion in the *Masses* case had established him as a leading voice for free speech in the face of government repression.[22]

By 1949, Hand had become a living legend. A regular correspondent and friend of Holmes, he was widely considered the best appellate judge in the country. Yet Roosevelt never appointed him to the Court. In 1942, when Jimmy Byrnes left the Court to run war mobilization, Frankfurter had launched a vigorous campaign on Hand's behalf.[23] Born in 1872, Hand was a little old; Roosevelt had claimed as part of his court-packing plan that justices should not serve beyond the age of seventy. Hand had also written a lower court opinion striking down the NIRA as unconstitutional, which could not have endeared him to Roosevelt. But these seemed like minor objections to

Frankfurter, who enlisted numerous distinguished lawyers to remind the president of Hand's superior intellect and qualifications.

"Do you know how many people asked me today to name Learned Hand?" Roosevelt asked his poker-playing friends the night before the decision. "Twenty, and every one a messenger from Felix Frankfurter." According to Douglas, who was there, Roosevelt had reached the point of exasperation. "By golly, I won't do it," he said. "This time, Felix overplayed his hand."[24]

Regardless, Hand's judicial reputation was unmatched. Even without the appointment to the Court for which he always yearned, he was sometimes called the tenth justice. Yet when the convictions of the Communist leaders came before him, Hand did not rule as he had in 1917. The applicable legal test, he said, was not his—which was never adopted by the Court—but a famous test penned by Holmes. Did the defendants' conduct create a clear and present danger?[25] If it did, they could be convicted. If not, their speech was protected by the First Amendment.

The way to decide whether the Communist leaders had created a clear and present danger, Hand proposed, was to consider the probability of harm resulting from their advocacy relative to the gravity of the harm that might occur as a result of it. This interpretation of "clear and present danger" echoed another view that had made Hand famous. Hand had proposed that whether a defendant exercised "reasonable care" to prevent an accident could be measured by weighing the probability of the accident relative to the gravity of the harm it caused.[26] Now he was applying his reading of tort law to the Constitution.

In practice, when applied to the Communist Party, Hand's test for clear and present danger protected civil liberties much less than had his youthful opinion in the *Masses* case. The Communist leaders' teachings were not themselves very likely to cause immediate violence, he acknowledged. But, he explained, the potential for harm posed by Soviet Communism itself was enormous: "[N]o such movement in Europe of East to West had arisen since Islam."[27] According to his test, a low probability of harm could be outweighed if the harm itself was very serious. Hand upheld the convictions. The stage was now set for an appeal to the Supreme Court.

CHAPTER 37

Clear and Present Danger

By the time the case reached the Supreme Court under the name *Dennis v. United States*, the composition of the Roosevelt Court had changed substantially. Although five justices were Roosevelt appointees, Truman had by 1950 named four justices of his own. One of them, Tom Clark, could not participate in the case, because he had himself initiated the prosecution while he was attorney general. The others—Chief Justice Fred Vinson, Justice Harold Burton, and Justice Sherman Minton—all voted to affirm the convictions that were a product of Truman administration policy.

One Roosevelt holdover, Stanley Reed, joined these three Truman men. Since only eight justices were sitting on the case, these four votes guaranteed that Learned Hand's opinion would be upheld and that the Communist leaders would stay in prison. Chief Justice Vinson's opinion applied the clear and present danger test just as it had been glossed by Hand. The four very average justices who signed the opinion deemed it the best course to rely on the famous appellate judge.

Roosevelt's four leading justices, however, could not accept the Court's opinion—and for four different reasons. Frankfurter and Jackson each produced concurring opinions that accepted the convictions, though not for the reasons expressed by Learned Hand and adopted by the Court. Black and Douglas each wrote important and memorable dissents. Each of the men was eager to express his distinctive constitutional philosophy—and to distance himself from Truman's unpopular policies.

Black's opinion was the simplest. In a ringing and concise

dissent—two pages to Frankfurter's forty-two—Black came as close as he ever would to announcing that the right to free speech was absolute. He based his argument on the text of the First Amendment: "Congress shall make no law...abridging the freedom of speech." Black would walk around his office reciting a catechism to himself: "What does the Constitution say?" went the question. "It says 'no law,'" went the answer. "That means no law. It doesn't make for any exceptions."[28] For Black, the key to the case was simply that the Smith Act flatly prohibited speech.

Applying Holmes's clear and present danger test, the Supreme Court had never before taken the command of the First Amendment literally. As usual, Black was willing to jettison precedent, even when it came from the pen of the great Holmes.[29] If the doctrine did not match the text, then the doctrine must be wrong.

To abandon the clear and present danger test in favor of absolute free speech was an act of constitutional bravery—and like most brave acts, it left the hero unguarded and alone. Even Douglas, usually friendly to Black, could not agree with him: "The freedom to speak," he wrote in his own dissent, "is not absolute."[30] As Holmes had explained in formulating the clear and present danger test, the First Amendment could not possibly protect someone who falsely shouted *fire* in a crowded theater. Frankfurter charged Black with the sin of formalism: "Such literalness treats the words of the Constitution as though they were found on a piece of outworn parchment,"[31] or as "barren words found in a dictionary."[32]

Frankfurter considered *Dennis* "a great case"—the kind that posed a fundamental conflict "of the utmost concern to the well-being of the country."[33] On the one hand was the inherent right of the state "to maintain its existence" against a serious threat.[34] On the other hand was the right to free speech, which Frankfurter had supported during his long association with the ACLU. Indeed, one of the Communist leaders who had been convicted, William Z. Foster, had served with Frankfurter on the ACLU national committee—and Frankfurter had been questioned about him in his confirmation hearings.[35]

Grasping for a solution to the conflict between self-preservation and freedom, Frankfurter turned to his master theory: judicial restraint. In the presence of a conflict of values, Frankfurter reasoned, it was not up to the Court to "balance the relevant factors and ascertain which interest is in the circumstances to prevail."[36] Courts, after all, are not "representative bodies. They are not designed to be a good reflex of a democratic society."[37] Responsibility for balancing the competing interests of self-preservation and free speech lay with Congress. Of course the Court could overturn the law if it so chose, but Frankfurter advised against it: "We must scrupulously observe the narrow limits of judicial authority even though self-restraint is alone set over us."[38]

Frankfurter understood perfectly well that the CPUSA posed little threat domestically. He quoted George Kennan, the country's most prescient student of the Soviet Union and the author of Truman's doctrine of containment. "The American Communist party is today, by and large, an external danger," Kennan had written in the *New York Times Magazine.* "It represents a tiny minority in our country; it has no real contact with the feelings of the mass of our people; and its position as the agency of a hostile foreign power is clearly recognized by the overwhelming mass of our citizens."[39]

Acknowledging that the Communist leaders were basically harmless, Frankfurter wanted to duck the question of whether they belonged in jail. He could, he thought, uphold the Smith Act and the convictions without endorsing crude anti–Communism. He wanted to believe he was following Holmes, who had patented the trick of saying that a given law was a bad one while simultaneously upholding it as constitutional.

But there was a catch. In all his writing on the freedom of speech, Holmes had never said that the courts should defer to the legislature. Neither had Brandeis, Frankfurter's other judicial hero. Frankfurter had always claimed that judicial restraint was the invention of these two great justices and of Professor James Bradley Thayer. But now he was forced to confront the one area where Holmes and Brandeis had both been activists. Both men believed that the courts should carefully review restraints on free speech, permitting them to remain in place only when there was, in fact, a clear and present danger.

Frankfurter could not admit that he was deviating from the legacy of Holmes. As Douglas once cruelly joked, "Know why Frankfurter never had any children? Because Holmes didn't."[40] So Frankfurter tried to claim that he was actually applying the "clear and present danger" test flexibly, as Holmes would have: "It does an ill-service" to Holmes, Frankfurter wrote, "to make him the victim of a tendency which he fought all his life, whereby phrases are made to do service for critical analysis by being turned into dogma."[41]

This was a striking piece of overreaching, especially for someone who had devoted his life to emulating Holmes. The clear and present danger test was designed to protect free speech from encroachment by government officials armed with broad legislative authority. When it came to the First Amendment, Holmes could not credibly be made into an advocate of deference to the legislature.

Frankfurter had allowed the theory of judicial restraint to take him outside of Holmes's legacy. In so doing, he found himself misrepresenting Holmes and Brandeis in the bargain. When forced to choose between his mentors and the theory he had invented to explain them, he went with the theory. Instead of looking principled, Frankfurter ended up looking benighted. His theory of judicial restraint itself came to seem like a cover for tolerating violation of the most basic civil liberties. Frankfurter would pay dearly for this deviation. Black pointed out the problem in his opinion: If the Court defers to a "reasonable" judgment by Congress to abridge free speech, then the First Amendment is no longer a law, but "little more than an admonition to Congress."[42] Although he did not know it, Frankfurter's decision in the *Dennis* case marked the moment that he could no longer be fairly described as a liberal.

If Frankfurter in the *Dennis* case was misled by his own constitutional theory, for Jackson the case was a test of whether a country lawyer turned international statesman could apply his own pragmatism correctly. His early experience with domestic anti-

Communism had left him skeptical of its efficacy. As a young man in Jamestown, he had been a member of the American Protective League, formed originally in 1917 as an auxiliary to the Department of Justice in order to ferret out pro-German sentiment across the country.[43] Jackson considered the League's activities amateur and absurd; after the war, the League became anti-Communist and antilabor, which Jackson later called "a complete perversion of its original purpose."[44]

During his year at Nuremberg, however, Jackson had seen Communism from a different angle. The Soviet lawyers and judges with whom he worked were, he knew, taking their orders from Moscow. In occupied Germany, with its different zones controlled by different states, it had been obvious how the world was becoming divided between the Soviets and the Western powers. More than his colleagues, Jackson had been exposed to the ground zero of the Cold War—and he felt he understood the operation of Communism firsthand.

Jackson began his opinion by acknowledging that under the "clear and present danger" test as it had been formulated some thirty years before, the Communist leaders could not be found guilty. The test, he reasoned, belonged to the age of "anarchist terrorism"—of Sacco and Vanzetti. Anarchists, Jackson asserted, lacked coordinated plans, and so it made sense to deal with them by prohibiting their speech only when it was in danger of causing imminent harm.

Communism, on the other hand, was something entirely different. The "antithesis of anarchism," it relied on a highly disciplined cadre of leaders to coordinate the long-term takeover of the government it sought to subvert. "The Communists," Jackson wrote, "have no scruples against sabotage, terrorism, assassination, or mob disorder; but violence is not with them, as with the anarchists, an end in itself. The Communist Party advocates force only when prudent and profitable.... Force or violence...may never be necessary, because infiltration and deception may be enough."[45]

With his single year of formal legal education in Albany, Jackson had not been a protégé of Holmes and had no instinct to treat him as a legal god. Holmes was for him simply a judge of a previous generation, whose "clear and present danger" test was obsolete. If it were used, it would mean "that the Communist plotting is protected during its period of incubation," and that "its preliminary stages of organization and preparation are immune from the law."[46] The government would be allowed to make arrests "only after imminent action is manifest, when it would, of course, be too late."[47]

Like his opinion in the case of the anti-Semitic priest Terminiello, Jackson's argument drew from what he had learned about the rise of Nazism. "Totalitarian groups," he wrote, "perfected the technique of creating private paramilitary organizations to coerce both the public government and its citizens."[48] Jackson, led astray by his own experiences, concluded that what had happened in Europe could happen at home. "The Communist Party realistically is a state within a state, an authoritarian dictatorship within a republic," he wrote.[49] In reality, the CPUSA and its Soviet handlers might have aspired to such discipline and power, but they were very far from achieving it.

Jackson's assessment of the Communist threat was not the only part of the *Dennis* opinion in which he was influenced by Nuremberg. He also drew on the tribunal for what he considered the cure. The right tool to combat the Communists' long-term strategy, Jackson argued, was to put them on trial for conspiracy.

"The basic rationale of the law of conspiracy," he explained, "is that a conspiracy may be an evil in itself, independently of any other evil it seeks to accomplish."[50] Conspiracy law made sense because Communism was itself a conspiracy—an ongoing, collective enterprise designed to accomplish the takeover of government by any expedient means. The essence of the conspiracy charge was to impose responsibility on different people within complex organizations for the actions of all. At Nuremberg, Jackson had argued that Nazism itself amounted to the greatest criminal conspiracy the world had ever known.

Douglas put no stock in Jackson's use of conspiracy at Nuremberg. Earlier in the year, in a case involving investigation of subversive groups, Douglas had lashed out at what he called "guilt by association." It was, he said, "one of the most odious institutions of history"—un-American and unconstitutional. "The fact that the technique of guilt by association was used in the prosecutions at Nuremberg does not make it congenial to our constitutional scheme. Guilt under our system of government is personal. When we make guilt vicarious you borrow from systems alien to ours and ape our enemies."[51] Douglas had a point. At Nuremberg, Jackson had been participating in a trial that included the Soviets, who considered law strictly as a tool for political ends.

In his *Dennis* dissent, Douglas went after Jackson once more. "Invoking the law of conspiracy," he charged, "makes speech do service for deeds which are dangerous to society."[52] It turned mere words into acts of sedition: "Never until today has anyone seriously thought that the ancient law of conspiracy could constitutionally be used to turn speech into seditious conduct. Yet that is precisely what is suggested."[53]

As Douglas took pains to demonstrate, the CPUSA defendants had been accused of nothing more than speaking. The men had taught the doctrines of four Communist texts. These books were perfectly lawful in the United States. If they could be on the shelves, Douglas asked, how could it be a crime to teach what was in them?[54] Douglas admitted that the Communist leaders believed the teachings of the books in question, but to rely on that charge to convict them was "to make freedom of speech turn not on what is said, but on the intent with which it is said."[55] This, in its essence, was mind control.

Douglas had always claimed to be the true heir to Brandeis.[56] Now he invoked that legacy with pride, quoting Brandeis's most trenchant free speech passage: "Fear of serious injury cannot alone justify suppression of free speech and assembly. Men feared witches and burnt women. It is the function of speech to free men from the bondage of irrational fears."[57] While Jackson was pontificating about world communism and Frankfurter was flailing in a maelstrom of theory, Douglas embodied the values of Brandeis. The mantle of liberalism had passed to his shoulders.

The core of Douglas's liberal free-speech theory was that advocating ideas was different from conduct. The state has the power to prohibit "teaching the techniques of sabotage, the assassination of the President...the planting of bombs...and the like."[58] It did not have the authority to prohibit abstract ideas. "I repeat that we deal here with speech alone, not with speech plus acts of sabotage or unlawful conduct. Not a single seditious act is charged in the indictment."[59] The absence of action made all the difference. In violation of liberal principle, the leaders of the CPUSA were being convicted only for their ideas.

Douglas did more than insist on the all-important difference between ideas and action. He provided an original explanation for why the liberal state must protect ideas, even those that might seem dangerous: "The airing of ideas releases pressures which otherwise might become destructive.... Full and free discussion keeps a society from becoming stagnant and unprepared for the stresses and strains that work to tear all civilizations apart."[60] Threatening ideas could not be suppressed without creating potentially destructive pressures on the whole system. Allowing the unspeakable to be spoken would, Douglas suggested, safeguard the civilization against destruction from within. The argument reflected Douglas's familiarity with the version of Freudian psychology that he had experienced himself when George Draper cured him of his fear of peritonitis.

Not content with abstract arguments for free speech, Douglas also gave a practical one. Jackson had emphasized the tremendous threat of Communism worldwide. But Douglas insisted that Communism was not a threat domestically, because it lacked popular support. "Communists in this country have never made a respectable or serious showing in any election. I would doubt that there is a village, let alone a city or county or state, which the Communists could carry."[61] And why was Communism so unpopular in the United States? "Communism has been so thoroughly exposed in this country that it has been crippled as a political force. Free speech has destroyed it as an effective political party."[62] Douglas was arguing that liberal democracy could only be subverted through a broad-based popular movement. To believe that Communists "are placed in such critical positions as to endanger the Nation is to believe the incredible," Douglas wrote.[63] In the event of war with Russia, "they will be picked up overnight as were all prospective saboteurs at the commencement of World War II."[64] In fact, the CPUSA was "the best known, the most beset, and the least thriving of any fifth column in history."[65]

The upshot of Douglas's profession was that liberalism must rest itself on the will of the people. "Our faith should be that our people will never give support to these advocates of revolution, so long as we remain loyal to the purposes for which our Nation was founded."[66] Seen in these terms, it would actually be unpatriotic to interpret the Communist threat as dire. True patriotism relied upon the enduring power of popular support for liberal values and ideals.

Douglas's argument effectively refuted the paranoia that gripped even liberal anti-Communism in the early 1950s. In the face of speculation—much of it in retrospect well justified—that international Communism sought to take advantage of liberalism in order to subvert it, Douglas insisted that liberalism was more than strong enough to resist the challenge. As Jackson and Frankfurter doubted the strength of liberalism, they began to stray from the values they had once striven to protect. Douglas kept his eye on the ball, never believing that Communism could make serious inroads into American society. History vindicated his opinion. The major reason Douglas emerges as a hero of liberalism in the anti-Communist moment is simply that he was right.

CHAPTER 38

Seizure

By the spring of 1952, with his last months in office approaching, Harry Truman was exhausted. His presidency, he believed, had not been a success. The public agreed. Gallup reported that only 22 percent of the public approved of the job he was doing as president—lower than the 24 percent mark that Nixon would hit at the nadir of the Watergate scandal and still the lowest ever recorded.[67]

The reasons for Truman's unpopularity were not hard to divine. The labor unrest that had plagued his first term had never fully abated. And the Korean War, which dominated his second term, had gone badly. Beginning as a limited war against Communist forces from North Korea, it had turned into a much more serious conflict when General Douglas MacArthur had provoked China to send hundreds of thousands of troops across the Yalu River.

Poorly conducted, the war cost more than fifty thousand American lives in addition to the lives of nearly a quarter of a million South Korean soldiers; at least the same number of civilians died. Truman would not even manage to end the war during his presidency: When he left office in January 1953, it still had another six months to run before the armistice was signed. The war ended in a stalemate, with Korea split into two separate countries. If this was Truman's containment doctrine in action, it did not seem to bode well for the future.[68]

Truman wanted very much to choose his own successor. Alben Barkley, his vice president, was too old for the job. Truman dangled his endorsement—for what it was worth—before Dwight Eisenhower, who politely declined. He was a lifelong Republican who had disagreed with Truman's labor policies and felt he could not change parties just to run for president. The same day, Truman welcomed the justices of the Supreme Court for their annual presidential reception. In a conversation with a group that included Douglas as well as all four of Truman's Supreme Court appointees, Truman mentioned his chat with Eisenhower. Douglas went home and called Arthur Krock, who published the story of Truman's offer to Eisenhower in the next day's *New York Times*. The White House brazenly denied the account, with Truman commenting that he would have expected it from a gossip columnist, not from Krock.[69]

As it turned out, it was not a coincidence that Truman had mentioned the Eisenhower story to a group that included his best friend in Washington, Chief Justice Fred Vinson. In February, Truman offered the Democratic nomination to the chief justice. Truman and Vinson had been close for nearly twenty years, since Truman had been a senator and Vinson a Democratic congressman from Kentucky. Vinson, who played in Truman's regular, high-stakes poker game, had become secretary of the treasury soon after Truman became president. When the Jackson-Black fracas had made Jackson unappointable as chief justice, Truman had chosen Vinson for the job.

This time, however, Vinson said no, declining the presidential nomination. First he claimed that he did not think the Court should be a stepping stone to politics. When Truman pointed to Hughes's run for the presidency, Vinson admitted the real reason: He feared his health was not up to it.[70]

Now concerned that he might not be able to anoint a plausible Democrat to succeed him, Truman approached Adlai Stevenson, the governor of Illinois. When Stevenson initially demurred, Truman spent some ten days thinking about running again himself. On the evening of March 29, at a black-tie Democratic dinner in Washington, Truman announced to the senior figures in the party that he would not run. Some applauded, and some called out "No," but the overwhelming feeling among Democrats was relief. Arthur

Schlesinger Jr. captured the moment. "I found myself shouting 'No' with vigor. Then I wondered why the hell I was shouting 'No,' since this is what I had been hoping would happen for months."[71]

Having taken himself out of the race, Truman immediately faced yet another crisis. The steelworkers union, which had been in contract negotiations since the previous November, was coming dangerously close to declaring a work stoppage. Both telephone and telegraph workers were already out on strike. By this time, Truman had become accustomed to the cycle of labor disputes. But steel was something else again. The United States was still at war. And in modern war, steel was the single most important commodity to keep the soldiers fighting.

Truman's advisers confirmed the seriousness of the situation. His secretary of defense told him that "any curtailment of production . . . would endanger the lives of our fighting men."[72] Supplies of some kinds of ammunition were running low. Although fighting had died down as truce negotiations continued, there was always the risk of a flare-up if China believed that U.S. supplies were likely to be depleted.[73]

From Truman's perspective, the stumbling block to a settlement with the steelworkers was the steel companies. Truman's Wage Stabilization Board, the organization with the job of managing labor difficulties during the war, had proposed raising the workers' hourly wage by twenty-six cents. Management was in principle willing to accept the pay raise. In exchange, they wanted permission from the government to increase the price of steel by twelve dollars a ton. Since the U.S. government was by far the largest purchaser of American steel, the steel industry's counteroffer essentially called for the taxpayers to subsidize their employees' wage hike. Truman flatly rejected this option.

But Truman also wanted to avoid a strike in one of the nation's largest and most important industries. Korea aside, the United States had promised weapons to its allies as part of its broader Cold War strategy. Dean Acheson, now Truman's secretary of state, told him that a steel slowdown would hurt U.S. credibility as the leader of the free world and encourage Soviet aggression. Domestically, a halt in steel production would interfere with the postwar growth that the economy so much needed. It would affect the production of ships, airplanes, highways, and bridges.[74]

The solution was to force the steel companies to take the deal. Abandoning negotiation, Truman adopted the most radical approach possible. In a televised speech on the evening of April 8, 1952, he announced an executive order taking temporary possession of the steel production industry on behalf of the U.S. government. Outright takeover of an entire major American industry by presidential fiat was a shock to the public and the business community alike. The relevant labor law, known as the Taft-Hartley Act, would have allowed the president to postpone the strike for eighty days. Truman ignored it as a half measure. Plagued by difficulties in Korea and frustrated by industry intransigence, he wanted to solve a complicated problem with a single bold stroke.

The decision seemed like self-dealing on the part of an unpopular president immersed in a war that was going badly. Once the president "owned" the mills, Truman could dictate any policy he chose to avoid the strike—including paying the workers what the Wage Stabilization Board had recommended. As the major consumer of steel, the government naturally wanted to buy it at the lowest possible price. Seizing the mills allowed Truman to set a price that the manufacturers did not consider sufficiently profitable. Price setting for wartime commodities was already in place. But this particular episode of price setting seemed particularly aggressive to contemporary observers. Indeed, Truman's director of defense mobilization resigned over the decision.

Apart from the economic wisdom of the decision, Truman was worried about its constitutionality. Justice Tom Clark, Truman's former attorney general, had advised him while in that role that the president enjoyed an inherent constitutional power to stop the national economy from grinding to a halt as the result of a strike.[75] And Truman himself was wont to say that the president had the power to save the country from falling apart.[76] Nevertheless, the Supreme Court might overturn his decision and thwart his plans. So Truman sought expert legal advice before acting.

The expert Truman chose was his friend Vinson. The president privately asked the chief justice whether seizing the mills was constitutional.[77] Vinson replied that in his view, it was. A careful Court watcher could certainly have predicted that the justices would find in Truman's favor. He had appointed four of them—Vinson, Tom Clark, Harold Burton, and Sherman Minton. Two of these, Vinson and Clark, had specifically taken broad views of presidential power. Jackson had been a great advocate of expansive executive authority when he was Roosevelt's attorney general and had authorized Roosevelt to take over various factories to resolve labor disputes. Even if Black and Douglas came out against the seizure, five votes seemed relatively secure, even allowing for the uncertainty of Frankfurter.

It was of course improper for Truman to consult with Vinson. Both men knew their conversation was outside the bounds of ordinary propriety, and it remained secret for some years. But the norms of the 1940s and 1950s with respect to contacts between judges and the executive branch were different than they are today. Roosevelt had stayed in touch with Frankfurter (albeit through intermediaries) during the saboteurs' case. The steel seizure was connected to the war effort. Perhaps Vinson should have resisted, but there is every reason to think that he considered the national interest in the war against Communism to be paramount.

What makes this episode of backdoor conversation particularly interesting—and apt as a coda to the Truman era—is how it backfired. Public opinion generally supported the seizure when it happened in April. Truman's poll numbers even enjoyed a brief resurgence.[78] But fairly quickly, as the implications of what Truman had done set in, attitudes began to turn. Ten days after the seizure, on April 18, Truman was asked at a press conference, "Mr. President, if you can seize the steel mills under your inherent powers, can you in your opinion also seize the newspaper or/and the radio stations?" Truman did not hesitate. "The President of the United States had to do what was best for the country," he replied.[79]

Truman was free to exercise the lame duck's privilege of speaking frankly. He was not, however, helping his case with the public or the courts. By the end of the month, a federal district court issued an injunction to reverse Truman's action. The government sought an expedited review by the Supreme Court, which heard arguments on May 12 and 13, barely a month after the initial seizure.

On June 2, with speed befitting a national crisis, the Supreme Court decided against Truman. By a 6–3 vote, the Supreme Court ruled in *Youngstown Sheet & Tube Co. v. Sawyer* that the president's seizure of the steel mills was unconstitutional. Two of Truman's appointees actually voted against him. One was Harold Burton, a Republican who had served with Truman in the Senate and was appointed in a gesture of bipartisanship that was in this case not reciprocated. A frustrated Truman told his poker-partners, Justices Vinson and Minton, that Burton appeared not to understand how important the steel seizure case was to maintaining support for his presidency.[80] The other turncoat, by Truman's estimation, was Tom Clark, the former attorney general who had given Truman his broad notion of executive authority in the first place. This reversal by the Texan whom Truman had elevated from the middle levels of the Justice Department was one that Truman would never forgive. Truman would later call Clark's appointment his biggest mistake as president. "It isn't so much that he's a *bad* man," Truman said cannily. "It's just that he's a dumb son of a bitch."[81]

But it was the Roosevelt appointees on the Court who led the charge against Truman. Frankfurter and Jackson were willing to vote on the same side as Black and Douglas, who were by now their judicial archenemies. It is hard to escape the conclusion that this was their chance to repudiate Truman, the ineffectual non–New Dealer who was presiding over the corpse of Roosevelt-style liberalism.

Truman had expected the Court to allow him the same broad authority that Roosevelt had exercised in wartime. To Roosevelt's justices, the police action in Korea—never declared a war by Congress—was not the total war of World War II. Frankfurter and Jackson could have found grounds to uphold the seizure had they wanted to do so. That they did not reflected their contempt for Truman. At the same time, it also furnished Jackson with the opportunity to write one of the most influential opinions of the last half century.

CHAPTER 39

The Zone of Twilight

The Supreme Court over the years has come to treat Jackson's concurrence as though it were the opinion of the Court. Yet Jackson commanded exactly one vote for his opinion—his own. The opinion for the Court was written by Hugo Black. Its simplicity probably explains why the other five justices were prepared to join it; it also explains why it has been essentially forgotten. Black's approach grew out of his own text-oriented originalism. The authority for Truman's action, Black wrote, must come either from a statute passed by Congress or from some specific provision of the Constitution.[82] Truman had not relied on any statute, and his lawyers had not "claimed that express constitutional language grants this power to the President." Instead they had maintained, more or less as Truman had in his press conference, that the president had the inherent authority under the Constitution to do what was necessary to save the country.

Relying on the text of the Constitution, Black rejected Truman's claim that the president's power as commander in chief implicitly authorized the seizure. The seizure, he pointed out, had not taken place in the theater of war[83]—a point that Jackson would echo and expand. Then, in a more aggressive act of reliance on the words of the Constitution alone, Black said that the president's "executive power" was limited to executing the laws passed by Congress. The seizure did not rely on any congressional enactment, and the order was therefore beyond the president's power to execute.

The justices knew that Black's opinion was unconvincing. The growth of the president's authority during Roosevelt's administration made such a cramped view totally unworkable. The reason they joined it at all was their perception that if the Court was going to reverse a presidential decision in wartime, there was safety in numbers. Every single one of those who joined Black's opinion also wrote his own concurring opinion, each with a different stance on the correct division between presidential and congressional power under the Constitution. Frankfurter even wrote an unusual separate statement, printed immediately after Black's opinion but separately from Frankfurter's own concurrence, the better to ensure that Black's opinion would not be treated as the majority opinion it technically was.

Frankfurter's own concurrence in *Youngstown* laid out his theory of how the separation of powers could be figured out: by asking what government had in fact done in the past. Black was wrong to look to the text: "It is an inadmissibly narrow conception of American constitutional law to confine it to the words of the Constitution and to disregard the gloss which life has written upon them."[84]

The "gloss" Frankfurter had in mind was actual practice, what he called "deeply embedded traditional ways of conducting government." The Constitution was "a framework for government," not a rigid set of unchanging rules. The binding nature of constitutional law in fact depended on the binding nature of constitutional practice. "The way the framework has consistently operated fairly establishes that it has operated according to its true nature."[85] Frankfurter was advancing an approach associated with the unwritten British constitution. He was looking at practice and asserting that legality is constructed out of tradition. The great benefit of such an approach lies in its historical continuity coupled with its situational flexibility.[86] It represents, of course, an outright rejection of originalism.

The most surprising aspect of Frankfurter's opinion was his conclusion that Truman could not rely on precedent to seize the steel mills. The proof, he said, lay in the past practice of Congress, which since 1916 had enacted at least sixteen different seizure provisions (he listed them in an appendix). These were the relevant precedents, since they made it clear that seizure was allowed only with congressional authorization. Yet Frankfurter failed to account for those instances in which the modern wartime presidents, Roosevelt and Wilson, had engaged in seizures without congressional authorization. Frankfurter explained these away by saying that wartime was different. But of course it was wartime, even if Truman had never bothered to have Congress declare war in Korea, preferring to call the conflict a police action.

Even distinguishing wartime from peace still left Frankfurter with three seizures Roosevelt had made during the six months of 1941 before Pearl Harbor. These now-embarrassing incidents seemed precisely parallel to what Truman had done. Frankfurter simply asserted without explanation that they had been different and temporary. In doing so he demonstrated the great danger of his approach to presidential power: The result depends completely on how the judges choose to define the circumstances in which the presidential power is exercised.

Douglas's solution to the seizure problem was much less complicated than Frankfurter's. But he found room to inject his own judicial philosophy: a concern for civil liberties vis-à-vis the government. This was no easy matter in a case that pitted organized labor against big business. On the face of it, the *Youngstown* case involved no individual liberties at all, but simply the question of the separation of powers.

With creative flair, Douglas insinuated individual rights into the case. The government, he said, certainly had the power to seize private property to settle a labor dispute. But under the Fifth Amendment, every such seizure, no matter how brief, needed to be compensated. Since only Congress had the power to tax, only Congress would have the power to pay for such a seizure. It followed, Douglas said, that a presidential seizure could only be lawful if it were immediately validated by Congress. This view was not especially logical. Even if the seizure had to be paid for, the president might still have the authority to order it. But logic was not Douglas's priority. The right to compensation was the only conceivable individual right that could be introduced to the case, even if it belonged here to the owners of the steel factories.

The limitations of the other opinions serve to underscore the elegance of Jackson's effort in the steel seizure case. His opinion offered a precise match between the strange circumstances of the case and his distinctive theory of constitutional pragmatism. Jackson had no love for Truman, who had denied him the chief justiceship. But his concurring opinion went beyond this animus. Like the best products of the art of constitutional decision making, it transcended the politics of the moment to say something of lasting value.

What gave the opinion its drama, though, was something different still: It required Jackson to revisit and reverse the position on executive power that he had taken while working for Roosevelt and that had cemented his relationship with the president he so revered. Characteristically, Jackson began the opinion by acknowledging that his own experience as a presidential adviser on questions of executive power was the real basis for his judgment. "Anyone who has served as legal adviser to a president in time of transition and public anxiety," Jackson wrote, would understand both the advantages and dangers of "comprehensive and undefined presidential powers."[87] Although he had undergone an "interval of detached reflection" during his time as a judge, the "teachings of that experience" in the executive branch were "probably a more realistic influence on my views than the conventional materials of judicial decision."[88]

When Jackson was writing, judges never said explicitly that practical experience, not the law, was shaping their judgment. To be sure, judges describing the judicial process had been known to say that some aspects of decision making came from outside the law.[89] But recognizing outside influence is quite different from expressly discounting the importance of constitutional text and precedent. Jackson was stating the first principle of constitutional pragmatism: What matters is what works in the real world, not the law on the books.

Nor did Jackson stop there. He explained just why the law was of little help and why the judge should therefore draw on his own practical sense. The legal materials, he said, "seem unduly to accentuate doctrine and legal fiction."[90] *Doctrine* is not usually a dirty word to judges; it is, after all, the stuff of judicial decisions. In Jackson's hands, though, doctrine was associated with legal fiction and thereby drawn into the realm of invention and irrelevance.

The problem, Jackson said, was that the law did not answer the question. There was a "poverty of really useful and unambiguous authority applicable to concrete problems of executive power as they actually present themselves."[91] The judicial decisions were "indecisive."[92] As for the original intent of the framers, what they envisioned "or would have envisioned had they foreseen modern conditions, must be divined from materials almost as enigmatic as the dreams Joseph was called upon to interpret for Pharaoh."[93] No more pithy dismissal of originalism appears in the *U.S. Reports.*

With this opening salvo rejecting other methods of constitutional interpretation, Jackson went on to propose his own picture of how the separation of powers should be defined. It relied, he said, on a "somewhat oversimplified grouping of practical situations" that could confront the president and Congress.[94] The practical situations, Jackson asserted, were three: The president acts with the express or implied authorization of Congress; the president acts when Congress has neither granted nor denied him the authority to do so—what Jackson memorably called a "zone of twilight"; or the president acts contrary to what Congress had explicitly or implicitly told him to do.

For each of these three practical situations, Jackson proposed results. A president acting with Congress behind him is at the maximum point of his power, exercising his inherent authority and whatever additional authority Congress has chosen to give him. Where Congress is silent, there might be overlap between the president's inherent powers and those of Congress, but in any case, no good rule of conduct can be given: "In this area, any actual test of power is likely to depend on the imperatives of events and contemporary imponderables rather than on abstract theories of law."[95] In the twilight zone, Jackson was saying, there is no right legal answer.

Most important was Jackson's third category. When the president's action is "incompatible with the expressed or implied will of Congress, his power is at its lowest ebb, for then he can rely only upon his own constitutional powers minus any constitutional powers of Congress over the matter."[96] The word *minus* carried enormous weight. It meant that so long as Congress was acting within the scope of its vast constitutional powers, it could block the president from taking action—and the courts should uphold congressional authority over that of the president.

Jackson was careful to say that his three-part framework was not a formal doctrinal rule—he had, after all, impugned the value of doctrine as opposed to practical judgment. Yet the neatness of the three categories has unquestionably contributed to their becoming standardized as the law of the land. These categories came from nowhere in the history of the Constitution or the opinions of the Court. Nevertheless, they captured the notion that the Constitution contemplated a kind of contest between the different branches of government. According to Jackson's opinion, the role of the Court was to resolve this contest.

In this image of the referee adjudicating between contending sides, it was possible to see an extension of Jackson's earlier view, first expressed in his book on judicial supremacy, that the job of the courts was to resolve conflicts between contending social forces. In place of labor and capital, Jackson now inserted the president and Congress. These contending forces needed guidelines to cabin their potential for conflict. And although Jackson frankly admitted that in the "zone of twilight" no simple resolution was possible, the power of the opinion lay at least partly in the fact that a reasonably competent court could usually find some judgment of Congress—even if only implicit—that was arguably at stake.

Indeed, that was the strategy that Jackson pursued in the section of his opinion in which he applied his categories to Truman's seizure of the steel mills. Jackson reminded his readers of the Taft-Hartley Act, which allowed the president to block a strike for eighty days. That law, Jackson reasoned, amounted to an implicit congressional prohibition on using seizure to solve a labor dispute right away. If Congress had told the president he could block the strike by means of delay, it must have meant that he could not block it by means of a seizure.

Considered formally, this was probably the weakest part of Jackson's opinion. Although the topic had been debated in Congress before the law was passed, the Taft-Hartley Act said nothing about seizure, either to allow it or to ban it. From a practical standpoint, however, Jackson was right to suggest that the Taft-Hartley Act, passed over labor's objections and Truman's veto, expressed a congressional mood very different from Truman's aggressively prolabor policy of seizing the mills. Jackson was relying on his own astute political judgment in attempting to craft a constitutional result consistent with what Congress in fact would have wanted to do—not only when it passed the Taft-Hartley Act but right then, during the seizure crisis. Constitutional pragmatism, as Jackson himself acknowledged, required fine judgment in implementation.

Jackson did, however, face a serious difficulty: his own prior views. As attorney general, he himself had written a memo authorizing Roosevelt to seize a California aviation plant in June 1941, some six months before Pearl Harbor and the declaration of war. At the time, Jackson was in the middle of the debate over executive authority connected to the plan of sending war supplies to Britain. The aviation plant in question had suffered a strike by a rogue union faction, and Roosevelt had seized it to order the workers back into the saddle. The circumstances, in other words, were not so different from what Truman had faced, although the scale had been much smaller.[97]

Jackson made several rather weak attempts in his opinion to distinguish the two situations. He mentioned that the strike in California had occurred without the approval of the national union, and he suggested—somewhat absurdly—that government-owned machinery was lying unused in the aviation plant. He also argued, without much support, that the aviation seizure "was regarded as an execution of congressional policy."

But Jackson's key point was far more honest: Even if the aviation seizure counted as a precedent, he "should not bind present judicial judgment by earlier partisan advocacy."[98] Jackson the judge, he believed, should not be constrained by the views of Jackson the attorney general.

Jackson was not simply making the formal point that his opinion as attorney general could not bind him as a judge. Nor was he saying that experience can be misleading. He had, after all, begun the *Youngstown* opinion by saying that his experiences were precisely what led him to the result in the case. Jackson was instead arguing that different roles call for different forms of judgment. In words Jackson quoted in an earlier case, "the matter does not appear to me now as it appears to have appeared to me then."[99]

There was a final twist. Jackson still had to confront the Truman administration's argument that the president as commander in chief must be able to do all that was necessary to win the war. To Jackson, this argument recalled the German constitution of the prewar Weimar period. That document allowed the president of the Reich to suspend basic rights if "public safety and order are considerably disturbed or endangered."[100] Jackson knew of the provision from his work at Nuremberg, and he considered this model of the so-called state of emergency to be a recipe for totalitarianism. In thirteen years, he pointed out, individual rights were suspended 250 times under the Weimar constitution, until at last "Hitler persuaded President von Hindenburg to suspend all such rights, and they were never restored."[101]

Under the U.S. Constitution, Jackson explained, the president was not authorized to use the state of war to make exceptions to individual rights. In emergencies, Congress was supposed to authorize the president to act. Jackson acknowledged that when facing a true crisis the president might take action unilaterally, and no one would be able to do anything about it. But events in Korea did not amount to such a crisis. Although the president was without question commander in chief of the Army and Navy, he was not "Commander in Chief of the country." Advocates of strong executive authority thought that necessity gave the president unique powers, but the Korean War did not afford the president the power to intervene in the domestic sphere.

The later history of Jackson's opinion has underscored the power of this set of ideas about the contest between Congress and the president and the reach of presidential authority. The opinion proved essential in leading the Supreme Court to force President Richard Nixon to comply with a subpoena in the Watergate tapes case.[102] By the time of the second Bush presidency, a secret government memorandum was retracted by the Department of Justice largely because of its failure to cite Jackson's concurrence in the steel seizure case.[103]

But when the Supreme Court rebuffed Truman in 1952, all this was in the future. The president was furious, especially at Tom Clark. Invited to a dinner with the justices at Black's house, Truman studied the opinions closely in order to make his views known. Whether it was good manners or recognition of his declining political position, Truman softened once he was faced by the assembled justices. After the drinks were served, Truman turned to Black and simply said, "Hugo, I don't much care for your law but, by golly, this bourbon is good."[104]

Dislike of Truman was the glue that joined Black, Douglas, Jackson, and Frankfurter in the steel seizure case. Their four opinions reflected four very different perspectives on the Constitution; in their disagreement they were able to maintain their self-respect. Their next great challenge, the last the four men would confront together, required still greater finesse. To outlaw segregation, the scorpions in the bottle would have to stop fighting and agree on a single opinion—one that would change the course of American history.

Book Nine

BETRAYAL AND FULFILLMENT

CHAPTER 40

Segregation

After the war, Communism replaced Fascism as the great external challenge to the United States. On the domestic front, as the economy began to boom, prosperity was no longer the country's primary internal concern. Instead a very old American problem resurfaced, one that had been neglected during the period of economic crisis: the problem of race.

War changes not only political and economic realities but also ideas of right and wrong. Both the Civil War and World War II transformed national opinion about race. Lincoln originally launched the war to preserve the Union, not to free the slaves. But once the emancipation of Southern slaves had become a war end, Lincoln used it as justification for the death and destruction caused by the war. In his famous second inaugural address, he intimated that the enslavement of Africans was America's original sin, to be cleansed by the blood of the Civil War's martyrs on both sides. The Fourteenth Amendment, ratified in the aftermath of that war, was intended to redress the legacy of slavery by guaranteeing all Americans the equal protection of the laws.

Something similar happened in World War II. Roosevelt had embraced war not because of Nazi anti-Semitism, but to save the Western world and the position of the United States in it. Eventually, as had happened during the Civil War, the enemy's racial practices became part of the moral rationale for America's war efforts. The Nazis' racial codes became archetypes of the evil character of the Third Reich. By the time the war was over and the overtly racist powers of Germany and Japan had been defeated, it had become increasingly difficult to justify race-based segregation in the United States.

Yet as late as 1952, segregation was still the legal and cultural norm to many Americans. The promise of racial equality contained in the Fourteenth Amendment had not been enforced. After Lincoln's assassination, President Andrew Johnson had compromised with the South, undercutting the goals of Reconstruction. In the wake of this failure, formal segregation had been enacted in the states where slavery had once prevailed. Even Washington, D.C., subject to Congress's control, remained a segregated city. At the Mayflower Hotel, where Justice Stanley Reed lived with his wife, African-Americans could not sit down to eat in the restaurant, much less get a room.

The Soviet Union, eager to recruit allies, condemned the hypocrisy of American racism. The racially restrictive Nuremberg laws passed by the Third Reich had been based on the model of American segregation laws, with their quantum-of-blood measurements and their bans on miscegenation. The United States had punished German crimes against humanity, yet it was preserving Nazi-style practices at home—and enforcing segregation through its own courts.

In the Cold War, hearts and minds mattered to the foreign policies of both superpowers, and former imperial colonies were especially important. Racism was condemned by the member states of the newly constituted United Nations and by the Universal Declaration of Human Rights. For the United States to be seen as a racist nation was becoming a significant liability from the standpoint of national security.

Given the costs that segregation now imposed on U.S. interests, it would have been natural for Congress—perhaps with presidential leadership—to do something about it. Although white voters in the Southern states largely supported segregation (and blacks in the South were generally denied voting rights), the majority of voting Americans lived outside the South. African-Americans living in the North were slowly building economic and political power of their own, and Northern politicians increasingly sought to take account of their interests. A meaningful majority of Americans might well have been prepared to abolish the old ways. President Truman took advantage of this state of affairs to order the desegregation of the military in 1948. But his power to act unilaterally extended only to the military, which itself took three years to implement the order. As had been true since the end of Reconstruction, Congress was unable to act.

The chief impediment to a legislative reversal of segregation was the U.S. Senate. Designed by the Founding Fathers to weaken the power of the national majority by giving equal weight to small and large states, the Senate had developed its own procedures that took the entrenchment of minority veto power much further. The filibuster rule allowed senators to block any piece of legislation that did not receive a two-thirds vote. The Senate's procedures, coupled with the numbers of Southern and Southern-sympathizing senators, made it all but impossible for Congress to take on the issue of desegregation up through the 1950s.[1]

With the president's power limited and Congress's doors closed to them, civil rights activists turned to the courts—the only branch of the federal government left. Today, with the benefit of hindsight, the courts seem like the logical place for the great early advances in civil rights, and lawyers like Thurgood Marshall and the staff of the NAACP Legal Defense Fund seem like inevitable heroes. But in the 1940s and 1950s, the fit between the courts and civil rights was highly imperfect. The judiciary had no legacy of protecting racial or other minorities. At no time in the history of the United States had a judicial body stood in the vanguard of promoting progressive social change. For that matter, no judges in the world had ever done such a thing.

This backdrop helps explain the slow, stepwise progress of civil rights through the court system. As early as 1950, cases challenging the segregation of public schools were wending their way toward the Supreme Court, but a set of five consolidated public schools cases were not argued before the Court until the late fall of 1952—just a few months after the Court had rebuffed Harry Truman in the steel seizure case and a few weeks after Dwight D. Eisenhower had been elected president of the United States.

The Brown *Puzzle*

T he nine men who heard five hours of oral argument on December 9, 1952, and sat down to discuss the case in private conference the next Saturday, knew that *Brown v. Board of Education* would be the most important case they ever decided. Their opinions on what to do about it were deeply divided. In the conference, Chief Justice Vinson, Truman's former confidant, said in so many words that he did not think the Court should put an end to segregation. The entire case for desegregation rested on the assertion that the equal protection clause of the Fourteenth Amendment made racial separation inherently unequal. Yet after drafting and helping to enact the amendment—which gave Congress the power to pass enforcing legislation—Congress had never passed a law outlawing segregation.

Although Congress had direct control over Washington, D.C., the public schools in the District had been segregated for ninety years, as long as they had existed. The implication was twofold. First, those members of the Congress who drafted and presumably understood the Fourteenth Amendment did not think it outlawed segregation. Second, the Congress of 1952 had not changed its mind about what the amendment meant. For the Court to do what Congress had not done would therefore reflect its disagreement with the body designed, however imperfectly, to express the will of the American people.

Vinson was not a profound lawyer, and the reasons he gave to the other justices did not rely on any grand theories. Born in a small, nearly all-white town in the northeastern part of segregated

Kentucky, Vinson felt he understood the Southern mind-set. At the conference, Vinson said that he was worried about the consequences if a judicial decision mandated an immediate end to segregation. The Southern states, he warned, might abolish their entire public school systems in order to avoid having to educate black and white children together. This worry was not absurd. As it later turned out, a few cities and towns in the South did close their schools after *Brown*, and some shut down other public services like parks and swimming pools rather than allow their integration.[2]

Hugo Black was the longest-serving justice, and his seniority meant that he spoke next in the conference. From the Deep South, Black had even greater authority than Vinson when he described potential Southern reaction to a desegregation order. The reaction would, he predicted, be "serious" or "drastic."[3] Black had a reliable Southern source to support his prediction. Jimmy Byrnes, the former Supreme Court justice, "assistant President" to Roosevelt, and secretary of state, was now governor of South Carolina. Black, Frankfurter, and Jackson knew him well. He had made it clear to them that judicially mandated desegregation would result in closing the South Carolina schools.

Byrnes was considered a racial moderate. In his inaugural address as governor in 1951, he had insisted on maintaining segregation but also called for more funding to African-American schools.[4] Like other Southern moderates, Byrnes believed segregation should be ended gradually and voluntarily. A judicial decision forcing the issue would harden the commitment to segregation. His words about closing the schools were at once a warning and a threat, and they defined, or so Black thought, a political reality. Indeed, Black told his fellow justices on other occasions, the consequences of a desegregation decision would include riots so bad they would have to be put down by the U.S. Army. Southern liberals would be politically destroyed. Forced to support desegregation as a matter of conscience, they would be identified as allies of outside forces meddling with Southern tradition. Liberal Southern Democrats would be replaced by reactionary racists.[5] In short, Black thought the opposition to *Brown* would be overwhelming.

With this grim picture of Southern reaction to judicially man-dated desegregation in mind, another man might have thought twice about court-ordered social change. In addition to Black, there were three sitting justices who had experience with segre-gation: Vinson, Stanley Reed (from Kentucky, like Vinson), and Tom Clark, a Texan from segregated Dallas. At the December 1952 conference, none of these three was willing to hold segrega-tion unconstitutional.[6]

Yet despite his expectations, Black told the conference with complete certainty that the Court must overturn segregation. The reason he gave was based on what he considered the original mean-ing of the Fourteenth Amendment and its two Reconstruction-era companions: the Thirteenth Amendment, which prohibited slavery; and the Fifteenth Amendment, which barred racial discrimination in the right to vote. Together, Black believed, these amendments "had as their basic purpose the abolition of [racial] castes."[7] The purpose of segregation, he stated with perfect accuracy, was to show that "the Negro is inferior."[8] The opposition to desegregation in the South proved his point: Whites were attempting to hold on to their superiority. Because segregation was intended to subordinate African-Americans and so maintain a system of racial caste, it was in direct violation of the Constitution. The Court, Black asserted, had no choice but to say so.[9]

In framing segregation as a violation of the original meaning of the Constitution, Black reached the pinnacle of his constitutional achievement. For him to strike down the system of segregation took exceptional bravery—more so than for any of his colleagues. The former Ku Klux Klan member was the strongest internal voice on the Supreme Court calling for a unilateral end to segregation. His vote expressed an absolutist commitment to a single consti-tutional idea: that the original meaning of the text must be given effect without regard to consequences. The Constitution meant what it said, and it had to be elevated above political concerns.

For those who believe the Constitution should always be inter-preted according to its original meaning, Black's stance in *Brown* must count as heroic. Fidelity to the Constitution helped overcome the prejudices someone of Black's background might have held. The result is a testament not only to Black's deeply principled nature but to the ideal of the Constitution itself.

Black knew the importance of his vote, but he did not experience the moment as a triumph. At the time he voted to end segregation, Black was enmeshed in the most difficult period of his life. A year before, almost to the day, on December 7, 1951, Black's wife, Josephine, had killed herself in their family home in Alexandria, Virginia. Josephine had long suffered from depression. That fall the Blacks' daughter, JoJo, had gone off to college, leaving Josephine alone with Black. Her depression had mounted, and after a visit from her son, Sterling, she had gone to sleep in his childhood room, where she took an overdose of some medication from which she did not awake. Black was in the house at the time.

After hearing the terrible news, Hugo Jr. came home to find his father sitting at his desk with a half-finished opinion on a yellow pad in his hand. Tears were streaming down his cheeks. "Daddy, what happened?" his son asked. "Tell me how it happened." Black did not move. "I don't know," he replied."[10] In the manner of the era, the family announced that Josephine had died of natural causes. No autopsy was performed.[11]

In the months after Josephine's death, Black was surrounded by concerned friends. First one, then both of his law clerks moved into the Black house in Alexandria so that he would not have to be alone—an arrangement that lasted on and off for several years. With the clerks, Black told jokes and held court. Despite his denial, on some level he must have understood what had happened. Occasionally he would say to the clerks that Josephine might have been happier had they lived in Birmingham. Yet as a friend of Black's later put it, Black "went to his death not knowing two things. How to respond to being a member of the Klan and how Josephine died."[12]

Black, who remarried in 1957, may never have come to terms with Josephine's suicide. But in the desegregation decision, Black did find a way to overcome the taint of his association with the Klan. For that reason, if for no other, his vote in *Brown* demands further attention. As with any heroic act, the motivations run deeper than pure principle.

The first clue was that the original meaning of the Constitution regarding segregation was nowhere near as simple as Black maintained. The Reconstruction amendments put an end to slavery and required legal equality and suffrage for the former slaves. But the segregation of public schools was barely mentioned during debates about the amendments. Had it been discussed, it might well have been excluded from the requirement of equal protection. Even some Northern states maintained segregated public schools after the passage of the Fourteenth Amendment. If the drafters of the Fourteenth Amendment really meant to prohibit segregation in the schools or elsewhere, why didn't they say so?

It fell to Frankfurter to challenge Black's historical interpretation, and despite his own claims to scholarly expertise, Frankfurter once again passed on the responsibility to a younger man. Frankfurter had deputed Professor Charles Fairman to refute Black's view about the incorporation of the Bill of Rights into the Fourteenth Amendment by reference. This time, with secrecy a more significant factor, Frankfurter gave the assignment to one of his law clerks for the 1952–53 Supreme Court term, Alexander Bickel.

Many of Frankfurter's law clerks over the years were overachieving Jewish boys who resembled their boss in their biographies, but none came closer to matching Frankfurter's background and experience than the brilliant Bickel. He had come with his parents from Romania at the age of fifteen (Frankfurter had been twelve); shone at City College in New York (Frankfurter's alma mater); and been graduated from Harvard Law School with a sterling record just eleven years after arriving in the United States without a word of English.

Frankfurter told Bickel to delve deeply into the question of segregation and the Fourteenth Amendment, and to review the debates in Congress and the states. Bickel took a full year to do the research and write up his conclusions, completing the memo in August 1953. The resulting document was so thorough that Frankfurter had it typeset and printed by the Court's print shop for distribution to the other justices. Then, in 1955, after *Brown* had been decided, the memorandum, now revised, was published as a freestanding article in the *Harvard Law Review*.[13] At least partly on the strength of the piece, Bickel was hired as a professor at Yale Law School.[14]

Bickel's memorandum argued that nothing in the legislative history of the Fourteenth Amendment suggested any specific intent to end segregation, and certainly not in the public schools. Each time the radical Republicans who supported the amendment were accused of seeking to equalize blacks and whites socially, with respect to schools or marriage, they sought to avoid the charge. Ultimately, they compromised with "moderate" Republicans. The language they adopted was general enough to avoid the imputation that the amendment was going to create instant social equality while leaving open the possibility of future reinterpretation. According to Bickel, the original meaning of the Fourteenth Amendment did not absolutely preclude the Court from declaring segregation unlawful, but neither did it require that result.[15]

This historical ambiguity suggests that there must have been more to Black's understanding of the Fourteenth Amendment than simply the original meaning of the text. Today, with a certainty that would gratify Black, we believe the Constitution prohibits racial subordination. And segregation, as Black pointed out, was intended to subordinate African-Americans. In the deepest possible sense, Black was right. The Constitution should be interpreted to prohibit segregation. But even people who are right are influenced by outside factors.

Black had never fully recovered from the public humiliation after his Klan membership came to light. In general, the topic of the Klan was off limits in conversation with him.[16] When over the years his law clerks would gingerly approach it, Black would point out that as an aspiring politician he joined all sorts of civic organizations and that Klan membership in Alabama in the 1920s was no different than membership in the Elks or the Rotarians. The explanation rang hollow. Black had joined the Klan to get himself elected senator. That was precisely what made his exposure so shameful: He had done a deal with the devil for his own advancement.

The Klan membership was a terrible stain on his reputation and a crushing blow to a man jealous of his honor. Not only was honor a key feature of Southern civilization, it was also a central value in the classical Roman texts that Black read as part of his project of self-improvement. Black, too, admired and even idolized America's founding generation—which was itself dominated by honor-obsessed men like George Washington.[17] With this weight upon him, Black could not let his own dishonor stand permanently unaddressed. In the end, there was only one way for Black to prove, once and for all, that he was not a racist: to vote definitively to end segregation. To establish his independence from the values of the Klan, Black had to repudiate the Klan members who launched him into national office.

Black's decision in the Japanese-American internment cases was both a counterpoint to his position in *Brown* and a precursor to it. Writing for the Court, Black had upheld the constitutional authority of the federal government to intern Japanese-Americans based on nothing more than their ethnicity. With the war on, Black was disinclined to stand up for equality, even though his liberal, Catholic colleague Frank Murphy condemned the decision as pure racism. In any event, voting for the Japanese-Americans would have done little at the time to redeem Black's public honor; and it would have been extremely unpopular on the West Coast and perhaps even at the national level.

Yet embedded in Black's opinion in the *Korematsu* case was a hint that he had already begun to anticipate a route to rehabilitation through the rejection of racism. If the Japanese-Americans were being detained for racial reasons, he had written, this would have violated the Constitution. When the issue of segregation arose nearly a decade later, Black was as good as his word. This really was government discrimination based on race—and Black was prepared to rule it unconstitutional.

To many white Southerners, Black's vote in *Brown* was a betrayal of his origins, his race, his region, and his very identity. Black's willingness to acknowledge the likelihood of Southern resistance suggests that he, too, knew that his actions would be understood in this way. His son, Hugo Jr., had returned to Birmingham to practice law there, and after a gradual rapprochement with local political bosses, was approached about running for Congress in 1952. Well in advance of the election, Black wrote to his son that while he might get elected in 1952, his father's role on the Court would very shortly make life difficult for Hugo Jr.: "Next time they will get you unless, of course, you are willing to abuse the Supreme Court."[18]

Black was right. After *Brown* was decided, Hugo Jr. recalled, many Alabamians considered his father a "hateful renegade." Feelings against him in Alabama were so strong that when he returned occasionally to Birmingham, "invariably, someone would insult him on the street by saying, 'You are a traitor to the South.' . . . Then several times during the day and night we would get anonymous phone calls from people who blurted out brilliant things like, 'Hugo Black is a nigger lover.' "[19] Things got so bad for Hugo Jr. in Birmingham that he quit his law firm and moved to Miami. "We were so intimidated by the feeling against Daddy that I knew my partners would be better off without me and I would be more effective somewhere else. . . . I felt that I did not want to live any place where my daddy, who should have been respected beyond all other Alabama public figures, living or dead, could not come home without being treated like a leper."[20]

If Black was betraying racist Southerners, those same racists had betrayed him by disclosing his Klan membership to the press. The knife he was sticking into the Klan's heart with his *Brown* vote made good the debt of honor that he owed. As with Harlan Fiske Stone and Robert Jackson, two colleagues who had on different occasions impugned his honor, Black had taken a leisurely and complete revenge. The difference was that this time, Black's vindication of his honor was also an act of historical merit.

CHAPTER 42

Deliberate Speed

With Vinson for upholding segregation and Black for striking it down, the discussion at the December 1952 conference turned to Stanley Reed. True to his geographic origins, Reed weighed in to say that he would vote to uphold segregation. The South, he said, was making progress. But the process had to be gradual. In any case, he added, what had long been constitutional did not suddenly become unconstitutional unless the people actively changed their view, which in at least seventeen states had not happened.[21]

Now it was the turn of Frankfurter, who was never more attuned to his role than when he knew that history was being made. Bolstered by Bickel's research, Frankfurter believed that the case could not be decided on the basis of original meaning alone. Instead it would have to be evaluated through the lens of gradual constitutional development, the kind he had embraced in the steel seizure case. The difficulty, of course, was that the Southern states had no interest in such change. When it came to segregation, they wanted to preserve the status quo.

Frankfurter had always considered himself a racial liberal. He had served on the legal advisory committee to the NAACP in the 1930s, in the period when he was the nation's best-known liberal lawyer. In 1948, he had hired William Coleman, a Harvard Law School graduate, as the Court's first African-American law clerk— the only one for some two decades.[22] Frankfurter abhorred segregation, which undercut his idealistic belief that the American people were liberal in their instincts and aspirations.

The cost of segregation to America's reputation abroad was yet another reason for Frankfurter to desire a symbolic blow against it. One of his closest friends was Secretary of State Dean Acheson. Each morning, Frankfurter and Acheson would walk together from Georgetown to the State Department at Foggy Bottom, where a car (usually driven by a law clerk) would pick up Frankfurter to bring him to the Court. Acheson was convinced that segregation seriously harmed American interests. He would express his position in a letter that was included—possibly at Frankfurter's suggestion—in the government's brief in *Brown*:

> During the past six years, the damage to our foreign relations attributable to [segregation] has become progressively greater. The United States is under constant attack in the foreign press, over the foreign radio, and in such international bodies as the United Nations because of various practices of discrimination against minority groups in this country.... Soviet spokesmen regularly exploit the situation in propaganda against the United States.... The continuance of racial discrimination in the United States remains a source of constant embarrassment to this government in the day-to-day conduct of its foreign relations.[23]

Frankfurter knew politics well enough to understand that Congress might never act on its own. Any steps to improve America's reputation by counteracting segregation would have to come from the Court. Yet judicial intervention was, in principle, anathema to Frankfurter. A Supreme Court ruling that segregation was unconstitutional would be the most aggressive piece of judicial activism in American history. It was almost impossible to imagine how it could sit comfortably with the philosophy of judicial restraint. True, it could be said that the words "equal protection of the laws" more clearly excluded segregation than the words "due process of law" included the liberty of contract. But Frankfurter did not believe that the words alone resolved the case. For generations, the Supreme Court had accepted the assumption that what was separate could nevertheless be equal. The Court had been wrong about the facts, but that did not mean it had been wrong about the language.

This quandary was the most difficult one that Frankfurter faced in his judicial career. Segregation had to go. But voting against it would betray his essential judicial philosophy. Faced with this internal conflict, Frankfurter sought a compromise, just as he had when his loyalty to Roosevelt conflicted with his veneration of the Supreme Court at the time of the court-packing plan.

The compromise Frankfurter had in mind would ultimately have two parts. First, judicial activism, if it must be undertaken, should at least be adopted through judicial consensus. Frankfurter decided that the only way segregation should be struck down would be for the Court to support the result overwhelmingly. He would devote himself to the task of bringing his unruly colleagues together behind this goal.

The second part of Frankfurter's compromise, which would become clear a bit later, would prove to be more controversial. Attempting to reconcile activism and restraint, Frankfurter would try to end segregation gradually. If change must be ordered by the Court, at least the change should not have to take place in a single blow. Change ordered by judges was less desirable than change chosen by the people's representatives; but gradualism could reduce the conflict engendered by rapid social transformation. It was at least, Frankfurter thought, a way of mitigating the harms of judicial activism.[24]

By the time he spoke at the conference, Frankfurter already realized that consensus would be impossible to achieve at the time. With Chief Justice Vinson on his side to uphold segregation, Reed would be hard to move. Frankfurter could anticipate that the Texan Tom Clark would also be skeptical about whether the time was right for the Court to change the world so drastically. Jackson, moreover, was likely to be troubled by the idea of a decision that would cause social unrest rather than resolving it. Like Frankfurter, Jackson would have to deviate from his favored constitutional theory to reach the result Frankfurter now sought.

Frankfurter was loath to join Black, who was urging immediate action. Douglas, as Frankfurter must have expected, agreed with Black. If Black and Douglas had their way, the Court would have to issue a divided opinion. Frankfurter might have had to vote for activism without the cover of consensus; and he would have had to swallow his personal distaste and join Black and Douglas. In Frankfurter's view, expressed later to Judge Learned Hand, allowing these two "great libertarians" to get their way at this point would have been disastrous.[25] Division on the Court, Frankfurter believed, would have undercut the legitimacy of the Court's judgment and made it more difficult to enforce.

With this array of possible votes, Frankfurter sought tactical refuge in delay. He told his colleagues that he was ready to overturn segregation in the District of Columbia as a violation of the due process clause of the Constitution. But, he intimated, the question was harder with regard to the states, and required more thought. As a legal matter, this interpretation was contorted. Both due process and the equal protection clause applied to the states, as Frankfurter well knew.[26] Frankfurter was signaling to his colleagues that as an exponent of judicial restraint who believed in deference to state legislatures, he sympathized with those who were unwilling to strike down segregation.

Then Frankfurter suggested delay: Why not tell the parties to reargue the case afresh? This time, Frankfurter proposed, the parties should be told to add another element to their briefs. They should explain why segregation might be unconstitutional now even if it was constitutional when the Fourteenth Amendment was ratified. Once again, from a legal standpoint, there was no real reason to order reargument. Neither the facts nor the law had changed in the few days since the oral argument had occurred. The main purpose of the suggestion was to give the other justices another year to think through the problem, and Frankfurter another year to work on them. He may also have hoped that some of the Southern states would read the writing on the wall from the Court's directive. If they concluded they were about to lose before the Supreme Court, perhaps the states might take the hint and desegregate on their own.[27] That would enable the Court to avoid condemning segregation, and Frankfurter to uphold the principle of judicial restraint.

Frankfurter could hardly tell his colleagues that he wanted a delay in order to change their minds. Needing an excuse, he settled on the fact that President Eisenhower had just been elected—the closest thing to a new fact he could conjure. The Eisenhower administration would have to enforce any ruling, he pointed out. Reargument would give the new president the chance to express the views of his administration.

With this equivocation, Frankfurter left it deliberately unclear how he might vote that day if he were required to express an opinion. As a result, some historians have concluded that he was prepared to uphold segregation at the December 1952 conference—a view that the unsympathetic Douglas suggested in a memo for his files a year and a half later.[28] A more subtle interpretation of his motivation, however, is that Frankfurter had a characteristically complicated plan to avoid having to vote at all until consensus could emerge.[29] The implication that he might vote to preserve segregation, or at least that he was not sure how he would vote, was intended to create sympathy with the other justices who might vote against—in hopes of winning them over to his corner when he himself would later announce that he had been convinced.

The source that confirms Frankfurter's plans is his former law clerk, Philip Elman, who was then working on the segregation issue in the office of the solicitor general at the Department of Justice. By his own account, Elman was in constant touch with Frankfurter through this period. "At first," Elman later explained, Frankfurter "was talking to me, not as a lawyer in the SG's office, but as his law clerk for life and perhaps his closest confidant about his problems with fellow justices. He told me what he thought, what the other justices were telling him they thought. I knew from him what their positions were."[30] When the conversations began, the federal government had no official role in the case, which was a lawsuit between private individuals and the boards of education of cities with segregation. In that context, Frankfurter's disclosures were questionable but not completely improper.

On December 2, 1952, however, just a few days before the oral argument, the government filed a brief as a friend of the court.[31] Written by Elman, the brief argued that the federal government itself had an interest in seeing segregation overruled. Elman quoted Acheson at length, asserting on behalf of the government that striking down segregation would help counteract Soviet propaganda. After receiving the brief, Frankfurter called Elman to thank him. "Phil, I think you've rendered a real service to your country."[32] Elman, in turn, considered the brief "the one thing I'm proudest of in my whole career."[33]

Frankfurter especially appreciated Elman's suggestion in the government's brief that the Supreme Court did not need to insist on immediate implementation of its decision. Instead, Elman argued, the Court had the authority to order a careful, stepwise, and in effect gradual process of desegregation to be supervised by the federal courts. In an oral history he gave years later, Elman insisted that although he was in constant contact with Frankfurter, this idea was entirely his own: "I had had no discussion about it with Frankfurter beforehand."[34]

Regardless of whether this was true, Frankfurter adopted the idea as his own, turning it into the second prong of his strategy within the Court. Reargument would give him time to allay the concerns of his colleagues who were fearful of social conflict. The Court, he proposed, should hold that segregation was unconstitutional. But it should delay the remedy, instructing the states and lower courts to implement their decision "with all deliberate speed." The phrase, borrowed from an opinion by Holmes, would later become the touchstone for liberal criticism of *Brown* as insufficiently assertive.[35] For Frankfurter, however, gradualism was essential to his goal of unanimity.

Frankfurter, like Black, had decided that segregation had to end. But unlike Black, for whom the judge's job was to announce the true meaning of the Constitution and let justice be done even if the heavens should fall, Frankfurter saw the judge as a statesman, responsible for the consequences of his actions. He believed it was crucial for the country that the decision to end segregation be a success. In order to achieve that goal, he, like any other political actor, needed to muster all the resources he could put together.[36]

This political view of the process of ending segregation explains not only Frankfurter's willingness to compromise, but also the fact that his contacts with Elman continued after the government had joined the case. Frankfurter, Elman later claimed, "didn't regard me as a lawyer for any party; I was still his law clerk."[37] But he was a lawyer for a party. That was why he could be of service to Frankfurter. Elman clearly understood this: "He needed help, lots of help, and there were things I could do in the Department of Justice that he just couldn't do, like getting support of both administrations, Democratic and Republican, for the position he wanted the Court to come out with, so that it would not become a hot political issue."[38]

Frankfurter was familiar with this kind of backdoor machination from his days in the Roosevelt administration. As he had during World War II, Frankfurter thought that the historic importance of the struggle justified breaking the usual rules. From Elman's perspective, at least, these efforts were successful. "When the Court announced its decision," Elman explained, Frankfurter "wanted both the present and former presidents of the United States to be publicly on record as having urged [the] Court to take the position it had. And that's exactly the way it worked out."[39]

In the eyes of his onetime law clerk and political ally, the historic, unanimous judgment in *Brown v. Board of Education*, certainly the most important Supreme Court case of the last sixty years, was the result largely of Frankfurter's efforts. "There is no question that the grand strategist in all this inside the Court was FF. . . . The man stirring everything up inside the Court was Frankfurter."[40]

CHAPTER 43

The Individualists

For someone who was on his way to becoming the most unabashedly liberal, results-driven justice ever to sit on the Supreme Court, Bill Douglas paid little attention to the problem of segregation or the specific case of *Brown v. Board of Education*. Not that he faltered when his turn came to express his view. At the December conference, Douglas saw the issue as simple. The Court must not "play [the] factor of time," but must decide straightaway. He opposed Frankfurter's proposal for delay and reargument. Some of his motivation was no doubt a principled commitment to deciding the case like any other, but Douglas also clearly enjoyed the chance to needle Frankfurter.[41]

From that moment on, Douglas ceased to be a significant player in the drama of *Brown*. The weeks after the November 1952 election could not have been easy ones for Douglas. This was the first election since 1940 in which he had not come close to appearing on the ballot. The reason was Douglas's impending divorce, news of which hit the papers in the spring of 1952 ("Justice Douglas Wants Divorce To Wed; She's 30ish," according to the ever-subtle *New York Daily News*).[42] Even this distraction, however, cannot fully account for Douglas's lack of interest in the desegregation case. In the spring of 1953, as the case sat quietly on the Court's docket, Douglas immersed himself in the last-minute appeals to save the lives of Julius and Ethel Rosenberg, convicted of sending nuclear secrets to the Soviets. This time, Douglas took an active though ultimately ineffectual interest.

To his colleagues, Douglas's behavior was highly idiosyncratic.

In the fall of 1952, the Court had considered whether to take the Rosenbergs' case. At the time, Black was in favor of hearing the appeal. Frankfurter, too, believed the Court should hear the case, and another justice, Harold Burton, was willing to grant a hearing out of deference to Black and Frankfurter. Their three votes fell one shy of the four votes required before the Court would decide to hear the case under its ordinary rules. Douglas, with what Frankfurter considered "surprising vehemence," voted to deny a hearing.[43] In the spring of 1953 the Rosenbergs once again applied to the Court. Again only Black and Frankfurter were prepared to hear the case; again, Douglas voted to deny. Frankfurter asked his colleagues for a week to consider writing a dissent from the denial of review; during that time Jackson told Frankfurter he might well join such an opinion. Frankfurter ultimately decided not to issue the statement.[44]

At this point, when it was clear the case would not be heard (though the vote was not yet public), Douglas appeared to change his mind. He wrote his colleagues that he planned to issue a separate dissent from the denial of review. Jackson was furious. Already detesting Douglas, Jackson was certain that Douglas had no desire for the Court to hear the Rosenbergs' case: Douglas could have made that result far more likely by joining Black and Frankfurter only a few days earlier in voting to have the case heard. The only possible motive Douglas could have to issue a dissent from denial of review, Jackson believed, was to grandstand, drawing attention to his own liberal credentials without actually putting the Court in a position to hear the case. Jackson told Frankfurter that Douglas was bluffing. If there were actually enough votes to hear the case, Jackson predicted, Douglas would flip back and block the Court from taking it.[45]

At conference, Jackson called Douglas's bluff. After Black, Douglas, and Frankfurter voted to grant review, Jackson stated that he was willing to provide the fourth vote so that the Court would hear the Rosenbergs' case. At this point Douglas backed down and said he would withdraw his proposed dissent. Jackson then said he would withdraw his vote to grant a hearing. Without four votes to hear the case, the Court denied a hearing. Jackson believed he had proved his point. "That S.O.B.'s bluff was called," he said to Frankfurter.[46]

But the bizarre game was not yet finished. The Rosenbergs filed a final, last-ditch request for a stay of execution, which their lawyers directed solely to Douglas. This time, against the advice of Chief Justice Vinson, Douglas granted the stay on his own accord, as the Supreme Court's rules allowed him to do. For a day, this was front-page news. But the Court reconvened in an emergency session, only to overturn Douglas's stay by a 6–3 vote, clearing the way for the Rosenbergs to be executed.[47]

The way to reconcile Douglas's lack of interest in *Brown* with his engagement in the Rosenberg execution is to notice that only one afforded him the chance to act as a lone wolf. Whatever else it might be, the desegregation case never had the potential to be a decision that would express Douglas's individualist values. The Court's decision would be based on equality, not liberty. More important, it would be a collective act of the Court, one that did not depend on any individual member. *Brown* would be a team effort, and in it there was simply no special role for Douglas to play. Egotism, then, may explain why Douglas cared so little about *Brown*. If this formulation sounds harsh, it must be remembered that a nearly obsessive focus on the individual's autonomy and freedom of action sparked Douglas's contribution to modern constitutional thought. The love of liberty and the love of equality are not the same thing. It is no slur on Douglas's character to say that the one inspired him to great heights while the other elicited a vote only.

If Black and Douglas thought the Court should simply order segregation to be ended at once, and Frankfurter sought unanimity and a gradual process, all were clear on a course of action the Court should take at this historic moment. For Robert Jackson, the problem was substantially harder. It was not simply the lack of historical basis or judicial precedent to overturn segregation that troubled him. As he had written just a few months before in the steel seizure case, the law on the books could be insufficient to produce the correct outcome in constitutional cases. Jackson's difficulty in *Brown* went deeper—to the very heart of his constitutional philosophy.

Ever since he wrote his book on the judiciary, Jackson had believed that the role of the courts was to resolve social conflict—not to cause it. The constitutional system of divided powers assigned the role of making drastic social change to Congress. The mistake of the Court in the *Lochner* era had been to intervene on one side of the conflict between progressive and reactionary forces in the society, and to block Congress and the state legislatures from making the changes they deemed appropriate. For the Supreme Court to find segregation unconstitutional would, according to this view, be deeply illegitimate. It would create social conflict on a massive scale, contradicting the expressed preferences of state legislatures and the studied inaction of Congress. If indeed segregation needed to be overturned—and as an upstate New Yorker, Jackson had no sympathy for the practice—it was a job for Congress, not the Court.

Before the December conference, he discussed the issue at length with his two law clerks. The evidence of their discussions lies in two memoranda, one by each clerk, each reflecting a different kind of skepticism about holding segregation unconstitutional. The memos were eventually to become famous, not because of what they revealed about Jackson, but because one of the law clerks was William H. Rehnquist, subsequently appointed a justice by Richard Nixon and later chief justice by Ronald Reagan. Rehnquist's memo became a subject for debate both times he was up for confirmation.

One of the memos, initialed by the other clerk, Donald Cronson, was titled "A Few Expressed Prejudices on the Segregation Cases." The memo began by rejecting *Plessy v. Ferguson*, the infamous 1896 case in which the Supreme Court had said that separate was not inherently unequal. But the memo went on to argue that since "a whole way of life," namely segregation, had developed in the shadow of *Plessy*, the Court should not overturn that decision. Instead the Court should say that *Plessy* was wrong—and then leave it to Congress to do something about the problem.

The other memo was initialed by Rehnquist. Its title was "A Random Thought on the Segregation Cases." Striking down segregation just because liberal members of the Court did not like the practice, the memo said, would resemble the approach of the

Lochner-era Court, which interpreted the Constitution so as to satisfy its own policy preferences. The attempt by the Court to protect racial minorities, the memo asserted, would be no different than its past efforts to protect property holders. Indeed, the memo pointed out, nothing in the Constitution made civil rights any more important than property rights.

Then came the bombshell, at least for Rehnquist's later career and reputation: "I realize that it is an unpopular and unhumanitarian position, for which I have been excoriated by 'liberal' colleagues, but I think *Plessy v. Ferguson* was right and should be reaffirmed."[48] Confronted with the document at his first confirmation hearing, Rehnquist fell back on the law clerk's favorite defense: The boss made me do it. "The memorandum was prepared by me at Justice Jackson's request; it was intended as a rough draft of a statement of his views at the conference of the justices, rather than as a statement of my views."[49]

Rehnquist had never much liked Jackson, and at the time of his confirmation he had no particular reason to protect his former boss, who had been dead for seventeen years. Rehnquist's only goal was to deny that he had been skeptical of the Supreme Court's most important holding of the twentieth century. Attributing the words in the memo to Jackson helped Rehnquist get confirmed twice by the Senate.

Jackson's longtime secretary and Nuremberg companion, Elsie Douglas, who was as loyal to him as anyone on earth, was eager to protect Jackson from the charge that he might have entertained the now-heretical thought that *Plessy* could have been right. At the time of Rehnquist's confirmation hearings, she accused Rehnquist of "a smear of a great man." Jackson, she said, would never have sought a clerk's help in drafting remarks to be made to the conference.[50] Rehnquist himself admitted that the circumstances had been highly unusual.

Read carefully, Jackson's remarks at the conference suggest that the truth lay somewhere between Rehnquist's position and that of Elsie Douglas. According to one set of notes, Jackson did not want a vote to occur. He argued that nothing in the constitutional text, precedent, history, or statutes sufficed to make segregation unconstitutional. The brief filed by Thurgood Marshall and the NAACP

Legal Defense Fund was, Jackson said, sociological rather than legal. He himself was unwilling "to say that it is unconstitutional to practice segregation tomorrow." He might, however, be willing to join an opinion that gave the Southern states time to get rid of segregation. He seemed to say that the best result would be to label segregation as "bad," then require that it must be abolished within some period of time.[51]

The two law-clerk memoranda disagreed on a central question: Was *Plessy* correct when it was originally decided? At the conference, Jackson equivocated. If, as he said, the traditional legal materials allowed segregation, then that strongly implied the 1896 decision had been correct. Jackson's unwillingness to say that segregation was unconstitutional today implied there must be some possible constitutional basis for upholding it. At the same time, though, he also wanted to strike down segregation on constitutional grounds. Hence he could not have believed that *Plessy* ought to be reaffirmed, as Rehnquist's memo had it.

Instead, Jackson seems to have wanted the Court to issue some sort of an advisory opinion. What he envisioned may have been similar to his strange dissent in the Japanese-American internment cases, in which he had said that the law was unconstitutional but that the military should be allowed to continue the internment anyway. In *Brown*, Jackson seems to have imagined that the Court might say that segregation must be eliminated and, simultaneously, that the Southern states who had maintained it over the years had not violated the spirit of the Constitution.

This uniquely pragmatic Jacksonian position could not have been endorsed by any other member of the Court. It would have required the justices to admit that constitutional law could change based on contemporary pragmatic circumstances—that what had once been right must now be wrong. Jackson, his clerk the following year would say, "didn't want to accuse the south of behaving unconstitutionally all those years, especially since the history of the Fourteenth Amendment didn't really point to the conclusion that *Plessy* should be reversed. In short, he wanted the Court, in ending segregation, to admit that it was making new law for a new day."[52]

The intended effect of this honesty was to avoid making white Southerners feel the Court was telling them that their way of life was based on a constitutional mistake. This, in turn, might conceivably have reduced the social conflict to follow.

Given Jackson's complicated perspective, it seems likely that the two memoranda produced by the two law clerks actually did reflect the content of conversations with Jackson. Jackson must have been trying out arguments for and against explicitly repudiating *Plessy*, with the help of clerks who had their own preferences and views. Rehnquist was probably not lying when he said he was asked to prepare the memorandum.

The two memos do suggest, however, that each of the law clerks had his own view of the case, and that Jackson asked them each to summarize in memo form the viewpoint he had been expressing in conversation. Cronson generously wrote a public letter to Rehnquist at the time of the latter's nomination suggesting that both men had contributed to both memoranda. This was no doubt true, since in most Supreme Court chambers, collaboration is the rule. Yet the individual signatures on the memoranda are nonetheless telling. What pushed Rehnquist to his public position was the impossibility as a practical matter of telling the whole truth. Rehnquist was convinced that *Plessy* was correct—a view that Jackson partly adopted at the December conference.

For Jackson, then, there was no good option available in the desegregation case as of December 1952. His constitutional theory of pragmatism and mediation of social conflict counseled against a revolutionary decision that would change both the country and the position of the Court in it. The compromise he was beginning to favor—frank recognition that the Court was making new constitutional law—was unpalatable to his colleagues. This realization might have prompted a willingness to go along with Frankfurter's strategy of delay, which would at least give him more time to think about the issue. Jackson saw no reason for the Supreme Court's rush to make history in *Brown*; in fact, he was doubtful that the Court should ever make history at all.

CHAPTER 44

Ex Machina

In the usual practice of the Supreme Court, once a case has been discussed in conference by the justices, some disposition emerges. Usually a vote is taken and an opinion assigned. If the justices need more time for discussion, the case is "relisted," put back on the agenda for future conversation. Once in a long while, reargument might be set.

At the December 13 conference, though, the justices took no vote and reached no resolution.[53] And after the conference, nothing happened at all. As Frankfurter told Elman, "The cases are just sitting, Phil. Nothing's happening."[54] The Court was at an impasse— and no one had any very clear idea what to do about it. As the end of the term approached, Frankfurter decided it was time for an intervention. On May 27, 1953, he sent the other justices a specific proposal to issue an order for the cases to be reargued.

The questions Frankfurter recommended for reargument, drafted by Bickel, his outgoing law clerk, were exceptionally specific. To a careful reader, they revealed the division within the Court. The first two asked for historical evidence that the framers and ratifiers of the Fourteenth Amendment had intended to abolish segregation or to allow Congress or the Court to do so in the future. As Frankfurter already knew from Bickel's research, which was by then almost completed, the answer to these was that no such specific evidence existed. The third question asked whether, assuming the evidence was insufficient, the Court still had the power to abolish segregation—a question suggesting the quandary that was gripping Jackson in particular. Finally, the fourth and fifth questions asked whether the Court could abolish segregation gradually using its equity powers, either by appointing a special master for the purpose or else using the lower federal courts. This question was derived from Elman's brief for the Department of Justice proposing gradual implementation. It reflected the possibility that notwithstanding the Court's apparent difficulty in explaining why segregation should be struck down, there might well be enough votes to do so anyway.

Frankfurter acknowledged the incoherence of the document, admitting to his colleagues that his intention was for some of the questions to "give comfort to one side and some to the other." He recognized that discussing possible implementation hinted that a decision might have been reached already. But, he suggested, such a hint was actually desirable. It would begin the process of "an adjustment... in the public mind to such a possibility."[55] The key, Frankfurter suggested, was again gradualism: "For me the ultimate crucial factor in the problem presented by these cases is psychological—the adjustment of men's minds and actions to the unfamiliar and the unpleasant."[56] Nominally, Frankfurter was talking about the public perception of the Court's action. But he was also talking about the psychology of his colleagues themselves. On June 8, the Court issued the order for reargument.[57] Frankfurter had bought himself the time needed to achieve unanimity; and he had done so, for better or worse, at the cost of turning *Brown* into an exercise in gradual rather than rapid social change.

Time, as it turned out, was on Frankfurter's side in another way, one that he could not have anticipated. On September 8, just a few weeks before the new Supreme Court term was to begin, Fred Vinson died suddenly of a heart attack at the age of sixty-three. Vinson's service as chief justice had been unremarkable. If the tone among the justices was perhaps slightly less rancorous than it had been under Harlan Fiske Stone, it was not on Vinson's account. After the blowout between Jackson and Black that had led to Vinson's appointment, things could not possibly have gotten any worse. Indeed, had Vinson not died, his most significant contribution to the history of the Court might well have been leading a bloc that stood in the way of consensus on the issue of desegregation.

Frankfurter's reaction was callous. He had never liked Vinson. Once, after an acerbic comment by Frankfurter at a conference, Vinson had actually gotten out of his chair and walked around the table, threatening to hit Frankfurter with a clenched fist.[58] To Frankfurter, Vinson's untimely death was not a tragedy but an opportunity. When Frankfurter came into Washington, D.C., for the funeral, Elman, now working on the Department of Justice's response brief for the Eisenhower administration, met his former boss's train at Union Station. "I'm in mourning," Frankfurter said sarcastically. Then, in a characteristic gesture of excitement, he grabbed Elman by the arm with his "viselike grip" and looked him in the eye. "Phil," said Frankfurter, "this is the first solid piece of evidence I've ever had that there really is a God."[59]

Elman believed this piece of mordant wit was no joke.[60] Without divine intervention, the Court "would have remained bitterly divided, fragmented, unable to decide the issue forthrightly."[61] Now, however, a hole had been opened in the bloc of justices who opposed desegregation. Into it walked the man who would become the most liberal chief justice in the annals of the Court: California's three-time Republican governor Earl Warren.

Eisenhower's choice of chief justice had a political air about it from the first. Warren was a national figure who had been the Republican nominee for vice president in 1948, when Truman beat Thomas Dewey. Then, at the 1952 Republican convention, Warren, who had his home state's "favorite son" support, directed the California delegation to cast its votes for Eisenhower, assuring his nomination on the first ballot. Rumor had it that Warren had demanded the chief justiceship in return.[62]

Influenced by the political background of the choice, Frankfurter, at first, did not look kindly on Eisenhower's appointment of Warren. Warren lacked any sustained engagement with issues of constitutional law. His one high-ranking legal job, as attorney general of California, coincided with the internment of the state's Japanese-Americans during World War II, a policy he had advocated aggressively. Frankfurter, as he had when Black was appointed, felt that choosing a politician for the Court was an insult to the complexity of the judicial craft. Despite his grudging respect for Black's subsequent intellectual accomplishments, Frankfurter still thought a distinguished jurist would have been a better choice than a professional politician.

Quickly, though, as the new term began, Warren began to win over the other justices. By the time the reargument rolled around in December 1953, almost exactly a year after the first argument in *Brown*, Warren was giving Frankfurter reason for optimism.[63] At the Court's conference on December 12, 1953, Warren adopted a position that was almost equal parts Black and Frankfurter. With Black, he agreed that treating African-Americans as separate and equal was meant to keep them in a position of inferiority. That meant *Plessy* must be overruled. With Frankfurter, Warren suggested that acting too quickly could cause social unrest. Desegregation must be accomplished with "a minimum of emotion and strife," which was to say, gradually.[64]

It was surely no coincidence that Warren had adopted in essence the viewpoints of the two men on the Court with the most strongly held opinions—even if those were in some ways opposed. Warren was seeking a middle path that would lead to unanimity. The justice whom this affected most was Tom Clark. The previous year, the Texan Clark had made it clear that he would vote to uphold segregation. Now he indicated that he was ready to change his vote, provided the Court allowed Southern states discretion to implement desegregation in accordance with local conditions. Burton and Minton—the remaining Truman appointees—had already opted to end segregation, and their positions had not changed.[65] Now that Vinson was dead and Clark had jumped ship, only Stanley Reed was left of the original group of three who had been firmly committed to upholding segregation.

Jackson, for his part, was still troubled by the idea of an opinion announcing that *Plessy* had been wrongly decided. He explained, as he had in conference the previous year, that he could not endorse any opinion unless it stated overtly that the Court was acting politically and making new law. He indicated his intention to write a separate concurrence, blocking Warren's emerging plan for the

Court to speak with one voice. To achieve this unanimity, Warren needed time to work on the outliers, Reed and Jackson. As it had the previous year, the Court went into a holding pattern. Once again, the Court's ordinary procedures for scheduling discussion or resolution of a case were suspended. "Week by week, we discussed it, from the middle of November to the latter part of March, when we took a vote," Warren later recalled.[66] Indeed, so irregular was the process that no formal record of this final vote exists.

The strategy adopted by Warren during this period of delay was pure politics. He told his colleagues that he would use the chief justice's prerogative to write the opinion himself. Meanwhile, by endorsing Frankfurter's goal of gradual implementation, Warren encouraged the other justices to think about the remedy—the all-important question of how desegregation would be implemented. Urging the justices to focus on a common problem was designed to marginalize Jackson and Reed. Nevertheless, in February, as Warren worked on his draft, both Jackson and Reed put pen to paper to draft opinions of their own.

Reed's draft was a straightforward dissent. He argued, as the Southern states' lawyers had in court, that separate schools were perfectly constitutional so long as they were effectively equal. Some states had been working to improve that equality, he maintained. But his primary contention was that the words "equal protection of the laws" did not guarantee equal access to public facilities by all Americans; otherwise, the clause would be an invitation to state socialism. The issue, then, should properly be considered one of due process, not equal protection. Here Reed could fall back on the liberal critique of the property-protecting *Lochner* court to explain that the Constitution should not serve as a tool for implementing the personal preferences of the judges.[67] What made Reed's draft opinion threatening was the way it took the liberal, New Deal approach to the Constitution and marshaled it against the desegregation decision.

Jackson's draft concurrence ran to twenty-three pages, and attempted to achieve consistency with his philosophy of pragmatism. He asserted frankly that neither the original meaning of

the Constitution nor the history of its judicial interpretation sufficed to overturn segregation. He also rejected the idea that integration would address psychological harms to African-American
children. (The NAACP had included in its brief a controversial
social-psychological study suggesting that segregation caused poor
self-esteem in African-American children, a study that would ultimately be cited by the Court in a footnote to Warren's decision.[68])
Jackson's central argument was that while the Constitution had
not changed, African-Americans had. They were today "a different people" than they had been in the aftermath of slavery, both
because of improved educational opportunity and also because of
the mixing of races. Under these circumstances, Jackson wrote,
there could be no "just segregation effort."[69]

The law clerk who was working with Jackson on the opinion
was E. Barrett Prettyman Jr., later an important figure in Washington, D.C., legal circles. Prettyman's father was a judge on the U.S.
Court of Appeals for the D.C. Circuit—and the same man who
had been occupying the office of general counsel to the Bureau of
Internal Revenue the day Jackson arrived in Washington to take
his job, only to find that his predecessor had not yet been fired.
The younger Prettyman had served in World War II as an infan-
tryman in France and Germany, spending eight months afterward
in military hospitals recuperating from his wounds.[70] Mature and
experienced, Prettyman had more confidence than an ordinary
clerk. He now told Jackson bluntly that his draft opinion was weak.
It read as an apology, Prettyman said, rather than as a strong statement of principle.[71]

Whether Jackson planned to change the opinion or decline to
issue it on the basis of Prettyman's advice is difficult to know. On
March 30, some two weeks after the date on the last draft concurrence, Jackson suffered a major heart attack.[72] Confined to a hospital bed, Jackson lost his taste for writing a separate opinion. Warren
came to see him in the hospital, bringing his own draft opinion
with him. This was simultaneously an act of great solicitude and a
perfect example of a consummate politician putting on the screws.
Jackson, bedridden, had still not fully recovered. His law clerk was

with him when Warren arrived; Prettyman went out in the hall to wait. After Warren had left, Prettyman came back, and Jackson gave him the chief justice's draft to read. Prettyman went into the hall again to read the relatively short document. When he returned, he told Jackson that he "didn't find anything glaringly unacceptable in it."[73]

Warren was not finished. He came back to the hospital later the same day. Jackson managed two oral suggestions to Warren, who accepted one of them, a mention of African-American advancement in the contemporary period. In the light of his earlier concerns, Jackson cannot have been fully satisfied with the Warren opinion. But he agreed to join. Even sick—or perhaps precisely because he was seriously ill—he saw the need to compromise on his constitutional theory in favor of unanimity. Ending segregation by judicial fiat ran counter to Jackson's pragmatic constitutional philosophy. But Jackson signed the opinion in the service of his broader pragmatic principles.

That left only Reed. Warren, fresh from his victory with Jackson, knew how to deal with him. He put it bluntly: "Stan, you're all by yourself in this now."[74] Reed feared his lone opinion could be blamed for the resistance to *Brown* that he felt sure would come. Isolated and insecure, Reed folded under Warren's pressure. Plotted by Frankfurter, aided by the death of Vinson and Jackson's heart attack, and sealed by Warren's willingness to be brutal with Reed, a unanimous opinion had emerged. It would be the Supreme Court's greatest liberal moment; but it would also reveal the dangers of the very judicial activism that Frankfurter and Jackson feared.

The Supreme Court would announce that segregation was unconstitutional, and then wait for another opinion, known as *Brown II*, to lay out the remedy. A gradual process, supervised by federal district courts, and proceeding "with all deliberate speed," the desegregation effort of the 1950s, 1960s, 1970s, and even 1980s would in many important ways prove a failure. *Brown* became the ultimate symbol of equal justice under law—the phrase over the front entrance to the Supreme Court. But it also became a touchstone for criticism by those who believed either that the Court lacked the effective capacity to change society from the top or that the Court had mistakenly chosen gradual change when its orders should have been immediate and absolute.

The decision still had to be announced from the bench. On May 17, 1954, against doctor's orders, Jackson rose from his hospital bed and returned to the Supreme Court for the first time since his heart attack.[75] There were no leaks to the press that the desegregation decision was going to be announced. Nevertheless, Jackson's clerk later recalled, "the atmosphere was quite extraordinary.... The courtroom was filled because we were getting near the end of the term and everyone was waiting for the big one." Decisions in a few other cases were announced—and then Warren began to read. "When he reached the key point he inserted 'unanimously'— which was not in the opinion—'we unanimously hold,' and the courtroom took in a breath. You could actually hear it because no one had expected that. It was very dramatic."[76] Exhausted, Jackson went home to recover. He traveled for most of the summer, spending time at Bohemian Grove, the exclusive, all-male club-resort in California where the members, political and financial elites, socialized and sang and swam.

On the first Monday in October—it was October 4, 1954— Jackson appeared for his last time on the bench. The next Saturday morning, October 9, Jackson suffered a fatal heart attack. He was sixty-two years old.

The circumstances were awkward. Jackson died while in the apartment of Elsie Douglas, his longtime secretary and Nuremberg companion. Prettyman, Jackson's law clerk, was at his desk in the Supreme Court when he received a call from Frankfurter. "Justice Jackson is dead," Frankfurter told him. Before Prettyman could respond, Frankfurter continued: "We have a bit of a problem. He was in Elsie's house on Mass. Avenue." Then Frankfurter proposed a face-saving explanation to Prettyman: "The story is that he was headed to the Court and felt badly and went to her house to feel better."[77]

As it turned out, the official statement issued later that day by the Supreme Court did not say that Jackson had been headed to the Court, probably because Elsie Douglas's apartment at 5400 Massachusetts Avenue was nowhere near the route from McLean, Virginia, where Jackson lived, to the Supreme Court building on Capitol Hill. According to the Court's statement, Jackson drove into Washington, D.C., to shop at the Sears, Roebuck store on Wisconsin Avenue in Tenleytown. After shopping, Jackson was suddenly struck by what one newspaper report called a light seizure and another called a stroke.[78] Somehow, the story went, the stricken Jackson managed to get into his car and drive himself a mile and a third—southeast down Wisconsin Avenue, right on Nebraska Avenue, and then left onto Massachusetts Avenue where Elsie Douglas lived. When he arrived, she called his doctor, Hill Carter. At 11:45 a.m., shortly after the doctor arrived, Jackson died.

The cover story could barely withstand scrutiny. The Sears store—an elegant, Art Moderne facility—still stands, but it was not an obvious shopping destination from Jackson's home, nor was Jackson the kind of person who shopped at Sears. Jackson might conceivably have followed a homing instinct to the apartment of the woman who had been his stalwart professional colleague and companion for more than a decade. Yet the store opened at 10:00 a.m. on Saturdays, giving Jackson little time to have shopped, been taken ill, driven to the apartment, and awaited the doctor. The cause of his death was coronary thrombosis, a heart attack like the one Jackson had six months before, which was not consistent with the ability to drive and climb stairs before dying.

The newspaper versions also communicated suspicion. The *Washington Post* reporter made a point of saying that the Supreme Court did not announce Jackson's death for four and a half hours after it had occurred—suggesting that the reporter had doubts about whether the story was accurate. According to one source, J. Edgar Hoover, who had disliked Jackson since he was attorney general, vengefully told the press that Jackson had died in Elsie's apartment, which forced the Supreme Court press office to come up with the story.[79]

Jackson, then, was not shopping, but was already at Elsie Douglas's apartment when the blow came. The two had traveled together to Nuremberg and had secretly been a couple for years. Jackson had the solace of dying in the arms of someone he loved and who loved him.

For the first time since 1940, Roosevelt's justices no longer constituted a majority of the members of the Court. Eisenhower would replace Jackson with John Marshall Harlan II, a judge on the Second Circuit Court of Appeals, whose background could not have been more different from those of Roosevelt's self-made Supreme Court appointees. The grandson of a Supreme Court justice who shared his name, he was a Princetonian, a Rhodes scholar, and a distinguished corporate lawyer. He had briefly been an assistant U.S. attorney under the Coolidge administration and had shown no interest whatever in the New Deal. The Roosevelt Court had come to an end.

CHAPTER 45

Last Act

*B*rown v. *Board of Education* changed the constitutional universe. Once and for all, the Supreme Court came to be seen as rightly devoted to the protection of minorities—a conception that continues to be shared by many in the United States, and increasingly by constitutional judges in other countries across the world. Despite the criticism to which the case was subjected almost immediately, it also became an emblem for the Constitution in general and the Court in particular. The possibility that, as a law clerk, William Rehnquist might have written a memo prior to the decision suggesting a different outcome was almost enough to derail his nomination to the Supreme Court.

When Robert Bork, then among the country's leading originalists, was nominated to the Supreme Court by Ronald Reagan in 1987, he was obliged to declare that he supported the holding in *Brown*. This must surely have galled Bork, a former colleague of Alexander Bickel's at Yale Law School. The originalist argument to strike down segregation was equivocal at best. In the end, endorsing *Brown* was not enough to get Bork past Senate opposition driven by the drumbeat argument that his originalist views were "out of the mainstream." But the fact that even Bork found it necessary to say that *Brown* was rightly decided indicates the leading position that the case assumed in the hierarchy of American constitutional thought.

Because Earl Warren joined the Court before *Brown* was decided, and because of its importance as a symbol of the Court delivering justice to the oppressed, *Brown* is often thought of as the first act of the Warren Court. That Court, whose era would last until 1969, became a byword for judicial activism. Venerated by a generation of liberal activists and scholars, it was also excoriated by the judicial conservatives who came into power starting with the election of Richard Nixon and later flourishing under Reagan and the two Bushes.

Yet the composition of the Court at the time of the *Brown* decision also makes that landmark case the last significant act of the Roosevelt Court. It was the last important case on which Roosevelt's great justices—Black, Frankfurter, Douglas, and Jackson—sat together. It was also one of the only times that those fiercely independent men agreed on a common opinion in a case of great moment. Beginning as close liberal allies, they had come to disagree profoundly as each had developed his own majestic constitutional theory. When they managed to agree, as they had done in the cases of Japanese-American internment and the steel seizure case, it was only about the outcome, with each producing his own separate opinion.

To reach their heroic agreement in *Brown*, Roosevelt's justices had to go beyond their individual philosophies and self-interests, and to work once more together as a coherent unit. It was a configuration that Roosevelt himself would have recognized. Liberal and results driven, it was shaped by Black's moral clarity, Frankfurter's aspiration to judicial leadership, Douglas's political instincts, and Jackson's frank pragmatism. In this respect, *Brown* may be seen not only as the last act of the Roosevelt Court but as its greatest.

Yet in the unanimity of the decision in *Brown* also lay its greatest flaw: that it was a compromise and, in that sense, incoherent as a statement of constitutional law. The mess that the Court and the country made of *Brown* in the years that followed reflected this incoherence. Was *Brown* a strong statement that the Constitution demanded desegregation? Then why did its sequel, *Brown II*, contemplate a gradual and stepwise remedy, one that was not even specified in detail? Was *Brown* based on the original meaning of the Constitution or on changed circumstances that required the Constitution itself to change? The Court's utter—and wholly intentional—failure to answer these questions cast the whole problem of constitutional interpretation into decades of turmoil. It undercut the legitimacy of the Warren Court's activism, it drove the Burger Court's ambivalence, and it fueled the Rehnquist Court's confused and incomplete turn to originalism.

The limitations and failures of *Brown* suggest that what made the Roosevelt Court great was precisely that its justices ordinarily did not compromise on their deeply held constitutional visions. Their struggles with one another, their personal resentments and even hatreds, expressed their profound commitment to working out the meaning of the Constitution through the lens of liberalism.

The fact that two of their constitutional theories—judicial restraint and originalism—came to be seen as conservative, not liberal at all, illustrates the tremendous generative power of their constitutional ideas. Douglas's vision of the autonomy-expanding, living Constitution would come to be the dominant philosophy of the Warren Court. Pragmatism would increasingly come to dominate the Court in the years of Rehnquist's chief justiceship, as Justice Sandra Day O'Connor became the constant swing vote and the person who left her mark most clearly on the jurisprudence of that body. Indeed, the Rehnquist Court might more accurately be called the O'Connor Court, just as the present Roberts Court so far would be more fairly named for Justice Anthony Kennedy.

The constitutional theories of Roosevelt's justices live on. But that is not all. Today, more than half a century after the last time those justices sat together as a group, their distinctive constitutional theories cover the whole field of constitutional thought.

Epilogue

AFTER THE ROOSEVELT COURT

CHAPTER 46

Hollow Men

After Jackson's untimely death, Frankfurter's feelings for his colleague gradually grew warmer. By the standards of Frankfurter's intense, intimate friendships, he and Jackson were not close. Asked by the *Harvard Law Review* for a remembrance of Jackson, Frankfurter delivered a tribute so guarded it was almost ungenerous. The central theme was Jackson's great verbal facility and his skill in translating his manner of speaking directly to the page. Frankfurter seemed to suggest that Jackson's "specially endowed" talent for advocacy had exceeded his accomplishments as a judge. He quoted Brandeis as saying that Jackson should be solicitor general for life. Finally he hinted at judicial promise incompletely fulfilled. Toward the end of Jackson's life, Frankfurter said, "his aims increasingly groped beyond that of mere advocacy. He steadily cultivated his understanding in the service of these aims; the advocate became the judge. Deeper insight made him aware that the best of phrases may be less than the truth and may even falsify it."[1]

The condescension was compounded by Frankfurter's passing observation that Holmes (and not Jackson) was "a literary genius." Frankfurter's own prose tended to purple. A brutal parody, probably by Jerome Frank, translated the Gettysburg Address into the style of Frankfurter: "A semi-centennial, three decades and seven solstices preceding the present, our paternal progenitors gestated and regurgitated upon the western hemisphere [49 longitude, 38 latitude] a pristine commonwealth."[2] It was as if Frankfurter, with his gibe at Jackson, wanted to head off the judgment of history—which is that with the possible exception of Holmes, Jackson is the greatest writer ever to have sat on the Court.

Yet reserved as Frankfurter was in his own public pronouncements about Jackson, he soon found reason to fight for his memory. First Frankfurter hired Elsie Douglas as his secretary, creating a bond of continuity between the men through the woman whom Jackson had loved. Then, after sending Jackson's former clerk William Rehnquist a copy of his tribute to Jackson, Frankfurter received in return a coruscating dismissal of Jackson's judicial legacy and character. Jackson had reached the peak of his career as solicitor general, Rehnquist asserted. He had "a tendency to go off half-cocked." His judicial opinions did not "seem to go anywhere," and he had no lasting influence on the Court. To top it off, Rehnquist presumptuously complained that Jackson had not become his personal friend during the time of his clerkship.[3]

Frankfurter's loyalty to his "law clerks for life" was limitless, and his expectations of loyalty comparably expansive. Rehnquist's posthumous betrayal of Jackson upset him.[4] Frankfurter sent the letter to E. Barrett Prettyman Jr., Jackson's last law clerk, asking him to write a response—not for public distribution, but aimed squarely at the historical record.

Prettyman's reply began with Jackson's service at Nuremberg. At the distance of a decade, Prettyman wrote, it was still not clear "whether Nuremberg will be rated one of the world's great achievements—or a bad political bust. If it turns out to be the former, the Justice's place in history will center upon that event."[5] Today, after more than sixty years, most historians consider the Nuremberg tribunal to have been a highly consequential historical event. With all its flaws, the tribunal helped create the modern international legal order. No history of human rights, international law, or postwar transitional justice could be written without it.

Prettyman presciently added that it was also too soon to assess Jackson's judicial influence. It would be nearly half a century before pragmatism of the kind Jackson developed would be rediscovered as a coherent constitutional philosophy. What are today some of Jackson's most famous constitutional opinions—in the steel seizure case, and the once-obscure decision about whether the Constitution applied abroad—have become canonical only in recent years.

To counteract Rehnquist's claim that Jackson was impetuous, Prettyman cited the fact that Jackson had ultimately overcome his skepticism and joined the Court's opinion in *Brown*: "Certainly any man with the Justice's views who could join the segregation opinions could hardly be characterized as going off half-cocked." Jackson had agreed to do so only from his sickbed, and at Prettyman's urging. Nevertheless, in joining the unanimous *Brown* opinion, Jackson showed the capacity to allow his broader judgment to overcome his particular view of the case. His last important judicial act was to participate in judicial consensus, not to write a lone opinion that history might later redeem.

Prettyman's deepest insight was his response to Rehnquist's charge that Jackson's opinions did not "go anywhere." The same criticism, Prettyman wrote, was sometimes leveled at his father, who sat on the D.C. Circuit. "This kind of reasoning," he continued, "makes me slightly ill. The idea that a judge has to stick to some 'philosophy,' no matter where it leads him in individual cases, is repulsive to me." Jackson was not unprincipled. He "had certain basic, established beliefs which formed a rock bed for his opinions; but I don't think he let these beliefs carry him along without looking into each set of merits; I don't think he 'tagged,' or categorized, cases and let the tag control."[6]

In maintaining that a judge should not stick with a single overarching judicial philosophy, Prettyman was restating the judicial philosophy of pragmatism that would make Jackson great. As Prettyman noted, Jackson lacked the kind of predictability that follows from specific ideology and helps a judge gain influential supporters who can make (or break) his reputation after he is retired or dead. No doubt that was part of the reason it took so long for Jackson's judicial prominence to emerge. But eventually, the absence of ideology made Jackson a role model and a symbol of a particular approach to judging. Combined with the fact that Jackson's most important work focused on the perennially important issue of executive power under the Constitution, this ensured the resuscitation of his reputation.

Beyond ideology, the other feature that helps a justice achieve historical reputation is a network of friends who are in the business of framing judicial accomplishment. Frankfurter, who had canonized Holmes, Brandeis, and to a lesser degree Cardozo, understood this thoroughly. Frankfurter was on close terms with an astonishingly wide circle of intellectuals, journalists, and of course judges and lawyers. His friends included influential contemporaries like Arthur Schlesinger Jr., who would eventually help him win a Presidential Medal of Freedom (with distinction, a detail Frankfurter would not have wanted omitted). More important still for Frankfurter were his students and law clerks, whom he placed in professorships, government jobs, and judgeships, and who would be the shapers of his historical reputation.[7]

When it came to friends, among his professional contemporaries and even his law clerks, Jackson could not have posed a starker contrast with Frankfurter. To put it bluntly, among this cohort Jackson had no close friends at all. The fact that Frankfurter had asked Prettyman to refute Rehnquist's attack on Jackson captured the extremity of the situation. Frankfurter's closeness to Jackson's clerks exceeded that of Jackson himself.

Prettyman did not hide this distance from Jackson in his letter for Frankfurter's files. Addressing Rehnquist's complaint that "he never felt that he became a personal friend of the Justice's," Prettyman began by acknowledging that Jackson "was an extremely complicated person." When the clerkship began, Prettyman "thought he must not like me; I thought I just wasn't getting through to him." Over time, though, by recognizing "the small signs that meant friendship, displeasure, etc.," Prettyman began to feel that some relationship was developing. He eventually "got to feel, perhaps mistakenly, that he liked me."

The parenthetical "perhaps mistakenly" says a lot; but Prettyman's one anecdote to suggest a friendship with Jackson is even more striking: "He took me on a fishing trip once," Prettyman wrote. "Coming back in the evening, as we were chatting in the back of the boat, he came as close as he ever did to saying: We're having a good year, aren't we?; we like each other, and we get along fine."[8] Prettyman deserves credit for intuiting the awkward attempt to create human connection. "For me," he said, "this peculiar friendship meant more than I could ever express." But he was not whitewashing Jackson's character, either: "I think few people ever *felt* that he was completely revealing himself to them. I think he was often quite lonely."[9]

Jackson's loneliness was also the central theme in a letter written to Frankfurter by Harlan B. Phillips of Columbia's Oral History Research Office, a man to whom any biographer of Jackson and Frankfurter owes a debt. In 1952, Phillips convinced Jackson to give him an extraordinarily extensive interview—a kind of "this is your life" from beginning to end. Their conversations ultimately lasted seventy-four hours, recorded on 16.8 miles of reel-to-reel audio tape.[10] In July 1955, trying to convince Frankfurter to sit for an oral history of his own,[11] Phillips wrote to him disagreeing with Frankfurter's statement that Jackson's charm was not merely "surface glitter." Phillips believed Jackson's charm was a defense mechanism designed to get him through the misery of social interactions that he fundamentally did not enjoy with people he fundamentally disliked.[12]

According to Phillips, Jackson had considered Frankfurter the only regular visitor to his office whose company he appreciated. Jackson "told me once," Phillips wrote, "that the only caller—and he had many—whose talk and companionship he 'thoroughly enjoyed' was you." Jackson had enjoyed their "clash of minds," Phillips flatteringly told Frankfurter. Then came the kicker: "He loved to rassle with your quality, and, I suspect, this was the only kind of love unhappy circumstance permitted him."[13] The "unhappy circumstance" referred to the fact that Jackson's relationship with Elsie Douglas had necessarily remained secret. But Phillips also had in mind Jackson's gnawing ambition to be chief justice. "Keeping our eyes on the 'bird on the wing,'" he wrote, "sometimes encourages such ambition that we devour our young."

Phillips was circling around something deeper and more terrible that haunted Jackson: "In the midst of comfort and the acclaim which attended his performances, he was the loneliest figure, but one, I've met, and, with the end in sight and eagerly reaching for the release it would bring, I believe he considered himself fundamentally a hollow man. 'Tis sad, but I believe it true."[14] Frankfurter would certainly have understood the reference to T. S. Eliot's "The Hollow Men," one of the iconic modernist poems of his generation. It suggested death before death: a futility of existence that could not have been more unlike Frankfurter's own zest for life and optimistic self-conception. It hinted, in short, that Jackson died believing he had been a failure.

CHAPTER 47

Kaddish

Frankfurter, vital as he was, could not accept this picture of Jackson. He became a one-man police force, scouring the world for any quotation or description, however minor, that cast aspersions on the man who became a closer friend to him in death than he had been in life.[15] The underlying source of Frankfurter's impulse to make Jackson into his responsibility was that some time soon, his own historical legacy would be on the line. Unable to control the results (though he certainly tried), Frankfurter could at least manage his colleague's legacy and model good reputational stewardship for the last time.

During the same period in his life that he was defending Jackson, Frankfurter's own work as a justice was notably in decline. Unlike his heroes Holmes and Brandeis, some of whose most important judicial opinions came very late in life, Frankfurter made few significant contributions to constitutional thought in his last eight years on the Court. After shepherding *Brown* to fruition, Frankfurter had just one more great opinion left in him, one of the more controversial dissents of his career. It came in an important case about voting rights, a precursor to the Supreme Court's eventual holding that the Constitution guaranteed "one man, one vote." The issue was whether it was within the power of the Supreme Court to hold that Tennessee must alter its traditional mechanism for setting up the districts for the state assembly. Redistricting had long been a political matter, decided by the state legislature. Geographical districts could remain unchanged even when population shifted. As a result, urban areas that had grown large might have the same number of representatives as sparsely populated rural districts. Maintaining the old district border could be, and often was, a cover for racial discrimination.

For Frankfurter, the case, *Baker v. Carr*, provided the perfect and indeed crowning example of where judicial restraint was appropriate. It was not only that legislatures had always been in charge of redistricting, but rather that the act of designing districts was the most inherently political act possible. Once the courts got into the business of such design, there would be no way for them to craft a judicial remedy that was not simply more politics. Putting the courts in the redistricting business, Frankfurter predicted, would undercut the legitimacy of the Court. It would not be only futile, but actively destructive of judicial authority.

Frankfurter fought long and hard for his position that the courts must not venture into what he called the "political thicket."[16] According to one report, the seventy-nine-year-old harangued the other justices in conference for four and a half hours. At first, in April 1961, the Court seemed to be evenly divided, with one justice, the Eisenhower appointee Charles Evans Whittaker, on the fence. The case was reargued in October. Before a decision could be reached, Whittaker suffered a nervous breakdown and resigned. His distraught son blamed Frankfurter for having pressured his father to the point of collapse.[17] Whittaker was replaced by Byron White, and Frankfurter's side ended up losing decisively. William Brennan, the emerging liberal leader of the Warren Court, wrote the opinion. In landmark terms, it held that although there were some "political questions" that the Court must not address, redistricting was not one of them.

Frankfurter's dissent urging judicial restraint helped consolidate his reputation as a conservative. To the generation of lawyers and law professors who clerked for the justices of the Warren Court, especially for Brennan and later Thurgood Marshall, redistricting would become a touchstone of the new liberal constitutional thought. With time, it came to seem impossible that a justice who opposed judicial enforcement of voting rights could be considered liberal.

Frankfurter had hoped his former clerks would preserve the association between judicial restraint and liberalism. The professor-clerks remained loyal, none more so than Alexander Bickel, who ended up in the hostile terrain of Yale Law School, with its connections to Douglas and intellectual sympathy for Black. Yet during the tumultuous decade of the sixties and well into the seventies, it proved impossible as a matter of political reality to trumpet judicial restraint while remaining a liberal. Now that liberals enjoyed a majority on the Court, the activists would have their day.

Bickel, perhaps Frankfurter's most intellectually influential former clerk, would make a fundamental contribution to American constitutional thought by reformulating the doctrine of judicial restraint into a conflict between the Court on the one hand and the democratic majority on the other. What he called the "counter-majoritarian difficulty" was the challenge of how the Court could use the Constitution to declare rights that went against the preferences of the voting public. For at least a generation after he posed this problem in 1962—the same year as Frankfurter's *Baker v. Carr* dissent—the field of academic constitutional law was obsessed with solving it. Yet Bickel himself was often seen as a conservative, not a liberal. Over time, still expanding on Frankfurter's philosophy, he may even have become one.[18]

The dissent in the redistricting case would be the last opinion Frankfurter ever wrote. Just a few days after it was handed down in April 1962, Elsie Douglas came into his chambers at the Court and discovered him lying on the floor. Frankfurter had suffered a stroke that left him partially paralyzed.[19] As it became clear that Frankfurter would have to retire from the Court, his friend Dean Acheson did him the kindness of asking President John F. Kennedy to meet Frankfurter in his chambers. All three men understood that the visit paralleled Roosevelt's call on Holmes that Frankfurter had arranged for his idol's ninetieth birthday. Frankfurter gamely played the role of Holmes. After Kennedy left the office, Frankfurter, who had detested Joe Kennedy, commented to Acheson that although he had never noticed it before, "that young man has grace."[20]

Frankfurter retired from the Court later that summer. On February 21, 1965, Frankfurter, by now in the hospital, looked to his aide and said, "I hope I don't spoil your Washington's birthday." With those words, he turned his head and died.[21]

The next morning, Hugo Black, who had been visiting his son in Miami, sat down to breakfast and saw the newspaper headline announcing the death of his old adversary. "Ohhh, Felix is dead," moaned Black. Then he began to cry.[22]

Frankfurter's memorial service was held in his apartment, as Brandeis's had been. The speakers were chosen from among the scores of protégés and law clerks who now occupied some of the most important positions in the legal academy. One of them, Paul Freund of Harvard Law School, who had like Frankfurter turned down the job of solicitor general—and was widely considered a possible Supreme Court nominee—recalled the "iron grip on the arm" that accompanied every conversation with the justice. Then Freund read the same words from *Pilgrim's Progress* that Frankfurter had read at Brandeis's memorial twenty-four years earlier: "My sword I give to him that shall succeed me in my pilgrimage."

As his faith, Frankfurter had consciously substituted Americanism for Judaism. At the end, though, he chose to acknowledge his religious heritage. "I came into the world as a Jew," he said, "I think it is fitting I should leave as a Jew." Frankfurter was childless, but at his request, a favorite former clerk, Louis Henkin, closed the memorial by reciting the *kaddish* prayer for the dead.[23] Those assembled, many of them Jewish-Americans, knew they had lost a father figure whose love of country and influence in the world of legal thought would not soon be equaled.

CHAPTER 48

The Pine Box

For Black, the years after *Brown* were bittersweet. He continued to refine his theory of the original meaning of the Constitution's text in opinions and speeches, focusing especially on the First Amendment. More and more—though never, quite, in opinions for the Court—he began to say that the First Amendment "means what it says,"[24] and that as a result, "there *are* absolutes in our Bill of Rights."[25] Frankfurter's students, supporters, and friends would never let this perspective go unchallenged. Such an absolutist notion of the Constitution, they believed, could not possibly be implemented even if it were desirable to do so.

Nor did the Supreme Court as a whole ever adopt Black's opinion about the First Amendment. Black could take pleasure in the great expansion of the protections for free speech that were achieved under the Warren Court, and he was not above taking the credit. But in truth the real victor in the First Amendment cases of the 1960s was not Black but Brennan. Even a landmark decision like *New York Times v. Sullivan*, which barred libel suits against public figures unless falsehoods had been spread with actual malice, fell short of absolute First Amendment protection—a result Black could not wholly embrace. At oral argument, the *New York Times* and the cause of free speech were represented by Alexander Bickel. "It's too bad the *Times* couldn't get someone who believes in the First Amendment," Black witheringly observed.[26]

To Black's chagrin, even his historical claims for the strong nature of the First Amendment came to be challenged. Scholars researching the free-speech practices of the founding generation concluded that the original meaning of freedom of speech was highly limited.[27] It was frustrating for Black to see his sweeping interpretation undercut. Nonetheless, the emergence of this serious scholarly work on the origins of the Constitution was a testament to Black's influence. Much as Fairman and Bickel had been directed by Frankfurter to the history of the Fourteenth Amendment in order to confront Black's powerful arguments, a whole generation of constitutional scholars now found that originalism demanded that they retool and become serious historians. Through the influence of his originalism, Black helped create the flourishing and ever-improving field of U.S. constitutional history.

The ascendance of professional constitutional history would have struck Black as an ambivalent legacy. He liked originalism precisely because he hoped it would provide clear answers that were not subject to judicial manipulation. Professional historians, though, specialize in ambiguity, uncertainty, and doubt. The populist in Black also liked to think that anyone could go to the books to understand the meaning of the Constitution in its original context, as he had done. Yet the work of professional historians is technical and requires training. As a result, originalism today, despite its aspirations, is not a populist constitutional theory.

Hints of these tensions within originalism were evident to Black already in the 1960s, and he responded by emphasizing constitutional text over historical context. His important opinion in *Gideon v. Wainwright*, guaranteeing that indigent defendants would have counsel appointed for them if they could not afford it, was a masterpiece of textual legerdemain.[28] There was not a shred of historical evidence to suggest that when the framers of the Sixth Amendment guaranteed the accused "the assistance of counsel," they intended that the government would pay for a lawyer. They meant simply that the government could not deny the defendant the chance to have a lawyer appear on his behalf. Black, though, read the guarantee as promising a lawyer to every defendant.

After *Gideon*, Black's brilliant former law clerk Professor Charles Reich of Yale—whose philosophy was in fact much closer to that of Douglas, with whom he was also close—wrote an article attempting to ascribe the notion of the "living Constitution" to Black.[29] Black privately rejected the attempt.[30] It went flatly against his whole approach to think that the Constitution evolved. But he must have realized that the historical component of originalism was waning even in his own work.

When it came to the protection of privacy—the greatest constitutional innovation of the 1960s—Black again relied on text rather than history. He pointed out that the word *privacy* appeared nowhere in the Constitution. The Fourth Amendment protected the people against "unreasonable" searches and seizures. Instead of seeking a historical meaning for the word *unreasonable*, Black restricted himself to explaining that the word could not extend so far as the majority of the Warren Court sought to bring it. While the Warren Court transformed the landscape of constitutional law to protect individual autonomy, Black remained squarely in dissent.[31]

Indeed, in Black's later years, he found that his originalism was turning him into a judicial split personality: now liberal, now conservative. When it came to free speech, Black was in principle the most liberal member of the Court, with only Douglas approaching his impulse toward the absolute.[32] When it came to privacy, however, Black dissented from the rights expansion that was occurring under Douglas's influence.

Black served on the Court for so long that he became a transitional figure in the history of the constitutional philosophy he himself invented. He sat long enough—from 1937 to 1971—to see originalism transformed from a liberal theory of constitutional law into a conservative one. The shift had much to do with the way the Warren Court expanded individual liberties and enforced the integration of the schools. Black's liberalism relied on original meaning to create basic rights to liberty and equality. But as the Court went further and further, Black came to believe the text and history did not support these expansions. And so, with the exception of the First Amendment, he hesitated. Eventually Black stopped voting with the other liberals on the Court and began to seem conservative.

In August 1971, Black's health started to fail. Before entering the hospital, he composed and signed a letter of resignation, leaving the date blank. Then, in what he called "Operation Frustrate the Historians," he instructed Hugo Jr. to burn all his Supreme Court papers. Like others charged with the task of destroying a writer's unpublished work, Black's son was ambivalent. He gave his father a note to sign authorizing him to destroy papers selected "in his discretion." "Good Lord," Black said, when he read over the document. "Can't anybody do anything right?" From his hospital bed, Black took a pen and added the words, "so long as he destroys them all."[33] Hugo Jr. burned many of the papers in a fireplace—but he left behind notes and letters between the justices, as well as drafts of Black's opinions.[34]

Black held out until September 17—the anniversary of the date in 1787 when the framers of the Constitution signed the document that would become the focus of Black's professional life. With the beginning of the term coming into view, Black realized he had to retire. Elizabeth, his second wife, who had been his secretary after Josephine's death, fulfilled both duties and typed in the date on his resignation. Within a week Black was dead. He was eighty-five years old.

In Black's final hours, the South embraced him as it had not during his thirty-four years on the bench. The Alabama legislature passed a resolution praying for him, "confident that history will regard Justice Black as one of the true giants of jurisprudence."[35] Black's own efforts in *Brown* had helped create the conditions for the rise of the New South—a state of mind as much as a place. After the struggles of the civil rights movement, Southerners were coming to embrace integration even as they shared some of Black's skepticism of the new individual rights the Warren Court was inventing. In this new world, Black was not a traitor, but a native son made good.

His family buried Black in a plain pine box—an echo of the unfinished pickets of the fence in front of his family's house in Clay County. At his funeral, his favorite childhood hymns were sung. Buried with him in his pocket was his constant companion in life: a printed pamphlet copy of the Constitution of the United States.[36]

CHAPTER 49

The Wilderness—and a Triumph

For Douglas, who outlasted even Black, the later years presented a tableau of ever-increasing professional triumph and ever-declining personal satisfaction. It took the political skills of William Brennan and a liberal majority to make Douglas's views law. But the Supreme Court's privacy revolution in the 1960s and 1970s was intellectually the work of Douglas and his constitutional theory.

It began with the Supreme Court finding a constitutional right to contraception for married couples in their bedrooms. It moved on to include abortion rights. In our era, privacy has expanded to include a right of sexual expression with a partner of one's choice. Someday it may include the right to same-sex marriage. These developments mark one of the most epochal shifts in the history of our constitutional law. Embraced by liberals and excoriated by conservatives, the Court's privacy cases reflect the distinctive philosophy of a living Constitution, one in which new rights to personal autonomy can be discovered and announced based on some collective intuition about what is central to human flourishing.

In 1965, it was Douglas who framed the crucial constitutional opinion that gave the underpinning to this line of cases. Several years earlier, in a case challenging a state ban on contraceptives, Douglas had written a dissent. There he had argued for a right to privacy that "emanates from the totality of the constitutional scheme under which we live."[37] Now, in another contraception case, with prodding from Brennan, Douglas filled in what he meant. In the case of *Griswold v. Connecticut*, Douglas famously said that "specific

guarantees in the Bill of Rights have penumbras, formed by emana-
tions from those guarantees that help give them life and substance."[38]
He argued that aspects of the First, Third, Fourth, Fifth, and Ninth
amendments together created "zones of privacy" that included
marital intimacy. None of these amendments mentioned privacy or
marriage, much less contraception or sex.[39]

Although his opinion in *Griswold* was written with characteristic brio and brevity, Douglas understood that he was discovering new constitutional rights that seemed to reflect the preferences
of the justices. As a former New Dealer and a Roosevelt justice,
Douglas knew that he had to provide some explanation for why
this ruling was different from *Lochner*, which also discovered an
unmentioned right—the liberty of contract—in the deep principles of constitutional structure. Douglas's answer was, bluntly,
that privacy was different. It was not about economic rights, but
personal freedom: "We do not sit as a super-legislature to determine the wisdom, need, and propriety of laws that touch economic
problems, business affairs, or social conditions. This law, however,
operates directly on an intimate relation of husband and wife."[40]

Insisting that privacy was special just because it was—that personal autonomy belonged to a category of its own—was Douglas's
signal contribution to modern constitutional law. Its roots could
be traced to Brandeis, who himself had coauthored a famous law
review article arguing for privacy as a right to be let alone.[41] For
Brandeis, though, privacy protected personal communication
against wiretapping as well as the right to keep one's own counsel.
Douglas deserves the credit—or the blame—for extending privacy
to cover intimate matters of sex and procreation.

The rhetorical technique that Douglas employed to press this
extended conception of privacy was to present sex within the con-
fines of marriage ("an intimate relation of husband and wife"[42]) as
the ultimate expression of private choice. As if to deflect attention
from the fact that the right was not to marriage itself, but to sexual
autonomy within it, Douglas closed his opinion with a paean to
marital union:

We deal with a right of privacy older than the Bill of Rights—older than our political parties, older than our school system. Marriage is a coming together for better or for worse, hopefully enduring, and intimate to the degree of being sacred. It is an association that promotes a way of life, not causes; a harmony in living, not political faiths; a bilateral loyalty, not commercial or social projects. Yet it is an association for as noble a purpose as any involved in our prior decisions.[43]

The contrast between Douglas's constitutional triumph and the ongoing collapse of his personal life is captured poignantly in this passage. Or perhaps no justice was better placed to sing the glories of marriage. Douglas, after all, loved the institution so much he entered into it four times.

Douglas's accomplishments in his later years on the Court were by no means limited to his historic victories in expanding privacy rights. Spurred by his love of the outdoors, Douglas became a major figure in the early environmental movement. In 1954, he organized a hike along the C&O Canal outside Washington, D.C.—180 miles in eight days—to protest plans to turn it into a freeway. The hike made headlines, and the canal was eventually turned into a national park. Then Douglas did it again, and again—for a total of more than a dozen such hikes over the next two decades. He campaigned successfully to preserve the Couger Lakes in Washington State, which were ultimately included by Congress in the William O. Douglas Wilderness Area. And he wrote several books urging environmental preservation, including two volumes under the title *My Wilderness* and a third, *The Wilderness Bill of Rights*, laying out legal strategies for conservation.[44]

As a justice, Douglas set the groundwork for legal environmentalism with a series of opinions seeking to expand individuals' rights to challenge government decisions that impinged on the environment.[45] In one famous dissent, Douglas poetically suggested that the inanimate objects of nature—the "valleys, alpine meadows, rivers, lakes, estuaries, beaches, ridges, groves of trees, swampland, or even air"—should be treated as parties with the right to have their continued existence considered by a court.[46] Douglas was taking the same creative impulse he had applied to individual autonomy and expanding it to the preservation of nature.

And on several memorable occasions, Douglas took the kind of unilateral political action as a justice that would put him on the front pages of the nation's newspapers. One astonishing episode took place in 1973, while Douglas was on summer vacation in Washington State. Thousands of miles away, a handful of American pilots in Thailand were facing court martial for refusing to fly bombing missions over Cambodia. Arguing on their behalf in New York, ACLU attorney Burt Neuborne convinced a federal judge that the pilots could not be found guilty because the bombing itself was illegal, since there had been no declaration of war on Cambodia. The court of appeals issued a stay blocking the judge's order, but Neuborne had the idea of trying to get Douglas to put the order back in place.

The ACLU had a "Douglas watch" so that they could find their favorite justice at a moment's notice. In an evocation of the last-minute efforts to save Sacco and Vanzetti, Neuborne flew to Washington State and knocked on the door of Douglas's cabin in Goose Prairie. Douglas, in jeans and boots, met with him on the steps. But unlike Brandeis, who turned away the lawyer for the Italian anarchists when he came to his door, Douglas agreed to hear argument. The next morning, in his birthplace of Yakima, fifty miles away, Douglas convened an impromptu hearing in the post office. After considering arguments made by Neuborne and, on the other side, a hastily alerted assistant U.S. attorney, Douglas ruled. He lifted the stay issued by the court of appeals, reinstating the lower court's ruling. In effect, Douglas was ordering the government of the United States to stop bombing Cambodia.

The other justices overturned the order within hours, the first time they had ever voted by telephone rather than convening for a formal meeting. But the charges against the pilots were dropped, and they were honorably discharged. Douglas had made a grand point, and done it in style.[47]

Yet despite his role on the Warren Court as the author of the regnant liberal constitutional philosophy, Douglas was never fully embraced either by his colleagues or by Court watchers. Remembered as a liberal justice and as an idiosyncratic personality, he is not recognized for what he was: the intellectual father of the rights-expanding school of constitutional thought. One reason history has shortchanged Douglas is that legal realism as a constitutional theory can seem embarrassingly results driven. Struck by Douglas's results-oriented approach and his outsize personality, one influential legal historian has argued that Douglas was not so much a judge as an "anti-judge."[48] His "indifference to the approved sources of judicial constraint"[49] seemed strikingly out of the mainstream traditions of constitutional interpretation.

By comparison, Black's originalism carried the prestige of history. Frankfurter's judicial restraint could boast a theory of which government institutions are best suited for different tasks. Even Jackson's pragmatism had the pedigree of American common sense as well as the objective of balancing competing interests in society. Douglas's constitutional realism acknowledged full-on that because judges inevitably will make the law, they should do it right. If this constitutional vision was much bolder than the others, it also seemed much cruder.

But the theoretical drawbacks of constitutional realism do not fully explain why Douglas is not generally seen as central to the liberal constitutional revolution. Justices William Brennan and Thurgood Marshall got the credit that might have been Douglas's for the liberal ideal of what came to be called "the living Constitution." While its name sounded mellifluous—and owed much to Brandeis's notion of "the living law"[50]—the theory of the living Constitution was subject to the same criticism as Douglas's realism: that it made the Constitution mean whatever liberals wanted it to mean.

The core of the problem with crediting Douglas lay in his character, which made him an unsuitable hero for liberal constitutional thought. His contemporaries took his speed in opinion writing for laziness and his isolation for contempt—and perhaps they were right. Above all, Douglas's resistance to the strictures of conventional morality in his own life made it look as though his undisciplined search for personal freedom was driving his constitutional thought. The man who would most aggressively advocate the freedom of the marital bedroom from government intrusion was precisely the man who tore through marriages. From the standpoint of conventional morality, Douglas seemed to exemplify the kind of social breakdown that might follow from expanding individual rights. For liberals, it was infinitely preferable to have as their public champion someone like Thurgood Marshall, a legitimate hero of the civil rights movement, or Brennan, a New Jersey Catholic who was married to his first wife for fifty-five years until her peaceful death.

Douglas's increasingly difficult personality also injured his reputation. If he and Black had never been intimate friends, they had at least been close judicial allies. During the 1960s, however, the two men actually stopped speaking for several years, a result of their constitutional positions growing apart and Black's distaste at Douglas's personal peregrinations.[51] Douglas's circle of intimates shrank with his greater remove from political life. He entertained the fantasy of being named the candidate for vice president should Lyndon B. Johnson have won the Democratic nomination in 1960, but his divorces apart, Douglas no longer had political allies left.[52]

Where other justices might have been turned into heroes by their former law clerks, Douglas was generally met with a disdain that almost matched the attitude with which he had treated law clerks himself. Douglas was reported to have observed that a law clerk was "the lowest form of human life."[53] Douglas rarely addressed his clerks, and when he did, his language could be abusive.[54] According to others who clerked alongside them in different chambers, Douglas's clerks lived in some combination of fear and loneliness. He would "fire" them regularly, until they learned to ignore him and show up for work the next day.[55] Once, after he had retired—forced unhappily into the decision by a debilitating stroke—Douglas ordered a clerk to bring an "opinion" he had written to the Court's printing shop for publication. Although Douglas would not or could not admit it, he was no longer a sitting justice, and the clerk refused. Douglas turned on him. "You are a traitor," the retired justice told his clerk.[56]

Of course Douglas also did not need his clerks very much. He wrote fast and well and relied on them only to check his opinions for errors. But that fact alone could not account for the distant contempt in which he held his clerks. The explanation lay in Douglas's frustration with having to rely on judicial opinions as his method of exerting influence—a frustration that Roosevelt, as a politician who grappled with the Court, would certainly have understood. Roosevelt was not wrong in judging that among the justices whom he appointed, Douglas was the one most fitted to politics—because he most yearned for that form of public acclaim.

Frankfurter was born to be a justice. By his lights, he sought to become a great one, through consistency with a single philosophy.[57] What frustrations he felt derived from the way the world did not seem to recognize that consistency was the hallmark of judicial quality. Perhaps, too, Frankfurter suffered from the lack of a Felix Frankfurter to make him into a judicial icon as he had done for Holmes and Brandeis.

Black enjoyed the Senate and thought about the presidency, but he also embraced the role of judge from the start. With the model of Jefferson before him, he set out to achieve greatness in the job he occupied. He succeeded because he developed a constitutional vision that grew from and complemented his populist liberalism.

Jackson, who lacked the special "it" necessary for electoral politics, welcomed the judicial role. He yearned for the chief justiceship as a way to make a permanent mark on history, and took the Nuremberg prosecutor's job as an alternative. He died doubting that he had succeeded. Yet it was through the very act of judging pragmatically and explaining openly what he was doing that he ended up being recognized many years after his death as one of the great justices, probably the most influential for our current era.

These were extraordinary, self-made men: brilliant, ambitious, proud, arrogant, and independent to a fault. Douglas was the most independent of them all. He alone made his independence into the basis of a constitutional philosophy. And he alone was so independent that he could not be truly happy in a role defined by being just one of nine. His liberalism was, in the end, perfectly compatible with his personal remove. It has probably never been more truly said of anyone that he loved humanity and hated people.

Douglas served for thirty-six years on the Supreme Court, longer than any other justice, including his successor, John Paul Stevens, who served thirty-five years. His record is likely to stand even in this era of increasing life expectancy, because it is correspondingly difficult to get appointed to the Supreme Court so young.[58] Douglas's accomplishments on the Court were vast—and they were those of a brilliant, irascible individualist, not a team player.

In this sense, Douglas was simply a more extreme version of the other great Roosevelt justices. These four men all turned out to be among the most important and influential justices ever to have sat on the Court. They started as political allies of the president, but their alliance was not what made them great. Indeed their alliance faltered once they were all on the Court, and it fractured irreparably once Roosevelt could no longer hold them together.

Their greatness came to pass precisely because each went his own way, each developing a constitutional vision distinctive to his own personality and worldview. The great decisions of the Roosevelt Court are not unanimous or even 5 to 4. They include independent concurrences and dissents by all four men, writing seriatim in the manner of the British common law justices of old. Only *Brown v. Board of Education* breaks this rule—and to reach that historic result, Roosevelt's justices had to break rules of their own.

Consensus can be valuable for an institution that must take decisive and unpopular action. In *Brown*, its last act, the Roosevelt Court showed its justices still had some of the political wisdom they had learned from the most successful politician in American history. But the justices of the Roosevelt Court also demonstrate that agreement is not the most important value for the members of the institution charged with interpreting the Constitution.

There is no one way to interpret the Constitution, and the lives of the greatest justices reflect that reality. Driven by prudence, by principle, by pragmatism, or by policy, the justices at their best make the Constitution their own. Arguing about its true meaning, striving to make sense of its contours and its commands, is the essence of what makes us loyal to it. To interpret the Constitution by one's own best lights is to be an American.

ACKNOWLEDGMENTS

In researching and writing this book over the last five years I incurred many debts. I would especially like to thank those who generously read and commented on the entire manuscript, including Daniel Aaron, John Q. Barrett, Seth Berman, Norman Dorsen, Andrew Kaufman, Michael Klarman, Sandy Levinson, Frank Michelman, Bill Rubenstein, Mark Tushnet, and Ted White. They improved the draft enormously and saved me from many errors; those that remain are my own. I benefited from interviews and conversations with Norman Dorsen, Andrew Kaufman, E. Barrett Prettyman Jr., John Mansfield, Frank Sander, and Victor Brudney, all of whom knew many of the subjects of the book personally. Margaret Koster and Joseph Koerner guided me in art-historical matters. I had excellent research assistance from Glenna Goldis, Neeraj Gupta, Brian Hauss, Zachary Schauf, Lauren Kuley, Jonathan Truppman, Garrett Coyle, Ian Samuel, Lucas Issacharoff, Stephanie Finn, and Aaron Voloj Dessauer. Elizabeth M. Farley helped with the photos. Ben Owen masterfully coordinated editing and sourcing. My gratitude to my wife, Jeannie Suk, for what I owe her, intellectually and otherwise, cannot be adequately captured here.

NOTES

1. The quotation is often attributed to Oliver Wendell Holmes Jr. See, for example, Max Lerner, *Nine Scorpions in a Bottle: Great Judges and Cases of the Supreme Court* (New York: Arcade, 1994). But there is no evidence Holmes ever said it or anything like it. For the attribution to Bickel, see Dennis J. Hutchinson, "The Black-Jackson Feud," *Supreme Court Review* 1988: 203, 238. Kent Olson of the University of Virginia Law School Library points out that in the July 1953 issue of *Foreign Affairs*, J. Robert Oppenheimer compared the US-USSR arms race to "two scorpions in a bottle, each capable of killing the other, but only at the risk of his own life." Oppenheimer, "Atomic Weapons and American Policy," *Foreign Affairs* 31 (1953): 525, 529. Olson writes: "This metaphor received some coverage in the newspapers at the time, and the application to the Supreme Court may well have started out as a play on Oppenheimer's phrase." Bickel was a law clerk from 1952 to 1953, and so would have been finishing his clerkship when Oppenheimer used the phrase. Kent Olson, personal communication to the author, July 22, 2009.

Book One   CONTACTS

1. "Frankfurter v. Pupils," *Time*, June 12, 1933 (Frankfurter "still had an accent" in 1906).

2. Jerome Karabel, *The Chosen: The Hidden History of Admission and Exclusion at Harvard, Yale, and Princeton* (Boston: Houghton Mifflin, 2005), 16–17.

3. See, for example, a cover story on Theodore Jr.'s Porcellian induction: "Initiate Young Roosevelt; Porcellian Club at Harvard Compels Him to Adore Pigs' Feet," *New York Times*, February 19, 1907, 1. Archibald, Theodore's third son, was not a member. See Patricia O'Toole, *When Trumpets Call: Theodore Roosevelt after the White House* (New York: Simon & Schuster, 2005), 336.

4. President William McKinley was shot on September 5, 1901, and died on September 14, 1901.

5. A comparison I made of the membership of the Institute of 1770 and the *Crimson* editorial board for 1903, 1904, and 1905, shows that between one-third and one-half of the *Crimson* board members had been chosen for the Institute. For FDR's experiences see Karabel, *The Chosen*, 14–15.

6. *Felix Frankfurter Reminisces: Recorded in Talks with Dr. Harlan B. Phillips* (New York: Reynal, 1960), 18.

7. H. N. Hirsch, *The Enigma of Felix Frankfurter* (New York: Basic Books, 1981), 13 (linens); Michael E. Parrish, *Felix Frankfurter and His Times: The Reform Years* (New York: Free Press, 1982), 12 (fur and silks).

8. The degree was structured by a mandatory core curriculum that included Latin and even some Greek. *Felix Frankfurter Reminisces*, 9–11.

9. Id., 11.

10. Id., 12.

11. Id., 17.

12. Id., 19.

13. Id., 38.

14. Gerald T. Dunne, *Grenville Clark: Public Citizen* (New York: Farrar, Straus and Giroux, 1986), 14–15.

15. *Felix Frankfurter Reminisces*, 21, 235.

16. Id., 109.

17. Parrish, *Frankfurter*, 76 (Harold Laski and Holmes thought Marion resembled a painting by Bernardo Luino and nicknamed her "Luina"); for the relative heights of Marion and Frankfurter see, for example, the photograph reproduced in this book.

18. Hirsch, *Enigma*, 50, citing Denman to Frankfurter, early October 1916, Felix Frankfurter papers, Library of Congress, Folder 33 in Box 5.

19. Id., 53, citing Frankfurter to Denman, June 21, 1917, Felix Frankfurter Papers, Library of Congress, Folder 35 in Box 5.

20. At the time the secretaries of the Army and the Navy were full cabinet appointments; assistant secretary therefore counted as a subcabinet appointment.

21. Frankfurter was one of only a few Jews on the entire Harvard University faculty at the time. The first Jew on the Harvard faculty was Judah Monis, appointed to teach Hebrew in 1722 after a public conversion to Christianity. The next, Charles Gross, was appointed instructor in medieval history in 1888 and full professor in 1901. Susanne Klingenstein, *Jews in the American Academy, 1900–1940: The Dynamics of Intellectual Assimilation* (New Haven: Yale University Press, 1991), 211 n.18. Another, Leo Wiener, was appointed instructor of Slavic languages in 1896, assistant professor in 1901, and full professor in 1911. Id., 11–12.

22. Parrish, *Frankfurter*, 108 and 293 n.16 (citing Eleanor Roosevelt to Sara Delano Roosevelt, May 12, 1918, in Eleanor Roosevelt Papers, Hyde Park). Eleanor continued to refer to Jews in such terms into the 1930s. See Blanche Wiesen Cook, *Eleanor Roosevelt* (New York: Viking, 1992), vol. I, 390 ("ER's anti–Semitism was impersonal and casual, a frayed raiment of her generation.... She did not remove it until the era of the Holocaust caused her to consider deeply, actually study, her own feelings."); for her shift, see Cook, vol. II, 304–34.

23. "Mooney Pardoned; To 'Dedicate Life To Common Good'; Absolved of Guilt," *New York Times*, January 8, 1939, 1. The pardon was granted by California governor Culbert Olson.

24. Theodore Roosevelt to Felix Frankfurter, December 19, 1917; see Parrish, *Frankfurter*, 99.

25. Felix Frankfurter to Theodore Roosevelt, January 7, 1918; see ibid.

26. Frankfurter's attitude to the Bolshevik Revolution as a pro-war progressive was that the United States should not interfere. For context, see Christopher Lasch, *The American Liberals and the Russian Revolution* (New York: Columbia University Press, 1962).

27. Paul Avrich, *Sacco and Vanzetti: The Anarchist Background* (Princeton: Princeton University Press, 1991), 153–56; Bruce Watson, *Sacco and Vanzetti: The Men, the Murders, and the Judgment of Mankind* (New York: Viking, 2007), 8–10.

28. James Roosevelt and Sidney Shalett, *Affectionately, FDR* (New York: Harcourt, Brace, 1959), 60–61.

29. Id., 62; Stanley Coben, *A. Mitchell Palmer: Politician* (New York: Da Capo Press, 1972), 205–06; Jean Edward Smith, *FDR* (New York: Random House, 2007), 171–72 and n.32; Watson, *Sacco and Vanzetti*, 10. Smith reports that Roosevelt drove Mrs. Palmer and her daughter to safety; other sources say Palmer and his wife were alone in the house.

30. Ruling of Judge George W. Anderson, June 23, 1920. The case was *Colyer v. Steffington*, 265 F. 17 (1920).

31. Parrish, *Frankfurter*, 125–28.

32. Matthew Josephson, "Profiles: Jurist-II," *The New Yorker*, December 7, 1940, 46.

33. The pamphlet, called *La salute è in voi* ("Health Is in You!), was adopted from another guide to explosives written by another Italian anarchist, a professor of chemistry in Milan. See Avrich, *Sacco and Vanzetti*, 98–99.

34. Id., 204–06. Buda escaped to Italy. For more on the bombing and Buda's probable role, see Beverly Gage, *The Day Wall Street Exploded: A Story of America in Its First Age of Terror* (Oxford: Oxford University Press, 2009), 325–26; see also Mike Davis, *Buda's Wagon: A Brief History of the Car Bomb* (London: Verso Books, 2007).

35. Felix Frankfurter, *The Case of Sacco and Vanzetti: A Critical Analysis for Lawyers and Laymen* (Boston: Little, Brown, 1927).

36. On the Mexican sojourn, see Avrich, *Sacco and Vanzetti*, 58–72.

37. Parrish, *Frankfurter*, 179 and n.14 (citing *The Sacco-Vanzetti Case: Transcript of Record* 5: 5253, 4: 3579 [New York: Holt, 1928–29]).

38. Daniel Aaron, *Writers on the Left: Episodes in American Literary Communism* (New York: Columbia University Press, 1992), 170.

39. Papers of Elizabeth Glendower Evans, Schlesinger Library, Harvard. For a catalogue see http://oasis.lib.harvard.edu/oasis/deliver/~sch00026.

40. Linda Simon, *William James Remembered* (Lincoln: University of Nebraska Press, 1996), 58–60.

41. Moshik Temkin, *The Sacco-Vanzetti Affair: America on Trial* (New Haven: Yale University Press, 2009), 19.

42. In his oral history, Frankfurter claimed that one day he "saw" that Thompson had been hired to represent Sacco and Vanzetti. *Felix Frankfurter*

Reminisces, 210. In fact, though, a letter to Frankfurter from Brandeis, dated December 7, 1924, tells Frankfurter, "Auntie B. seems much relieved by what you did re W. G. Thompson." Melvin I. Urofsky and David W. Levy, eds., *Half Brother, Half Son: The Letters of Louis D. Brandeis to Felix Frankfurter* (Norman: University of Oklahoma Press, 1991), 183 and n.12. The strong implication is that Frankfurter played a role in bringing Thompson on board—and that Glendower Evans had something to do with it. Further support for this conclusion may be derived from the memoirs of Elizabeth Gurley Flynn, a key figure in the radical defense team, who recalled that Frankfurter had recommended Thompson to the committee. Elizabeth Gurley Flynn, *Rebel Girl: An Autobiography, My First Life (1906–1926)* (New York: International Publishers, 1973), 330. I owe this point about Flynn to Moshik Temkin, who noticed the discrepancy between it and Frankfurter's story. Temkin, *Sacco-Vanzetti Affair*, 234–35 n.51.

43. Some scholars of the case have argued that Proctor at no point believed that it was possible to prove from ballistic analysis that any particular bullet had come from any particular gun. They hypothesize that Proctor came forward because he was eager for attention and possibly money, and was jealous of another prosecution ballistics expert whose testimony followed his. The same scholars, though, also argue that the bullet introduced into evidence was not the one taken from the bodyguard's body but was actually a substitute bullet that had been test-fired through Sacco's gun by the police and then used as part of an attempt to frame Sacco at trial. See William Young and David E. Kaiser, *Postmortem: New Evidence in the Case of Sacco and Vanzetti* (Amherst: University of Massachusetts Press, 1985), 106–23.

44. *Felix Frankfurter Reminisces*, 213.

45. With an assistant's help. See Hirsch, *Enigma*, 91 and n.101.

46. Parrish, *Frankfurter*, 179 and n.19.

47. Frankfurter, *Sacco and Vanzetti*, 92–101.

48. Parrish, *Frankfurter*, 187–88.

49. Attributed to John Collins Bossidy. See Robert Andrews, ed., *Famous Lines: A Columbia Dictionary of Familiar Quotations* (New York: Columbia University Press, 1996).

50. *Time*, June 21, 1926. See also the obituary in *Time*, January 18, 1943.

51. Parrish, *Frankfurter*, 71–72.

52. Karabel, *The Chosen*, 86–109; on Frankfurter especially see 95, 100; Penny Feldman, *Recruiting an Elite: Admission to Harvard College* (New York: Garland, 1988), 8, 18; Parrish, *Frankfurter*, 155–56.

53. Compare Temkin, *Sacco-Vanzetti Affair*, 283–84 n.52. Gardiner Jackson, who worked with Frankfurter on the case, was "satisfied that the intensity of Lowell's animosity to Felix was a very large factor in what happened to his mind in the face of the evidence."

54. *Felix Frankfurter Reminisces*, 217; and see Parrish, *Frankfurter*, 187. Note that the source of the story is Frankfurter, who attributed it to Norman Hapgood's contemporaneous report. For Wigmore's perspective, see William R.

Roalfe, *John Henry Wigmore: Scholar and Reformer* (Evanston, IL: Northwestern University Press, 1977), 150–53.

55. Watson, *Sacco and Vanzetti*, 323 (Thompson resignation), 328 (Hill takes over).

56. Id., 339–40; Melvin I. Urofsky, *Louis D. Brandeis: A Life* (New York: Pantheon, 2009), 644. Through Auntie Bee, Rosina Sacco (Sacco's wife) had actually stayed at Brandeis's house in Boston.

57. Josephson, "Profiles: Jurist-II," 46; see also Parrish, *Frankfurter*, 177.

58. See National Civil Liberties Bureau Free Speech Report, 1921. I owe this reference to Laura Weinrib. On Frankfurter's relationship with Roger Baldwin, founder of the ACLU, see Peggy Lamson, *Roger Baldwin, Founder of the American Civil Liberties Union: A Portrait* (Boston: Houghton Mifflin, 1976), 130.

59. On Brandeis see Urofsky, *Louis D. Brandeis*, 21–23 (education in Vienna and Dresden), 31 (average grades of 97/100 "would not be duplicated in his lifetime"). On Brandeis's Harvard Law School record see also Arthur E. Sutherland, *The Law at Harvard: A History of Ideas and Men, 1817–1967* (Cambridge: Harvard University Press, 1967), 198 n.44.

60. See Samuel D. Warren and Louis D. Brandeis, "The Right to Privacy," *Harvard Law Review* 4, no. 5 (1890): 193; Louis D. Brandeis, *Other People's Money and How the Bankers Use It* (New York: Stokes, 1914).

61. *Half Brother, Half Son*, 212 (quoting letter from Louis D. Brandeis to Felix Frankfurter, September 24, 1925).

62. Bruce Allen Murphy, *The Brandeis/Frankfurter Connection: The Secret Political Activities of Two Supreme Court Justices* (New York: Oxford University Press, 1982), 41–42; Hirsch, *Enigma*, 225 n.69, citing Frankfurter to Brandeis, September 29, 1924, Felix Frankfurter Papers, Library of Congress, Folder 493 in Box 29.

63. On Brandeis and Zionism, see Urofsky, *Louis D. Brandeis*, 515–44.

64. See Avi Shlaim, *Collusion Across the Jordan: King Abdullah, the Zionist Movement, and the Partition of Palestine* (New York: Columbia University Press, 1988). Abdullah was Faisal's brother; negotiations between Abdullah and the Zionist movement began when Abdullah became prince of Transjordan.

65. James Bradley Thayer, "The Origin and Scope of the American Doctrine of Constitutional Law," *Harvard Law Review* 7, no. 3 (1893): 129, reprinted in Thayer, *Legal Essays* (Cambridge: Harvard University Press, 1927), 1.

66. It has been argued that Roosevelt may in fact have had Guillain-Barré syndrome, a different auto-immune disorder. Armond Goldman et al., "What Was the Cause of Franklin Delano Roosevelt's Paralytic Illness?" *Journal of Medical Biography* 11 (2003): 232.

67. "F. D. Roosevelt Ill of Poliomyelitis," *New York Times*, September 16, 1921.

68. "The President's Niece Engaged: Miss Corinne Douglas Robinson to Marry George Draper," *New York Times*, March 30, 1907. Robinson later broke off the engagement. Betty Boyd Caroli, *The Roosevelt Women* (New York: Basic Books, 1999), 301–02. For other family ties, see Geoffrey C. Ward, *A First-*

Class Temperament: The Emergence of Franklin D. Roosevelt (New York: Harper and Row, 1989), 602 n.2.

69. On Draper's career and approach, see Sarah W. Tracy, "George Draper and American Constitutional Medicine, 1916-1946: Reinventing the Sick Man," *Bulletin of the History of Medicine* 66, no. 1 (Spring 1992): 53.

70. Ward, *First-Class Temperament*, 605; see also Tony Gould, *A Summer Plague: Polio and Its Survivors* (New Haven: Yale University Press, 1997), 35.

71. Gould, *Summer Plague*, 35, 42–44.

72. Ward suggests that in February 1924, two years after the illness struck, Roosevelt was affected by Draper's "devastating verdict" that he had reached the limits of his recovery. *First-Class Temperament*, 675–86. But Draper delivered that message in a letter to Lovett (id., 675), to whom he was accustomed to reporting the medical facts as he understood them. There is no evidence that he said the same thing directly to Roosevelt. The depression that Missy LeHand reported Roosevelt as feeling in the mornings on a boat trip in February could easily have come from his own efforts at making sense of his condition.

73. *Roosevelt and Frankfurter: Their Correspondence, 1928–1945*, annotated by Max Freedman (Boston: Little, Brown, 1967), 38 (October 9, 1928).

74. Ibid.

75. Id., 39 (November 8, 1928).

76. Id., 44 (January 17, 1930).

77. Id., 112–13 (undated memorandum by Frankfurter of conversation with Roosevelt on March 8, 1933).

78. Matthew Josephson, "Profiles: Jurist-I," *The New Yorker*, November 30, 1940, 28 (stubborn pig), 26 (General Hugh Johnson, a former Roosevelt aide and director of the National Recovery Administration turned critic, called Frankfurter the most influential individual).

79. Robert H. Jackson, *That Man: An Insider's Portrait of Franklin D. Roosevelt* (New York: Oxford University Press, 2003), 3.

80. Ibid.

81. Reminiscences of Robert H. Jackson (1952), in the Columbia University Oral History Research Office Collection, 58–59.

82. John Q. Barrett, "Albany in the Life Trajectory of Robert H. Jackson," *Albany Law Review* 68 (2004–2005): 513, 517.

83. Barrett, "Albany in the Life Trajectory of Robert H. Jackson," 520-25, explains that this was the last year Albany Law School allowed students who had studied in a law office to receive their certificate of graduation after one year of study rather than two. Barrett also corrects the misimpression that Jackson combined two years of coursework in a single year, id. at 523.

84. *West's Encyclopedia of American Law*, 2d ed. (2008), q.v. "patronage."

85. Jackson, *That Man*, 5. Roosevelt's choice to maintain his connections to upstate Democrats reflected the fact that he was still keen on New York politics, harboring hopes of a U.S. Senate seat in 1914. By then the Constitution had been amended so that senators would be directly elected. Roosevelt, trying to take on Tammany Hall, ran in the Democratic primary—and lost badly.

86. Ibid.

87. He was also frustrated with his marginalization on the state committee. See William Domnarski, *The Great Justices, 1941–54: Black, Douglas, Frankfurter, and Jackson in Chambers* (Ann Arbor: University of Michigan Press, 2006), 48–50.

88. Harold Jackson Adams, "A Tribute to Robert Jackson by His Nephew," *Albany Law Review* 68 (2004–2005): 1. For the ice-skating, see Barrett, "Albany in the Life Trajectory of Robert H. Jackson," 526.

89. Jackson, Reminiscences, 76.

90. Id., 80.

91. Id., 76–77, 128.

92. Id., 77–79.

93. Id., 80–81.

94. Id., 163. For the conversion, see Samuel H. Williamson, "Six Ways to Compute the Relative Value of a U.S. Dollar Amount, 1790 to Present," *MeasuringWorth*, 2009, http://www.measuringworth.com/uscompare/.

95. Jackson, Reminiscences, 249. I am grateful to John Q. Barrett, author of a forthcoming Jackson biography, for pointing me to the right lake as well as for many other helpful Jackson references.

96. Id., 236–37.

97. Id., 237.

98. Ibid.

99. Id., 237–39.

100. Jackson, *That Man*, 6.

101. Id., 8.

102. Jackson, Reminiscences, 252–55.

103. Roger K. Newman, *Hugo Black: A Biography* (New York: Fordham University Press, 1997), 158.

104. Id., 159–60.

105. John P. Frank, *Mr. Justice Black: The Man and His Opinions* (New York: Knopf, 1949; reprinted by Greenwood Press, 1973), 4–5.

106. Gerald T. Dunne, *Hugo Black and the Judicial Revolution* (New York: Simon and Schuster, 1977), photograph following page 288.

107. Newman, *Hugo Black*, 16.

108. For an exhaustive list see id., 99.

109. "Hugo L. Black, Who Will Today Occupy Bench in the Recorder's Court," *Birmingham Age-Herald*, April 12, 1911, 1.

110. Charles. H. Mandy, "Evidence of Hospitality," *Birmingham Age-Herald*, November 22, 1911, 5.

111. Interview with Virginia Foster Durr, March 13, 14, 15, 1975, Interview G-0023-1, Southern Oral History Program Collection (#4007), available at http://docsouth.unc.edu/sohp/G-0023-1/G-0023-1.html, 71–72 (hereafter Virginia Foster Durr Oral History Interview I); see also Hugo L. Black Jr., *My Father: A Remembrance* (New York: Random House, 1975), 65 ("blown $500,000 and had no income").

112. Virginia Foster Durr Oral History Interview I, 136.

113. Id., 22.

114. I owe this analysis to the sociolinguist Anne Fitts. Fitts, personal communication on file with the author, comparing Virginia Foster Durr's speech with that of Black. See also Anne Malone Fitts, "Dialect Boundaries in Alabama: Evidence from LAGS," in *From the Gulf States and Beyond: The Legacy of Lee Pederson and LAGS*, ed. Michael B. Montgomery and Thomas E. Nunnally (Tuscaloosa: University of Alabama Press, 1998), 147.

115. In 1925. Newman, *Hugo Black*, 69.

116. David M. Chalmers, *Hooded Americanism: The History of the Ku Klux Klan* (Durham: Duke University Press, 1981), 28–38, 78–84. In 1926, Klansmen David Bibb Graves and Charles C. McCall were respectively elected governor and attorney general (id., 80), while the bitterly anti-Catholic Klan member Thomas Heflin served as Alabama's senator throughout the period (id., 305).

117. For a thorough treatment of this case see Sharon Davies, *Rising Road: A True Tale of Love, Race, and Religion in America* (New York: Oxford University Press, 2010). Gussman's name was an Anglicization of Guzmán. Id., 95.

118. Newman, *Hugo Black*, 73; at trial, Stephenson testified he had said, "You have ruined my home! That man is a Negro." Davies, *Rising Road*, 251.

119. Newman, *Hugo Black*, 83-87; Davies, *Rising Road*, 283.

120. Newman, *Hugo Black*, 104. "Hugo could make the best anti-Catholic speech you ever heard," according to the later recollection of Grand Dragon James Esdale.

121. According to the scholar who has studied the election the most closely, "the final tally showed Black's total number of votes closely paralleled the total Klan membership in the state," suggesting that most of his votes had come from Klansmen. Id., 115.

122. On their first meeting see William O. Douglas, *Go East, Young Man: The Early Years* (New York: Random House, 1974), 124. For a contemporary description of Douglas, see "Walla Walla to Washington," *Time*, January 27, 1936, 50; for the ungovernable cowlick, see Arthur M. Schlesinger Jr., "The Supreme Court 1937," *Fortune*, January 1947, 73.

123. Bruce Allen Murphy, *Wild Bill: The Legend and Life of William O. Douglas* (New York: Random House, 2003), 20–24. This biography has been criticized; as with all other secondary sources, I have tried to verify cited material from primary sources whenever possible.

124. Douglas, *Go East, Young Man*, 97–98.

125. Murphy, *Wild Bill*, 37.

126. Id., 40–42.

127. Douglas, *Go East, Young Man*, 133-34.

128. Jerome Frank is often credited as the source of the quip, but the saying's origins are disputed. Frederick Schauer, *Thinking Like a Lawyer: A New Introduction to Legal Reasoning* (Cambridge: Harvard University Press, 2009), 129.

129. Douglas, *Go East, Young Man*, 149.

130. Id., 177–82; George Draper, *Disease and the Man* (New York: Macmillan, 1930), 155–57; Murphy, *Wild Bill*, 55, 65–66. Murphy deserves the credit for matching up the episode in Draper's book with Douglas's own account in his memoir.

131. Douglas, *Go East, Young Man*, 178 (psychoanalysis), 182 (seminal influence).

132. Indeed, the casebooks were so innovative they could not find a market, since almost no professor taught the subjects that way. See Laura Kalman, *Legal Realism at Yale, 1927–1960* (Chapel Hill: University of North Carolina Press, 1986), 86–87.

133. Douglas, *Go East, Young Man*, 75.

134. Without Frankfurter's help. See *Half Brother, Half Son*, 592 n.1.

135. Donald A. Ritchie, *James M. Landis: Dean of the Regulators* (Cambridge: Harvard University Press, 1980), 198–200. Landis entered a guilty plea in federal court and was sentenced to thirty days' imprisonment and a year of probation. By then he was so sick that he served the sentence in the hospital: first in a Public Health Service prison-hospital facility, then, after the intervention of Attorney General Robert Kennedy, in Columbia Presbyterian Hospital, where two guards sat outside his room until the sentence ended. Landis died in his own swimming pool less than a year later; his biographer concludes from the autopsy report that it was not suicide. Id., 201.

Book Two POWER

1. Virginia Foster Durr Oral History Interview I, 157.

2. Black, *My Father*, 69.

3. Virginia Foster Durr Oral History Interview I, 157, 163.

4. Newman, *Hugo Black*, 155.

5. Virginia Foster Durr Oral History Interview I, 158.

6. Interview with Virginia Foster Durr, March 13, 14, 15, 1975, Interview G-0023-2. Southern Oral History Program Collection (#4007), available at http://docsouth.unc.edu/sohp/G-0023-2/G-0023-2.html, 3 (hereafter Virginia Foster Durr Oral History Interview II).

7. Newman, *Hugo Black*, 155.

8. The main source for this meeting is an oral history interview with Black. See Oral History Project, draft of interview with Hugo Black, LBJ Presidential Library, n.d., Hugo L. Black Papers, Box 518. See also Howard Ball, *Hugo L. Black: Cold Steel Warrior* (New York: Oxford University Press, 1996), 77; Newman, *Hugo Black*, 155.

9. North Carolina State Board of Health, Standard Certificate of Death, Sept. 22, 1932, on file with the author; "Insurance Man, Hunting, Killed," *New York Times*, September 22, 1932, 8. On the company, see "Jefferson-Pilot Corporation," in *International Directory of Company Histories* (Farmington Hills, MI: Thomson Gale, 1995), http://www.encyclopedia.com/doc/1G2-2841500078.html. Jefferson acquired Pilot Insurance in March 1931, see

"Insurance Companies Plan To Consolidate," *New York Times*, March 26, 1931, 47. Gold was working for Pilot at the time of his death. For the letter, see Hugo L. Black to Albert Lee Smith, October 1, 1932, in the Hugo LaFayette Black Papers, Library of Congress, Box 50. Newman mistakenly says the suicide was Smith's brother-in-law, not father-in-law. Thanks to Zach Schauf for unraveling the mystery and finding the death certificate.

10. See T. H. Watkins, *The Hungry Years: A Narrative History of the Depression* (New York: Henry Holt, 1999), 135.

11. Eugene C. Gerhart, *America's Advocate: Robert H. Jackson* (Indianapolis: Bobbs-Merrill, 1958), 128.

12. When Lowenthal's participation met with resistance, Frankfurter let the matter drop. Parrish, *Frankfurter*, 211.

13. Thomas McCraw, *Prophets of Regulation: Charles Francis Adams, Louis D. Brandeis, James M. Landis, Alfred E. Kahn* (Cambridge: Harvard University Press, 1984), 210–11.

14. Indeed, Gen. Hugh Johnson, director of the NRA, who devised the Blue Eagle, sympathized with fascist economic theory and distributed literature expounding its ideas to other cabinet members. For a subtle account of the relationship between fascism, corporatism, and the New Deal, and on Johnson in particular, see James Q. Whitman, "Of Corporatism, Fascism, and the First New Deal," *American Journal of Comparative Law* 39 (1991): 747, 763–69. See also Stanley G. Payne, *A History of Fascism, 1914–1945* (Madison: University of Wisconsin Press, 1995), 230 n.65 (Johnson was the only New Deal figure "who seemed to look on fascist corporatism as a kind of model"); Frances Perkins, *The Roosevelt I Knew* (New York: Viking, 1946), 206.

15. Robert Jackson, "The Bar and the New Deal," *West Virginia Law Quarterly* 41 (1935): 103, 105.

16. See Michael Parrish, *Securities Regulation and the New Deal* (New Haven: Yale University Press, 1970), 32–33.

17. Jackson, "The Bar and the New Deal," 105.

18. *Roosevelt and Frankfurter*, 425. The phrase actually appears in a letter from Frankfurter to Charles Burlingham, which Frankfurter sent to Roosevelt.

19. William Lasser, *Benjamin V. Cohen: Architect of the New Deal* (New Haven: Yale University Press, 2002), 72–79.

20. On Corcoran see David McKean, *Tommy the Cork: Washington's Ultimate Insider from Roosevelt to Reagan* (New York: Steerforth, 2003), 41. See also Michael Janeway, *The Fall of the House of Roosevelt: Brokers of Ideas and Power from FDR to LBJ* (New York: Columbia University Press, 2003), 15, and more generally 13–27 ("Corcoran and the New Dealers' Gospel"). The historian was Cabell Phillips. See also Allan J. Lichtman, "Tommy the Cork: the Secret World of Washington's First Modern Lobbyist—Thomas G. Corcoran," *Washington Monthly*, February 1987.

21. See Ward, *First-Class Temperament*, xiii–xv. It is worth noticing that even in Ward's telling, there is some uncertainty about whether Holmes was speaking about Franklin Roosevelt or Theodore Roosevelt when he gave his judgment.

22. The British had adopted a similar model a few years before, and the drafters referred to it.

23. McKean, *Tommy the Cork*, 39, 41.

24. *Roosevelt and Frankfurter*, 115-36.

25. Id., 157.

26. McKean, *Tommy the Cork*, 55.

27. Acheson believed that the purchases violated clear federal law. See Dean Acheson, *Morning and Noon* (Boston: Houghton and Mifflin, 1965), 187–92.

28. McKean, *Tommy the Cork*, 45–46.

29. The note described Corcoran as a "person of entire dependability" who could speak on Frankfurter's behalf. *Roosevelt and Frankfurter*, 156.

30. Elliott Roosevelt, *An Untold Story: The Roosevelts of Hyde Park* (New York: Putnam, 1973).

31. McKean, *Tommy the Cork*, 47 (piano), 53–54 (house appearance and Roosevelt call).

32. Id., 74.

33. Janeway, *The Fall of the House of Roosevelt*, 16 ("little by little"), 14 ("hatchet-man").

34. Arthur Schlesinger Jr., "Who Was Henry A. Wallace? The Story of a Perplexing and Indomitably Naive Public Servant," *Los Angeles Times*, March 12, 2000 (urinal and bar).

35. McKean, *Tommy the Cork*, 58. In another, possibly related story that Roosevelt later told, Frankfurter once drank with Garner from four until seven o'clock, then went to the White House for cocktails and dinner with the president, where he spoke (unusually for him) "in slow and deliberate tones...and did not show in any way that he had been drinking except by his careful enunciation." Garner, according to Roosevelt's rather doubtful conclusion, "had to be helped home." *The Secret Diary of Harold L. Ickes* vol. ii (New York: Simon and Schuster, 1953), 610 (entry for March 18, 1939).

36. Arthur Krock, *Memoirs: Sixty Years on the Firing Line* (New York: Funk and Wagnalls, 1968), 169–71. See also McKean, *Tommy the Cork*, 62–63.

37. Krock, *Memoirs*, 170.

38. Id., 171.

39. "Hopson Guilty," *Time*, January 13, 1941.

40. Hopson showed early signs of other sorts of corruption as well as the moral sort. He managed to be tried and sentenced under a false name, then to have his sentence waived on appeal, all apparently because of his connections to the powerful Public Service Commission officials and the governor. See "Annoyer Set Free Was Howard Hopson; Albany Public Service Official Who Insulted Women Hid Behind a False Name," *New York Times*, October 27, 1912, Picture Section 9.

41. "Lobbies, Social et al," *New York Times*, August 25, 1935, E1.

42. "Hopson Guilty," *Time*.

43. Newman, *Hugo Black*, 185.

44. Id., 186.

45. For an exposition of the issue, see Rondall Ravon Rice, *The Politics of Air Power: From Confrontation to Cooperation in Army Aviation Civil-Military Relations* (Lincoln: University of Nebraska Press, 2004), 115–23. For Elliott's role, see Elliott Roosevelt and James Brough, *A Rendezvous with Destiny: The Roosevelts of the White House* (New York: Putnam, 1975), 101.

46. Newman, *Hugo Black*, 188.

47. Ibid.

48. Id., 190, citing Lippmann, *New York Herald Tribune*, March 5, 1936.

49. David Cannadine, *Mellon: An American Life* (New York: Knopf, 2006).

50. Cannadine, *Mellon*, 525.

51. Jackson, Reminiscences, 314, quoting *New York Herald Tribune*, May 11, 1934.

52. Id., 318–20.

53. "Taxation: Rich Men Scared," *Time*, March 11, 1935. Hogan, a founding partner of the firm Hogan & Hartson, is not to be confused with New York County district attorney Frank S. Hogan, who served in that post for more than thirty years.

54. Jackson, Reminiscences, 328.

55. Cannadine, *Mellon*, 527-35.

56. Jackson, Reminiscences, 327.

57. "Justice Jackson Dead at 62 of Heart Attack in Capital," *New York Times*, October 10, 1954.

58. Douglas Warrenfels, "Duveen Jokes in Testimony on Mellon Tax: Peer Cheerily Testifies Ex-Secretary Has Finest Collection in World," *Washington Post*, May 10, 1935, 1.

59. Cannadine, *Mellon*, 130–31.

60. Meryle Seacrest, *Duveen: A Life in Art* (New York: Knopf, 2004), 299–302.

61. Seacrest, *Duveen*, 314–17.

62. "Protest Against Soviet Manganese; American Producers Assert That 'Dumping' Here Keeps Their Plants Idle. Anxious For Protection Declare Russian Ore Sells 30% Below the Profit Level in This Country. Steel Industry as Market. Says Soviet Cuts Prices," *New York Times*, February 15, 1931, 41.

63. Seacrest, *Duveen*, 315–16.

64. Jackson, Reminiscences, 330–31.

65. "The function of this trust," Jackson wrote, "is to get the beneficial use of this valuable art collection to the next generation without gift or inheritance tax, and with deduction from income tax, and the use of the forms of a charitable trust is but a mask for that purpose." He continued, "When considered in connection with the way the trust has actually operated this strange set-up is strongly suggestive that the purpose of the trust was...tax avoidance." "Mellon Art Gift Held Tax Evasion," *New York Times*, April 7, 1935, 22.

66. "Mall Site Selected for Gallery of Arts; Gift of Unidentified Donor To Be Constructed on B Street at 12th," *Washington Post*, November 9, 1927, 20;

Seacrest, *Duveen*, 308. David Doheny, *David Finley: Quiet Force for America's Arts* (Washington, DC: National Trust for Historic Preservation, 2006), 112, reports that Mellon mentioned a possible national gallery twice in his diaries for 1928, and that Mellon told his associate and art consultant David Finley about his plans in 1927.

67. Jackson, Reminiscences, 332.

68. Seacrest, *Duveen*, 346. Indeed, Duveen did make further enormous sales to Mellon for the National Gallery—$21 million in one sale, by far the largest sale of Duveen's career. Id., 356.

69. Jackson, Reminiscences, 338; Seacrest, *Duveen*, 345.

70. Seacrest, *Duveen*, 346 (quoting Marquis Childs oral history, National Gallery of Art); Warrenfels, "Duveen Jokes in Testimony on Mellon Tax."

71. Cannadine, *Mellon*, 526–27.

72. Jackson, Reminiscences, 432–33. Just a few weeks earlier, Jackson had heard Roosevelt say he was considering "outright defiance of the court" and that "he just could not accept an adverse decision" on the issue of his confiscation of gold. Id. at 430; and see Jeff Shesol, *Supreme Power: Franklin Roosevelt vs. the Supreme Court* (New York: W. W. Norton, 2010), 96. Jackson explained later that his speech was made "against the background of experience we were having with the courts." Jackson, Reminiscences, 432. Jackson did not know of the court-packing plan in advance, but he did know that the issue of the Court's intransigence was bothering Roosevelt.

73. *Hammer v. Dagenhart*, 247 U.S. 251 (1918) (5–4 decision striking down law excluding products of child labor from interstate commerce).

74. In *Lochner v. New York*, 198 U.S. 45 (1905), the Court struck down a state maximum hours law. In *Morehead v. New York ex rel. Tipaldo*, 298 U.S. 587 (1936), the Court struck down a state minimum wage law, relying on *Adkins v. Children's Hospital*, 261 U.S. 525 (1923), which invalidated a similar federal law that applied to the District of Columbia.

75. David E. Bernstein, "The Story of *Lochner v. New York*," in *Constitutional Law Stories*, ed. Michael Dorf (New York: Foundation Press, 2009), 309.

76. Felix Frankfurter, "Hours of Labor and Realism in Constitutional Law," *Harvard Law Review* 29, no. 4 (1916): 371.

77. For example, in *Muller v. Oregon*, 208 U.S. 412 (1908), the Court accepted the argument of then attorney Louis Brandeis that a law setting maximum working hours for women on the basis of the "inherent difference between the two sexes" was constitutional. And in *Bunting v. Oregon*, 243 U.S. 427 (1917), the Court upheld a maximum hours law for women and men.

78. Most famously in *Adkins v. Children's Hospital*, 261 U.S. 525 (1923), which struck down a D.C. minimum wage law for women as violating the liberty of contract.

79. Felix Frankfurter, "Mr. Justice Holmes and the Constitution: A Review of His Twenty-Five Years on the Supreme Court," *Harvard Law Review* 41, no. 2 (1927): 144.

80. Id., 145.

81. Id., 142.

82. *A. L. A. Schechter Poultry et al. v. United States*, 295 U.S. 495 (1935).

83. Id. at 553 (Cardozo, J., concurring).

84. *United States v. Butler et al.*, 297 U.S. 1 (1936).

85. Samuel Hendel, *Charles Evans Hughes and the Supreme Court* (New York: King's Crown Press of Columbia University Press, 1951), 204. For the text of McReynolds's dissent, which does not mention Nero, see *Norman v. Baltimore & O.R. Co.*, 294 U.S. 240, 316 (1935) (McReynolds, J., dissenting). Dean Acheson wrote that when McReynolds announced the dissent from the bench, he departed from his prepared text, became incensed, "almost beside himself with feeling," and said that "the Constitution, as we have known it, is gone." Acheson, *Morning and Noon*, 73–74. See also Shesol, *Supreme Power,* 103.

86. Morton Keller and Phyllis Keller, *Making Harvard Modern: The Rise of America's University* (Oxford: Oxford University Press, 2001), 7 (quoting letters of complaint and Lowell's letter to FDR).

87. "Whose Child Are You?" unsigned editorial, *Harvard Crimson*, September 26, 1936.

88. Arthur M. Schlesinger Jr., *A Life in the Twentieth Century: Innocent Beginnings, 1917–1950* (New York: Houghton Mifflin, 2002), 122.

89. The Judiciary Act of 1801 would have shrunk the Court to five at the next vacancy, but it did not remain in effect long enough for a vacancy to occur.

90. "Reed Assails Court Plan: Former Missouri Senator Warns of Roosevelt Dictatorship," *New York Times*, February 6, 1937, 11.

91. W.J.C., "Dictatorship Seen in the Offing," *New York Times*, February 9, 1937, 21.

92. Barry Cushman, *Rethinking the New Deal Court: The Structure of a Constitutional Revolution* (Oxford: Oxford University Press, 1998), 16.

93. Though Justice Cardozo opposed the court-packing plan, he also opposed the letter, believing the Court "ought to remain aloof from the political struggle." See Andrew Kaufman, *Cardozo* (Cambridge: Harvard University Press, 1998), 525.

94. *Roosevelt and Frankfurter,* 377.

95. *Roosevelt and Frankfurter,* 378.

96. See Samuel I. Rosenman, *Working with Roosevelt* (New York: Harper and Brothers, 1952), 149–50.

97. *Roosevelt and Frankfurter,* 381.

98. Id., 372.

99. Murphy, *The Brandeis/Frankfurter Connection*, 180.

100. Jackson, Reminiscences, 436–37.

101. Jackson downplayed the fact that several of the key programs, including the NIRA, had been struck down by large margins.

102. Except for Brandeis, who puritanically refused to occupy his oak-paneled office and came to the Court only for conferences and to sit on the bench.

103. Cushman, *Rethinking the New Deal Court*, 99.

104. *West Coast Hotel v. Parrish*, 300 U.S. 379 (1937).

105. *Nebbia v. New York*, 291 U.S. 502 (1934).

106. *Morehead v. New York ex rel. Tipaldo*, 298 U.S. 587 (1936).

107. See especially Cushman, *Rethinking the New Deal Court*, 84–105.

108. Id., 45, 96–97. See also Felix Frankfurter, "Mr. Justice Roberts," *University of Pennsylvania Law Review* 104 (1955): 311, 314–16.

109. See Cushman, *Rethinking the New Deal Court*, 92–105. On Frankfurter's efforts and the historical accuracy of Roberts's memo, see Michael Ariens, "A Thrice-Told Tale, or Felix the Cat," *Harvard Law Review* 107, no. 3 (January 1994): 620–76; Richard D. Friedman, "A Reaffirmation: The Authenticity of the Roberts Memorandum, or Felix the Non-Forger," *University of Pennsylvania Law Review* 142, no. 6 (June 1994):1985–1995.

110. *Roosevelt and Frankfurter*, 392.

111. *Half Brother, Half Son*, 594 n.1; see also Ariens, "A Thrice-Told Tale," 630.

112. *NLRB v. Jones & Laughlin Steel Corp.*, 301 U.S. 1 (1937).

113. *Roosevelt and Frankfurter*, 397; Jackson, Reminiscences, 450.

114. Jackson, *That Man,* 53–54; Jackson, Reminiscences, 442. Cf. Cushman, *Rethinking the New Deal Court*, 22 ("The replacement of one conservative with another would result in no net gain for Roosevelt's constitutional agenda").

115. Indeed, Roosevelt's delay in appointing Robinson—which the senator sorely resented—suggests he was considering just that. Cf. Cushman, *Rethinking the New Deal Court*, 22.

116. Shesol, *Supreme Power,* 489.

117. Robert H. Jackson, *The Struggle for Judicial Supremacy: A Study of a Crisis in American Power Politics* (New York: Knopf, 1941).

118. Id., 10. According to Jackson, the framers of the Constitution understood "that they were creating not only a political government but an instrument of economic control as well." Id., 7.

119. Jackson, *That Man*, 3.

120. G. Edward White, *The American Judicial Tradition: Profiles of Leading American Judges* (New York: Oxford University Press, 1988), 185, calls Jackson a flashy dresser; but that formulation is not quite right. I owe to John Q. Barrett the fact of Jackson's sartorial honor. For purposes of comparison, another political recipient of the dubious "best-dressed" honor was the perfectly groomed Secretary of State Dean Acheson—a man whose elite credentials (Groton, Yale, Harvard Law School, clerkship for Justice Brandeis) needed no reinforcement whatever. "Ultra-meticulous" is the judgment of the *New York Times* in Jackson's obituary. See "Justice Jackson Dead at 62 of Heart Attack in Capital," *New York Times*, October 10, 1954.

121. Jackson, Reminiscences, 487.

122. Id., 614.

123. Jackson, *That Man*, 31–32.

124. Id., 34-38.

125. Id., 38.

126. *The Secret Diary of Harold L. Ickes* vol. ii, 593 (entry for March 14, 1939).

127. *The Secret Diary of Harold L. Ickes* vol. iii, 378–79 (entry for December 1, 1940).

128. "Justice Jackson Dead at 62."

129. William H. Chafe, *The Achievement of American Liberalism: The New Deal and its Legacies* (New York: Columbia University Press, 2003), 75. For Jackson's threat to resign if not appointed attorney general, see *The Secret Diary of Harold L. Ickes* vol. ii, 628 (Entry for May 6, 1939) ("Bob Jackson is getting restive....Murphy has done a fine job as Attorney General, but Bob Jackson is a far abler lawyer and this place has definitely been promised to him. Bob is threatening to resign.").

130. In order, they were Hugo Black, Stanley Reed, Felix Frankfurter, William O. Douglas, Frank Murphy, Jimmy Byrnes, Harlan Fiske Stone (made chief), Robert Jackson, and Wiley Rutledge. Only two justices, Owen Roberts and Stone, came on the Court before Roosevelt and outlasted him, and of course Roosevelt appointed Stone as chief.

Book Three JUDGES

1. On Black as "radical," see Newman, *Hugo Black*, 226 (Joseph Alsop and Truner Catledge called Black "probably the most radical man in the Senate"). The other Southerners were Lucius Lamar, Joseph Lamar, Howell Jackson, and Edward White. Horace Lurton and Brandeis were from Kentucky.

2. Not counting Stanley Reed and Fred Vinson, both of Kentucky; Tom Clark of Texas; and Thurgood Marshall, born in Maryland.

3. Newman, *Hugo Black*, 234, citing Joseph P. Lash, *Dealers and Dreamers: A New Look at the New Deal* (New York: Doubleday, 1988), 311.

4. Newman, *Hugo Black*, 235.

5. Id., 169, 171–72.

6. Id., 174.

7. Id., 241.

8. Id., 242.

9. Id., 243.

10. Id., 121.

11. A note from his cousin (and possibly lover) Margaret Suckley, on September 29, before Black's speech, may have captured FDR's attitude: "I may be all wrong—but I've felt from the beginning of all this Klan talk...that perhaps he did belong to the Klan—but that did not necessarily mean that he might not make a very great Judge on the Supreme Court—*On verra*! [We'll see!]" Geoffrey C. Ward, ed., *Closest Companion: The Unknown Story of the Intimate Friendship Between Franklin Roosevelt and Margaret Suckley* (Boston: Houghton Mifflin, 1995), 101.

12. Newman, *Hugo Black*, 259.

13. Id., 271–72.

14. *Abington School Dist. v. Schempp*, 374 U.S. 203 (1963) (Bible-reading); *Engel v. Vitale*, 370 U.S. 421 (1962) (school prayer).

15. Philip Hamburger, *Separation of Church and State* (Cambridge: Harvard University Press, 2002), 429–34, and Noah Feldman, *Divided by God: America's Church–State Problem—And What We Should Do About It* (New York: Farrar, Straus and Giroux, 2005), 173–77.

16. *NAACP v. Alabama*, 357 U.S. 449 (1958).

17. The two most important instances are Chief Justice Roger Taney in the infamous *Dred Scott* case and Chief Justice Morrison Waite in *Reynolds v. United States*, a case about whether Latter Day Saints church members had the right to plural marriage. See *Dred Scott v. Sandford*, 60 U.S. (19 How.) 393, 404–27, 432–42 (1857); *Reynolds v. United States*, 98 U.S. 145, 162–66 (1878). Neither case uses originalism in a text-centered way.

18. For this insight and for much else I am indebted to my teacher Sanford Levinson. See Sanford Levinson, *Constitutional Faith* (Princeton: Princeton University Press, 1988), 31–33. Levinson's own title was borrowed from Hugo Black, *A Constitutional Faith* (New York: Knopf, 1968).

19. *Connecticut General Life Ins. Co. v. Johnson*, 303 U.S. 77, 85 (1938) (Black, J., dissenting).

20. Black also offered history to support his claim. He explained that the purpose of the Fourteenth Amendment was to repudiate racially discriminatory state laws enacted in the Southern states. At the time of its ratification in 1868, no one publicly mentioned that it might cover corporations. It was not until 1882 that the Supreme Court was presented with the argument that a secret committee discussion in the Congress that drafted the amendment had considered the inclusion of corporations in the word *person*. Black asserted that such secret deliberations, unavailable to the public that ratified the amendments, ought not to be given any authority.

21. He had found the claim first in the writings of the radical constitutional historians Charles and Mary Beard. Newman, *Hugo Black*, 157–58.

22. *Connecticut General Life Ins. Co. v. Johnson*, 303 U.S. 77, 83 (Black, J., dissenting).

23. It is unlikely but not completely impossible that Black knew of these references, which appear in James Bradley Thayer's essay on judicial review that Frankfurter was fond of citing. Frankfurter did send Black some of his articles in August 1937 (see Newman, *Hugo Black*, 274); Black could have run down a footnote from those. But Black did not cite Thayer or any other source on the "beyond a reasonable doubt" standard.

24. Newman, *Hugo Black*, 278–79; 274 and 673 n.10, citing FF to LDB, May 20, 1938.

25. *Roosevelt and Frankfurter*, 408.

26. Newman, *Hugo Black*, 267. The student, Bernard Monaghan, was unimpressed that Black had chosen a Catholic secretary and an African-American messenger who was himself a Catholic.

27. Id., 275, 278–79.

28. *Roosevelt and Frankfurter*, 457.

29. Ibid.

30. Alpheus Thomas Mason, *Harlan Fiske Stone: Pillar of the Law* (Hamden, CT: Archon Books, 1968), 472.

31. Ibid.

32. Marquis William Childs, "The Supreme Court To-day," *Harper's Magazine*, May 1938, 586.

33. Id., 474.

34. *Roosevelt and Frankfurter*, 446.

35. Frankfurter's letters to Estelle, signed "Filly," are collected at the Harvard Law School. See "Frankfurter, Felix. Letters to His Sister Estelle, 1933–1964: Finding Aid," available at http://oasis.lib.harvard.edu/oasis/deliver/~law00106.

36. See G. E. R. Gedye, "Nazis List 1742 Jailed in Austria," *New York Times*, March 23, 1938, 8 (giving his professional title, Hofrat ["court-counsellor"] Frankfurter, and explaining he was arrested because he was "president of the Jewish Lodges, an organization resembling the Freemasons"). The phrase "unguarded remarks" comes from Nancy Astor's recounting of what she was told by the German ambassador in London, *Roosevelt and Frankfurter*, 473. The explanation sounds as though it might be apologia. The content of the remarks comes from Max Freedman's annotation, id., 472, presumably based on personal communication from Frankfurter.

37. Rabbi Mayer Kopfstein to Frankfurter, March 23, 1938, Felix Frankfurter Papers, Harvard Law School, Folder 6 in Box 1.

38. On the Cliveden Set, see Norman Rose, *The Cliveden Set: Portrait of An Exclusive Fraternity* (London: Pimlico, 2001).

39. *Roosevelt and Frankfurter*, 473; Rose, *The Cliveden Set*, 183–84.

40. "Frankfurter's Kin Freed: Vienna Nazis Release Uncle of Harvard Professor, U.S. Hears," *New York Times*, March 26, 1938, 21 (identifying Hofrat Frankfurter as Frankfurter's uncle and stating he had been released "from a hospital in Vienna where he had been taken after Nazi authorities arrested him").

41. *Roosevelt and Frankfurter*, 472. The letter seems also to have been forwarded to Brandeis. See *Half Brother, Half Son*, 612–13. Brandeis complimented him for writing "frankly."

42. *The Secret Diary of Harold L. Ickes* vol. iii, 149 (entry for March 10, 1940) ("Felix Frankfurter, I think, wants us to go further than any of the rest of us do. I believe that he actually would be willing to go to war.").

43. Id., 129 (entry for February 11, 1940).

44. *Roosevelt and Frankfurter*, 461.

45. Ibid.

46. Id., 463.

47. *Felix Frankfurter Reminisces*, 281.

48. Parrish, *Frankfurter*, 275, quoting a letter to Farley.

49. Id., 274.

50. *Felix Frankfurter Reminisces*, 146; for Frankfurter's account of the trip, see 145–53.

51. *Roosevelt and Frankfurter*, 481–82; *The Secret Diary of Harold L. Ickes* vol. ii, 470-71 (entry for September 18, 1938); Parrish, *Frankfurter*, 276.

52. *The Secret Diary of Harold L. Ickes* vol. ii, 424 (entry for July 16, 1938); Parrish, *Frankfurter*, 274.

53. Gerhart, *America's Advocate*, 165.

54. Id., 165–66.

55. "Transcriptions of Conversations Between Justice William O. Douglas and Professor Walter F. Murphy, 1961–1963," Special Collections, Seeley G. Mudd Library, Princeton University, Cassette no. 6, January 18, 1962, available online at the Mudd Library website, http://www.princeton.edu/~mudd/finding_aids/douglas/ (hereafter Douglas Oral History Interview with Walter Murphy).

56. For the account, in Frankfurter's words, see *Felix Frankfurter Reminisces*, 282–84, 288.

57. Ibid.

58. Id., 284.

59. Matthew Josephson, "Profiles: Jurist-II," *New Yorker*, December 7, 1940, 36. For the transcript, see Nomination of Felix Frankfurter: Hearings Before a Subcomm. of the S. Comm. on the Judiciary, 76th Cong. 126 (1939) (hereafter Frankfurter Hearings).

60. Frankfurter Hearings, 124–25. On the challenge to Frankfurter's citizenship, see *Felix Frankfurter Reminisces*, 286; Acheson, *Morning and Noon*, 201–02, says that Learned Hand found the relevant records.

61. *Felix Frankfurter Reminisces*, 285.

62. Frankfurter Hearings, 126.

63. Acheson, *Morning and Noon*, 208.

64. Id., 211–12.

65. The photograph is reproduced in this book.

66. Ritchie, *James M. Landis*, 77; Murphy, *Wild Bill*, 117.

67. Murphy, *Wild Bill*, 127.

68. Id., 132–33.

69. Id., 141, quoting "SEC Study to Seek Reasons for Rise and Fall of Market," *New York Herald Tribune*, November 4, 1937.

70. Ron Chernow, *The House of Morgan: An American Banking Dynasty and the Rise of Modern Finance* (New York: Simon and Schuster, 1991), 421.

71. "Sorely Mistaken," *Time*, May 9, 1938. For a further exposition of Whitney's fall, see Murphy, *Wild Bill*, 144–54.

72. "Sorely Mistaken."

73. Douglas, *Go East, Young Man*, 289.

74. Id., 289–90.

75. Chernow, *House of Morgan*, 428–29.

76. Douglas, *Go East, Young Man*, 290.

77. Krock, *Memoirs*, 177.

78. Murphy, *Wild Bill*, 171–72.

79. *Roosevelt and Frankfurter*, 490.

80. *The Secret Diary of Harold L. Ickes* vol. iii, 601 (entry for March 22, 1939). The poker game was March 21; Douglas had been nominated March 20. Ickes suggested that Douglas be invited, as he was "lots of fun with his inimitable wit."

81. Rosenman, *Working with Roosevelt*, 150.

82. Douglas, *Go East, Young Man*, 330–31 (setup of games and stakes); Smith, *FDR*, 338 (Garner's quip). See also Byron Liggett, "William O. Douglas, Supreme Court Justice and Poker Player," *Poker Player*, June 27, 2005.

83. *The Secret Diary of Harold L. Ickes* vol. ii, 601 (entry for March 22, 1939); *The Secret Diary of Harold L. Ickes* vol. iii, 53 (entry for November 3, 1939) (mentioning the same hand); Douglas, *Go East Young Man*, 330-31.

Book Four ALLIES

1. Gerhart, *America's Advocate*, 155.

2. Lillian Gobitis, "The Courage to Put God First," *Awake!* July 22, 1993, 13. The family name was spelled Gobitas at the time, but court papers rendered it Gobitis, and the spelling stuck. For a good overview, see Shawn Francis Peters, *Judging Jehovah's Witnesses: Religious Persecution and the Dawn of the Rights Revolution* (Lawrence: University Press of Kansas, 2000), 33–40.

3. David R. Manwaring, *Render Unto Caesar: The Flag Salute Controversy* (Chicago: University of Chicago Press, 1962), 30–31.

4. Id., 81–82.

5. Gobitis, "The Courage to Put God First," 13–14.

6. Id., 13 (mob violence threat);

7. On the wartime context, see Richard Danzig, "How Questions Begot Answers in Felix Frankfurter's First Flag Salute Opinion," *Supreme Court Review* 1977: 257–74; Richard Danzig, "Justice Frankfurter's Opinions in the Flag Salute Cases: Blending Logic and Psychologic in Constitutional Decision-making," *Stanford Law Review* 36 (1984): 675; see also Peters, *Judging Jehovah's Witnesses*, 53–54.

8. *The Secret Diary of Harold L. Ickes* vol. iii, 199 (entry for June 5, 1940).

9. *Minersville School Dist. v. Gobitis*, 310 U.S. 586 (1940).

10. Murphy, *Wild Bill*, 188, citing Joseph L. Rauh Jr., "An Unabashed Liberal Looks at a Half Century of the Supreme Court," *North Carolina Law Review* 69 (1990): 221.

11. On Murphy's sexual orientation, see Joyce Murdoch and Deb Price, *Courting Justice: Gay Men and Lesbians v. the Supreme Court* (New York: Basic Books, 2001), 18–21.

12. Sidney Fine, *Frank Murphy: The Washington Years* (Ann Arbor: University of Michigan Press, 1984), 79–98 (giving history of the civil liberties unit, or CLU).

13. *The Secret Diary of Harold L. Ickes* vol. ii, 628 (entry for May 6, 1939).

14. Gerhart, *America's Advocate*, 167.

15. Jackson, Reminiscences, 787.

16. Fine, *Frank Murphy,* 224-25 (plan of return to Philippines), 477 (plan to become ambassador to India).

17. This is the famous Carolene Products Footnote 4, in which Stone had raised the possibility that it might be appropriate for the Court to engage in especially searching judicial inquiry where prejudice against "discrete and insular minorities" might have interfered with the operation of the political process. *United States v. Carolene Products Co.,* 304 U.S. 144, 152 fn.4 (1938).

18. Mason, *Harlan Fiske Stone,* 533.

19. "Maine Mob Burns Jehovah Sect Home: Action Follows Shooting of Two Kennebunk Men by Group Barricaded in House," *New York Times,* June 10, 1940, 19. The Witnesses who had fired from inside the building were arrested and charged with assault.

20. Mason, *Harlan Fiske Stone,* 32.

21. See David N. Atkinson, *Leaving the Bench: Supreme Court Justices at the End* (Lawrence: University Press of Kansas, 1999).

22. Lash, *Dealers and Dreamers,* 404; Charles Michelson, *The Ghost Talks* (New York: G. P. Putnam's Sons, 1944), 175–76.

23. On Powell's alcoholism and his snobbery about his wife's family, see the unedited transcript of "Conversations with Mr. Justice Frankfurter," Interviews conducted between 1953 and 1955 by Harlan B. Phillips, Oral History Research Office, Butler Library, Columbia University, New York, 1956; and compare to the parallel edited passages in *Felix Frankfurter Reminisces,* 292–99.

24. Douglas, *Go East, Young Man,* 147–48. See also Melvin Urofsky, ed., *The Douglas Letters: Selections from the Private Papers of Justice William O. Douglas* (Bethesda, MD: Adler and Adler, 1987), 372–86.

25. *The Secret Diary of Harold L. Ickes* vol. iii, 241 (entry for July 19, 1940). Harry Hopkins, the president's closest adviser, told Ickes he believed "the leading possibilities" were Hull, Wallace, and Douglas; Ickes believed Hopkins favored Wallace. Roosevelt later told Ickes that he had offered the vice presidency to Hull, who turned it down, and that "they told me Bill Douglas would not do because he was not well enough known." *The Secret Diary of Harold L. Ickes,* vol. iii, 286 (entry for August 4, 1940). James Farley, Roosevelt's former close ally who wanted the presidency for himself, wrote in his memoir that he told Roosevelt "all the talk about Douglas was asinine and he readily agreed." James A. Farley, *Jim Farley's Story: The Roosevelt Years* (New York: Whittlesey House, 1948), 253. Murphy, *Wild Bill,* 189, says that "FDR announced to his staff that his choice was coming down to either Wallace or Douglas." I have not been able to substantiate this statement.

26. John Culver and John Hyde, *American Dreamer: The Life and Times of Henry A. Wallace* (New York: W. W. Norton, 2000), 137.

27. Culver and Hyde, *American Dreamer,* 131–32; on Roerich's collaboration with Diaghilev, see Karl E. Meyer and Shareen Blair Brysac, *Tournament of Shadows: The Race for Empire in Central Asia and the Great Game* (Washington, DC: Counterpoint, 1999), 452–53. The vestige of the museum's collections may be seen at the Roerich Museum at 319 W. 107th Street, New York. See also http://www.roerich.org.

28. Nicholas Roerich, *Shambhala* (New York: Stokes, 1930). The work may have been one of the sources for James Hilton's Shangri-La in his *Lost Horizon* of 1933. See Meyer and Brysac, *Tournament of Shadows*, 454.

29. Culver and Hyde, *American Dreamer*, 134. On Roerich more generally, see Ruth A. Drayer, *Nicholas and Helena Roerich: The Spiritual Journey of Two Great Artists and Peacemakers* (Wheaton, IL: Quest, 2007); Meyer and Brysac, *Tournament of Shadows*, 450–91.

30. On Roerich's journey, see Culver and Hyde, *American Dreamer*, 136–41.

31. Culver and Hyde, *American Dreamer*, 232; Meyer and Brysac, *Tournament of Shadows*, 490.

32. Culver and Hyde, *American Dreamer*, 234; Smith, *FDR*, 473–74. For the Democrats' tapes of Willkie, as well as a self-serving account of the broader affair, see Douglas Oral History Interview with Walter Murphy, Cassette no. 9, May 23, 1962. See also Murphy, *Wild Bill*, 190.

33. Murphy, *Wild Bill*, 190 and 592 n. (relying on an interview with Eliot Janeway).

34. Douglas Oral History Interview with Walter Murphy, Cassette no. 14, April 5, 1963, 295–97; Murphy, *Wild Bill*, 89.

35. Jackson, *That Man*, 76.

36. He was extraordinarily good at it: In the previous term, Jackson had won twenty-two of the twenty-four cases that he argued for the Court. Gerhart, *America's Advocate*, 175. The Office of Legal Counsel had been founded in 1934 as part of the office of the Solicitor General. But as Jackson's advisory role, which continued once he had become attorney general suggests, the role was naturally that of the attorney general.

37. *The Secret Diary of Harold L. Ickes* vol. ii, 628 (entry for May 6, 1939) ("Bob is threatening to resign").

38. *The Secret Diary of Harold L. Ickes* vol. iii, 53 (entry for November 3, 1939). The poker game had been at Ickes's house the previous Saturday, October 27, 1939. See also Gerhart, *America's Advocate*, 184.

39. Randolph S. Churchill and Martin Gilbert, *Winston S. Churchill* (Boston: Houghton Mifflin, 1988), 6:345–46.

40. Lasser, *Benjamin V. Cohen*, 225; Jackson, *That Man*, 95.

41. Acheson, *Morning and Noon*, 221–23; Lasser, *Benjamin V. Cohen*, 226–27.

42. Acheson, *Morning and Noon*, 223.

43. Jackson, *That Man*, 97.

44. Gerhart, *America's Advocate*, 217.

45. Jackson, *That Man*, 99.

46. Id., 102.

47. Gerhart, *America's Advocate*, 226, quoting March 27, 1941, speech. A version of this speech appears in *American Bar Association Journal* 27 (May 1941): 275–79.

48. Ibid.

49. *The Secret Diary of Harold L. Ickes* vol. iii, 417 (entry for January 26, 1941).

50. Id., 542 (entry for June 15, 1941).

51. Douglas Oral History Interview with Walter Murphy, Cassette no. 3, December 20 and 27, 1961.

52. Mason, *Harlan Fiske Stone*, 279 (giving the story and rejecting it as inaccurate).

53. Douglas Oral History Interview with Walter Murphy, Cassette no. 2, December 20, 1961, beginning.

54. Gerhart, *America's Advocate*, 165.

55. *The Secret Diary of Harold L. Ickes* vol. iii, 534 (entry for June 8, 1941) (Frankfurter "is hoping that Bob Jackson will be appointed to fill the vacancy").

56. Douglas thought so. "There is no question in my mind that [Frankfurter] was responsible," he wrote to Black. See *The Douglas Letters*, 107 (Douglas to Black, June 22, 1941).

57. Robert Harrison, "The Breakup of the Roosevelt Supreme Court: The Contribution of History and Biography," *Law and History Review* 2 (1984): 165, citing the diary of Homer Cummings, Roosevelt's former attorney general, for July 11, 1941. Manuscript in the Alderman Library, University of Virginia.

58. Brandeis, who believed tired people made poor judgments, insisted on going home by 4:30 on Saturdays. Douglas Oral History Interview with Walter Murphy, Cassette no. 1, December 20, 1961, end.

59. Id., Cassette no. 2, December 20, 1961, beginning.

60. Ibid.

Book Five   LOYALTIES

1. *Roosevelt and Frankfurter*, 618.

2. Ibid.

3. Frankfurter still had one living mentor from his early career, Henry Stimson. And with Frankfurter's help, Stimson had reentered national life as Roosevelt's secretary of war. But Frankfurter had never mythologized Stimson as he did Holmes and Brandeis and even to an extent Cardozo.

4. *Roosevelt and Frankfurter*, 623.

5. Jackson, *That Man*, 104.

6. MacArthur received a message at 3:30 a.m. Manila time on December 8, 1941, informing him of the Pearl Harbor attack. William H. Bartsch, *December 8, 1941: MacArthur's Pearl Harbor* (College Station: Texas A&M University Press, 2003), 260. Clark Field, the U.S. air base forty-five miles from Manila, was bombed at 12:35 p.m. that day. Id., 262, 311–40. Iba Field at Luzon was bombed five minutes later. Id., 341–57.

7. Frankfurter's insights were up-to-date, including comparisons with the difficulties faced by Britain and France in war preparedness; but they drew on his experiences coordinating labor-defense relationships during World War I. *Roosevelt and Frankfurter*, 628–32.

8. Id., 644.

9. Id., 107.

10. Murphy, *Wild Bill*, 197.

11. Michael Dobbs, *Saboteurs: The Nazi Raid on America* (New York: Knopf, 2004), 15–34 (training and mission).

12. *Ex Parte Quirin*, 317 U.S. 1, 22 (1942).

13. Dobbs, *Saboteurs*, 82.

14. Id., 129.

15. Id., 93.

16. Id., 94–95, 105.

17. Id., 119–22.

18. Id., 125–26.

19. Id., 127–28.

20. Christopher Lydon, "J. Edgar Hoover Made the F.B.I. Formidable With Politics, Publicity and Results," *New York Times*, May 3, 1972.

21. Dobbs, *Saboteurs*, 139–41.

22. Id., 145–47.

23. Francis Biddle, *In Brief Authority* (Garden City, NY: Doubleday, 1962), 330; Dobbs, *Saboteurs*, 195–96 (memo), 204 (unaware of Dasch's role).

24. Dobbs, *Saboteurs*, 223–24.

25. Biddle, *In Brief Authority*, 331; Dobbs, *Saboteurs*, 196.

26. Biddle, *In Brief Authority*, 336.

27. Id., 328.

28. Biddle, who was married to a poet, could also be literary. He once wrote of Roosevelt, "He was not a knight in shining armor. He wore his own rather complicated armor, and knew how to make it shine before the faces of the people. They did not want to hear the truth. They might suspect the complexities, sometimes devious, that actually were his. But they felt his greatness. Though like ordinary men, he was no ordinary man." Id., 142.

29. Rosenman, *Working with Roosevelt*, 321, 323 (giving time as State of the Union preparation); Dobbs, *Saboteurs*, 199–200.

30. Biddle, *In Brief Authority*, 331.

31. David Danelski, "The Saboteurs' Case," *Journal of Supreme Court History* 1 (1996): 66.

32. Ibid; Dobbs, *Saboteurs*, 239; G. Edward White, "Felix Frankfurter's 'Soliloquy' in *Ex Parte Quirin*: Nazi Sabotage and Constitutional Conundrums," *Green Bag* 5 (2002): 423.

33. Danelski, "The Saboteurs' Case," 66; Dobbs, *Saboteurs*, 239.

34. Dobbs, *Saboteurs*, 235.

35. Id., 236.

36. 71 U.S. 2 (1866).

37. Biddle, *In Brief Authority*, 328.

38. Dobbs, *Saboteurs*, 273.

39. Jack Goldsmith, "Justice Jackson's Unpublished Opinion in *Ex Parte Quirin*," *Green Bag* 9 (2006): 225.

40. David J. Barron and Martin S. Lederman, "The Commander in Chief at the Lowest Ebb—Framing the Problem, Doctrine, and Original Understanding," *Harvard Law Review* 121, no. 3 (2008): 772–799. A similar position had been taken by the great justice Joseph Story in an early nineteenth-century

case, though he had not commanded a majority of the Court for his view. See *Brown v. United States*, 12 U.S. 110, 129, 153-54 (1814) (Brown, J., dissenting).

41. White, "Felix Frankfurter's 'Soliloquy,'" 432; see also Michael Belknap, "Frankfurter and the Nazi Saboteurs," *Supreme Court Historical Society, 1982 Yearbook*, 67; Jack Goldsmith, "Justice Jackson's Unpublished Opinion in *Ex Parte Quirin*," *Green Bag* 9 (2006): 223.

42. White, "Felix Frankfurter's 'Soliloquy,'" 434.

43. Ibid. Here was an express statement of one component of the doctrine of judicial restraint. Constitutional questions, according to Frankfurter, should be avoided because the Court would inevitably impinge on the other branches of government in deciding them. Justice Brandeis had in fact given formal expression to this notion in a case where he suggested that the Supreme Court should not reach constitutional questions unless obligated to do so. *Ashwander v. Tennessee Valley Authority*, 297 U.S. 288, 345–56 (1936). More than sixty years later, John Roberts, as a judge on the D.C. Circuit before his elevation to chief justice, would express essentially the same idea in the pithy formulation that "if it is not necessary to decide more, it is necessary not to decide more." *PDK Laboratories Inc. v. DEA*, 362 F.3d 786, 799 (D.C. Cir. 2004) (Roberts, J., concurring in part and concurring in the judgment).

44. See *Schneiderman v. United States*, 320 U.S. 118 (1943); for the facts concerning his age and background see his memoir, William Schneiderman, *Dissent on Trial: The Story of a Political Life* (Minneapolis: MEP Publications, 1983), 11–18; 84.

45. Felix Frankfurter, *From the Diaries of Felix Frankfurter*, ed. Joseph P. Lash (New York: W. W. Norton, 1975), 214.

46. Id., 211.

47. Id., 211–12.

48. *Schneiderman*, 320 U.S. 118.

49. In Jackson's opinion in *West Virginia State Board of Education v. Barnette*, 319 U.S. 624, 627–28 (1943), the Court noted objections to the salute on these grounds—objections unmentioned in *Gobitis*.

50. *Jones v. City of Opelika*, 316 U.S. 584, 623–24 (1942) (Black, J., dissenting).

51. *The Secret Diary of Harold L. Ickes* vol. iii, 199 (entry for June 5, 1940) ("Apparently there was a good deal of feeling between Bob Jackson and Felix" over the opinion at a dinner hosted by Archibald MacLeish.).

52. *Barnette*, 319 U.S. at 638.

53. Id. at 642.

54. Norman I. Silber, *With All Deliberate Speed: The Life of Philip Elman, an Oral History Memoir* (Ann Arbor: University of Michigan Press, 2004), 112.

55. *Barnette*, 319 U.S. at 646–47.

56. Frankfurter, *Diaries*, 254.

57. Ibid.

58. Id., 254–55.

59. Ibid.

60. Ibid.

61. For an alternative view, see Norman Dorsen, Book Review, *Harvard Law Review* 95, no. 1 (1981): 367 (reviewing Hirsch, *The Enigma of Felix Frankfurter*).

62. Cf. Dorsen, Book Review, *Harvard Law Review* 95.

63. *Barnette*, 319 U.S. at 646–47.

64. *Gitlow v. New York*, 268 U.S. 652, 673 (1925) (Holmes, J., dissenting).

65. Holmes to Harold Laski, May 13, 1919, in Mark DeWolfe Howe, ed., *The Holmes-Laski Letters: The Correspondence of Mr. Justice Holmes and Harold J. Laski, 1916–1935* (Cambridge: Harvard University Press, 1953).

66. Sanford Levinson, "The Democratic Faith of Felix Frankfurter," *Stanford Law Review* 25 (1973): 430.

67. The most up-to-date scholarly work on the Japanese internment is Greg Robinson, *A Tragedy of Democracy: Japanese Confinement in North America* (New York: Columbia University Press, 2009). See also Greg Robinson, *By Order of the President: FDR and the Internment of Japanese Americans* (Cambridge: Harvard University Press, 2001); and Wendy L. Ng, *Japanese American Internment During World War II: A History and Reference Guide* (Westport, CT: Greenwood Press, 2002); Eric L. Muller, *American Inquisition: The Hunt for Japanese-American Disloyalty in World War II* (Chapel Hill: University of North Carolina Press, 2007). On the legal aspects of the case, the definitive source remains Peter Irons, *Justice at War* (New York: Oxford University Press, 1983). For an overview of the Japanese-Americans who brought the test cases, see Robinson, *A Tragedy of Democracy*, 218–19; Irons, *Justice at War*, 81–103; Neil Gotanda, "The Story of Korematsu: The Japanese-American Cases," in *Constitutional Law Stories* (see book 2, note 74), 231, 247–251. On Yasui, see the oral history of Yasui in John Tateishi, *And Justice for All: An Oral History of the Japanese-American Detention Camps* (New York: Random House, 1979), 62–93; on Yasui's family, see Lauren Kessler, *A Stubborn Twig: Three Generations in the Life of a Japanese Family* (New York: Random House, 1993).

68. Robinson, *A Tragedy of Democracy*, 128.

69. See the oral history of Endo in Tateishi, *And Justice for All*, 60–61; see also Robinson, *A Tragedy of Democracy*, 219.

70. Steven A. Chin, *When Justice Failed: The Fred Korematsu Story* (Austin, TX: Raintree, 1992), 70.

71. See, for example, "Nips Work Prisoners to Death in Jungles," September 1, 1945; "Nip Ship Sunk Off Solomons," March 2, 1943; "Jap Girl Awarded Vacation Wages," December 28, 1943 (all from the *Los Angeles Times*).

72. Attack on Pearl Harbor by Japanese Armed Forces, S. Doc. No. 77-2, at 12 (1942), available at http://www.ibiblio.org/pha/pha/roberts/roberts.html.

73. Irons, *Justice at War*, 45.

74. Biddle, *In Brief Authority*, 218–19.

75. Robinson, *A Tragedy of Democracy*, 84–85. See Walter Lippmann, "Facts Demanded on Coast Danger," *New York Times*, February 15, 1942; "Pacific Coast Aliens," *New York Times*, February 15, 1942.

76. Robinson, *A Tragedy of Democracy*, 220–21.

77. *Hirabayashi v. United States*, 320 U.S. 81 (1943).

78. *Hirabayashi*, 320 U.S. at 93 (quoting Charles Evans Hughes, War Powers under the Constitution, 42 A.B.A. Rep. 232, 238).

79. Id., 97.

80. Id., 100.

81. Ibid. From a doctrinal perspective, the crucial move here was Stone's assertion that despite the fact that Fourteenth Amendment equal protection did not ordinarily bind the federal government, the Court could nevertheless "assume that these considerations [i.e., equal protection concerns] would be controlling here" were it not for the distinctive conditions of wartime.

82. Id., 112 (Murphy, J., concurring).

83. Id., 111.

84. Frankfurter, *Diaries*, 251.

85. *Hirabayashi*, 320 U.S. at 105–6 (Douglas, J., concurring).

86. Id., 107–8. On the vetting process, see Muller, *American Inquisition*.

87. Irons, *Justice at War*, 237–39.

88. *Hirabayashi*, 108 (Douglas, J., concurring).

89. *Korematsu v. United States*, 323 U.S. 214, 216 (1944).

90. Id., 223–24.

91. Id., 223.

92. Ibid.

93. Robinson, *By Order of the President*, 55, 133.

94. *Ex Parte Endo*, 323 U.S. 283 (1944).

95. Douglas denied this. Douglas Oral History Interview with Walter Murphy, Cassette no. 8, May 23, 1962.

96. Irons, *Justice at War*, 345.

97. *Endo*, 323 U.S. at 302.

98. As Peter Irons argues in his book on the internment, California politicians urged Roosevelt's staff not to repatriate the internees before the November 1944 election lest anti-Japanese prejudice cost Roosevelt and the Democratic Party votes. Irons, *Justice at War*, 269.

99. And indeed, Douglas's opinion arguably implied without saying so that the Constitution would prohibit the detention of loyal Americans. Patrick O. Gudridge, "Remember *Endo*?" *Harvard Law Review* 116 (2003): 1933, 1952–53.

100. William O. Douglas, "The Bill of Rights Is Not Enough," *New York University Law Review* 38 (1963): 223.

101. Frankfurter, *Diaries*, 250.

102. Douglas Oral History Interview with Walter Murphy, Cassette no. 1, December 20, 1961.

103. Id., Cassette no. 8, May 23, 1962.

104. Fine, *Frank Murphy*, 259, 261.

105. *Korematsu*, 323 U.S. 246 (Jackson, J., dissenting).

106. Ibid.

107. Ibid.

108. Id., 247–48.

109. Id., 224 (Frankfurter, J., concurring).

110. Id, 225.

111. Ibid.

112. Eugene Rostow, "The Japanese American Cases—A Disaster," *Yale Law Journal* 54 (1945): 489.

113. *Korematsu v. United States*, 584 F. Supp. 1406 (N.D. Cal. 1984).

Book Six BETRAYALS

1. Jackson, *That Man*, 154–55.

2. Smith, *FDR*, 618.

3. Robert Sherwood, *Roosevelt and Hopkins: An Intimate History* (New York: Harper, 1948), 881. James Roosevelt "came away with the distinct impression that [FDR] really preferred Justice William O. Douglas as the vice-presidential nominee." Roosevelt and Shalett, *Affectionately, FDR*, 351.

4. McKean, *Tommy the Cork*, 71.

5. Id., 120.

6. Lash, *Dealers and Dreamers*, 449.

7. Lasser, *Benjamin V. Cohen*, 246.

8. McKean, *Tommy the Cork*, 152.

9. The assistant was James Rowe—a protégé of Corcoran's. For Frankfurter's conversation with Rowe, see Lasser, *Benjamin V. Cohen*, 245–46. For his memorandum to Roosevelt, citing "FF," see Lash, *Dealers and Dreamers*, 449–50.

10. Letter from Frankfurter to Learned Hand, November 5, 1954, Learned Hand, Papers, 1840–1961, Harvard Law School Library, Box 105; see also Fine, *Frank Murphy*, 253.

11. Douglas Oral History Interview with Walter Murphy, Cassette no. 3, December 20 and 27, 1961.

12. Murphy, *Wild Bill*, 215, citing Ed Kelly, "Tells Why Wallace Isn't Nation's Chief Executive," *Chicago Herald-American*, May 14, 1947.

13. Janeway, *The Fall of the House of Roosevelt*, 51 and 238 n.24 (citing a memorandum by Edwin Pauley in the Truman library).

14. Id., 52.

15. Robert H. Ferrell, *Choosing Truman: The Democratic Convention of 1944* (Columbia: University of Missouri Press, 1994), 83.

16. Murphy, *Wild Bill*, 227; see also Janeway, *The Fall of the House of Roosevelt*, 53. Elliott Roosevelt suggests that there were in fact two notes, each with the names in a different order, at Hannegan's request. Roosevelt and Brough, *A Rendezvous with Destiny*, 374.

17. Merle Miller, *Plain Speaking: An Oral Biography of Harry S. Truman* (New York: Berkley: 1974), 181.

18. See Miller, *Plain Speaking*, 180–81; Eliot Goldman, "Justice William O. Douglas: The Vice-Presidential Nomination and His Relationship with Roosevelt," *Presidential Studies Quarterly* 12 (1982): 377; see also James F. Simon, *Independent Journey: The Life of William O. Douglas* (New York: Harper and Row, 1980), 265 unnumbered footnote.

19. Janeway, *The Fall of the House of Roosevelt*, 55.

20. Harry Hopkins, cited in Simon, *Independent Journey*, 264–65.

21. Miller, *Plain Speaking*, 181–82.

22. Jackson, *That Man*, 167–69; see also Biddle, *In Brief Authority*, 361–62.

23. Merlo Pusey, "The Roosevelt Supreme Court," *American Mercury* lviii (1944): 596, quoted in Robert Harrison, "The Breakup of the Roosevelt Supreme Court" (see book 4, note 50), 168.

24. Fine, *Frank Murphy*, 325.

25. *Jewell Ridge Corp. v. Local No. 6167, United Mine Workers of America*, 325 U.S. 161, 196 (1945) (Jackson, J., dissenting).

26. Robert L. Stern, Eugene Gressman, Stephen M. Shapiro, and Kenneth S. Geller, *Supreme Court Practice* (Washington, DC: The Bureau of National Affairs, 2002), 726–27.

27. It was highly unusual when, in 2004, Justice Antonin Scalia issued a lengthy opinion explaining why he had not recused himself from a case about executive privilege after attending a duck hunt with Vice President Dick Cheney. *Cheney v. U.S. District Court for the District of Columbia*, 541 U.S. 913 (2004).

28. Newman, *Hugo Black*, 256–57.

29. Fred Rodell, "Justice Hugo Black," *American Mercury* lix (August 1944): 137.

30. Gerhart, *America's Advocate*, 242 n.24, citing an interview with Arthur Krock.

31. Wesley McCune, *The Nine Young Men* (New York: Harper and Brothers, 1947), 179.

32. Jackson, Reminiscences, 1581. Of course Black and Douglas may only have been hoping to win over Roberts with flattery. Compare Fine, *Frank Murphy*, 261.

33. For the date see Newman, *Hugo Black*, 322, 678 n.3.

34. Douglas Oral History Interview with Walter Murphy, Cassette no. 4, December 27, 1961.

35. Douglas Oral History Interview with Walter Murphy, Cassette no. 4, December 27, 1961; compare Jackson, Reminiscences, 1588–99.

36. Gerhart, *America's Advocate*, 321.

37. Id., 308, 322.

38. Jackson, Reminiscences, 1163.

39. Id., 1164.

40. Gerhart, *America's Advocate*, 316–17.

41. Jackson, Reminiscences, 1165.

42. Mason, *Harlan Fiske Stone*, 715.

43. Biddle, *In Brief Authority*, 428. Andrey Vyshinsky, the Soviet permanent representative to the United Nations, had been a prosecutor in the show trials. See also Gary J. Bass, *Stay the Hand of Vengeance: The Politics of War Crimes Tribunals* (Princeton: Princeton University Press, 2000).

44. International Conference on Military Trials, London, 1945, Minutes of Conference Session of July 23, 1945. Available at http://avalon.law.yale.edu/imt/jack44.asp.

45. Ibid.

46. Ibid.

47. Jackson, Reminiscences, 1391.

48. Id., 716.

49. Ibid. (quoting letter from Stone to Sterling Carr, Dec. 4, 1945).

50. Compare Judith N. Shklar, *Legalism* (Cambridge: Harvard University Press, 1964), 156-60.

51. Jackson, Reminiscences, 1392.

52. Avalon Project, Yale University, republishing: Nazi Conspiracy and Aggression, Office of the United States Counsel for Prosecution of Axis Criminality (Washington, DC: U.S. Government Printing Office, 1946), chapter 5, "Opening Address for the United States." Available at http://avalon.law.yale.edu/imt/chap_05.asp [hereafter Opening Address].

53. Ibid.

54. Ibid.

55. The only treaty on which Jackson could rely was the Kellogg-Briand Pact of 1928. Its signatories, including Germany, condemned "war for the solution of international controversies." They renounced such war "as an instrument of national policy." To condemn and renounce war, though, was not the same as to make it a crime. In 1941, as attorney general, Jackson had claimed that Germany violated the Kellogg-Briand Pact by starting the war. But in international law, breaching a treaty is not ordinarily a crime. And there was nothing in the pact that made war itself into a crime. After all, the Allies had also engaged in war, and the 1928 treaty did not distinguish defensive war from aggressive.

56. Opening Address.

57. Ibid.

58. Ibid.

59. Cf. Shklar, *Legalism,* 160 (rejecting the dualism of legalism versus expediency).

60. Jackson, Reminiscences, 1405; for the text of the letter, dated December 20, 1945, see John Q. Barrett, "Jackson in the Holiday Season," available at http://new.stjohns.edu/media/3/471e63b0fd1a4fe1842575e936994956.pdf.

61. Jackson letter, quoted in Barrett, "Jackson in the Holiday Season."

62. John Q. Barrett, "Christmas Celebration, Nuremberg, 1945," available at http://new.stjohns.edu/media/3/7287a7aca09c4dfc8627349d03ae27b7.pdf.

63. Jackson letter, quoted in Barrett, "Jackson in the Holiday Season."

64. Francis Biddle's first request from Truman on being asked to become a judge of the tribunal was to bring his wife, Katherine; she arrived in March of 1946. Biddle, *In Brief Authority*, 372. Herbert Wechsler, a staff member of Biddle's and later an important professor at Columbia Law School, also brought his wife. Id., 420.

65. Ronald Kessler, *The Bureau: The Secret History of the FBI* (New York: St. Martin's Press, 2002), 66, 67.

66. Moritz Fuchs, "Robert H. Jackson at the Nuremberg Trials, 1945–1946 as Remembered by His Personal Bodyguard," *Albany Law Review* 68 (2004): 14.

67. Jackson, Reminiscences, 1405–06.

68. Id., 1407–08.

69. Admiral Karl Doenitz, also on trial, had become Reich president briefly after Hitler's suicide; and Rudolf Hess had held the title of deputy führer before his bizarre flight to Scotland in 1941.

70. The literature on Goering leaves much to be desired. The first full-length English-language biography was Roger Manvell and Heinrich Fraenkel, *Hermann Göring* (London: Heinemann, 1962). More recently there is a 573-page biography by Holocaust-denier David Irving, *Göring: A Biography* (New York: William Morrow, 1989). It includes passages like this one about Hermann von Epenstein, Goering's Jewish godfather: "He…may have imprinted on young Hermann's character traits that were not always wholesome—the conclusion, for instance, that money could buy everything, and a contempt for morality." Id., 27. Irving describes the Nuremberg cross-examination with great sympathy to Goering, "this lion of a man" who "fought back" with "resonant oratory, scattering immortal lines before this last arbitrary tribunal of mortal enemies." Id., 493.

71. Jackson, Reminiscences, 1419.

72. Id., 1428.

73. General William "Wild Bill" Donovan, who had headed the Office of Strategic Services (precursor to the Central Intelligence Agency) during the war, strongly disagreed with Jackson's emphasis on the use of documentary evidence, believing that success at Nuremberg required dramatic public proof, preferably in the form of testimony. Donovan quit the prosecution team over this disagreement. Jackson, Reminiscences, 1427.

74. Norman Birkett, quoted in Manvell and Fraenkel, *Hermann Göring*, 9.

75. Jackson, Reminiscences, 1431.

76. Id., 1432–33.

77. Biddle, *In Brief Authority*, 365–66.

78. See Telford Taylor, *The Anatomy of the Nuremberg Trials: A Personal Memoir* (New York: Knopf, 1992), 94–95 (Jackson disappointed at Truman's suggestion of Biddle); Jackson, Reminiscences, 1321–28, and especially 1325 (Jackson tells Biddle he would not have picked him); Biddle, *In Brief Authority*, 372.

79. Jackson, Reminiscences, 1433.

80. Cited in Gerhart, *America's Advocate*, 514 n.37, citing Helen Kirkpatrick, "Goering's Oral Sparring Flattens U.S. Prestige," *Chicago Daily News*, March 19, 1946, and "Goering Names Jew-Baiters," March 20, 1946.

81. Birkett, cited in Manvell and Fraenkel, *Hermann Göring*, 9.

82. Cited in Gerhart, *America's Advocate*, 513 n.36.

83. Id., 514 n.37.

84. Avalon Project, Yale University, republishing: Trial of the Major War Criminals Before the International Military Tribunal, vol. 9 (Nuremberg, Germany: [s.n.], 1947-1949), March 19, 1946, "Testimony of Reich Marshal, Defendant Hermann Goering." http://avalon.law.yale.edu/imt/03-19-46 .asp#Goering6 (hereafter "Goering Testimony").

85. Ibid.

86. Biddle, *In Brief Authority*, 410-11. Jackson later renewed his threat to

resign, leading Biddle to comment in a letter to his wife that "this is not new." Taylor, *Anatomy of the Nuremberg Trials,* 359.

87. Goering Testimony, March 20, 1946, http://avalon.law.yale.edu/imt/03–20–46.asp#Goering7.

88. Ibid.

89. Janet Flanner, Letter from Paris, *New Yorker,* March 30, 1946, 76.

90. Id., 78.

91. Jackson was as well-dressed as ever in Nuremberg. In most images he wears a suit in lieu of the tailcoat and striped flannel trousers affected by Fyfe; but in at least one image he is sitting at the prosecution table wearing the formal striped trousers and dark coat.

92. Norbert Ehrenfreund, *The Nuremberg Legacy: How the Nazi War Crimes Trials Changed the Course of History* (New York: Palgrave Macmillan, 2007), 81; Biddle, *In Brief Authority,* 385.

93. Biddle, *In Brief Authority,* 384–86.

94. Jackson, Reminiscences, 1591.

95. Cf. Dennis J. Hutchinson, "The Black-Jackson Feud," *Supreme Court Review* 1988: 213–14.

96. Id., 215. Hutchinson says that there was a column, but research reveals this is inaccurate; no such column appeared on that day—it therefore must have been a radio broadcast.

97. Newman, *Hugo Black,* 341–42, 430.

98. Id., 341 and 680 n.7.

99. Ernest Lindley, "Chief Justiceship: Many Factors Temper Selection," *Washington Post,* April 26, 1946, 7.

100. Newman, *Hugo Black,* 343.

101. Jackson, Reminiscences, 1207–08. Eagleton was the father of Thomas Eagleton, who would serve as Democratic senator from Missouri and briefly be George McGovern's running mate, only to lose the spot on the ticket when revelations of his treatment for mental illness became public.

102. Doris Fleeson, *Evening Star,* May 16, 1945.

103. Frank Sher to RHJ, May 17, 1946, cited in Hutchinson, "The Black-Jackson Feud," 216.

104. Hutchinson, "The Black-Jackson Feud," 220.

105. Lewis Wood, "Split of Jackson and Black Long Widening in Capital," *New York Times,* June 11, 1946, 2.

106. *Yale Law Journal* 56 (1946–1947): 636.

107. "The Supreme Court: 1947," *Fortune,* January 1947, 73, 78.

108. Biddle, *In Brief Authority,* 163.

109. Id., 411.

110. Ibid.

Book Seven FRACTURE

1. Janeway, *The Fall of the House of Roosevelt,* 80–81 (quoting transcripts of Corcoran's wiretapped phone conversations).

2. Id., 61 (LBJ), 77 (Corcoran).

3. Douglas Oral History Interview with Walter Murphy, Cassette no. 16, June 5, 1963.

4. Janeway, *The Fall of the House of Roosevelt*, 77 (quoting transcripts of Corcoran's wiretapped phone conversations).

5. Simon, *Independent Journey*, 217, quoting Elizabeth Peer, "The Mind of a Maverick," *Newsweek*, November 24, 1976. I have not been able to identify the other person to whom Frankfurter may have been referring.

6. Simon, *Independent Journey*, 216, citing Frankfurter, *Diaries*, 76.

7. Fine, *Frank Murphy*, 254, citing Douglas to Frank Murphy, May 11, 12, 16, 1943.

8. Harrison, "The Breakup of the Roosevelt Supreme Court" (see book 4, note 50), 165, deserves credit for noticing the way these allies fractured. For Harrison, the cause lay in several "lessons" the justices had learned from their experiences as liberals during the 1920s and 1930s.

9. The details may all be found in Richard Cortner, *The Supreme Court and the Second Bill of Rights: The Fourteenth Amendment and the Nationalization of Civil Liberties* (Madison: University of Wisconsin Press, 1981), 139–43.

10. See *Adamson v. People of State of California*, 332 U.S. 46, 55 (1947) ("Generally, comment on the failure of an accused to testify is forbidden in American jurisdictions."); id. at 50 (assuming without deciding that the inference would violate the Fifth Amendment if the trial were held in federal court).

11. *Barron v. Baltimore*, 32 U.S. (7 Pet.) 243 (1833). In *Twining v. New Jersey*, 211 U.S. 78 (1908), the Supreme Court had specifically held that the right against self-incrimination did not extend to the states.

12. See Eric Foner, *Reconstruction: America's Unfinished Revolution, 1863–1877* (New York: Harper and Row, 1988), 241 (describing Bingham as a moderate rather than a radical Republican).

13. *Adamson*, 332 U.S. at 71–72 and n.5.

14. Id. at 72.

15. Newman, *Hugo Black*, 359.

16. Black had been able to rely for some material on an obscure historical book, Horace Edgar Flack, *The Adoption of the Fourteenth Amendment* (Baltimore: Johns Hopkins Press, 1908). Otherwise the research was original.

17. *Adamson*, 332 U.S. at 63 (Frankfurter, J., concurring).

18. Id. at 65.

19. See Richard J. Aynes, "Charles Fairman, Felix Frankfurter, and the Fourteenth Amendment," *Chicago-Kent Law Review* 70 (1995): 1223.

20. Frankfurter to Black, November 13, 1943, Felix Frankfurter Papers, Harvard Law School, Folder 2 in Box 169.

21. See *Slaughter-House Cases*, 83 U.S. (16 Wall.) 36 (1873). Charles Fairman, *Mr. Justice Miller and the Supreme Court, 1862–1890* (Cambridge: Harvard University Press, 1939).

22. Frankfurter, *Diaries*, 312. In Frankfurter's diary for April 25, 1947, when the justices were still working on their *Adamson* opinions, Frankfurter recorded

his conversation with Hughes. Not only did the two men discuss Fairman, but Frankfurter reported Justice Samuel Miller's remark about Justice Stephen Bradley, his great nineteenth-century rival. Fairman had also studied Bradley; see Aynes, "Charles Fairman," 1213.

23. Charles Fairman, "Does the Fourteenth Amendment Incorporate the Bill of Rights? The Original Understanding," *Stanford Law Review* 2 (1949–1950): 5. The piece appeared as the lead article in the second-ever volume of the *Stanford Law Review*. In one respect, Fairman's research actually strengthened Black's case. He pointed out that one senator supporting the Fourteenth Amendment had actually said outright that it would incorporate the first eight amendments of the Constitution by reference. Black had mentioned this passage in his original appendix without fully emphasizing its significance. Id., 57–58.

24. Flack, *The Adoption of the Fourteenth Amendment.*

25. Hugo Black to John P. Frank, January 10, 1950, cited in Newman, *Hugo Black*, 355–56.

26. Newman, *Hugo Black*, 383. Newman emphasizes Black's personal fondness for Truman (id. at 380, 385); but this is at odds with his apparent interest in supplanting him and with his at least partial alliance to Douglas and Corcoran, who disdained Truman.

27. Janeway, *The Fall of the House of Roosevelt*, 60.

28. In his diaries, Frankfurter related an exchange with Justice Reed about the role of politics on the Supreme Court. Reed insisted that politicians like Hugo Black could not ignore their political instincts just because they joined the Court. Frankfurter's reaction was, "But what about Bill Douglas? You can have no such excuse for him. He's never been a politician, he was a professor." Reed, in Frankfurter's telling, replied, "But he is a politician now....I had assumed he had put all thoughts of the Presidential nomination in '44 out of his head, but plainly not." See Frankfurter, *Diaries*, 184.

29. See Murphy, *Wild Bill*, 254.

30. Id., 255.

31. Id., 240–41.

32. Id., 258, comments to Eliot Janeway.

33. Id., 263.

34. Id., 271.

35. Id., 274.

36. Id., 276–77, citing interview with a law clerk.

37. On these peregrinations see id., chapters 24, 30, and 32.

38. Janeway, *The Fall of the House of Roosevelt*, 65 n.

39. Murphy, *Wild Bill*, 291.

40. Id., 293. Janeway's son notes that Murphy overstates the permanence of the break between Douglas and Corcoran, who reconciled at least once, in 1957. Janeway, *The Fall of the House of Roosevelt*, 65 n.

41. Douglas, *Go East, Young Man*, 39; see White, *The American Judicial Tradition* (see book 2, note 118), 371, identifying the themes of "loneliness, fear, and the strengthening and calming effects of the wilderness."

42. William O. Douglas, *The Court Years* (New York: Random House, 1980), 394; White, *The American Judicial Tradition* (see book 2, note 118), 369. The reference was very probably to Walt Whitman's poem "Darest Thou Now, O Soul," which issues a challenge to go to the "Unknown Region," where these is no map or guide, where "ties loosen" and no "darkness, sense, nor any bounds, bound us."

43. Patrick Schmidt, " 'The Dilemma to a Free People': Justice Robert Jackson, Walter Bagehot, and the Creation of a Conservative Jurisprudence," *Law and History Review* 20 (2002): 519.

44. Ibid.

45. *Terminiello v. Chicago*, 337 U.S. 1, 16–17 (1949)

46. Schmidt, "The Dilemma to a Free People," 520.

47. See "American Civil Liberties Union," in Encyclopedia of Chicago History, available at http://www.encyclopedia.chicagohistory.org/pages/20.html.

48. *Terminiello*, 337 U.S. at 3.

49. Id. at 4.

50. *Chaplinsky v. New Hampshire*, 315 U.S. 568, 571–72 (1942); the rule has never been directly followed by the Court afterward.

51. *Terminiello*, 337 U.S. at 23 (Jackson, J., dissenting).

52. Id. at 1, 24–25, internal citations omitted.

53. *Hirota v. MacArthur*, 388 U.S. 197 (1949); *In re Yamashita*, 327 U.S. 1 (1946).

54. Charles Lane, "Habeas Schmabeas: The 60-Year-Old Case That Will Decide Guantanamo," *Slate,* April 14, 2004, available at http://www.slate.com/id/2098817/.

55. *Johnson v. Eisentrager*, 339 U.S. 763, 793 (1950) (Black, J., dissenting).

56. *Eisentrager v. Forrestal*, 174 F.2d 961 (D.C. Cir. 1949).

57. *Johnson*, 339 U.S. at 779.

58. Id. at 791.

59. West Pediment Information Sheet, Office of the Curator, Supreme Court of the United States. Available at http://www.supremecourtus.gov/about/westpediment.pdf.

60. *Johnson*, 339 U.S. at 796.

61. Id. at 797.

62. Id. at 798.

63. Ibid.

64. In a telling footnote, Black explained that his vision of a people who "choose to maintain their greatness by justice rather than violence" came from Rome. Ibid.

Book Eight COMMUNISM

1. "Harvard Law School Celebrates Its Black Alumni," *The Journal of Blacks in Higher Education* no. 31 (Spring 2001): 85–87.

2. Gerald Horne, *Black Liberation/Red Scare: Benjamin Davis, Jr. and the Communist Party* (Cranbury, NJ: Associated University Presses, 1994).

3. Id., 31.

4. Id., 27–31.

5. Benjamin Jefferson Davis, *Communist Councilman from Harlem: Autobiographical Notes Written in a Federal Penitentiary* (New York: International Publishers, 1991), 222; Horne, *Black Liberation/Red Scare*, 36.

6. Horne, *Black Liberation/Red Scare*, 38.

7. Davis, *Communist Councilman from Harlem*, 222.

8. Horne, *Black Liberation/Red Scare*, 38.

9. Davis, *Communist Councilman from Harlem*, 222.

10. Horne, *Black Liberation/Red Scare*, 38.

11. Harvey Klehr and John Earl Haynes, *The American Communist Movement: Storming Heaven Itself* (New York: Twayne Publishers, 1992), 99.

12. Horne, *Black Liberation/Red Scare*, 143.

13. Michal R. Belknap, *Cold War Political Justice: The Smith Act, the Communist Party, and American Civil Liberties* (Westport, CT: Greenwood Press, 1977), 45–53.

14. Irving Howe & Lewis Coser, *The American Communist Party: A Critical History* (New York: Praeger, 1962), 339.

15. Harvey Klehr, John Earl Haynes, and Fridrikh Igorevich Firsov, *The Secret World of American Communism* (New Haven: Yale University Press, 1995), 259–63.

16. Id., 233–38.

17. Id., 323.

18. Michael Gold, *Jews Without Money* (New York: Carroll and Graf, 1996), 309 (originally published 1930).

19. John Earl Haynes and Harvey Klehr, *Venona: Decoding Soviet Espionage in America* (New Haven: Yale University Press, 2000), 15. Eugene Dennis was mentioned just twice in the intercepts, without enough context to show him guilty of anything. Id. at 222. Browder, the former CPUSA general secretary who was not tried, was mentioned in twenty-six messages and implicated in espionage. Id at 210.

20. William M. Wiecek, *The Birth of the Modern Constitution: The United States Supreme Court, 1941–1953* (New York: Cambridge University Press, 2006), 555.

21. Horne, *Black Liberation/Red Scare*, 210.

22. On Hand see Gerald Gunther, *Learned Hand: The Man and the Judge* (New York: Knopf, 1994). See 151–70 for *The Masses*; and 598–612 for the *Dennis* case.

23. Gunther, *Learned Hand*, 554–62.

24. Douglas, *Go East, Young Man*, 332. Francis Biddle, attorney general at the time, would also write that he "heard later that [FDR] resented what he called the 'organized pressure' in Hand's behalf." Biddle, *In Brief Authority*, 194.

25. *Schenck v. United States*, 249 U.S. 47 (1919).

26. *United States v. Carroll Towing Co.*, 159 F.2d 159 (2d Cir. 1947).

27. *United States v. Dennis*, 183 F.2d 201, 213 (2d Cir. 1950).

28. Newman, *Hugo Black*, 404.

29. *Dennis*, 341 U.S. at 580 (Black, J., dissenting), quoting *Bridges v. California*, 314 U.S. 252, 263 (1941).

30. Id., 581 (Douglas, J., dissenting).

31. Id., 521.

32. Id., 523.

33. Id., 519.

34. Ibid.

35. Powers, 34–5.

36. *Dennis*, 341 U.S. at 525 (Frankfurter, J., concurring).

37. Ibid.

38. Id., 526.

39. Id., 554 (quoting George F. Kennan, "Where Do You Stand on Communism?" *New York Times Magazine*, May 27, 1951, 53).

40. Janeway, *The Fall of the House of Roosevelt*, 82.

41. Ibid.

42. *Dennis*, 341 U.S. 494, 580 (Black, J., dissenting).

43. Jackson, Reminiscences, 116.

44. Id., 121.

45. *Dennis*, 341 U.S. at 564–65 (Jackson, J., concurring).

46. Id. at 570.

47. Ibid.

48. Id., 577.

49. Ibid.

50. Id., 573.

51. *Joint Anti-Fascist Refugee Committee v. McGrath*, 341 U.S. 123, 178–79 (1951); see Murphy, *Wild Bill*, 304, noting reference to Jackson here.

52. *Dennis*, 341 U.S. at 584 (Douglas, J., dissenting).

53. Ibid.

54. Id., 583.

55. Ibid.

56. Cf. privacy cases, *On Lee v. US* and streetcar case, discussed in Murphy, *Wild Bill*, 312.

57. *Dennis*, 341 U.S. at 586 (Douglas, J., dissenting), quoting *Whitney v. California*, 274 U.S. 357, 376 (1927) (Brandeis, J., concurring).

58. *Dennis*, 341 U.S. at 581.

59. Id., 584.

60. Ibid.

61. Id., 588.

62. Ibid.

63. Id., 589.

64. Ibid.

65. Ibid.

66. Id., 591.

67. George W. Bush's lowest approval rating was 25 percent, in October 2008. See Lydia Saad, "Bush Presidency Closes With 34% Approval, 61%

Disapproval," Gallup, January 14, 2009 (giving data throughout Bush presidency). On the other hand, Bush's disapproval rating in April 2008 was 69 percent, higher than Truman's high of 67 percent in 1952. See Frank Newport, "Bush's 69% Job Disapproval Rating Highest in Gallup History," Gallup, April 22, 2008, available at http://www.gallup.com/poll/106741/bushs-69-job-disapproval-rating-highest-gallup-history.aspx.

68. Truman's claim to greatness depends ultimately on his response to Communism and the way that response played out in American foreign policy over the next four decades. This view, and the implicit comparison to Reagan, were advanced in particular by David McCullough in his biography, *Truman* (New York: Simon and Schuster, 1992).

69. Krock, *Memoirs* (see book 2, note 36), 268–69. See also McCullough, *Truman*, 887–88.

70. McCullough, *Truman*, 888.

71. Id., 893; John Bartlow Martin, *Adlai Stevenson of Illinois* (New York: Doubleday, 1976), 547.

72. Maeva Marcus, *Truman and the Steel Seizure Case: The Limits of Presidential Power* (New York: Columbia University Press, 1977), 74 (quoting Truman's *Memoirs*, vol. 2 [New York: Doubleday, 1955–1956], 531–32).

73. Marcus, *Truman and the Steel Seizure Case*, 74–75.

74. Id., 75.

75. McCullough, *Truman*, 1066.

76. Ibid.

77. Robert J. Donovan, *Tumultuous Years: The Presidency of Harry S. Truman, 1949–1953* (New York: W. W. Norton, 1982), 382–91; see also McCullough, *Truman*, 897, referring to John Snyder, then secretary of the treasury.

78. George Gallup, "President's Popularity Inches Up," *Washington Post*, May 11, 1952, B5.

79. "Seizure of Press Called Doubtful; White House Says Right Exists Only for Remote Crisis—Law Permits Radio Shutdown," *New York Times*, April 19, 1952, 6.

80. "Supreme Court Law Clerks' Recollections of October Term 1951, Including the *Steel Seizure Cases*," *St. John's Law Review* 82, no. 4 (Fall 2008): 1239, 1281 (recollection of Abner Mikva).

81. Miller, *Plain Speaking* (see book 6, note 17), 225–26.

82. *Youngstown Sheet & Tube Co. v. Sawyer*, 343 U.S. 579, 587 (1952).

83. Ibid.

84. Id., 610 (Frankfurter, J., concurring).

85. Ibid.

86. On Burke's constitutional thought, see J. G. A. Pocock, *The Ancient Constitution and the Feudal Law: A Study of English Historical Thought in the Seventeenth Century* (New York: Cambridge University Press, 1987).

87. *Youngstown*, 343 U.S. at 634 (Jackson, J., concurring).

88. Ibid.

89. Benjamin N. Cardozo, *The Nature of the Judicial Process* (New Haven: Yale University Press, 1921).

90. *Youngstown*, 343 U.S. at 634 (Jackson, J., concurring).

91. Ibid.

92. Id., 635.

93. Ibid.

94. Id., 635

95. Id., 637.

96. Ibid.

97. See Patricia L. Bellia, "The Story of the Steel Seizure Case," in *Presidential Power Stories*, ed. Christopher H. Schroeder and Curtis A. Bradley (New York: Foundation Press, 2009).

98. *Youngstown*, 343 U.S. at 649 n.17.

99. *McGrath v. Kristensen*, 340 U.S. 162, 178 (1950), quoting *Andrews v. Styrap*, 26 L.T.R. (N.S.) 704, 706.

100. Weimar Constitution, Article 48.

101. *Youngstown*, 343 U.S. at 651 (Jackson, J., concurring).

102. *United States v. Nixon*, 418 U.S. 683, 707 (1974).

103. Jack Goldsmith, *The Terror Presidency: Law and Judgment Inside the Bush Administration* (New York: W. W. Norton, 2007).

104. Douglas, *Go East, Young Man*, 450.

Book Nine   BETRAYAL AND FULFILLMENT

1. See Robert Caro, *Master of the Senate: The Years of Lyndon Johnson* (New York: Knopf, 2002), 3–105. Until 1949, the filibuster rules required two-thirds of those present for cloture. Then the rule was changed to require two-thirds of all the senators, a higher bar.

2. Michael Klarman, *From Jim Crow to Civil Rights: The Supreme Court and the Struggle for Racial Equality* (New York: Oxford University Press, 2004), 293–94.

3. Richard Kluger, *Simple Justice: The History of Brown v. Board of Education and Black America's Struggle for Equality* (New York: Knopf, 1975), 593, relying on Burton and Jackson notes. Some of the notes taken at the conference are consolidated in Del Dickson, ed., *The Supreme Court in Conference, 1940–1985: The Private Discussions Behind Nearly 300 Supreme Court Decisions* (New York: Oxford University Press, 2001), a source which can be confusing because of the manner of its formulation. For a more recent overview of the conference, see Klarman, *From Jim Crow to Civil Rights*, 292–311.

4. See "The Governor," *Time*, January 29, 1951. I owe this point to Michael Klarman.

5. Kluger, *Simple Justice*, 593–94.

6. Id., 589–91 (Vinson), 595–96 (Reed), 611–12 (Clark).

7. Newman, *Hugo Black*, 431, citing Black.

8. Ibid.

9. Ibid.

10. Black, *My Father* (see book 1, note 109), 177.

11. Newman, *Hugo Black*, 406–07. So sensitive was the issue that Newman, who worked closely with the family until his book was published in 1994, never states explicitly that the death was a suicide. Hugo Black Jr.'s book does not describe the death as a suicide. Black, *My Father* (see book 1, note 109), 177–81.

12. Newman, *Hugo Black*, 407.

13. Alexander M. Bickel, "The Original Understanding and the Segregation Decision," *Harvard Law Review* 69, no. 1 (1955): 58–59. Lest it be thought that it was published only because of Frankfurter's influence, note that its ambivalent conclusion did the Court and the justice no good once *Brown* had already been decided.

14. Why Bickel ended up at Yale rather than Harvard is a complex story, connected at least partly to the circumstances of Bickel's divorce and the reaction from Harvard's dean Erwin Griswold. Personal communication with Norman Dorsen.

15. For the original memorandum see Bickel to Frankfurter, August 22, 1953, Frankfurter Papers, part 2, reel 4, frs. 212–14, cited in Klarman, *From Jim Crow to Civil Rights*, 544 n.24.

16. See Newman, *Hugo Black*, 96–100.

17. George S. Wood, "The Statist," review of *Alexander Hamilton: Writings*, ed. Joanne B. Freeman (New York: Library of America, 2001), *The New Republic*, October 15, 2001. Available at http://www.tnr.com/article/books/the-statist.

18. Newman, *Hugo Black*, 430.

19. Black, *My Father* (see book 1, note 109), 211; cf. Ball, *Hugo L. Black: Cold Steel Warrior* (see book 2, note 8), 222.

20. Black, *My Father* (see book 1, note 109), 214–16.

21. Dickson, *The Supreme Court in Conference*, 649.

22. Klarman, *From Jim Crow to Civil Rights*, 304.

23. Brief for the United States as Amicus Curiae, *Brown v. Board of Education*, No 8 (S. Ct. filed Dec 2, 1952). On this brief see Mary Dudziak, *Cold War Civil Rights: Race and the Image of American Democracy* (Princeton: Princeton University Press, 2000), 99–102; Mary Dudziak, "The Court and Social Context in Civil Rights History," *University of Chicago Law Review* 72 (2005): 448–49.

24. Mark Tushnet with Katya Lezin, "What Really Happened in Brown," *Columbia Law Review* 91 (December 1991): 1908, 1918, takes the position that Frankfurter's conflict left him in a position where he was paralyzed. I agree that Frankfurter was deeply conflicted and to that extent agree with Tushnet; but paralysis was not in Frankfurter's personality, as his private conversations with Elman indicate. See also Dennis J. Hutchinson, "Unanimity and Desegregation," *Georgetown Law Journal* 68 (1979–1980): 1–96.

25. Kluger, *Simple Justice*, 603.

26. See Richard Primus, "Bolling Alone," *Columbia Law Review* 104, no. 4 (May 2004): 975–1041.

27. See Tushnet, "What Really Happened in Brown," 1918–20.

28. Klarman, relying on Douglas's notes of the conference and a memo that Douglas dictated to his files on May 17, 1954, holds the view that Frankfurter was inclined to vote against desegregation at the December conference. See Klarman, *From Jim Crow to Civil Rights*, 304 and n.24 (quoting Douglas to the effect that Frankfurter had said "*Plessy* is right"). In Tushnet's view, which seems persuasive to me, Douglas was unreliable on the topic of his archenemy Frankfurter. See Tushnet, "What Really Happened in Brown," 1908, 1918. However, it is entirely plausible that Frankfurter communicated at conference that he was torn, for the strategic reason I have suggested. For Klarman's valuable references to the full sets of existing conference notes, see Klarman, *From Jim Crow to Civil Rights*, 543 n.6. The other secondary treatments of the conference, which Tushnet calls "orthodox," are those of Kluger and of Bernard Schwartz, *Super Chief, Earl Warren and His Supreme Court: A Judicial Biography* (New York University Press, 1983). My interpretation generally accords with those, modified slightly by my agreement with Tushnet that Frankfurter was conflicted at the conference.

29. Silber, *With All Deliberate Speed* (see book 5, note 53), 198–99. To those inclined to discredit Elman given his loyalty to Frankfurter, it may be said that in revealing that the two were speaking extensively during the period of deliberation, Elman did Frankfurter's historical legacy no favors.

30. Id., 203.

31. Brief for the United States as Amicus Curiae, *Brown v. Board of Education*, No 8 (S. Ct. filed Dec 2, 1952).

32. Id. at 206.

33. Kluger, *Simple Justice*, 558; see also Silber, *With All Deliberate Speed* (see page 461, note 54), 202; Philip Elman and Norman Silber, "The Solicitor General's Office, Justice Frankfurter, and Civil Rights Litigation, 1946–1960: An Oral History," *Harvard Law Review* 100 (1987): 817, 827.

34. Silber, *With All Deliberate Speed*, 205.

35. The phrase appears in *Virginia v. West Virginia*, 222 U.S. 17, 20 (1911). For a cogent example of the criticism of *Brown II*, see Klarman, *From Jim Crow to Civil Rights*, 320 (the decision "encouraged defiance" and "undermined... moderates").

36. It is true that Black joined *Brown II*, with its controversial "all deliberate speed" remedy. This, though, did not go to Black's particular jurisprudential preoccupation, which was the meaning of the Constitution—the issue in *Brown I*.

37. Silber, *With All Deliberate Speed*, 208.

38. Ibid.

39. Ibid.

40. Id., 207–08.

41. Douglas apparently said that perhaps the D.C. case should be reargued but not the state cases—the exact opposite of Frankfurter's slightly absurd proposal. Kluger, *Simple Justice*, 602–03.

42. Murphy, *Wild Bill*, 292.

43. On this complex episode, see Brad Snyder, "Taking Great Cases: Lessons from the *Rosenberg* Case," forthcoming, *Vanderbilt Law Review* 63, (May 2010): 101ff.

44. Id., 118.

45. Id., 119-21.

46. Id., 122.

47. As a result of the stay, even today some observers, including the Rosenbergs' children, see Douglas as a hero. See letter by the children, Michael Meeropol and Robert Meeropol, "June '53: The Court and Our Parents, the Rosenbergs," *New York Times*, June 17, 2009, A36. In fact Douglas was unwilling on two occasions to cast the decisive vote to have the case heard.

48. Kluger, *Simple Justice*, 606. On the memos, see Bernard Schwartz, "Chief Justice Rehnquist, Justice Jackson, and the *Brown* Case," *Supreme Court Review* 1988: 245–67.

49. Kluger, *Simple Justice*, 606 n.

50. "Rehnquist's View on Memos Disputed by Aide to Jackson," *New York Times*, August 11, 1986.

51. Dickson, *The Supreme Court in Conference*, 652.

52. Kluger, *Simple Justice*, 609.

53. As Klarman notes, the justices wanted to preserve flexibility and confidentiality. Klarman, *From Jim Crow to Civil Rights*, 298.

54. Silber, *With All Deliberate Speed* (see book 5, note 53), 208.

55. Kluger, *Simple Justice*, 618.

56. Ibid.

57. The vote was 5 to 4. Id., 301.

58. Douglas Oral History Interview with Walter Murphy, Cassette no. 11, June 9, 1962.

59. Silber, *With All Deliberate Speed* (see book 5, note 53), 219; see also Kluger, *Simple Justice*, 656.

60. Indeed, according to Douglas, Frankfurter was "very, very bitter" about Vinson, and he refused to accompany the special funeral train that brought Vinson's body to Kentucky. Douglas Oral History Interview with Walter Murphy, Cassette no. 11, June 9, 1962.

61. Silber, *With All Deliberate Speed* (see book 5, note 53), 219.

62. Krock, *Memoirs* (see book 2, note 36), 287–88. The Minnesota delegation similarly cast its votes for Eisenhower rather than favorite son Harold Stassen. Eisenhower made a point of considering Robert Jackson. However, Jackson's feud with Black and his support for the court-packing plan swayed Eisenhower against him. It was the third time Jackson would be passed over for the job. Id., 302–03.

63. Kluger, *Simple Justice*, 696.

64. Id., 678–80.

65. Id., 680–82.

66. Id., 694.

67. Id., 690–91.

68. The reliance on social science in the footnote has been the subject of extensive discussion. See Edmond Cahn, "Jurisprudence," *New York University Law Review* 30 (1955): 159–60. It was also relied on by the trial court. See Justice Robert H. Jackson, Memorandum, March 15, 1954, Library of Congress, Jackson Papers, Brown file.

69. See Jackson's Memorandum; Kluger, *Simple Justice*, 689–90.

70. Author interview with E. Barrett Prettyman Jr., January 29, 2010.

71. Kluger, *Simple Justice*, 694–95.

72. Klarman, *From Jim Crow to Civil Rights*, 545 n.26 (giving date of March 15).

73. Kluger, *Simple Justice*, 701.

74. Id., 698.

75. Klarman, *From Jim Crow to Civil Rights*, 302; author interview with E. Barrett Prettyman Jr., January 29, 2010.

76. Cullen Couch, "Behind the Scenes of Brown: E. Barrett Prettyman, Jr. '53 Sensed History in the Making," *UVA Lawyer* (Fall 2004), available at http://www.law.virginia.edu/html/alumni/uvalawyer/f04/prettyman.htm.

77. Author interview with E. Barrett Prettyman Jr., January 29, 2010.

78. Chalmers M. Roberts, "High Court Member Dies Seeking Aid After Stroke," *Washington Post and Times Herald*, October 10, 1954, M1; "Justice Jackson Dead at 62" (see page 450, note 57).

79. Kessler, *The Bureau* (see book 6, note 63), 68. According to *Chicago Tribune* Washington bureau chief Walter Trohan, Hoover leaked the information through his public relations officer, Louis B. Nichols, as revenge for Jackson's opposition to warrantless wiretapping while he had been attorney general. See also Walter Trohan, *Political Animals* (New York: Doubleday, 1975), 406.

Epilogue AFTER THE ROOSEVELT COURT

1. Felix Frankfurter, "Mr. Justice Jackson," *Harvard Law Review* 68, no. 6 (1955): 939.

2. Janeway, *The Fall of the House of Roosevelt*, 81–82.

3. Although Rehnquist's letter has been lost, its content can be reconstructed from passages quoted or paraphrased in Prettyman's response to Frankfurter, October 13, 1955, Felix Frankfurter Papers, Harvard Law School, Folder 6 in Box 170.

4. Rehnquist's letter prefigured his later betrayal of Jackson's reputation in attributing the content of his anti-desegregation memorandum to Jackson rather than to himself.

5. Prettyman to Frankfurter, October 13, 1955.

6. Ibid.

7. Indeed, so gregarious was his personality, so keen his eye for talent—and, a cynic might add, so powerful his urge to influence—that Frankfurter even befriended the law clerks of other justices while they were working at the Court, a rare phenomenon under the Court's usual social norms. See Norman Dorsen, "The Supreme Court and Its Justices Fifty Years Ago, Felix Frankfurter

Pt. 2," *Green Bag Almanac* 47 (2008): 267; cf. John Knox, *The Forgotten Memoir of John Knox*, ed. Dennis J. Hutchinson and David J. Garrow (Chicago: University of Chicago Press, 2002), 61–67 (discussing the close relationship between John Knox, a McReynolds clerk, and Cardozo); Howard Ball and Phillip Cooper, "Fighting Justices: Hugo L. Black and William O. Douglas and Supreme Court Conflict," *American Journal of Legal History* 38 (1994): 12 (discussing the close relationship between Charles Reich, a Black clerk, and Douglas).

 8. Prettyman to Frankfurter, October 13, 1955. Punctuation and capitalization as in the original.

 9. Ibid.

 10. See the introduction to Jackson, Reminiscences.

 11. Frankfurter's were eventually published in edited form, while Jackson's have remained unpublished in the Columbia University archives for half a century.

 12. William Domnarski, *The Great Justices, 1941–54: Black, Douglas, Frankfurter and Jackson in Chambers* (Ann Arbor: University of Michigan Press, 2006), 56–57; Harlan B. Phillips to Felix Frankfurter, July 10, 1955, Felix Frankfurter Papers, Harvard Law School, Folder 6 in Box 170.

 13. Phillips to Frankfurter, July 10, 1955.

 14. Ibid.

 15. To give just one example of many, in December 1955 Frankfurter wrote a note of protest to Edward Dumbauld, who had worked under Jackson when he was attorney general. Dumbauld had published an essay in the *University of Pennsylvania Law Review* about Chief Justice John Marshall. It included the comment that Marshall's greatness stemmed from his intellect, not his position as chief justice. In his final footnote, Dumbauld commented that it was a mistake for Jackson to have aspired to the chief justiceship, since even the best chief justices (he named some) were not especially significant figures: "In desiring to be Chief Justice, did not Robert H. Jackson miscalculate the true nature of his own greatness? Ought he to have wished that posterity would number him with names such as Ellsworth, Waite, Fuller, Chase, or White, because of the exalted station they held, rather than with Holmes of the laurel crown?" Edward Dumbauld, "John Marshall and the Law of Nations," *University of Pennsylvania Law Review* 104 (1955): 56 n.96. The observation—again, from someone who had worked closely with Jackson—aroused Frankfurter's ire. He wrote to Dumbauld: "Of course it would have pleased [Jackson] to become Chief Justice, just as it would have pleased Holmes. . . . But in conveying the impression that Jackson, like Taft, was preoccupied with becoming Chief Justice or made it a driving ambition, you are wholly wrong. That notion, too widely bruited about, derives from ignorant interpretations of his outburst from Nürnberg after the appointment of Vinson. I have the best of reasons for knowing that he was not in the grip of ambition for office. Quite the contrary. . . . [He] was about as uncorrupted by ambition for place and the glitter of power as the best of men who have sat on this Court." Frankfurter to Edward Dumbauld, December 19, 1955, Felix Frankfurter Papers, Harvard Law School, Folder 6 in Box 170. This was how Frankfurter always sounded when he was on the defensive: overstated,

and relying on undisclosed private evidence and vague historical analogy. By December 1955, Frankfurter had made Jackson's memory into a cause. Six months later, in June 1956, Frankfurter was writing to Jackson's son, Bill, to warn him that an impending biography of Jackson by Eugene Gerhart was sure to be "naïve" like its author, and ought if possible to be delayed. Frankfurter to William H. Jackson, June 21, 1956, Id., Folder 7 in Box 170. In November 1956, Frankfurter wrote to Charles Evans Hughes's biographer, Merlo Pusey, to assure him that Hughes had told Frankfurter that he had recommended the appointment of Jackson when he went to see Truman after Stone's death, before Jackson's Nuremberg blow-up. Frankfurter to Merlo J. Pusey, November 27, 1956, Id., Folder 20 in Box 169. In April 1957, Frankfurter was drafting a memorandum responding to Gerhart's draft biography of Jackson, this time spending four pages insisting rather desperately that Jackson's outburst at Nuremberg had nothing whatever to do with "frustrated ambition," but was a response to Black's conduct "over the years carried on under the protective privacy of the Supreme Court." Id., Folder 7 in Box 170. A few years later, when the second volume of Francis Biddle's autobiographical memoir was published, Frankfurter wrote to Biddle's wife, Katherine, to complain about Biddle's account of Jackson's cross-examination of Goering. Id., November 26, 1962.

16. *Baker v. Carr*, 369 U.S. 186 (1962).

17. Newman, *Hugo Black*, 518.

18. Bickel, however, supported Robert Kennedy's presidential bid in 1968. He died in 1974 at fifty.

19. Frankfurter, *Diaries*, 89.

20. Ibid.; see also Melvin I. Urofsky, *Felix Frankfurter: Judicial Restraint and Individual Liberties* (Boston: Twayne Publishers, 1991), 173 (noting parallel to FDR's call on Holmes).

21. Leonard Baker, *Brandeis and Frankfurter: A Dual Biography* (New York: Harper and Row, 1984), 490.

22. James F. Simon, *The Antagonists: Hugo Black, Felix Frankfurter, and Civil Liberties in Modern America* (New York: Simon and Schuster, 1989), 261.

23. Frankfurter, *Diaries*, 89. Henkin explained that he chose the kaddish because Frankfurter had told him that he wanted him to speak because he knew Hebrew and was an orthodox Jew—and then added, "You do what you want." Ibid.

24. Newman, *Hugo Black*, 514.

25. Hugo Black, "The Bill of Rights," *New York University Law Review* 35 (1960): 865; Newman, *Hugo Black*, 512.

26. Newman, *Hugo Black*, 615–16.

27. See Leonard Levy, *Legacy of Suppression: Freedom of Speech and Press in Early American History* (Cambridge: Harvard University Press, 1960). Levy substantially moderated his position with his later book, *Emergence of a Free Press* (New York: Oxford University Press, 1985).

28. *Gideon v. Wainwright*, 372 U.S. 335 (1963). See also Anthony Lewis, *Gideon's Trumpet* (New York: Random House, 1964).

29. Charles Reich, "Mr. Justice Black and the Living Constitution," *Harvard Law Review* 76, no. 4 (1963): 673.

30. Newman, *Hugo Black*, 529.

31. For the right to privacy, see *Griswold v. Connecticut*, 381 U.S. 479 (1965) (Black, J., dissenting). For the Fourth Amendment, see *Vale v. Louisiana*, 399 U.S. 30 (1970) (Black, J., dissenting) (only Black and Chief Justice Burger dissented).

32. This did not always make him the most speech-protective vote, however, because Black only favored absolute protection for what he counted as speech. Thus he voted against protecting a jacket with the words "Fuck the Draft" on it because he considered the clothing not to be speech. See *Cohen v. California*, 403 U.S. 15 (1971).

33. Black, *My Father* (see book 1, note 109), 253.

34. Id., 254–56; Newman, *Hugo Black*, 621–22.

35. Black, *My Father*, 265.

36. Id., 266; Newman, *Hugo Black*, 623–24.

37. *Poe v. Ullman*, 367 U.S. 497, 521 (Douglas, J., dissenting).

38. *Griswold*, 381 U.S. 479, 482. Douglas's first draft in *Griswold* mentioned only the right of association, not the emanation that he had mentioned twice in his *Poe v. Ullman* dissent, nor the right to privacy mentioned there, nor the Third Amendment right against having troops quartered in one's home, which also appeared in the *Poe* dissent. Brennan, concerned by the brevity of the draft, asked his law clerk, Richard Posner, to draft a note to Douglas suggesting that he add various other amendments. Douglas acquiesced. David J. Garrow, *Liberty and Sexuality: The Right to Privacy and the Making of Roe v. Wade* (Berkeley: University of California Press, 1994), 246–48.

39. The amendments mentioned free speech and assembly (First); a right against having troops quartered in people's houses (Third); protection against unreasonable searches and seizures (Fourth); a right against self-incrimination (Fifth); and a general statement that rights not specifically mentioned in the Constitution were nevertheless retained by the states or the people (Ninth).

40. *Griswold*, 381 U.S. at 482.

41. See Warren and Brandeis, "The Right to Privacy" (see book 1, note 60), 193.

42. *Griswold*, 381 U.S. at 482.

43. Id. at 486.

44. Douglas, *Go East, Young Man*, 212–13; Adam M. Sowards, *The Environmental Justice: William O. Douglas and American Conservation* (Corvallis: University of Oregon Press, 2009), 22–23. For Douglas's environmentalism generally, see Sowards.

45. *Udall v. Federal Power Commission*, 387 U.S. 428 (1967); *Puyallup Tribe v. Washington Game Department*, 391 U.S. 392 (1968); Sowards, *The Environmental Justice*, 123–24; Charles F. Wilkinson, "Douglas and the Public Lands," in

He Shall Not Pass This Way Again: The Legacy of Justice William O. Douglas, ed. Stephen L. Wasby (Pittsburgh: University of Pittsburgh Press, 1990), 239.

46. *Sierra Club v. Morton*, 405 U.S. 727, 743 (1972) (Douglas, J., dissenting).

47. See James L. Moses, "William O. Douglas and the Vietnam War: Civil Liberties, Presidential Authority, and the 'Political Question,'" *Presidential Studies Quarterly* 26 (1996): 1029; Joseph Berger, "Creative Counsel," *The Law School* (Autumn 2004), 18, available at http://www1.law.nyu.edu/pubs/magazine/autumn2004/p16_23.pdf; Burt Neuborne, personal communication; "Douglas Hears Cambodian Case and Promises a Decision Soon," *New York Times*, August 4, 1973, 5; and Warren Weaver Jr., "Douglas Upholds Halt in Bombing But Is Overruled," *New York Times*, August 5, 1973, 1.

48. White, *The American Judicial Tradition* (see book 2, note 118), 369.

49. Id., 390.

50. Louis Brandeis, "The Living Law," *Illinois Law Review* 10 (1916): 461.

51. Newman, *Hugo Black*, 532.

52. Murphy, *Wild Bill*, 347.

53. Id., 408; cf. Newman, *Hugo Black*, 367 (quoting Douglas as calling his clerks "the lowest form of animal life").

54. Murphy, *Wild Bill*, passim. Most of the very little warmth that comes through in Murphy's book comes from Charles Reich, the visionary Yale Law School professor, environmentalist, and novelist, who in fact clerked for Black, not Douglas, and got to know Douglas well only after leaving the job. But see Marshall L. Small, "William O. Douglas Remembered: A Collective Memory by WOD's Law Clerks," *Journal of Supreme Court History* 32 (2007): 297.

55. Murphy, *Wild Bill*, 412.

56. Simon, *Independent Journey*, 453.

57. Dorsen, Book Review, *Harvard Law Review* 95, argues that Frankfurter was ultimately not consistent.

58. Clarence Thomas, appointed at the age of forty-two, is the justice with the best chance of doing so.

BIBLIOGRAPHY

Aaron, Daniel. *Writers on the Left: Episodes in American Literary Communism* (New York: Columbia University Press, 1992).

Acheson, Dean. *Morning and Noon* (Boston: Houghton Mifflin, 1965).

Andrews, Robert, ed. *Famous Lines: A Columbia Dictionary of Familiar Quotations* (New York: Columbia University Press, 1996).

Ariens, Michael. "A Thrice-Told Tale, or Felix the Cat." *Harvard Law Review* 107, no. 3 (January 1994): 620.

Atkinson, David N. *Leaving the Bench: Supreme Court Justices at the End* (Lawrence: University Press of Kansas, 1999).

Avalon Project, Yale University.

Avrich, Paul. *Sacco and Vanzetti: The Anarchist Background* (Princeton: Princeton University Press, 1991).

Baker, Leonard. *Brandeis and Frankfurter: A Dual Biography* (New York: Harper and Row, 1984).

Ball, Howard. *Hugo L. Black: Cold Steel Warrior* (New York: Oxford University Press, 1996).

Ball, Howard, and Phillip Cooper. "Fighting Justices: Hugo L. Black and William O. Douglas and Supreme Court Conflict." *American Journal of Legal History* 38 (1994): 1.

Barron, David J. and Martin S. Lederman. "The Commander in Chief at the Lowest Ebb—Framing the Problem, Doctrine, and Original Understanding." *Harvard Law Review* 121, no. 3 (2008): 772.

Bartsch, William H. *December 8, 1941: MacArthur's Pearl Harbor* (College Station: Texas A&M University Press, 2003).

Bass, Gary J. *Stay the Hand of Vengeance: The Politics of War Crimes Tribunals* (Princeton: Princeton University Press, 2000).

Belknap, Michal R. "Frankfurter and the Nazi Saboteurs." Supreme Court Historical Society, 1982 Yearbook, 67.

Belknap, Michal R. *Cold War Political Justice: The Smith Act, the Communist Party, and American Civil Liberties* (Westport, CT: Greenwood Press, 1977).

Bickel, Alexander M. "The Original Understanding and the Segregation Decision." *Harvard Law Review* 69, no. 1 (1955): 1.

Biddle, Francis. *In Brief Authority* (Garden City, NY: Doubleday, 1962).

Black, Hugo. L. "The Bill of Rights." *New York University Law Review* 35 (1960): 865.

Black, Hugo. L. *A Constitutional Faith* (New York: Knopf, 1968).

Black, Hugo L. *One Man's Stand for Freedom: Mr. Justice Black and the Bill of Rights.* Irving Dilliard, ed. (New York: Knopf, 1963).

Hugo L. Black Papers, LBJ Presidential Library.

Hugo LaFayette Black Papers, Library of Congress.

Black, Hugo L., Jr. *My Father: A Remembrance* (New York: Random House, 1975).

Bobbitt, Philip. *Constitutional Interpretation* (Cambridge, MA: Blackwell, 1995).

Bobbitt, Philip. *Constitutional Fate: Theory of the Constitution* (New York: Oxford University Press, 1982).

Brandeis, Louis D. *Other People's Money and How the Bankers Use It* (New York: Stokes, 1914).

Brandeis, Louis D. "The Living Law." *Illinois Law Review* 10 (1916): 461.

Brands, H. W. *Traitor to His Class: The Privileged Life and Radical Presidency of Franklin Delano Roosevelt* (New York: Doubleday, 2008).

Burns, James MacGregor. *Roosevelt: The Lion and the Fox* (New York: Harcourt, Brace & World, 1956).

Burns, James MacGregor. *Roosevelt: The Soldier of Freedom, 1940-1945* (New York: Harcourt Brace Jovanovich, 1970).

Burt, Robert A. *Two Jewish Justices: Outcasts in the Promised Land* (Berkeley: University of California Press, 1988).

Cahn, Edmond. "Jurisprudence." *New York University Law Review* 30 (1955): 150.

Cannadine, David. *Mellon: An American Life* (New York: Knopf, 2006).

Caro, Robert. *Master of the Senate: The Years of Lyndon Johnson* (New York: Knopf, 2002).

Caroli, Betty Boyd. *The Roosevelt Women* (New York: Basic Books, 1999).

Chafe, William H. *The Achievement of American Liberalism: The New Deal and Its Legacies* (New York: Columbia University Press, 2003).

Chalmers, David M. *Hooded Americanism: The History of the Ku Klux Klan* (Durham: Duke University Press, 1981).

Chernow, Ron. *The House of Morgan: An American Banking Dynasty and the Rise of Modern Finance* (New York: Simon & Schuster, 1991).

Childs, Marquis. Oral History, National Gallery of Art.

Chin, Steven A. *When Justice Failed: The Fred Korematsu Story* (Austin, TX: Raintree, 1992).

Churchill, Randolph S., and Martin Gilbert. *Winston S. Churchill* (Boston: Houghton Mifflin, 1988).

Coben, Stanley. *A. Mitchell Palmer: Politician* (New York: Da Capo Press, 1972).

Coker, Francis W. Review of *Nine Men: A Political History of the Supreme Court from 1790 to 1955*, by Fred Rodell. *Yale Law Journal* 65 (1956): 583.

Cook, Blanche Wiesen. *Eleanor Roosevelt, Volume One, 1884-1933* (New York: Viking, 1992).

Cook, Blanche Wiesen. *Eleanor Roosevelt, Volume Two, 1933-1938* (New York: Viking, 1999).

Cortner, Richard. *The Supreme Court and the Second Bill of Rights: The Fourteenth Amendment and the Nationalization of Civil Liberties* (Madison: University of Wisconsin Press, 1981).

Culver, John C., and John Hyde. *American Dreamer: The Life and Times of Henry A. Wallace* (New York: W. W. Norton, 2000).

Cushman, Barry. *Rethinking the New Deal Court: The Structure of a Constitutional Revolution* (Oxford: Oxford University Press, 1998).

Danelski, David. "The Saboteurs' Case." *Journal of Supreme Court History* 1 (1996): 61.

Danzig, Richard. "How Questions Begot Answers in Felix Frankfurter's First Flag Salute Opinion." *The Supreme Court Review* 1977: 257.

Danzig, Richard. "Justice Frankfurter's Opinions in the Flag Salute Cases: Blending Logic and Psychologic in Constitutional Decisionmaking." *Stanford Law Review* 36 (1984): 675.

Davies, Sharon. *Rising Road: A True Tale of Love, Race, and Religion in America* (New York: Oxford University Press, 2010).

Davis, Benjamin Jefferson. *Communist Councilman from Harlem: Autobiographical Notes Written in a Federal Penitentiary* (New York: International Publishers, 1991).

Davis, Mike. *Buda's Wagon: A Brief History of the Car Bomb* (London: Verso Books, 2007).

Desmond, Charles S., Paul A. Freund, Potter Stewart, and Lord Shawcross. *Mr. Justice Jackson: Four Lectures in His Honor* (New York: Columbia University Press, 1969).

Dickson, Del, ed. *The Supreme Court in Conference, 1940-1985: The Private Discussions Behind Nearly 300 Supreme Court Decisions* (New York: Oxford University Press, 2001).

Dobbs, Michael. *Saboteurs: The Nazi Raid on America* (New York: Knopf, 2004).

Doheny, David A. *David Finley: Quiet Force for America's Arts* (Washington, DC: National Trust for Historic Preservation, 2006).

Domnarski, William. *The Great Justices, 1941-54: Black, Douglas, Frankfurter, and Jackson in Chambers* (Ann Arbor: University of Michigan Press, 2006).

Donovan, Robert J. *Tumultuous Years: The Presidency of Harry S. Truman, 1949-1953* (New York: W. W. Norton, 1982).

Dorf, Michael, ed. *Constitutional Law Stories* (New York: Foundation Press, 2009).

Dorsen, Norman. Book Review. *Harvard Law Review* 95, no. 1 (1981): 367 (reviewing Hirsch, *The Enigma of Felix Frankfurter*).

Dorsen, Norman. "The Supreme Court and Its Justices Fifty Years Ago, Felix Frankfurter Pt. 2." *Green Bag Almanac* 47 (2008).

Douglas, William O. *Go East, Young Man: The Early Years* (New York: Random House, 1974).

Douglas, William O. *The Court Years* (New York: Random House, 1980).

Draper, George. *Disease and the Man* (New York: Macmillan, 1930).

Drayer, Ruth A. *Nicholas & Helena Roerich: The Spiritual Journey of Two Great Artists and Peacemakers* (Wheaton, IL: Quest, 2007).

Dudziak, Mary. "The Court and Social Context in Civil Rights History." *University of Chicago Law Review* 72 (2005): 429.

Dumbauld, Edward. "John Marshall and the Law of Nations." *University of Pennsylvania Law Review* 104, no. 1 (1955): 38.

Dunne, Gerald T. *Grenville Clark: Public Citizen* (New York: Farrar, Straus and Giroux, 1986).

Dunne, Gerald T. *Hugo Black and the Judicial Revolution* (New York: Simon & Schuster, 1977).

Durr, Virginia Foster. Interviews. March 13, 14, 15, 1975. Southern Oral History Program Collection (#4007). Interviews G-0023-1 and G-0023-2. Available at http://docsouth.unc.edu/sohp/.

Elman, Philip and Norman Silber. "The Solicitor General's Office, Justice Frankfurter, and Civil Rights Litigation, 1946-1960: An Oral History." *Harvard Law Review* 100, no. 4 (1987): 817.

Fairman, Charles. *Mr. Justice Miller and the Supreme Court, 1862-1890* (Cambridge: Harvard University Press, 1939).

Fairman, Charles. "Does the Fourteenth Amendment Incorporate the Bill of Rights? The Original Understanding." *Stanford Law Review* 2 (1949–1950): 5.

Feldman, Noah. *Divided by God: America's Church–State Problem—And What We Should Do About It* (New York: Farrar, Straus and Giroux, 2005).

Feldman, Penny. *Recruiting an Elite: Admission to Harvard College* (New York: Garland, 1988).

Ferrell, Robert H. *Choosing Truman: The Democratic Convention of 1944* (Columbia: University of Missouri Press, 1994).

Fine, Sidney. *Frank Murphy: The Washington Years* (Ann Arbor: University of Michigan Press, 1984).

Flack, Horace Edgar. *The Adoption of the Fourteenth Amendment* (Baltimore: Johns Hopkins Press, 1908).

Flynn, Elizabeth Gurley. *Rebel Girl: An Autobiography, My First Life (1906-1926)* (New York: International Publishers, 1973).

Foner, Eric. *Reconstruction: America's Unfinished Revolution, 1863-1877* (New York: Harper and Row, 1988).

Frank, John P. *Mr. Justice Black: The Man and His Opinions* (New York: Knopf, 1949) (reprinted by Greenwood Press, 1973).

Frankfurter, Felix. *The Case of Sacco and Vanzetti: A Critical Analysis for Lawyers and Laymen* (Boston: Little, Brown, 1927).

Frankfurter, Felix. "Hours of Labor and Realism in Constitutional Law." *Harvard Law Review* 29, no. 4 (1916): 371.

Frankfurter, Felix. "Mr. Justice Holmes and the Constitution: A Review of His Twenty-Five Years on the Supreme Court." *Harvard Law Review* 41, no. 2 (1927): 144.

Frankfurter, Felix. "Mr. Justice Jackson." *Harvard Law Review* 68, no. 6 (1955): 937.

Frankfurter, Felix. "Mr. Justice Roberts." *University of Pennsylvania Law Review* 104 (1955): 311, 314-16.

Frankfurter, Felix. *Of Law and Life & Other Things That Matter: Papers and Addresses of Felix Frankfurter, 1956-1963.* Philip B. Kurland, ed. (Cambridge, MA: Belknap, 1965).

Felix Frankfurter Papers, Library of Congress.

Felix Frankfurter Papers, Harvard Law School.

Felix Frankfurter Reminisces: Recorded in Talks with Dr. Harlan B. Phillips (New York: Reynal, 1960).

"Conversations with Mr. Justice Frankfurter." Interviews conducted between 1953 and 1955 by Harlan B. Phillips. Oral History Research Office, Butler Library, Columbia University, New York, 1956.

Freedman, Max. *Roosevelt and Frankfurter: Their Correspondence, 1928-1945* (Boston: Little, Brown, 1967).

Friedman, Leon, and Fred L. Israel, eds. *The Justices of the Supreme Court: Their Lives and Major Opinions*, vol. I (New York: Chelsea House Publishers, 1997).

Friedman, Leon, and Fred L. Israel, eds. *The Justices of the Supreme Court: Their Lives and Major Opinions, 1789-1969*, vol. IV (New York: Chelsea House Publishers, 1969).

Fuchs, Moritz. "Robert H. Jackson at the Nuremberg Trials, 1945–1946, as Remembered by His Personal Bodyguard." *Albany Law Review* 68 (2004): 14.

Gage, Beverly. *The Day Wall Street Exploded: A Story of America in its First Age of Terror* (Oxford: Oxford University Press, 2009).

Garrow, David J. *Liberty and Sexuality: The Right to Privacy and the Making of Roe v. Wade* (Berkeley: University of California Press, 1994).

Gerhart, Eugene C. *America's Advocate: Robert H. Jackson* (Indianapolis: Bobbs-Merrill, 1958).

Gerhart, Eugene C. *Supreme Court Justice Jackson: Lawyer's Judge* (Albany, NY: Q Corporation, 1961).

Elizabeth Glendower Evans Papers. Schlesinger Library, Harvard.

Gobitis, Lillian. "The Courage to Put God First." *Awake!* July 22, 1993, 13.

Gold, Michael. *Jews Without Money* (New York: Carroll & Graf, 1996).

Goldman, Armond, et al. "What Was the Cause of Franklin Delano Roosevelt's Paralytic Illness?" *Journal of Medical Biography* 11 (2003).

Goldman, Eliot. "Justice William O. Douglas: The Vice-Presidential Nomination and His Relationship with Roosevelt." *Presidential Studies Quarterly* 12 (1982): 377.

Goldsmith, Jack. "Justice Jackson's Unpublished Opinion in *Ex Parte Quirin*." *Green Bag* 9 (2006): 225.

Goldsmith, Jack. *The Terror Presidency: Law and Judgment Inside the Bush Administration* (New York: W. W. Norton, 2007).

Gould, Tony. *A Summer Plague: Polio and Its Survivors* (New Haven: Yale University Press, 1997).

Gudridge, Patrick O. "Remember Endo?" *Harvard Law Review* 116 (2003): 1933.

Gunther, Gerald. *Learned Hand: The Man and the Judge* (New York: Knopf, 1994).

Hamburger, Philip. *Separation of Church and State* (Cambridge: Harvard University Press, 2002).

Learned Hand Papers, 1840–1961. Harvard Law School Library.

Harrison, Robert. "The Breakup of the Roosevelt Supreme Court: The Contribution of History and Biography." *Law & History Review* 2 (1984): 165–168.

Hendel, Samuel. *Charles Evans Hughes and the Supreme Court* (New York: King's Crown Press, Columbia University, 1951).

Hirsch, H. N. *The Enigma of Felix Frankfurter* (New York: Basic Books, 1981).

Hockett, Jeffrey D. *New Deal Justice: The Constitutional Jurisprudence of Hugo L. Black, Felix Frankfurter, and Robert H. Jackson* (Lanhan, MD: Rowman & Littlefield, 1996).

Horne, Gerald. *Black Liberation/Red Scare: Benjamin Davis, Jr. and the Communist Party* (Cranbury, NJ: Associated University Presses, 1994).

Howe, Irving, and Lewis Coser. *The American Communist Party: A Critical History* (New York: Praeger, 1962).

Howe, Mark DeWolfe, ed. *The Holmes-Laski Letters: The Correspondence of Mr. Justice Holmes and Harold J. Laski, 1916-1935* (Cambridge: Harvard University Press, 1953).

Hutchinson, Dennis J. "The Black-Jackson Feud." *Supreme Court Review* 1988: 203.

Hutchinson, Dennis J. "Unanimity and Desegregation." *Georgetown Law Journal* 68 (1979-1980): 1.

Ickes, Harold L. *The Secret Diary of Harold L. Ickes* (New York: Simon and Schuster, 1953).

Irons, Peter. *Justice at War* (New York: Oxford University Press, 1983).

Irving, David. *Göring: A Biography* (New York: William Morrow & Co., 1989).

Jackson Adams, Harold. "A Tribute to Robert Jackson by His Nephew." *The Albany Law Review* 68 (2004-2005).

Jackson, Robert H. *The Struggle for Judicial Supremacy: A Study of a Crisis in American Power Politics* (New York: Knopf, 1941).

Jackson, Robert H. *The Supreme Court in the American System of Government* (Cambridge: Harvard University Press, 1962).

Jackson, Robert H. *That Man: An Insider's Portrait of Franklin D. Roosevelt* (New York: Oxford University Press, 2003).

Jackson, Robert H. "The Bar and the New Deal." *West Virginia Law Quarterly* 41 (1935): 103.

Reminiscences of Robert H. Jackson (1952), in the Columbia University Oral History Research Office Collection.

Janeway, Michael. *The Fall of the House of Roosevelt: Brokers of Ideas and Power from FDR to LBJ* (New York: Columbia University Press, 2003).

Josephson, Matthew. "Profiles: Jurist-I." *The New Yorker*, November 30, 1940.

Josephson, Matthew. "Profiles: Jurist-II." *The New Yorker*, December 7, 1940.

Kalman, Laura. *Legal Realism at Yale, 1927-1960* (Chapel Hill: University of North Carolina Press, 1986).

Karabel, Jerome. *The Chosen: The Hidden History of Admission and Exclusion at Harvard, Yale, and Princeton* (Boston: Houghton Mifflin, 2005).

Kaufman, Andrew. *Cardozo* (Cambridge: Harvard University Press, 1998).

Keller, Morton, and Phyllis Keller. *Making Harvard Modern: The Rise of America's University* (Oxford: Oxford University Press, 2001).

Kessler, Lauren. *A Stubborn Twig: Three Generations in the Life of a Japanese Family* (New York: Random House, 1993).

Kessler, Ronald. *The Bureau: The Secret History of the FBI* (New York: St. Martin's Press, 2002).

Klarman, Michael. "*Brown* and *Lawrence* (and *Goodridge*)." *Michigan Law Review* 104 (December 2005): 431.

Klarman, Michael. *From Jim Crow to Civil Rights: The Supreme Court and the Struggle for Racial Equality* (New York: Oxford University Press, 2004).

Klehr, Harvey, and John Earl Haynes. *The American Communist Movement: Storming Heaven Itself* (New York: Twayne Publishers, 1992).

Klehr, Harvey, John Earl Haynes, and Fridrikh Igorevich Firsov. *The Secret World of American Communism* (New Haven: Yale University Press, 1995).

Klingenstein, Susanne. *Jews in the American Academy, 1900-1940: The Dynamics of Intellectual Assimilation* (New Haven: Yale University Press, 1991).

Kluger, Richard. *Simple Justice: The History of Brown v. Board of Education and Black America's Struggle for Equality* (New York: Knopf, 1975).

Knox, John. *The Forgotten Memoir of John Knox.* Dennis J. Hutchinson and David J. Garrow, eds. (Chicago: University of Chicago Press, 2002).

Krock, Arthur. *Memoirs: Sixty Years on the Firing Line* (New York: Funk and Wagnalls, 1968).

Lamson, Peggy. *Roger Baldwin, Founder of the American Civil Liberties Union: A Portrait* (Boston: Houghton Mifflin, 1976).

Lasch, Christopher. *The American Liberals and the Russian Revolution* (New York: Columbia University Press, 1962).

Lash, Joseph P. *Dealers and Dreamers: A New Look at the New Deal* (New York: Doubleday, 1988).

Lash, Joseph P., ed. *From the Diaries of Felix Frankfurter* (New York: W. W. Norton, 1975).

Lasser, William. *Benjamin V. Cohen: Architect of the New Deal* (New Haven: Yale University Press, 2002).

Levinson, Sanford. "The Democratic Faith of Felix Frankfurter." *Stanford Law Review* 25 (1973): 430.

Levinson, Sanford. *Constitutional Faith* (Princeton: Princeton University Press, 1988).

Levy, Leonard. *Legacy of Suppression: Freedom of Speech and Press in Early American History* (Cambridge: Harvard University Press, 1960).

Levy, Leonard. *Emergence of a Free Press* (New York: Oxford University Press, 1985).

Lewis, Anthony. *Gideon's Trumpet* (New York: Random House, 1964).

Lichtman, Allan J. "Tommy the Cork: The Secret World of Washington's First Modern Lobbyist—Thomas G. Corcoran," *Washington Monthly*, February 1987.

Liggett, Byron. "William O. Douglas, Supreme Court Justice and Poker Player." *Poker Player*, June 27, 2005.

MacLeish, Archibald, and E. F. Prichard, Jr., eds. *Law and Politics: Occasional Papers of Felix Frankfurter, 1913-1938* (Gloucester, MA: Peter Smith, 1971).

Manvell, Roger, and Heinrich Fraenkel. *Hermann Göring* (London: Heinemann, 1962).

Manwaring, David R. *Render Unto Caesar: The Flag Salute Controversy* (Chicago: University of Chicago Press, 1962).

Marcus, Maeva. *Truman and the Steel Seizure Case: The Limits of Presidential Power* (New York: Columbia University Press, 1977).

Martin, John Bartlow. *Adlai Stevenson of Illinois* (New York: Doubleday, 1976).

Mason, Alpheus Thomas. *Harlan Fiske Stone: Pillar of the Law* (Hamden, CT: Archon Books, 1968).

McCraw, Thomas. *Prophets of Regulation: Charles Francis Adams, Louis D. Brandeis, James M. Landis, Alfred E. Kahn* (Cambridge: Harvard University Press, 1984).

McCullough, David. *Truman* (New York: Simon & Schuster, 1992).

McCune, Wesley. *The Nine Young Men* (New York: Harper & Brothers, 1947).

McKean, David. *Tommy the Cork: Washington's Ultimate Insider from Roosevelt to Reagan* (New York: Steerforth, 2003).

Mendelson, Wallace. *Felix Frankfurter: The Judge* (New York: Reynal & Company, 1964).

Mendelson, Wallace. *Justices Black and Frankfurter: Conflict in the Court* (Chicago: University of Chicago Press, 1966).

Mennel, Robert M., and Christine L. Compston, eds. *Holmes and Frankfurter: Their Correspondence, 1912-1934* (Hanover, NH: University Press of New England, 1996).

Meyer, Karl E., and Shareen Blair Brysac. *Tournament of Shadows: The Race for Empire in Central Asia and the Great Game* (Washington, DC: Counterpoint, 1999).

Michelson, Charles. *The Ghost Talks* (New York: G. P. Putnam's Sons, 1944).

Miller, Merle. *Plain Speaking: An Oral Biography of Harry S. Truman* (New York: Berkley, 1974).

Montgomery, Michael B., and Thomas E. Nunnally, eds. *From the Gulf States and Beyond: The Legacy of Lee Pederson and LAGS* (Tuscaloosa: University of Alabama Press, 1998).

Moses, James L. "William O. Douglas and the Vietnam War: Civil Liberties, Presidential Authority, and the 'Political Question.'" *Presidential Studies Quarterly* 26 (1996): 1029.

Murdoch, Joyce, and Deb Price. *Courting Justice: Gay Men and Lesbians v. the Supreme Court* (New York: Basic Books, 2001).

Murphy, Bruce Allen. *The Brandeis/Frankfurter Connection: The Secret Political Activities of Two Supreme Court Justices* (New York: Oxford University Press, 1982).

Murphy, Bruce Allen. *Wild Bill: The Legend and Life of William O. Douglas* (New York: Random House, 2003).

National Civil Liberties Bureau Free Speech Report, 1921.

Newman, Roger K. *Hugo Black: A Biography* (New York: Fordham University Press, 1997).

Ng, Wendy L. *Japanese American Internment During World War II: A History and Reference Guide* (Westport, CT: Greenwood Press, 2002).

Olson, Kent. Personal communication to the author, July 22, 2009.

Oppenheimer, Robert J. "Atomic Weapons and American Policy." *Foreign Affairs* 31 (1953): 525.

Parrish, Michael E. *Felix Frankfurter and His Times: The Reform Years* (New York: Free Press, 1982).

Parrish, Michael. *Securities Regulation and the New Deal* (New Haven, CT: Yale University Press, 1970).

Payne, Stanley G. *A History of Fascism, 1914-1945* (Madison: University of Wisconsin Press, 1995).

Pearson, Drew, and Robert S. Allen. *The Nine Old Men* (Garden City, NY: Doubleday, Doran & Company, 1936).

Perkins, Frances. *The Roosevelt I Knew* (New York: Viking, 1946).

Peters, Shawn Francis. *Judging Jehovah's Witnesses: Religious Persecution and the Dawn of the Rights Revolution* (Lawrence: University Press of Kansas, 2000).

Pocock, J. G. A. *The Ancient Constitution and the Feudal Law: A Study of English Historical Thought in the Seventeenth Century* (New York: Cambridge University Press, 1987).

Pollak, Louis H. "'We're Going to Miss You on the Court Because We Need You.'" Review of *The Antagonists: Hugo Black, Felix Frankfurter and Civil Liberties in Modern America*, by James F. Simon. *Yale Law Journal* 99 (1990): 2091.

Powe, L. A., Jr. Review of *Division and Discord: The Supreme Court Under Stone and Vinson, 1941-1953,* by Melvin I. Urofsky. *Constitutional Commentary* 18 (2001): 259.

Prettyman, E. Barrett, Jr. Author interview, January 29, 2010.

Primus, Richard. "Bolling Alone." *Columbia Law Review* 104, no. 4 (May 2004): 975.

Rauh, Joseph L., Jr. "An Unabashed Liberal Looks at a Half Century of the Supreme Court." *North Carolina Law Review* 69 (1990): 221.

Ray, Laura Krugman. "Judicial Personality: Rhetoric and Emotion in Supreme Court Opinions." *Washington and Lee Law Review* 59 (2002): 193.

Reich, Charles. "Mr. Justice Black and the Living Constitution." *Harvard Law Review* 76, no. 4 (1963): 673.

Rice, Rondall Ravon. *The Politics of Air Power: From Confrontation to Cooperation in Army Aviation Civil-Military Relations* (Lincoln: University of Nebraska Press, 2004).

Ritchie, Donald A. *James M. Landis: Dean of the Regulators* (Cambridge: Harvard University Press, 1980).

Roalfe, William R. *John Henry Wigmore: Scholar and Reformer* (Evanston, IL: Northwestern University Press, 1977).

Robinson, Greg. *A Tragedy of Democracy: Japanese Confinement in North America* (New York: Columbia University Press, 2009).

Robinson, Greg. *By Order of the President: FDR and the Internment of Japanese Americans* (Cambridge: Harvard University Press, 2001).

Rodell, Fred. "Justice Hugo Black." *American Mercury* lix (August 1944): 137.

Rodell, Fred. *Nine Men: A Political History of the Supreme Court from 1790 to 1955* (New York: Random House, 1955).

Roerich, Nicholas. *Shambhala* (New York: Stokes, 1930).

Roosevelt, Elliott. *An Untold Story: The Roosevelts of Hyde Park* (New York: Putnam, 1973).

Roosevelt, Elliott, and James Brough. *A Rendezvous with Destiny: The Roosevelts of the White House* (New York: Putnam, 1975).

Roosevelt, James, and Sidney Shalett. *Affectionately, FDR* (New York: Harcourt, Brace, 1959).

Rose, Norman. *The Cliveden Set: Portrait of An Exclusive Fraternity* (London: Pimlico, 2001).

Rosenman, Samuel I. *Working with Roosevelt* (New York: Harper and Brothers, 1952).

Rostow, Eugene V. "The Japanese American Cases—A Disaster." *Yale Law Journal* 54 (June 1945): 489.

Schauer, Frederick. *Thinking Like a Lawyer: A New Introduction to Legal Reasoning* (Cambridge: Harvard University Press, 2009).

Schlesinger,, Arthur M. Jr. *A Life in the Twentieth Century: Innocent Beginnings, 1917-1950* (New York: Houghton Mifflin, 2002).

Schlesinger, Arthur M. Jr. "The Supreme Court 1937." *Fortune,* January 1947, 73.

Schmidt, Patrick. "'The Dilemma to a Free People': Justice Robert Jackson, Walter Bagehot, and the Creation of a Conservative Jurisprudence." *Law and History Review* 20, No. 3 (2002): 517.

Schroeder, Christopher H., and Curtis A. Bradley, eds. *Presidential Power Stories* (New York: Foundation Press, 2009).

Schwartz, Bernard. *Super Chief, Earl Warren and His Supreme Court: A Judicial Biography* (New York: New York University Press, 1983).

Schwartz, Bernard. *The Unpublished Opinions of the Warren Court* (New York: Oxford University Press, 1985).

Seacrest, Meryle. *Duveen: A Life in Art* (New York: Knopf, 2004).

Sherwood, Robert. *Roosevelt and Hopkins: An Intimate History* (New York: Harper, 1948).

Shesol, Jeff. *Supreme Power: Franklin Roosevelt vs. the Supreme Court* (New York: W. W. Norton, 2010).

Shklar, Judith N. *Legalism* (Cambridge: Harvard University Press, 1964).

Shlaim, Avi. *Collusion Across the Jordan: King Abdullah, the Zionist Movement, and the Partition of Palestine* (New York: Columbia University Press, 1988).

Silber, Norman I. *With All Deliberate Speed: The Life of Philip Elman, an Oral History Memoir* (Ann Arbor: University of Michigan Press, 2004).

Simon, James F. *Independent Journey: The Life of William O. Douglas* (New York: Harper and Row, 1980).

Simon, James F. *The Antagonists: Hugo Black, Felix Frankfurter, and Civil Liberties in Modern America* (New York: Simon & Schuster, 1989).

Simon, Linda. *William James Remembered* (Lincoln: University of Nebraska Press, 1996).

Small, Marshall L. "William O. Douglas Remembered: A Collective Memory by WOD's Law Clerks." *Journal of Supreme Court History* 32 (2007): 297.

Smith, Jean Edward. *FDR* (New York: Random House, 2007).

Sowards, Adam M. *The Environmental Justice: William O. Douglas and American Conservation* (Corvallis: University of Oregon Press, 2009).

Stephenson, D. Grier, Jr. *An Essential Safeguard: Essays on the United States Supreme Court and Its Justices* (New York: Greenwood Press, 1991).

"Supreme Court Law Clerks' Recollections of October Term 1951, Including the Steel Seizure Cases." *St. John's Law Review* 82, no. 4 (Fall 2008): 1239.

Sutherland, Arthur E. *The Law at Harvard: A History of Ideas and Men, 1817-1967* (Cambridge: Harvard University Press, 1967).

Tateishi, John. *And Justice for All: An Oral History of the Japanese-American Detention Camps* (New York: Random House, 1979).

Temkin, Moshik. *The Sacco-Vanzetti Affair: America on Trial* (New Haven: Yale University Press, 2009).

Thayer, James Bradley. *Legal Essays* (Cambridge: Harvard University Press, 1927).

"Transcriptions of Conversations Between Justice William O. Douglas and Professor Walter F. Murphy, 1961-1963." Special Collections, Seeley G. Mudd Library, Princeton University.

Trohan, Walter. *Political Animals* (New York: Doubleday, 1975).

Tugwell, Rexford G. *The Democratic Roosevelt: A Biography of Franklin D. Roosevelt* (Baltimore: Penguin, 1957).

Tushnet, Mark, with Katya Lezin. "What Really Happened in Brown." *Columbia Law Review* 91 (December 1991): 1867.

Urofsky, Melvin I. "Conflict Among the Brethren: Felix Frankfurter, William O. Douglas and the Clash of Personalities and Philosophies on the United States Supreme Court." *Duke Law Journal* 1988: 71.

Urofsky, Melvin I. *Division and Discord: The Supreme Court Under Stone and Vinson, 1941-1953* (Columbia: University of South Carolina Press, 1997).

Urofsky, Melvin I., ed. *The Douglas Letters: Selections from the Private Papers of Justice William O. Douglas* (Bethesda, MD: Adler & Adler, 1987).

Urofksy, Melvin I. *Felix Frankfurter: Judicial Restraint and Individual Liberties* (Boston: Twayne Publishers, 1991).

Urofsky, Melvin I. *Louis D. Brandeis: A Life* (New York: Pantheon, 2009).

Urofsky, Melvin I. "William O. Douglas and Felix Frankfurter: Ideology and Personality on the Supreme Court." *The History Teacher* 24, no. 1 (November 1990): 7.

Urofsky, Melvin I,. and David W. Levy, eds. *"Half Brother, Half Son": The Letters of Louis D. Brandeis to Felix Frankfurter* (Norman: University of Oklahoma Press, 1991).

Ward, Geoffrey C., ed. *Closest Companion: The Unknown Story of the Intimate Friendship Between Franklin Roosevelt and Margaret Suckley* (Boston: Houghton Mifflin, 1995).

Ward, Geoffrey C. *A First-Class Temperament: The Emergence of Franklin D. Roosevelt* (New York: Harper and Row, 1989).

Warren, Samuel D., and Louis D. Brandeis. "The Right to Privacy." *Harvard Law Review* 4, no. 5 (1890).

Wasby, Stephen L., ed. *He Shall Not Pass This Way Again: The Legacy of Justice William O. Douglas* (Pittsburgh: University of Pittsburgh Press, 1990).

Watkins, T. H. *The Hungry Years: A Narrative History of the Depression* (New York: Henry Holt, 1999).

Watson, Bruce. *Sacco and Vanzetti: The Men, the Murders, and the Judgment of Mankind* (New York: Viking, 2007).

White, G. Edward. *The American Judicial Tradition: Profiles of Leading American Judges* (New York: Oxford University Press, 1988).

White, G. Edward. "Felix Frankfurter's 'Soliloquy' in Ex Parte Quirin: Nazi Sabotage & Constitutional Conundrums." *Green Bag* 5 (2002): 423.

White, Graham, and John Maze. *Henry A. Wallace: His Search for a New World Order* (Chapel Hill: The University of North Carolina Press, 1995).

Whitman, James Q. "Of Corporatism, Fascism, and the First New Deal." *American Journal of Comparative Law* 39 (1991): 747.

Wiecek, William M. *The Birth of the Modern Constitution: The United States Supreme Court, 1941-1953* (New York: Cambridge University Press, 2006).

Wyllie, James. *The Warlord and the Renegade: The Story of Hermann and Albert Goering* (Stroud, UK: Sutton Publishing, 2006).

Yarbrough, Tinsley E. *Mr. Justice Black and His Critics* (Durham: Duke University Press, 1988).

Young, William, and David E. Kaiser, *Postmortem: New Evidence in the Case of Sacco and Vanzetti* (Amherst: University of Massachusetts Press, 1985).

INDEX

ABOUT TWELVE

TWELVE

TWELVE was established in August 2005 with the objective of publishing no more than one book per month. We strive to publish the singular book, by authors who have a unique perspective and compelling authority. Works that explain our culture; that illuminate, inspire, provoke, and entertain. We seek to establish communities of conversation surrounding our books. Talented authors deserve attention not only from publishers, but from readers as well. To sell the book is only the beginning of our mission. To build avid audiences of readers who are enriched by these works—that is our ultimate purpose.

For more information about forthcoming TWELVE books, please go to www.twelvebooks.com.